A SERIOUS MAN

David Storey was born in 1933 in Wakefield, and studied at the Slade School of Art. His eight previous novels have won many prizes, including the Macmillan Fiction Award, the Somerset Maugham Award, the Faber Memorial Prize and, in 1976, the Booker Prize for *Saville*. He is also the author of fifteen plays. He lives in London.

ALSO BY DAVID STOREY

Novels
This Sporting Life
Flight into Camden
Radcliffe
Pasmore
A Temporary Life
Saville
A Prodigal Child
Present Times

Plays
The Restoration of Arnold Middleton
In Celebration
The Contractor
Home
The Changing Room
The Farm
Cromwell
Life Class
Mother's Day
Sisters
Phoenix
Early Days
The March on Russia
Stages
Caring

Poetry
Storey's Lives

General
Edward
(with drawings by Donald Parker)

David Storey

A SERIOUS MAN

V

VINTAGE

Published by Vintage 1999

2 4 6 8 10 9 7 5 3 1

Copyright © David Storey 1998

The right of David Storey to be identified as the author of
this work has been asserted by him in accordance with
the Copyright, Designs and Patents Act, 1988

First published in Great Britain in 1998
by Jonathan Cape

Vintage
Random House, 20 Vauxhall Bridge Road,
London SW1V 2SA

Random House Australia (Pty) Limited
20 Alfred Street, Milsons Point, Sydney
New South Wales 2061, Australia

Random House New Zealand Limited
18 Poland Road, Glenfield,
Auckland 10, New Zealand

Random House South Africa (Pty) Limited
Endulini, 5A Jubilee Road,
Parktown 2193, South Africa

Random House UK Limited Reg. No. 954009

A CIP catalogue record for this book
is available from the British Library

ISBN 0 09 927475 2

Papers used by Random House UK Ltd are natural,
recyclable products made from wood grown in sustain-
able forests. The manufacturing processes conform to the
environmental regulations of the country of origin

Printed and bound in Norway by
AIT Trondheim AS, 1999

1

HARRIET SAYS I'm going to die.

It's true, she had, moments before she told me, lost her temper (who wouldn't with a man of sixty-five who behaves as if he were approaching ninety?); yet she had been talking to Raynor (was ensconced with him this morning for half an hour and when she came out looked very peaked), and though Raynor has only made the one examination he has, she says, consulted Maidstone, the Sub-Dean of the Medical School and the Longcroft Professor of Psychiatry at the North London Royal, by telephone as well as letter.

Two and a half years in Boady Hall (and the same again at the N.L.R.) have not done me, on the whole, a lot of good. I say 'in', but, to be more accurate, in and out: yet when I was out the threat of re-internment never left me. When, for instance, she said, 'You are going to die,' my immediate response was to say, 'Is that a clinical judgement or merely a comment on the nature of life?' and might have gone on to announce, 'I haven't lived long enough. There's so much still I'd like to do,' but since, moments later, she walked out of the room I was unable to decide precisely what she meant and could only call after her, 'That's what I want. To put an end to all this pain.'

Why she's brought me to this house I've no idea: over the past five years I've come to hate as well as fear the mention of its name. 'I can't leave you in this hovel,' she declared, meaning my home in Taravara Road I shared with Vi, and when I replied, 'I love this place. Vivienne and I were very happy,' she instantly

1

responded, 'Don't talk to me about her. You know how much you despised her.'

'I didn't despise her at all,' I told her, totally confused.

'Why do you think she killed herself?' she asked.

'The pain,' I said, 'became too much. More,' I went on, 'than people like you, with humdrum jobs and humdrum minds (with humdrum feelings and humdrum reflections) can possibly imagine.'

I make her cruel. It's a charge other people have made in the past. 'You make me cruel. Cruel and wicked. I don't know why you do it,' Bea would say.

'Cruel to be kind,' I'd tell her, and, from time to time, might add, 'There's a wicked streak in all of us that's all the better for being out.'

'But why directed at me?' she would ask. 'Someone you've chosen to share things with.'

'I've never had much patience with rectitude,' I'd tell her.

'In that case,' she'd say, 'we shouldn't have married,' and when, later, poor Vi came on the scene, 'Why, for instance, didn't you marry *her*?'

Harriet always loved this house, even as a child, when she skipped about its lawns and through its wood, climbed its trees and dug its garden (rode the neighbours' horses – and one or two of the old shires from Freddie's yard – and held picnics with the neighbours' children by the porch, the steps set out with the contents of a hamper which had been carried by Rosie, the Corcorans' 'woman', around the house, from the kitchen door a distance of no more than twenty-five yards).

'I can't do anything here but die,' I told her when she brought me to the place the other night.

'If that's what you have in mind,' she said.

'Why are you so malevolent?' I asked.

'You make me cruel, Father!' she cried, in much the same way as Bea would cry when, in the last years of our marriage, I told her lies – lies about work, lies about art (lies about God, reality, etc.).

'So much of my past is bound up in this place,' I said. 'It was by those trees that I courted your mother. It was by that lawn that I fell in love. It's the worst place you could have chosen. Ask Maidstone. He'll tell you.'

'It was his idea,' she said, 'I should bring you.'

'It wasn't, in that case,' I said, 'from the kindness of your heart.'

'Kindness and heart are not words I care to associate with our relationship,' she told me. 'And haven't done so now for quite some time.'

When we reached the house the other night Charlie had left the gates wide open and the lamps, mounted on their quaint, cast-iron poles, burning in the drive. Only the leafless trees, however, and the lightless hulk of the place itself were visible against the moonlit sky. I shuddered as I stepped out from the car and Harriet, solicitous for me, suddenly enquired, 'Are you all right?' assuming it was the journey and not the place that had suddenly upset me.

'This place,' I said, 'will kill me.'

'It will,' she said, 'if you allow it. You're mad,' she had gone on. 'Why should I listen to anything you say?'

'You told me years ago I had a touch of genius,' I had told her, recalling having lunch in the restaurant at the Tate after supervising the hanging of several of my pictures and, taken aback to see how well they stood up to – or out from – the Picassos and Matisses, she had said, 'You have a touch of genius, Father,' like she might, after half a lifetime, have suddenly announced, 'You have red hair. All these years I took it to be brown.'

'You did have a touch of genius,' she said (her new-found philosophy à la Gurdjieff coming to the fore). 'What difference does it make? You can't take genius with you. Relationships are more important.'

'But don't earn any money.'

She hated me in my mocking mood: as a child, coming home from school with her latest cult which I, in those days, instantly destroyed, she would rush to her room and, slamming the door, stay inside for hours.

'You were brilliant,' she said, 'but your mind,' the biter bit, 'has lost its effervescence.'

I've been ill; how ill I can't recall. Harriet suspects, by bringing me here, she will, as she describes it, 're-animate those areas of your mind that previously existed. Mum says you were at peace,' she had added, 'the times you came up here.'

But can she possibly imagine what my youth in and around this place was like; and, worst of all, could she imagine what life was like twelve miles away, at Onasett, to the north?

When I first came here the valley below the house was full of smoke: a slag heap smouldered from the brow of an adjoining hill; shunting engines chuntered in and out of the village street, hauling lines of trucks to and from the main railway line a mile and a half to the south. The place, morning, noon and night, was full of men with blackened faces and stout, broad-chested women. The school at which, during the war, Bea's mother taught stood at the foot of the colliery heap, its brickwork streaked with soot and smoke, and the marks, or so it seemed, of a million blackened fingers.

I first came to Ardsley late one night in the back of a car, my friend Otterton behind the wheel, the lugubrious Jenny, his girlfriend, beside him, delivering Bea from our last school party – the last time I saw Otterton, or Jenny, and the first time I had escorted B.

I recall drawing up at a green-painted door let into a tall stone wall – its sandstone texture visibly eroded – and, after disabusing me of the notion that she was 'one of those' (girls who allowed intimacies on the first acquaintance), her condescending to a goodnight kiss – a light brushing of her lips on mine – and, with a wave, she was gone – a glimpse, beyond the wall, of a lighted path before a bolt was drawn.

It sits, Ardsley Old Hall, halfway up a wooded hill, a flat-fronted, five-bayed Georgian structure with a central porticoed entrance. A beech hedge, at the front, circumscribes a lawn within which are set rectangular, round and crescent-shaped flowerbeds. Trellises, threaded with roses and, here and there, a fruit tree, run off on either side to where, in one direction, a wicket-gate gives access to an orchard and, in the other, a stone arch, inset in a buttressed wall, opens into an area at one time known as Corcoran's Yard, a cobbled precinct occupied, in the years before my first visit to the house, by Freddie's carts, his stabled horses and, latterly, by his large, tall-sided lorries. Enclosed by terraced, stone-built dwellings, it is known nowadays as Ardsley Close: a pair of recently-erected metal gates, permanently closed, occupy the arch, cutting off Harriet's and Charlie's grounds from this previous heart of Freddie's kingdom.

At the foot of the slope, and all but hidden by the trees, lies Ardsley village. The pit – Old Ardsley Main – has gone: a symmetrically landscaped slope, dotted with trees and shrubs, has replaced the colliery heap – a wedge of uniformly ascending grass which overlooks the terraced streets and, when the trees are bare, as now, the façade and the grounds of the house itself.

2

'I'VE BROUGHT you some tea,' Harriet said, coming into my room this morning. 'What would you like for breakfast?'

It must have been late: Lottie (ten) and Glenda (five) no doubt had gone to school; and Charlie, no doubt, had gone to work (some mornings, Etty has told me – although he only goes to Linfield, twelve miles away to the north – he leaves at seven): the driveway to the house is at the rear and vehicles approaching or leaving are seldom heard.

'I'm not that old. There's still some time to go. I can still get up for breakfast,' I said.

'So you shall. Providing,' she said, 'Mrs Otterman cooks it.'

'Neither Mrs Otterman nor anyone else is needed,' I said. 'I'm quite capable of cooking it myself.'

I watched her open the curtains: 'How she endeavours to indulge me,' I reflected. 'A pavlovian response,' she once remarked: 'I see an old man and my immediate response is to offer to help.'

Turning from the curtains, she said, 'You look older than at any other time I've known you. You even look older than Grandpa,' referring to a photograph of Freddie (Corcoran, the profligate haulage contractor, coal-merchant, insurance agent and landowner, Bea's father) about whom we had been talking the night before ('What youthful spirits!' etc.), the photograph (in a silver frame) standing on the mantelpiece in the living-room below. 'You look more frightened, too,' she went on, never slow, from childhood, to identify my ailments, a subliminal form of retribution which gave her, I had always thought, much charm.

'What is madness,' Maidstone had once enquired, his eyes half-shut, flicking the plastic top of his fountain pen, 'but our ability to see other people as they see themselves but not as other people see them?' and though there might have been a facetious truth in this, it has, throughout my life, been my inability to see myself as anything at all that has lain at the root of all my problems.

Etty, of course, has a vested interest in seeing me as not only old but mad.

'I shall have bacon and egg,' I said. 'With sausage and tomato. Toast, marmalade. Fruit juice and coffee.'

'You never eat it,' she complained.

'I shall today,' I said. 'I feel quite well.'

'What are you planning?' she suddenly enquired.

It had been something about the way she had come into the room – moving to the bed and then the curtains, the projection of her arm (after setting down the tea) – that had reminded me of Isabella.

'My life from now on is totally unplanned,' I said.

'That,' she said, 'is what I feared,' dark hair coiled loosely round her head, dark eyes, a thin-lipped mouth (inherited from Bea), a delicate nose, a slender neck: sharp-featured, querulous (Bea, too): nevertheless, I see a great deal of myself in Etty, not least when she contemplates, as she might through the wrong end of a telescope, what, in no other mood but this, she considers to be her blighted ambition. 'You've never gone in want of anything,' I tell her. 'When you and Matt (her elder sister) were young you were seldom out of my sight.'

They spent much of their time, in fact, in my studio, I allowing them, from time to time, to contribute to my pictures: much paint was splashed about (an expressionist phase): 'Just look at it, Mummy!' when Bea came in and globules of red or blue were flicked in her direction.

'What am I doing with my life?' she would ask (like Bea used to ask when they were children: 'What am I *doing* here if you have them all the while?').

'You're happily married. You have two wonderful children. Your husband loves you,' is my reply, followed by, as with Bea, 'But, of course, these things have been devalued. Paranoia, with women, has got the upper hand. The obligation is to go around with a cross strapped on their backs, like the colliers, in the old days, used to haul the waste-trucks to the top of the tip where, fortunately for them, the contents were emptied out. Nowadays, of course . . .' etc., etc.

'What about *me?*' she asks. 'Caring and affection are to do with other people (even if my husband and my children are people that I love).'

'Everything,' I tell her, 'is to do with other people. Isn't Charlie,' I go on, 'as dependent on you?'

'Like you, he,' she says, 'can work.'

'So,' I tell her, 'can you.'

'The centres of research are all in London, Paris and New York,' she says (to mention but a few).

'What centres of research?' My obtuseness, in the old days, drove her mad. 'Isn't life a centre of research? I'm surprised you don't see you're living in such a location now.'

She is the authoress of a single book: *The Caravaggio Papers*. The book, absurdly, despite its scholastic pretensions, was made into a film. Etty, despite my warnings, sold the rights for a single sum. It made, for everyone involved, except the author, a great deal of money. 'I told you not to sell it,' I'd said (rape, sodomy, murder: what more could they want?). 'But if you did,' I'd gone on, 'to guarantee yourself a percentage of the budget. All you said, if you recall, was, "I don't care what they do. The book will last." It has,' I'd added. 'For six months, in paperback, at every airport in the land.'

A tray appears around the door. 'What's put you into such a good mood?' she says.

It is, I have come to the conclusion, the trees, their trunks hidden by the steepness of the slope, that have reminded me not only of waking in this room but of the hours spent sitting or standing by the window splashing or scouring my way across a canvas (attached to an easel set at an angle to distract the southern light), or stooping over a sketchbook scratching with a pen or, more intensely, over a sheaf of paper writing what turned out to be my Onasett poem and the beginning of a novel.

'I've always liked the trees,' I tell her, and add, 'They look much grander (silver birch and chestnut) now they've taken down the elm.'

Laying down the tray, relieved at having something of no consequence to talk about, she says, 'I always regret you can never see the trunks.'

'You see those,' I tell her, 'from the lower windows. In the old days, when the trees had shed their leaves, from up here you could see the pit and hear the panting of the winding-gear and the rattle of the trucks. In the early mornings, too, you could hear the whining of the dynamo and, once the clatter of the miners' clogs had died, came the clatter of the women's as they set off to Moxon's, at Thorncliff. They made cloth for soldiers' uniforms throughout the Second World War.'

'Did you live here long?' she says: affection for the place, though canvassed for, in this case, fills her with unease.

'I only stayed,' I tell her, 'from time to time. Coming here, from Onasett, was like coming to a palace.' I add, 'I was always given this room. I think Corcoran thought he could keep an eye on me in here. Your mother had her bedroom at the back. Her parents, of course, had the one that you and Charlie share.'

Sitting on the edge of the bed she says, 'What about the other rooms?'

'Your grandfather – Grandfather Corcoran – had an office in the one your children have. Your great-grandfather, H.J. Kells, occupied two others. Your great-grandmother Corcoran occupied two more. She and Grandfather Kells were always at each other's throats. Your grandmother, Isabella, also had a room in which she did her thinking.'

'What sort of thinking?' Etty asks.

'She was a very peculiar woman.'

'I thought you liked her.'

'Enormously,' I tell her.

I am about to add, 'I loved her deeply. She was the greatest love of my life,' but, recalling Maidstone's injunction, 'Where your children and your wife are concerned I should leave your accounts of that woman alone,' I merely continue,' I didn't expect to have breakfast in bed. I could easily have come down.'

'It won't happen often,' she says and, a moment later, after getting up, adds, 'Are you all right?'

'Perfectly,' I tell her.

'You went quite pale a moment ago.'

'I can't see you,' I tell her, 'against the light,' and, as she moves to one side, continue, 'Most of the time I talk to myself. It's something to do with my illness. Maidstone, whom you never liked, made quite a point of stressing it.'

'I never said I disliked him,' she says.

'Loquaciousness, he suggested, was the indirect result of my spending too much time on my own. "How can I create?" I said. "Don't you realise, before you came here," he said, "creativity had been your downfall?" '

For a while she holds my hand, and neither of us speaks.

The room has little changed: a wallpaper of abstracted shapes has replaced the cubist one of roses: the bed still faces the sky above the village, and though the tang of coal smoke is no longer in the air, and the panting of the pit has gone – the rattle of trucks, the clacking of clogs (the echo, at night, of a whistle on the mainline to the south) – I find myself imagining that the movements below me in the house – Mrs Otterman about her housework, Etty about hers – are those of Isabella, those memorable occasions when – Grandfather Kells on one of his walks (Grandmother Corcoran fast asleep), Bea shopping in the village, Freddie in the yard – she would come up to my room, a cup of tea in one hand, a cake in the other, apologising as I scraped at a canvas or scribbled with a pen (in an old school exercise book stolen from King Edward's), and say, 'I hope I'm not intruding, Richard,' her pale, green-irised eyes alight, a coppery sheen her hair against the southern glow.

'Didn't you love Bea?' Etty enquired when I went down to the kitchen (no sign of Mrs Otterman at all).

'Ours,' I said, 'was a mystical conjunction.'

'All those women that you had,' she said.

'Where are they now?' I might have asked, but merely responded, 'There were scarcely any.'

'They were even in the papers, Dad.'

Her back to me at the sink, she glanced across her shoulder. Outside, in the yard, surrounded by a hedge, her car stood by the garage, a side-window lowered, a child's seat clipped in the back for Glenda.

She was – Mrs Otterman clearly not here – preparing food.

'There were other things,' I said, 'as well.'

'Such as?'

'Why,' I said, 'her own ambition.'

Instead of Etty, however, it was Isabella who was standing there and, in my imagination, I heard her say, 'It's my daughter, my dear, you're supposed to love.'

'I do love her,' I said aloud and, as Etty turned, half-startled, from the sink, I swiftly added, 'She is, they tell me, very good. The Medical Research Council are very pleased. You may have seen it announced. She's on the threshold of discovering, in the anti-coagulant properties of the moorland leech, a possible cure for cancer.'

'Scarcely,' she said, and added, 'Couldn't she have combined research and marriage? After all,' she frowned, 'you say it's what I ought to do.'

'But then,' I said, 'she fell in love.'

'That,' she said, and added, 'Albert.'

'You're talking like the kind of man you say I should despise,' I told her.

'After this wonderful relationship you say you had, it

surprises me,' she said, 'she should feel, at the age of fifty-two, the need to go off with another man.'

'Marriage is a morbidity,' I said, and added, 'You sympathised with her at the time. "I hope," you said, "I have the guts to do the same at fifty." '

'I thought she didn't mean it,' Etty said.

'When you discovered that she did,' I said, 'I suppose you changed your mind.'

She smiled (I could see her reflection in the kitchen window): the absurdity of what we were up to struck us both afresh.

'Before I came down,' I gestured overhead, 'I was thinking of a project. I thought it might amuse you. Much of the research you could do from here. I could even,' I went on, 'suggest a title.'

'*The Fenchurch Papers.*'

'Why not?'

'The idea,' she said, 'is quite absurd.'

'If, as you say, I am about to die, you haven't much time. Less,' I added, 'the more you leave it.' When, however, she didn't reply, I hastily continued, 'Science acknowledges that subjectivity is the most valuable tool it has. Who, for instance, would describe Vasari or Lockhart or Boswell as objective? It's not the inscrutability of the observer that qualifies his or her judgements but the warmth, the dedication, the love they bring to their subject.'

At home together, in our early days, Etty both liked and resented me theorising in this manner, fascinated by the conclusions that I drew at the same time as feeling chastened by them. Afterwards I would hear her presenting similar if not identical views (when, for instance, she was at the Courtauld) to her fellow students, Viklund, the accredited authority in her field, describing her as 'the most forward pupil I have', and since he taught me for several terms (evening lectures at the Drayburgh: 'Landscape and the European Mind' – describing me as 'too clever by half') I have been inclined to accept his judgement.

'You don't have to go on. I'm perfectly capable,' she said 'of making up my mind.'

I heard her go out later in the morning, once in the car and once on foot. We ate our lunch in silence at the kitchen table, listening to the news. Afterwards I went upstairs to sleep. When I woke she had gone to fetch the children and Mrs Otterman, to my surprise, was busy in the kitchen.

A tall, dark-haired woman, with cadaverous features, she was, like Etty before her, busy at the sink.

'How are you, Mr Fenchurch?' she said.

'I'm well,' I said, in no mood to be patronised.

'Mrs Stott came and fetched me,' she said.

'Did she?'

'In her car.'

'Why should she do that?' I asked.

'She didn't wish,' she turned from the sink, having previously watched me in the reflection in the kitchen window, 'to leave you on your own.'

She was performing, I could see, a needless task – washing-up from lunch – a task, at the time, I'd offered to do myself.

'You can wash those in the machine,' I said, indicating the device adjacent to the sink.

'It's hardly worth the trouble,' she said, her hands, inflamed, plying in the water.

When she withdrew them completely, however, I observed she was wearing rubber gloves.

Whereas Mrs Otterman regarded Charlie as a cut or two above herself – with all the obsequiousness of the northern working class that that implied – she looked on me as something of a rival, she the daughter of a miner, the wife of another, the mother of a third (the last two out of work), I merely the offspring of another: despite differences in sensibility, intelligence, taste and wealth – or almost any other human attribute I might dare to mention – it put us on an equal footing – if not, in my case, having, if not sold out, absented myself, on something less. On the morning after I arrived I heard her

13

talking on the telephone in Charlie's study (assuming I and Etty, no doubt, were out), referring to me as 'Mrs Stott's poor dotty Dad – just like that man in Clatherton Street they took away last night.'

On one occasion, in an attempt to explain the acquiescence of so many of the miners in the village to being out of work, I remarked to Etty, 'So many people in the south, particularly intellectuals, talk of victimisation without realising that true conservatism – the imperviousness to change – lies at the heart of a place like this. What was Ardsley,' I went on, 'before the Wintertons discovered coal, but a dozen farms, as many rows of cottages, a church, a rectory, and Ardsley Hall?'

'It's a commuter village, for that involves work, too,' she said, angered, as the grand-daughter of a miner, by a designation she secretly despised.

'For some,' I said. 'But not for most,' for around the nucleus of the village have been constructed several estates of yellow-brick houses (described on a billboard, at the outskirts of the village, as 'executive-dwellings'): boxes, but for a garage, not much larger than the original miners' cottages themselves. 'Why the theorists go on,' I added, 'looking for change in a place like this, beats me.'

At which, for the first time, she exclaimed, 'It's why those theorists – and not theorists only – despise your work!'

'Why my work?' I enquired.

'Where they might have been looking for an appetite for change – even for revolution – they never find it.'

'In me?' (much feigned surprise).

'If anyone's work has been produced by a place like this – and by these conditions – and from amongst these people,' she further exclaimed, 'it's yours!'

'I think you're a couple of vowels out,' I said. 'Revolution returns any point on a circumference to where it was before. You don't think I'd waste my time on that? It's not revolution,' I went on, 'but revelation you're on about. Unless hypocrisy can be described as a phenomenon with a dynamic all its own, neither religious nor political sentiment affects or has affected anything at all. Both are based on appetites which are undeclared, and not merely undeclared but dishonestly perceived. I, for one, have always believed in a true revolution – of the individual spirit which prefers not to put its faith in authority, but to disseminate the authority of faith.'

'Feathering your own nest is a better description. Faith,' she went on, 'like love, is only achieved through others.'

'Not through destroying them by political and religious bigotry,' I said.

Taking up a tea-towel, Mrs Otterman, having previously removed her gloves, began to dry the pots.

'Would you like me to dry?' I said.

'No, thank you, Mr Fenchurch.'

'I'm quite capable,' I said (while you could get on with something else).

There was nothing else, however, to get on with: the tea for the children was already prepared (and standing on the table), and the food to be cooked for the evening meal arranged in a variety of bowls and dishes.

'It's quite all right, Mr Fenchurch,' she said.

What she couldn't be sure of, in Etty's absence, was what 'Mrs Stott's poor dotty Dad' might next get up to: not a few of her neighbours, I had heard her explaining one morning to Etty, had in recent years been 'taken off' – to be returned a few weeks later looking, if not changed, markedly subdued: other than that, and the eccentricities, observed or reported, which had preceded their departure (the broken windows, the shattered doors, the peculiar incidents to do with a length of rope or a bottle of pills) she had had, as she had told Etty, 'not a lot to go on'.

It was not, however, Mrs Otterman I was seeing there but Isabella's Mrs Hopkins: the ebullient, broad-bosomed, insolent (high-heeled, broad-hipped – invariably with laddered stockings) 'Rose' – the woman, also a collier's wife, who came and 'did' (stealing a great deal in the process: 'One thing she can't take away: the cheerfulness she leaves behind' – Isabella), and who more than suggested, in her occasional glances, she knew what Isabella and I were up to.

Or did she? And, if so, in the face of so much passion, what could she have done?

'And what are you doing, young Richard?' when she found me in the kitchen, creeping down in the hope the sounds I'd heard were those of Isabella – and not disinclined herself to be hugged, her more than ample figure ill-concealed in a home-made sweater – one of a variety she knitted in a range, as I endeavoured to explain to her on more than one occasion, of uniquely ill-matched colours. 'I suppose you're looking for Bea?' ('The mother *and* the daughter!' she announced coming, one Christmas, upon Isabella and myself kissing under the mistletoe.) 'I wonder what Mrs C is like in bed?' she had whispered to me once having caught me gazing after Bella as she walked off, one evening, down the drive on the way to her weekly meeting of the W.I.

'Why Etty should ask you to come,' I told Mrs Otterman, 'I've no idea. Or did she arrange it earlier? It's a terrible nuisance, I'm sure,' I added.

'Not at all,' she said, putting the pots in the cupboard.

'It's extra income, of course,' I suggested.

'That's part of it,' she said. 'But I'd do it for nothing for Mrs Stott.'

'How are things in the village?' I asked.

'Three-quarters of them,' she said, 'are out of work.'

'I thought the official figure,' I said, 'was a third.'

'If you add to it those who've decided to retire, those who don't bother to sign on, those who are on training schemes, it soon comes up to three-quarters. Seventy per cent, the unions make out.'

'There must be a lot of ill-feeling,' I said.

'And drugs.'

'And drugs.'

'Drugs are the main industry round here,' she added.

'So where does that put us?' I said.

'Some of you can get out,' she said. 'As opposed to them that are carried.'

'It must seem odd,' I said, about to take a dish to put away but foiled by her quicker movement, 'seeing someone like me coming to a place like this when everybody else is desperate to leave.'

'In work, or out,' she said, 'it's home.' With a sideways look, she added, 'And where is your home, Mr Fenchurch?'

'I'm not sure where it is,' I told her. 'Another drug-infested street.'

'At least,' she said, 'you have the choice,' and, closing the cupboard door with a bang, added, 'Which is more than most of us can say at present.'

3

MUCH OF the village is visible from my room, the trees, their branches bare, coiled in a familiar frieze against a bifurcated backdrop of land and sky: a characterless scene without the pit. On the lower slopes are the screes of sooty houses, over-looked by the more recently-constructed 'executive-dwellings', each house with its view of Ardsley Dam, a stretch of water divided by a hump-backed bridge (built by the proprietors of Ardsley Hall, the Wintertons, long before coal was discovered on their land), and brought near to collapse in the recent past by the weight of (mainly) Corcoran lorries. On a quiet day, I'm told by Mrs Otterman, the hum of machinery comes over the hill at the back of the house from the outcrop mine at Fernley – another pit which, having been closed, has been replaced by opencast workings.

I've drawn most of the fields and woods, the hedgerows and houses (and, once in London, painted them from memory and sketches). Along most of those lanes I have walked with Bea – and along not many fewer with her mother. I can see the outcrop of rock at Ardsley Edge, an extrusion of fissured sandstone – and recall that amongst its grasses and ferns, and beneath the silver birch (couched by buttercups, anenomes and daisies) that grow in profusion amongst the rock-falls at its base, I have lain for hours, as a youth, with the mother of the girl I was about to marry.

Red hair which, as with Bea, had darkened in later life to magenta: a pallid, lightly-freckled skin, green-irised eyes, an incisive mouth – a robust, slim-waisted, high-breasted figure, the slightest contact with which, whether excised by clothes or not, went through me like a knife.

I met Bea at a Christmas Dance (the boys from King Edward's, the girls from Linfield High: two single-sex schools confronting each other across a city street). Several weeks previously, Harris, an anonymous fellow whose parents owned a shop in town and who lived at Fernley, remarked that he was bringing a girl from a nearby village whom he met from time to time on the train: she would, on the night, be staying in town: 'Ought that might have gone on,' he said, 'on the train back home has gone clean out of the window.' A few days later he pointed her out in the street: amongst the groups of uniformed figures drifting along the pavement hers was indistinguishable. 'She's gone,' he said and, pointing down a sidestreet, departed in the opposite direction towards his parents' shop.

Wandering to the end of the street I glanced along it: a tall coppery-haired figure of slender build, with the mandatory dark blue High School coat stretching to her ankles, was walking away from me. Instantly (inexplicably) the thought came to me, 'This is the girl I shall marry,' and, without glancing back, let alone going after her, I slowly walked away.

On the evening of the party I invited her to dance: even as I held her I was aware of things I would never like: the way, for instance, she did her hair (less to attract than distract, I thought, swept from her brow in the manner of a child), the freckles on her brow, the green-irised eyes, flecked minutely, I observed, with strands of brown: nor did I like – nor could I separate these features from – the sharpness of her glance. Later in the evening, when I invited her again to dance, without any interest, she turned me down.

Six months elapsed before we met again: a party was being held to which several of the boys and an equivalent number of girls who were leaving their respective schools that year had been invited, their numbers supplemented by girls from a lower year: amongst the latter was Bea. As at the dance, she wore a light green dress which complimented the colour of her hair and emphasised, if that's the word, the colour of her eyes and her complexion; gauche, she had little of the assurance of the girls from the year who were leaving, and had come – as, indeed, had I – without a partner.

I had, in fact, come with Otterton, a thin-featured, lugubriously-humoured youth, and his girlfriend, Jenny, the buck-toothed daughter of a dentist whose mother, with some misgivings, had lent Otterton her car.

It was the last Saturday of the last term of our final year at Edward's. Otterton, whose ineptitude at sport had endeared him to me throughout that year, was destined for the army (the Officer Training School at Sandhurst).

I, I had announced, intended to become an artist (more dramatic still, already was one).

The party was held in a garden which stretched along one side and round the back of a (to me) very large house. The sun, as I arrived, was on the point of setting: its light illuminated a greenhouse (incandescent) and an orchard (ethereal), as well as a series of trellised terraces upon which figures were already dancing. Beyond an area of hedged fields and woodland, comprising the lower slopes and the bed of a shallow valley, hills were mistily enclosed in the mellow light. It was an area I'd roamed through as a child: the distant hills, with the bleaker slopes of the moors above, I'd camped in as a youth: the Pennine foothills with their dammed-up streams and rushing falls, their silent ponds and crumbling abbeys.

Chinese lanterns had been strung above a lawn: a gramophone, manipulated by the hostess's sister, in the Fifth Form, played a melancholy tune. It was the one I'd danced to with Bea at the Christmas Party and, looking up, I experienced a secondary shock of recognition, not unmixed with pleasure, to see her chatting with a group of friends.

I invited her to dance.

'Are you cold?' I asked.

'I am, as a matter of fact,' she said. Her hand, as I took it, had trembled.

I drew her closer to me.

20

'Do you come here often?' I enquired.

'You said that the last time,' she replied, to which I instantly responded, 'I'm surprised that you remember.'

'I remember a lot of things,' she said, and when I enquired, 'Such as?' replied, 'About your reputation.'

'For doing what?' I asked.

'Everything, as far as I can make out, that's reprehensible.'

I drew her closer: I felt the tautness of her back and the heat that surged between us, and recalled that this was the girl I was destined to marry. ('Destined by whom?' I mentally enquired, to which, then as now – and particularly on that lantern-lighted evening – came no reply).

We sat the next dance out: prompted by the pastel-coloured lanterns that glowed from the darkening trees, I remarked, 'I know that landscape well: every hill and dell, every beck and pond, every wood and hedge.'

'I live beyond those hills,' she said. She gestured to the south. 'A place called Ardsley.'

'What does your father do?' I asked.

'He owns,' she said, 'a lot of lorries.'

'What do the lorries carry?' I asked.

After a while – not sure, I discovered later, how precisely to describe her father – she said, 'Principally coal.'

'A haulage contractor,' I suggested.

'I suppose he is,' she said, disinclined to discuss it. 'I hear,' she went on, 'from Harris,' (our mutual friend who, I noticed, had not been invited to the party) 'that you're going to be an artist.'

'I am,' I said.

'Why?' Within the constriction of the garden bench, she glanced at me directly. 'There isn't much in it, if,' she went on, 'you wish to earn a living. Particularly,' she paused, 'if you haven't any money.'

'I intend to get a job,' I said.

'And give up,' she said, 'your education.'

'What's education,' I enquired, 'if it hasn't already directed me to art?' A moment later, eliciting no response, I added, 'It's a calling. Like Paul on the Road to Damascus. Three years ago,' I went on, 'I was sitting in the sixth-form classroom when, in the midst of reading Verlaine's "Ode to Autumn", it occurred to me that art is the highest form of human knowledge. I saw the whole of my life before me: a house, a wife, a job, a car: a set of rails that ran as far as I could see. At that instant I decided to dedicate my life to doing something that no one else could do.'

'Weren't you going to university?' she asked.

'I was,' I said. 'I've given it up.' Gesturing at our peers, I added, 'They're going on to something they know and can already see.'

'You'll end up in the gutter,' she suddenly declared. ('Nothing,' she might have said, 'challenges me so much as someone who forsakes their friends, their family, common sense (the destiny chosen for him) in order to pursue what everyone recognises to be an impossible dream'; it was, in short, I suspected, that preliminary lack of faith that brought us both together).

'Do you feel inspired?' she added.

'It's hidden,' I said, 'by other things.'

'What?'

'Practicalities.' I paused. 'Unlike science, industry, or any of the professions, art is useless. You can do it for three hundred and sixty-five days of the year and no one owes you a penny. It's the next best thing,' I was about to add, 'to God,' but, for reasons which only now I am beginning to understand, I substituted, 'love.'

'Are you coming down?'

The sound of Lottie and Glenda came from the living-room below (and of Mrs Otterman from the kitchen: the converging domestic interests of food and television).

When I said, 'Do you remember that party at Allgrave, the last Saturday of the last term of my last year at King Edward's?' I saw my own confusion mirrored in Etty's face – in reality, Bea's face, for, though she had my hair, dark and prematurely

22

greying, she had her mother's features – and added, 'I visited it not long ago and the view was obscured, where not by trees, by speculative building. I used to camp out there. Not at Allgrave, which is on the edge of town, but across the valley at Broughton Wood.'

I was about to continue, 'Broughton Springs was the most magical camp-site in the world,' but suddenly enquired, in order to distract her, 'Don't you use this room?' for she had found me not in my bedroom but in the back upstairs room which Isabella, at one time, had used as a study.

She looked at me, for a moment, as Bea had looked at me on the evening of the Allgrave party: like someone observing an accident which they were not altogether sure had taken place ('Was that a leg? Was that an arm? Was that a *body*?').

'It used to be Gran's. She came in here,' I said, 'to have her thoughts.'

'I suppose, too,' Etty said, 'to write her diaries.'

'Diaries?'

'Mummy has them now, of course.'

'I never knew,' I said, 'she kept a diary.'

'In a lot of Grandpa's ledgers. The ones he used for his trucks. She always had,' she said, 'such terrible writing,' and added, 'She only kept them at the time she married. And when you and Mum were growing up.'

The floor was bare: other than a cupboard, there was no sign that anyone had occupied the room at all: it overlooked the stone-flagged yard at the back of the house – with Charlie's shooting-brake standing by the garage – and, beyond the yard's enclosing hedge, a lawn which, presently unmown, had been given over at one time to a tennis court: a thicker, darker growth of grass showed where the limed white lines had run. A sharply-ascending slope, engulfed by trees, obscured the view on either side, save where, at an angle, the tower of the church – sooty, square, a battlemented crest – and the stone-slabbed roof of the rectory were visible over an intervening wall: tall, buttressed, bowed, its brickwork marked by salt and long,

23

horizontal fissures, it was here, in the time of the Wintertons, allegedly, peaches and apricots grew.

Here, by the presently uncurtained window, Isabella had had her desk: there, by the soot-lined fireplace with its marble surround, she had had her couch and, facing the couch, her chintz-covered chair. On the walls she had had her books – mostly unread, and in glass-fronted cases – and the sketches (which she'd framed) of the house, done by myself.

'She was immensely beautiful,' I said, and added, 'Your mother,' under the absurd illusion I was talking to Bea.

'She'll be glad to hear it,' Etty said. 'Though a bit late in the day, I should think, to tell her,' and, seeing no alternative, took my arm. 'Come down and have some tea,' she added.

With no resemblance to Etty – round, moon-like faces with dark-irised, moon-like eyes ('The epitome of Charlie,' Etty remarked proudly after each of their births), the children were sitting on the couch on which, thirty-five years before, Isabella and I had sat watching the then black-and-white, now coloured television screen.

Although the couch confronted the fireplace, with its marble pilasters and cornice and its iron grate, its black-leaded bars curled upwards like the ends of a moustache, the children were sitting sideways, the unshod feet of the one impressed against the stockinged legs of the other.

'Here's Grandpa,' Etty said, and though the youngest one glanced up and the eldest frowned (and neither spoke) their gazes, dream-like at this intrusion, moved swiftly back to the screen.

'Back to the table,' Etty said, since both of them were chewing, the youngest, Glenda, with the fragments of a bun in her hand and on her knee.

'I've finished, Mummy,' Lottie said.

'No, you haven't,' Etty said, in a manner indistinguishable from that of Isabella.

'I have, Mummy.' Swallowing first, Glenda opened her mouth.

'I don't want that chair made sticky,' Etty said.

'It is sticky,' Lottie said. 'It was sticky when I got here.'

Both the children had thick, black hair, with only a hint of brown, or red – the faintest legacy from Bea; they had, however, a pallid skin on which, in certain lights, could be glimpsed a scattering of freckles: in a similarly favourable light I have, from time to time, detected in their eyes a flickering of green amidst the brown – nothing, for instance, that was visible now – and not at all, of course, from a distance. They had, I had always been relieved to see (in light of the taciturnity of their father) something of a temper, an unmistakable Kellsian or Isabellian trait.

With a cry, 'Oh, Mum!' they descended from the couch and scampered to the hall. From the kitchen came Mrs Otterman's, 'Something more to eat, then, loves?' followed by a wail and, in unison, 'We've got to wash our hands!'

'The bathroom would be better,' came the dutiful response, but already the feet were scampering back (followed by, from Mrs Otterman, 'What about the tap!') and, the door slammed back, breathless, red-faced, the two figures once more were sitting on the couch.

'Are those hands dry?'

'Yes, Mum!' (Eyes on the screen.)

'You've scarcely had time to wash them.'

'We have!' (Unison again.)

Etty would sit there, in the old days, on Isabella's knee: Corcoran, who, despite his lorries with their governors which, much to his satisfaction, restricted his otherwise reckless drivers' speeds, had an aversion to 'technological development' (hence his retention of his shire horses and his four-wheeled carts long after everyone else had given them up): he similarly resisted 'the television': '*Everyone* has got one,' Isabella said. 'Then that's all the damn more reason why we shouldn't,' he replied. As for colour, it wasn't, he protested, 'what you see', and when Isabella pointed out – as she was inclined to when her wishes were frustrated – 'everyone's got one' and that colours 'could be seen outside,' he responded, 'Maybe colours

can, but not the ones in theer (I prefer the black and white).'
Even in those days, the second generation of television
watchers, the advisability of watching prompted the same
exhortations to filial or domestic duty.

'Did it do much harm?' I asked.

'Harm?' Etty sat beside me on an adjoining couch. 'I never
watched like these two. If I let them,' she went on, 'they'd be
in front of it all night.'

'We rationed it, at their age, to an hour and a half each
evening,' I said.

'I don't remember that,' she said. 'Why,' she went on, 'they
scarcely look at a book,' and, indicating the younger of the
two, continued, 'I don't even know if Glenda can read.'

Short, white ankle socks on slippered feet, stocky calves and
bulbous thighs, a tiny skirt, a jumpered chest, a pale, broad-
featured, sensitive face: at the mention of her name she turned
in my direction.

'You used to equate it with eating plastic food,' Etty added.

'When you were older,' I replied.

'The arguments we had. Far longer than we used to watch.'
Her eyes, too, were fixed on the screen. 'You and Mum.'

'Look where she is now,' I said.

The curtains on the windows of the room had not been
drawn: visible outside, a frieze of starkly-silhouetted branches
were sheaved against a darkening sky: it was through the second
of the two uncurtained windows, furthest from the door, that
I'd first seen Isabella: sitting where Harriet, her grandchild,
and I were sitting now – sewing, her head bowed, her face
shadowed from the light of an overhead lamp, glancing up as
she heard our step (Bea bringing me home, for the first time,
to the house), and perceiving not so much my face, she told
me later, as a mask, half-lighted, gazing from outside.

'You could look at it,' Etty said, 'the other way around.'
Withdrawing her gaze from the screen, she added, 'What good,
for instance, does it do?'

I was, however, recalling that journey back from the Allgrave
party, stopping in Fernley (where, ironically, Harris lived),

Otterton getting out to buy a drink and, finding the off-licence closed, coming back with fish and chips (having, with characteristic generosity, offered to drive both Bea and I home). He, with the toothsome Jenny, sat in front, Bea and I behind, each of us eating what – leaning in the car window to present each of us with a steaming packet – he had presciently described as 'our final meal together'.

I never saw Otterton again: over the years I heard (on the radio) and read (in a newspaper) accounts of him 'on loan' to one of the Arab states (a major in one, a lieutenant-colonel in another).

'You in your attic,' he had said on that final occasion, 'painting pictures, me,' he had added, 'God knows where,' gazing through the windscreen, his and Jenny's heads silhouetted against the light of the village street.

It was, or so it seemed, only moments later that I first saw Ardsley – or, more specifically, the door in the wall – and received, after a rebuke, my first, if peremptory goodnight kiss from Bea.

'Off to your room,' Etty said as the programme came to an end and, getting to her feet, turned off the television. 'You can see a half hour later,' she added, 'when Lottie has done her homework and I've heard Glenda read her book.'

'I haven't any homework!' Lottie cried.

'I'll set you some, in that case,' Etty said.

'Oh, Mummy!' And, climbing on my knee, my daughter's eldest child enquired, 'Will you tell us a story, Grandpa?'

'I want you both,' Etty said, 'to read to yourselves.'

'Glenda can't read, Mummy,' Lottie said.

'She can.'

'I can't,' Glenda said (still ensconced on the couch).

'I've heard her,' Etty said.

'You've just told Grandpa she can't,' Lottie said.

'A lot,' Etty said. 'But she can read some.'

'Oh, do tell us a story, Grandpa!' Lottie placed her arm around my neck: in such a way her great-grandmother, in the most improbable places, would make her first approach.

'Grandpa,' Etty said, 'can tell you one before you go to bed.'

'Will you, Grandpa!' Glenda, crossing the space between us, climbed on my knee as well.

'Whenever your mother says you're ready,' I announced.

'Goody, goody!' Lottie said, removing her arm from around my neck (like Isabella, too, once she'd got what she'd wanted), adding, 'It's got to be one that frightens!'

'It'll be one that sends you to sleep. Up to your room,' their mother said, yet it was Etty who was descending from my knee and it was Isabella who was being beseeched, 'Will you tell us a story, Gran?' and the smile of Bea's mother was turning on me as she informed them, 'If your father lets me.'

'Oh, do, Daddy,' Etty has said and, covertly, two hours later, as Etty and her sister go to bed, I am standing at the bedroom door watching Isabella stoop to kiss their cheeks – as, moments later, outside the door, her head is raised and I stoop to kiss her mouth.

In the car, approaching Ardsley, I had said, 'Do you think I can see you again?' and Bea had replied – her skirt fortuitously drawn above her knee, the consequence of our movements as we cleared the interior of the papers from the fish and chips, 'If you like,' adding, as my hand enclosed the skin above her stockinged thigh, 'I'm not that kind of girl,' drawing down her skirt with – although sitting sideways I couldn't be sure – a great deal of indignation.

'Where shall we meet?' I asked, while Otterton, restricted by his driving, murmured endearments to Jenny in the seat in front.

'I'm going away,' she said.

'Where?' I asked, in some surprise (could someone, I reflected, go away after receiving the sort of confidences I'd confided earlier that night?).

'France,' she said. 'The Riviera. We go there every year.'

An immeasurable gap – we weren't, since her previous rebuke, even holding hands – opened up between us.

'You ought to go,' she added. 'If you ever get the chance.'

I began to suspect she had listened to little if anything I had told her: how could an artist, about to take leave of his friends (his parents, his school, his past) contemplate the expense of going overseas? I hadn't even had the money that evening to pay for the fish and chips. ('On me,' Otterton had announced, leaning in the car knowing I was broke. 'It's our final meal together.')

'How long are you going for?' I asked.

'Six weeks. Sometimes,' she went on, 'it's nearer eight.'

She might, in the light of our predicament, have said, 'Six years': there was little chance, after all that time, and the distractions of the Riviera, that she'd remember who I was.

'I could write to you,' I said.

'That's a good idea,' she said and, with the interior light turned on above our heads, and with a pencil borrowed from Otterton, and a piece of paper from the fish and chips, she wrote down her address.

'Will you write back?' I asked.

'Of course I will,' she said (she hadn't asked for mine).

'Who are you staying with?' I asked.

'Friends.'

'Friends?'

'Of Daddy's. He has lots of friends down there. We sometimes go at Christmas.'

My vision of a future with the daughter of a man who spent both the winter and the summer on the Riviera vanished with the sound of Otterton running the car across the kerb and Bea announcing, 'That doorway over there,' – a green-painted door, like the door to a house, let into a high stone wall.

We kissed, perfunctorily, goodnight.

'I'll write to you,' I said.

'I'll look forward to hearing from you,' she said, and the door was opened and I was given my first glimpse of the path which led, beneath the shadowed mass of trees and through pools of light, to the hidden house above.

4

'KIDS IN?'

Charlie had come in: an ebullient man, he rubbed his hands
against the cold and went to the fire, acquainted himself with
the fact that it wasn't lit, and, turning, with the same cheeriness
to me, went on, 'Had time to find your way about?'

'Etty got in Mrs Otterman when she went to fetch the
children,' I said.

'I told her that she should.' His tall, suited figure – a large,
square, round-featured head – was turned with its back to the
empty grate. 'Now you're up here,' he added, 'we don't want
you spending too much time on your own.'

'Most of my life I've been on my own,' I said. 'One way or
another.'

'Along with Bea.' He rubbed his ample hands together.

'Without support from anyone.'

'That's right.' His attention drifted to the ceiling: '*I got it
first!*' followed by one of the children's cries. 'In their room?'

'That's right.'

A barrister, his practice had, in recent years, confined him
principally to the north, briefs of astounding insignificance
taking him to Manchester and Leeds, to Liverpool and Hull,
Beverley and York (Halifax and Bradford – Wakefield, Castle-
ford, Durham and Shipley): 'Old age,' he had said when I had
chided him for this narrowing of his horizons for, as a younger
man, before his marriage, he had travelled as far afield as
South Africa and South America (the United States and Russia)
representing 'causes', a legacy, this, from his years in London,

both where he had studied and had met (and married) Etty before, on his father's death, returning north to take on the family practice. 'Why,' I had told him, 'you are still a child,' (he was, I'd estimated, in his middle thirties). 'You don't shut up shop until you're dead, and perhaps,' I'd gone on, 'not even then. The whole of life before you!'

Despite his upbringing, background and profession, he was chairman of the Ardsley and District Labour Party (dominated until recently by the National Union of Mineworkers), succeeding in the task through what I could only describe as (for a lawyer) a uniquely disingenuous nature (as well as the amount of time he was prepared to put in, together with the quality and quantity of legal advice he freely dispensed), his refusal to acknowledge malice in anyone earning him a reputation for what the *Ardsley and District Express* – shown to me by Etty, not him – had described as his 'probitious generosity': 'They even have to invent a word to describe him. Or do you think it's a misprint?' Etty enquired.

'I could sell the house,' he had once remarked when I pointed out the disparity between his own resources and those of the people whom he had chosen to represent. 'At least, Etty could, for it's hers, and I haven't the time. We could live in Second Avenue,' (a row of, at one time, gas-lit cottages, the most notorious street in the village) 'but, taking into account the circumstances, I can't see it would do either us or our critics any good. Those who don't like me living in The People's Palace,' (as the house was now known) 'would only get something worse for their pains, and both the Party and I would be handicapped for the lack of space. Party walls, to coin a phrase, in Second Avenue, aren't that thick, and the amount of work I'm obliged to do at home wouldn't be facilitated by the noise coming through from the other side. When the day comes to hand over our ill-gotten gains they'll get an idea of how much it costs to keep on a roof so that they can come up here most days and sound off as long and as loud as they like.'

When Etty first introduced him to our house in Belsize Park (as if he not I were its rightful owner: 'My genial giant,' she had proudly declared), she had said, 'He is a liberal of the kind which set the Labour Party on its feet: sentimental and, to the degree that it is often mistaken for passion, loyal to his class in ways of which he is unaware. He wouldn't turn a hair,' (indicating, with a swing of her arm – six years out of the Courtauld and still a child – the fourteen rooms of our Victorian mansion) 'at living here if he felt he could put it to good use. Quite a counterblast,' she had concluded, 'to you.'

'I'll give them a shock and go up,' he said. 'Etty's not expecting me back so soon.'

'Why's that?' I said.

'With having you here she's been on tenterhooks,' he said. 'I thought I'd get back early. After all,' he smiled, 'we want to do the best by you.'

A further smile from his brown-eyed, round-featured face – the same expansive look with which he had greeted me when I had first arrived – and he was gone. 'What are you two up to!' came the cry, followed by (a unified), '*Daddy!*'

The sound of a kiss as he greeted Etty, and of several more as, accompanied by the splashing of water (they were evidently in the bathroom), he lifted each of the children.

'What are you going to do?' My father stands in front of the black-leaded range in the living-room of our house at Onasett.

Onasett: Ona's Headland: His Place: a Viking warlord who cleared a space on the crest of the wooded ridge that projected southward to the river – taken over, subsequently, by Dane and Saxon and, previous to all of them, the Romans who built a side-road, west, from Watling Street, into the Pennine hills – passing to the north of Onasett as the road to Manchester still does (isolating, in the process, the between-the-two-world-wars housing estate of three thousand semi-detached houses – a scree of brick and tile, of hedged lawn and field and tarmac that climbs one side of Ona's original Sett to the brick-built school and hospital and the stone-built church that form a crustaceous backbone to the ridge).

Our house, in front of whose living-room fire my father

32

stands, lies halfway up the eastward-facing slope (catching in its principal windows the morning sun – and looking out to the higher ridge on which are poised, in silhouette, the principal buildings of the town: the County Hall dome, the Greek-porticoed entrance to the Courts of Law, the chisel-roofed tower of the French-Renaissance-styled Town Hall, the dog-toothed spire of the Gothic cathedral – a résumé of an architectural heritage poised, in its totality, as a reciprocal spine to this more imposing ridge on which Ona set his original dwelling).

'I've got a job.'

'Where?'

My father is in his fiftieth year: small, broad-shouldered, stocky, his eyes are dark, not unlike my own – darkened further, however, in his case, by the dust that never leaves the lids. In the past few years he has risen from an underground maintenance worker to a coal-face foreman: the responsibility, in charge of thirty-five men, has subdued his once ebullient nature: he comes home now too tired to eat, or, if he has eaten, too tired to undress, falling asleep in front of the fire, his eyes, in his exhaustion, half-open (eerily-gleaming beneath the half-closed lids, the mouth ajar, air roaring through his dust-filled nose).

'At Chamberlains,' I tell him.

'You could have gone theer when you wa're only fifteen,' he tells me.

I've worked, as it is, at Chamberlains for the previous four summers: a contractor and erector of marquees at agricultural shows and weddings.

'After all this time at school. And now,' he goes on, 'you're geving it up.'

The argument is one of several which have taken place over the previous weeks: 'All these years', 'A lifetime of effort', 'What have we done to deserve it?' 'Chucking it away.'

It is the week of my first letter to Bea: I am, amidst scenes of industrial dereliction, imagining her caught up in the distractions of a sun-baked beach, wine-laden tables, palm trees, yachts, a waveless sea: "Here I am, reproached by bickering parents, broke, with no prospects whatsoever, ridiculed for what

I intend to be (already am). My form-master has written to say, in giving up university, I have let down King Edward's: 'All these years of teaching' etc., in much the same way as my father says, 'All these years of working down a mine . . .' "

'All these years of working down the pit so you can go to King Edward's and all you do,' his eyes alight with a vehemence which outshines the glow of the fire behind, 'is chuck it in our face.'

'There's a difference between education, as you would define it, and enlightenment,' I tell him (a prick at the age of eighteen as I am at sixty-five).

'Enlightment,' he says, 'is not having to do work like an animal in a cave.'

He coughs: a moment later, he retches.

"You'll be surprised to hear," I go on in my letter, "I've taken a job as a labourer. It won't leave me any time to paint but will give me enough cash, with overtime, to silence the opposition. I've worked at this place over the past four years (since, in fact, the age of thirteen). We travel, seven days a week (double-time on Sundays) to showgrounds across the north of England – and to country houses where, on lawns across which are scattered ancient trees, we erect marquees for society weddings – tents into which the bride and groom occasionally wander and, hand in hand, inspect the coloured awnings, the parquet floor, the boxes and racks arranged with flowers, the metalwork tables and the metalwork chairs, and, once in a while, I hear one or other of the two remark, 'My darling, this is jolly,' and, 'I say, my dear, just look at this,' and imagine turning up one day at Ardsley Hall and setting up a tent in the grounds for the wedding of Miss Beatrice Corcoran to a man who spends in one evening taking you out what it takes me a month to earn with a fourteen-pound hammer."

'I'll never be a teacher,' I tell him. 'I'll never subvert the most precious thing I have – my individuality – to a common interest. Why should I compromise that to become one of a hundred thousand others – a teacher, a hack, a professional?'

'Because,' my father says, 'everybody does, king or miner,

teacher or priest. They have to earn a living. Otherwise,' he declares, 'they beg off others.'

'I'll work at Chamberlains,' I tell him.

'Chamberlains,' he tells me, 'employs the riff-raff of the town. They pay a quarter of what you'd earn as a teacher, or in any other job, if it comes to that.'

His face is lined: a file of coal-dust extends laterally beneath the skin where, in the past, a cut has healed.

"The first year I came here, at the age of thirteen, the first to arrive, I sat in the sun. Around me was an ash-filled yard enclosed by low, wooden sheds in which canvas was stored – poles, ropes, stakes, awnings and flooring – and in one of which, on the step of which I was sitting, the canvas was sewn on two rectangular, smooth-surfaced tables, two foot-pedalled sewing-machines attached to the sides. I was joined by a man with a snap-bag on his back who, crouching in the sun beside me, announced that he, too, was applying for a job. He had, he confided, just come out of prison and his application, as a consequence, would be accompanied by one or two lies. He had, in prison, he further confided, acquired a hobby: even as he spoke he was filing at a piece of metal – a 'connecting-rod', he told me, of a model locomotive – looking up as the door to the office was finally opened and the figure of a woman could be seen inside.

To my horror, Bea, when I went in, this woman – sitting at a crowded desk – exclaimed, '*Fenchurch!* What on earth are *you* doing here?' causing me to blush to the soles of my feet. I then realised – which, my dear Bea, you might have done already – that the celebrated (the redoubtable) Mrs Chamberlain, the school secretary at King Edward's, and the terror of the Heads of both that school and the High (not to mention the masters and mistresses) was the wife of one of the Chamberlain brothers (three in number, she the spouse of the eldest and the most retired): unknown to me, during the school holidays, she lent a hand in the Chamberlain office – in front of whose desk I was presently standing. 'Fenchurch!' she exclaimed –

much to the puzzlement of the ex-con beside me, 'what on *earth* are you doing *here?* A pupil of King Edward's!'

I have been a renegade, Miss Corcoran, all my life – at home, at work, at school, at play: the last in my year at King Edward's to be made a prefect (a history of beatings lower down the school for misbehaviour), 'a bolshie-headed bastard' in the words of the woodwork-master whom I foolishly confronted at fisticuffs when he discovered me writing in the library one lunch-hour when it was out of bounds – and for which, in my last year, not for the first time, I was threatened with expulsion: 'Don't you realise, Fenchurch,' said the Head (the Oxonian classics scholar P.G. 'Piggy' Norton) 'that Mr Barraclough, like you, *is a former member of the working-class?*'

Dear Bea, with whom I have danced on only one or two occasions and whom, as yet, I have never taken out, to you all this, I know, must sound absurd: reading a letter from someone whom, despite our tête-à-tête at Allgrave, you scarcely know, but – I have to complete this tale in the hope that I may, at the very least, capture your attention when distractions – for you – crowd in on every side. Since you are familiar with the broad-bosomed, tweed-suited Mrs Chamberlain ('Flossie' to her intimates, 'Bloody old Flo' behind her back), who strides between our schools like a policeman on the beat and talks to masters and mistresses – as well as our respective Heads – as ferociously as she does to the boys and girls ('What are you doing in the street, boy/girl, without your cap/hat? I shall report you to Mr Norton/Miss Quartermain!') I feel obliged to complete my account of our interview for, having come upon her in such unfortunate surroundings, I could only confess – as, indeed, I do to you – 'I've come for a job, Mrs Chamberlain,' to which, on this first occasion, she instantly responded, 'You've been a trouble-maker, Fenchurch, from the start,' while, to my equally instantaneous response, 'I have to get a job,' she roared, 'Have you taken leave of your senses! Are you aware of the sort of people who work down here?' gesturing to the sun-lit yard where I could see a group of men assembling, not a minority of whom, in my father's and no doubt Mrs Chamberlain's terminology, would have come under the generic heading of riff-raff. Indeed, attracted by her voice (it could, I discovered later, be heard in the street outside) the whole of this group, with their snap-bags and their morning papers, their disreputable and dishevelled dress, turned in our direction.

'How old are you, Fenchurch?' she enquired.

'Thirteen,' I said.

'Thirteen what?'

'Thirteen years,' I responded.

'Thirteen years what?' she further demanded.

'Thirteen years, Mrs Chamberlain,' I was reminded.

'How can you be thirteen, *Fenchurch*,' (made to sound like an ecclesiastical sewer) 'when last year you were in 5b and next year you'll be in 5 Upper?' (encyclopaedic recall).

'I passed the eleven-plus entrance exam when I was only nine,' I said.

'It's not usually taken until you are twelve,' (further evidence of dissemblement, trouble-making, mischief).

'They closed the loop-hole,' I said, 'the following year. It's to do with my birthday, and the time of the year, and that I was moved up two classes by mistake at primary school,' (further evidence of chicanery).

'We don't employ boys,' she said, 'who are only thirteen. Furthermore, we don't employ people whose minds will be polluted by all they hear from the workmen, let alone by what they are obliged to see. Wait until Mr Norton hears about this.'

'Hears about what?' said a voice behind my back.

Turning, I was confronted by a massive figure: a rock-shaped, square-featured, close-cropped head beamed down at me from the office door.

'This, Harry,' Mrs Chamberlain said, 'is a pupil from King Edward's who, believe it or not, is applying for a job.'

The square, ruddy-cheeked, blue-eyed face beamed at me more broadly.

'I was a pupil theer,' it said, 'myself.'

'That is hardly a comparison, Harry,' Mrs Chamberlain said.

'I'll shove him in my gang, Mother,' the figure replied. 'What d'ost think to that, then, young 'un? If you find it too rough you'll be out on your ear. I on'y have rough 'uns in my lot.'

'This is my son,' Mrs Chamberlain said. 'If you're not up to scratch you'll be out on your ear,' showing, in my experience, not only a surprising deference but a not any the less surprising command of colloquialism.

'What's thy first name, young 'un?' the son enquired.

'Richard,' I replied.

'Richard.' His blue-eyed look went up to the window and the row of curious faces outside. He gave a laugh – not the last I was to hear that day. 'I'll call you college-boy,' he said. 'Come outside and load a lorry.'

On this last occasion, when I arrived this summer, Mrs Chamberlain said, 'Do you mean to say, Fenchurch, you're giving up *varsity* to work down here? The Wainscliff Prize for English Verse, the Atterton Prize for Art, the Athletics' Team Representative in the 880 yards, and the *First Fifteen at Rugger.*'

'I have to get a job,' I said.

'Perversity in your life,' she said, 'I have to admit, has never known its limit.' "

'You've given up all we've done for you,' my father says and, as my mother intervenes ('He takes it all for granted. We've worked our fingers to the bone'), he adds, 'They'll be laughing fit to burst round here. All the neighbours' lads at fifteen were i' the mill or down the pit and he ends up at Chamberlains. Nowt but the bloody riff-raff theer.'

Facing me, his back to the fireplace – a glimpse, through the uncurtained windows, of the darkening trees – is Charlie, a figure whom I have, I believe, already addressed as 'Dad' – and then, more confusedly, as 'Harry'. 'I have to get a job,' I say, to which he replies, 'Your royalties are enough to cover your cost of living. On top of which,' he goes on, 'you have the Public Lending Right.'

'I never joined,' I tell him. 'I've never been a lackey. I've never had a penny from anyone I didn't earn. Have you seen the people who apply? Have you seen the *forms* you have to fill in?' I ramble on ('What's individuality and independence mean if you're subsumed by a bureaucratic function?') to find, or so it seems, the television turned on and Glenda sitting on Charlie's knee and Etty sitting with her arm around Lottie while I, assuming they had gone to bed, enquire, 'Have they had their bath?'

'Charlie wanted to bath them,' Etty says. 'He seldom gets the chance.'

'I could have bathed them both,' I tell her.

'Yes,' she says in a tone which suggests that, no matter how convenient to Charlie and herself, something as controversial as this will not be allowed.

'I used to bath all four of you,' I tell her.

'I remember,' Etty says while, to my astonishment, Lottie says, 'Do hush, Grandpa. We'll never hear.'

Maidstone, when the intensity of my illness began to abate, suggested I went on lithium. 'It won't suppress depression,' he said, 'but once you come out of it it will make its re-occurrence less severe.'

'How long do I have to take it?' I enquired.

'A lifetime,' he said. 'You don't, after all, want to go on living like this. I don't think anyone could stand it.'

When I said, 'I like my life the way it is,' he immediately responded, 'There's more than you, of course, involved.'

I liked him: a prematurely greying, portly figure with uniquely mobile features which he could flex at will into all manner of expressions: grim, kind, despairing and – most frequently – fatigued.

'Being on anti-depressants is bad enough. As for tranquillisers,' I said, 'I've given them up.'

The fact was, I was taking nothing: 'No human being can survive what you are going through. Everyone,' he told me, 'has to take something. In the old days it was Shepherd's Balm, but whether it was opiates, alcohol or, later still, barbiturates, this kind of illness demanded treatment by something.'

I was unhappier than I'd ever been: lying to those who

wanted to help ('You are taking them, I take it?' – the drugs prescribed: 'Of course I am,' I told him), which intensified, in turn, the desolation I felt each morning (noon and night): when I had taken the drugs I had merely lain on the bed and cried, 'Help!' no other formulation of thought or expression of feeling coming to mind.

'The fact is, without lithium, once this spell is ended, I don't think you could carry on.' His eyes examined mine.

'With what?' I said.

'Living,' he said, 'an adequate life.'

'What, by your definition, is adequate?' I said.

He smiled. 'Doing the things you've done before. Like you,' he went on, 'many of my patients are creative people. As a group, they are, like you, more susceptible to this illness than any other, and though they might, temporarily, come off lithium, under supervision – while, for instance, they complete a book, or perform in a concert, or mount an exhibition, they would be in no shape to do any of these things if they hadn't been on it in the first place. It's preferable to analysis, which is inclined to formalise your instinctual life. It's a disability, after all, like any other – an arthritic hip, an impediment of speech, a diabetic condition.'

'I'd describe none of those as an experiential illness,' I replied.

'In that case,' he said, 'you're mistaken. Over ninety per cent of the people in this hospital are here for what I would describe as psychological reasons. All illnesses are injuries to the body, and all injuries to the body are injuries incurred in the mind. Who's to know why a woman broke her leg, or a man has cancer, or a youth gonorrhoea? Yet when each patient comes in it's not for a "psychological" cure. All I'm offering you,' he went on, 'is practical support. I don't know anyone who doesn't have something unsatisfactory in their background, but the problem, as I see it, isn't "when?" and "how?" but "what?" and "which?" If, for instance, you had a broken hip, the remedy I'd apply would have nothing to do with when and how you came to do it. "When?" and "how?" are what the analysts go in for, with a clear-up rate consistent with not having intruded on the patient at all.'

'I don't think, if I had a broken hip, I'd think about the nature of God and have visions of hell that defy description,' I said.

'The effect of the anaesthetic, if the break had been severe, or the discomfort of the break itself, might induce you to think of any number of things, amongst which presentiments of hell would not be the least to be considered. Chemical activity synonymous with depression is not all that different from the effects, let's say, of acid in the stomach. Both can give you a disagreeable night and, despite the current mythologising of mental illness, the principle is much the same. The mind hallucinates, for instance, during fever. When we are over the worst, however, we don't look at the wallpaper and say, "Those roses are human faces. I saw them during my illness and I know them now to be real." '

'You discount,' I said, 'the experiences I'm having?'

'I examine them,' he said, 'to see how far you are past the worst.'

'I've tried to save you from working on your belly eight hours of the day or night, with two hundred yards of rock above your head, smelling like an animal, looking like an animal, thinking like an animal.'

My father's eyes are incandescent, like the fire behind his back.

'All you have done for me,' I tell him, 'I am putting to better use.' ('A use which,' I might have gone on, 'if all goes well, might well transcend our lives').

'What on earth is he talking about?' He turns to my mother, a half-startled, half-apprehensive figure, standing by his side, round-cheeked, round-faced, pale-eyed behind her reflecting glasses.

'Ask him,' she says, 'how he's going to get the money.'

'To do what?' I ask.

'To paint your pictures,' she says, 'and write your poems.

41

Your father can't go on providing for you. He's provided long enough.'

That night I write, "I wonder, with the objectivity that separation from this place must give you (even if it is the Riviera), what, if you were here, you would advise me to do . . ."

'A story, Grandpa!' Having left her father's knee, Glenda, clutching at my leg, waits to be lifted – like, for the better part of twelve years, I hoisted up her mother (even at the age of thirteen, Etty would say, 'Tell me a story! Oh, do!' sitting in my lap).

'Tell us a story, Grandpa.' Her sister sidles up (the television, the programme at an end, turned off).

'About?'

'Scouts.'

'Scouts?'

'The one you told us the other night.'

'We used to camp,' I tell her, 'at Broughton Woods, not many miles from here. It stood, the camp-site, at the edge of a wood, and was approached from the foot of a steep embankment. (You know what a steep embankment is?)'

'A steep rise in the ground,' says Lottie, who has heard the description before.

'We had to carry everything up in bits and pieces but, at the top, we came onto an area of grass in the shape of a horseshoe on which we pitched our tents, built our kitchen, erected our marquee and our flagpole. At the back of the camp-site was a dry stone wall, to one side of which stood a ruined gamekeeper's stone-built cottage in which we made use of the old earth closet, a lavatory,' I add to Glenda, 'where you don't have to pull the chain.'

'Oh,' she says and, grimacing, adds, 'Go on.'

'Across a meadow at the foot of the embankment ran a stream. Beyond it rose an area of spoil-heaps where the monks in the old days dug for coal. The whole area was overgrown, with only a herd of cows sent, from time to time, across it. The stream, in places, was very deep and, in one of the deepest pools, below a weir, where a line of stepping-stones led over to the farm where we got our milk, the newcomers to the camp, which, on the first occasion, of course, included me, were tossed in, in a ceremony known as "duffing". Two of the older scouts got hold of your arms and legs and, chanting, threw you in. Whereupon you scrambled out the other side and joined the other "duffers" who, after that, had to sing a song.'

'What song, Grandpa?' Lottie asks.

'The Scout Song, written by the first vicar of St Michael's Church at Onasett, which was built from the stone of a nearby mill, beam on beam and stone on stone, and which to this day looks not unlike a mill – thrust out on the slope above the valley but where, through its mullioned, clear-glass windows, I got my first glimpse of – do you know what a glimpse is, Glen?' I am about to add, 'Of God,' but, without waiting for an answer, add, ' "The Peewit Song" which, because I was a peewit, went, as Lottie knows, as follows:

I used to be a Peewit,
A jolly Peewit, too,
But now I've given up Pee-witting
I don't know what to do:
I'm growing old and weary
And I can Peewit no more,
So I'm going to work my passage if I can:

Back to Ona-sett,
Happy Land!
I'm going to work my passage if I can!
Of course, if you were a Swift, or an Owl, or a Cuckoo . . .'

'A cuckoo!' Lottie and Glenda laugh.

'You sang the appropriate word.'

'Back to Ona-sett!' sings Lottie.

'Happy Land!' we sing together.

'I'm going to work my passage if I can,' sings Glenda.

'Now we're all peewits,' I tell them. 'And when you're as old as I am you, too, will know what you have to do.'

'Work our passage,' Lottie says.

'Back to Onasett!' I cry.

'Don't get Grandpa upset,' says Etty, while Charlie says, 'Bed-time, I think, for one of these.'

'What happened then?' asks Lottie.

'Then we went about our usual duties.' I dry my eyes. 'Those who were the cooks, cooked, those who were responsible for fuel went into the wood and brought back branches, which we then chopped up, and those who had to fetch the water took dixies downstream to Broughton Springs. Finally, when we had had our competitions – to do with making implements, keeping the camp tidy and learning how to track and to read the weather and to tie knots and to do first-aid – we played our games.'

'What sort of games?' Glenda, with the threat of bed, snuggles closer to my chest.

'The ones I liked were where half the camp had to go to a rendezvous and retrieve a message hidden earlier in the day by one of the scouters and bring it back to camp, which the other half were obliged to defend. We each wore a coloured ribbon on our arm or around our chest which, if someone succeeded in removing it, made you their prisoner or, in some of the games, meant you were dead. Those were fights! Especially when we played at night, somebody dropping from a tree or rising from the ferns. And the stars and the moon, and the owls and the doves, and the shouts and the cries. Or,' I go on, 'we rode the woodcutters' trolley, a truck which ran on a rail and which, if you pushed it to the top of the wood, took you back, rattling, to the cutting-shed at the foot of the slope where the trees were sawn into planks. The smell of the dust and the wood and the oil from the cutter! For the place was deserted most of the time. There we'd be, hurtling down, the branches clipping by on either side, cowboys or brigands trying to stop us . . .'

'Go on,' says Glenda, her dark eyes shut against my chest, her thumb in her mouth.

'At night, when the last of the attackers had come into the

camp, and we'd counted up the tally of coloured ribbons, we'd make a dixie of cocoa and sing.'

'Your Peewit Song?' says Lottie, her eyes shut, too, against my chest.

'Like "Goodnight, Ladies"! and "Old MacDonald"! and "Michael Finnegan"!, and then we'd have a prayer and go back to our tents and get into our blankets and start telling stories all over again, like "The Ghost with the Golden Arm" while, outside, the moon shone, the dew dropped on the grass, the owls fluttered in the trees, the firelight glowed, lighting up the circle of tents in each of which six sleeping heads finally fell back against their make-shift pillows. Like Glenda's and Lottie's, you see, are falling now . . .'

"Dear Bea, I've been thinking of that incident I told you about some time ago. Do you recall? I was fourteen and twenty or thirty of us were coming home one sunny afternoon from our summer camp on the North Yorkshire Moors, singing songs on the back of a lorry. Ahead I heard a sound which, by its persistency and harshness, I judged to be that of a rusty machine. One corroded flange of metal rasped against another until, as if arrested by the sound itself, the lorry stopped.

The traffic on the opposite side of the road had disappeared – until that moment a steady stream of cars and coaches heading for the North Sea coast – and one of the three scouters who, in the absence of our scoutmaster-vicar, had been in charge of the camp, climbed onto our equipment and, leaning forward, looked over the cab. He was there for only a moment, climbing back down, pale beneath his tan and the reflected light of his glasses (a clerk in a local bank). 'No one look forward,' he said, at which, the troop's principal rabble-rouser, I immediately climbed over the equipment and looked.

Directly in front of the lorry lay the figure of a boy not much younger than myself: in particular I noticed the neatness of his woollen stockings folded beneath his knees, the cleanness of his brown-strap sandals, and the way his grey, short-legged trousers were matched by a light grey shirt. A tie, with an alternately red and blue diagonal stripe was fastened around his collar. Over his shirt he wore a checkered jumper with a similarly diagonal pattern, pale blue and grey. Where his head should have been was a pool of matter, light-grey, in which were scattered fragments of bone. The word 'matter' came to me as a way of explaining what, in those first few moments, my senses refused to acknowledge. A man, standing astride this figure, was endeavouring, unsuccessfully, to direct the traffic which, I now noticed, on both sides of the road, had come to a halt.

In the centre of the road, kneeling, was a second man. With a peculiarly rhythmical gesture he was beating his forehead against the tarmac: it, and the rest of his face, was covered in blood, a mask of blood from within which his tortured eyes gazed out.

Across the road, on the pavement, stood a woman, the source of the screeching sound I had earlier heard: retching, she produced the sound each time she exhaled, stooping, bent forward from the waist, keeping bizarrely in time to the similar movements of the man beating his head against the tarmac.

At the doors of several houses which overlooked the scene – large, detached, with driveways running down to the road – a man was enquiring, ineffectually, for something to cover the body. Finally, having watched his efforts, the man astride the body took off his jacket and covered the upper half with that. Beneath its lower edge its neatly-sandalled legs stretched out.

From a bystander we discovered that the woman screeching on the pavement was the victim's mother, and the man beating his head against the road her husband. They had, we discovered later, been driving in a car to the coast, the boy in the back, despite warnings, fiddling with the door catch. He fell out: a bus, full of holidaymakers, travelling immediately behind, despite swerving, ran over his head.

What I recall most vividly afterwards was the sense of outrage which, amongst other things, inclined me to the view that all vehicles should be destroyed, a feeling which was followed,

46

when our lorry finally moved off, by one of relief – growing, when our speed increased, into something little short of exhilaration. I hadn't, after all, been run over by a bus; and although I could vividly imagine those terrible last seconds – the fall, the cry, the approaching tyre – and share in the mother's grief and the father's anguish, I hadn't been – perhaps never would be – the one to suffer: war and famine, disease and disaster, madness and death had, with a peculiar consistency, passed me by. I hadn't, metaphorically, been obliged to step down from the lorry. Life – destiny – had sanctioned my existence in a way that nothing else quite could.

As I talked to the children tonight, in words though not with feelings far above their heads (and Etty has given me instructions never to get in touch with you again without seeking your permission – something of a contradiction), I couldn't help sitting down in this room where I have sat on so many previous occasions, a reading-lamp lit on the table beside me, the window looking through the trees to the lights of the village, and set down what might be described as a postscript to all the letters I have sent before, a declaration which, at this first effort, reads, 'I am kneeling in the road, beating my head against the tarmac, looking at all we have left of our life together in the hope (not terror but anticipation) that, at the end of another day, despite your marriage to a man whom you knew, when you chose him, I would only despise (the antithesis of all we ever fought for), you might (despite all that has happened to us, Bea) come home to me again . . ."

5

'THY'LL TAKE some stick,' Chamberlain said. 'Riding with me, tha knows, i' the cab.'

'Why?' I said, squashed up beside him, with two other workmen, squashed slightly less, on my other side.

'Dalton usually rides in here. He's up on top o' the load at present. When tha gets out thy'd better stay clear.' He swung the lorry's wheel beneath his hand. 'He's a reet good puncher, is Dolly.'

He laughed: the two men beside him – 'Dolly's pals, are these two,' – laughed as well.

'I'll go on the back, in that case,' I said.

'Nay, thy'll bloody well get blown off, thy's far too light. I asked you in,' he paused at a traffic light, then, with the ramming of the gear beside my leg, set the vehicle once more in motion, adding, 'for an intellectual conversation.'

The men beside me laughed again.

'Thick as planks, these two,' Chamberlain said.

'That's right, Mr Chamberlain,' the two men said.

'Do Latin, do you?' Chamberlain said.

'That's right,' I said.

'Amo, amas, amat. These two won't know what that adds up to.'

'Love,' I said.

'Does Battersby hit you with his stick?'

'That's right.'

The two men laughed again.

'How long were you there?' I asked.

'Not long.' Chamberlain's arm was raised from the wheel. 'My faither yanked me out. "Thy'll learn more about ought i' Chamberlains," he said, "than you'll learn i' theer," and though the old lady put up a fight he had me in the yard at sixteen wi' this bloody lot. Isn't that right, you lads?' he added.

'That's right, Mr Chamberlain,' the two men said.

'They leave it all to me, my faither and my uncles. Teks a man wi' brains to do the setting-up. Isn't that right, then, lads?'

'That's right, Mr Chamberlain,' the two men said.

'Bloody champions, these two,' Chamberlain said.

"The men, after four years at Chamberlains, are used to me, and Harry (the owner, now his uncles and father have retired) sets me off with a gang on my own to put up the smaller marquees. I've a feeling, in a week or so, he'll let me loose on a larger one. The other day I couldn't help contrasting this with the first day I came here: we'd arrived at a house on the outskirts of Linfield with a view to putting up a wedding marquee. The garden was enormous and the tent had to be carried down several flights of steps to a lawn at the back. Because of the weight of the pieces the men grew fractious. One of them, Dalton – a foul-mouthed character of enormous proportions whose place I'd taken in the cab – took objection to the, in his view, minimal amount I carried and picked a quarrel. 'I don't like college-boys,' he said. 'Do you know what I do with them?' at which he picked me up with one arm and dropped me in a bed of nettles. Pulling out a garden stake I ran at him. Hearing me coming, he swung aside and – laughing as he'd walked away with two of his chums – hit me such a blow I fell into a hole at the side of the path which, fortunately, full of compost, softened my fall.

I stank like a sewer and screamed like a child but quickly climbed out and ran at him again. He fought me then as he might a man, picking his blows (holding me, at one point, with one hand and beating me round the head with the other). It was only when Chamberlain came across – he'd watched the incident from a distance – and said, 'Hit him again, Dolly, and

49

thy'll be hitting me,' (he had arms like pit-props and legs to match), 'and you hit Dolly, college-boy, and you'll have to tek me on.'

The next fight I had I was more prepared, and though I was given something of a beating, I gave as much of a beating back, and the man who picked the fight is working with me now and asks me occasionally for the spelling (and meaning) of 'difficult words', not because, he says, he 'wants to know' but because 'he likes to hear my voice',

The place we're in is a municipal park in a town you've never heard of. The ground is rock solid. In groups of six we stand in a circle to drive in the stakes, our hammers, each with a fourteen-pound head, striking up a rhythm, each hammer-head no sooner on the stake and lifted than the next in line descends. The canvas is laid out, secured to the principal poles by metal rings, raised slightly from the ground, then laced together. Finally, in groups of four, we secure the guys and haul the canvas up, insert the side-poles and hang the walls. As darkness falls the tents loom like animals around what, before we arrived, had been a featureless arena.

Things at home are much the same. I hand in a wage which, with overtime, is the same, after deductions, as my father's. How are things on the Riviera?"

Bea gives place to Isabella (*née* Kells), her father the embryologist turned Government dietician who, during the Second World War, created the infamous Kell Cake which, according to my father (who, between 1943, when they were introduced, and 1946, when they finally disappeared, must have fried up several thousand), was comprised of granulated coal, senna pods and a sprinkling of vitamins A and D (the latter, it was subsequently discovered, an antidote to certain types of depression).

A tall, rangey man, with a tongue of white hair that flicked to and fro across his brow, his original claim to fame had been his publication in the 1920s of *The Life of the African Locust: the study of a central nervous system*, in which, digressing from his theme – that there was, in each cell, an imprint of its previous existence – he had offered the suggestion that golf was the one activity in life that would unite the middle and the working classes: 'on the links and in the club-house are where true spirits meet.' The son of a Dorsetshire labourer – the son himself of an Irish navvy – he had worked his way to Oxford and, from there, during the war, to the Ministry of Health – returning to post-war academic life to discover that his proposition that change was exclusive of environment had grown increasingly out of fashion and from where he retired, finally, to the home of his daughter and son-in-law, the 'Ardsley Ubiquitarian', as he described him, and where, in addition to playing golf, he spent much of his time teaching science to Bea – the principle influence, apart from myself, on Bea's life.

'Mum, initially, was against you coming.' Etty offers me a drink (which I refuse), Charlie upstairs seeing Lottie to bed ('He tells her a story, just like you, but is not so long about it'). The curtains are drawn, the fire lit – something which, while the children are being put to bed, I've been inclined to do myself (fetching logs from the yard at the back, or, since that supply is now depleted, from beneath the trees themselves). 'She doesn't like you coming,' (facing me across the hearth, curiously on edge whenever she and I are together and Charlie is around). 'Ever since your illness.'

'I wasn't aware of that.' I add, 'She loved this place. Especially as a child.'

'You ought to let Ardsley go,' she says. 'Don't think you have to hold on to it because of her.'

'I don't,' I tell her, and continue, 'Her father was a labourer's son, of Irish descent who won his way to Oxford and, believe it or not, into insect physiology. During the Second World War he was drafted into the Ministry of Health and became a dietician. He invented Kell Cakes, "the working-man's Yorkshire Pudding".'

'I thought Yorkshire Pudding was the working-man's Yorkshire Pudding,' she says, and laughs, having heard this story a thousand times, and adds, 'In any case, you're talking about Gran's father, not Mum's.'

'Bed-time, Lottie!' Charlie commands, halfway down the stairs, his feet returning to the children's door.

'In the first years of our marriage we came here every month. Certainly every summer,' I tell her.

' "He was always begging to come up," Mum says. "To see his mother-in-law," ' Etty tells me, imitating less Bea's voice than her tone.

'What mother-in-law?'

' "His beloved Isabella. It embarrassed all of us at times. She, of course, pretended not to notice. Father, of course, was always in the yard, or out driving on a lorry." '

'In addition to being a quarter Irish,' I lean back in my chair, 'your mother is Lebanese.'

'An eighth Sardinian,' Etty says.

'Her grandfather was Irish, her mother the daughter of a Lebanese tart.'

'The daughter of a Lebanese who, as was the custom at the time, happened to have had three wives. His daughter by his second marriage, to a Sardinian, she came over here to study science – for the daughter of a Lebanese merchant, far ahead of her time.'

'Corcoran met Isabella on the Riviera between the First and Second World Wars,' I tell her, 'and seduced her beneath a palm tree. As a child he took her back there and said, "That's where you were born," the tree itself still standing. At least, after one of her post-war holidays there, that's what your mother told me. It's what,' I go on, 'induces her moods, that mixture of the Mediterranean and the bogs of Connemara.' My eyes fixed on a space above Etty's head, I suddenly declare, 'It's what drove her back to science. Once she's discovered a cure for cancer in the non-coagulant properties of the moorland leech she'll turn to something else. Her and that bloody Albert, "the people's friend". Has she asked you to go and see him?'

'On several occasions,' Etty says.

'Before he met your mother he lived with another woman.'

52

'Rose.'

'She came to see me and asked me, would you believe it, if "I couldn't control my wife".'

She sips her drink, disinclined to talk about her mother 'behind', as she once told me, 'Mummy's back'.

'We used to sit in here for hours, Kells and I,' I tell her. 'I told you about his idea that golf was potentially the greatest unifier of mankind since time began. Something to do with the limitation, at any given time, on the numbers who could play it, the space required, and the utter fatuity of the exercise. He was, in my view, locusts apart, completely off his head. It's only now, in the last few years, that I've come to appreciate what a remarkable man he was. He never got on with your Grandfather Corcoran's mother. "Nan", as everyone was obliged to call her. A local woman with a ravaged face who lived to be nearly a hundred. The two of them shared a bathroom. The one you never use at the back. And used to call to each other through the door whenever they found it locked. "Are you going to be in there all day, woman?" and she'd shout back, "Go and eat your Kell Cakes!" Corcoran and Isabella and your mother would sit down here, laughing by the hour.'

As Charlie takes a drink already poured for him by Etty from a table behind the door, I add, 'I was telling Etty how Isabella's Lebanese and Celtic background may well have affected her blood. The sands of Araby.'

'Freddie's still talked about,' Charlie says, 'in the village. I don't think a meeting goes by without his name, in one form or another, coming up. "I wonder what he'd think now if he could see The People's Palace?" as they come grinning through the door.'

'I always liked Grandpa,' Etty says. More than any of our children (who, on the whole, responded more warmly to my father), she would cling to the burly, large-fisted man who, with his lorries and his yard (and, for relaxation, his 'Liberal Club'), had scarcely any time for her at all.

'Fighting his drivers,' Charlie says, 'if they offered him abuse.'

'He was driven,' Etty says, 'by the poverty he came from.'

'Like his son-in-law,' I tell her.

'His background,' Etty says, 'was a great deal worse than yours. He started out with a horse and cart as a youth and worked up,' she goes on, 'to a place like this. If anything, *his* father-in-law despised him.'

'Your Great-Grandfather Kells,' Charlie says, 'fell out with a fellow-Mick. Didn't Freddie's father have a horse and cart, and didn't Freddie himself take over? When he came from Linfield to Ardsley he moved into lorries.'

'I've a letter I ought to write,' I suddenly announce. 'And notes I ought to make. If Etty is going to write her book I intend to give her every help.'

'I'm writing nothing of the sort,' she says.

'I keep telling her,' says Charlie. 'She ought to write something. You know what they say about Ardsley? "First thy frizzles, then thy fries, then, if thy still hast nowt, thy dies." '

'That's when the pit was closed,' she says. 'We're not in that situation, my dear, ourselves.'

'I've a meeting at the Club,' he says, 'at nine.' (The Labour Club, ironically, is next door to the former Liberal Club in the village).

'What about this time?' Etty says.

'Do we oppose the Regional Health Board in the closing down of the Fever and Isolation at Sneighton or the Maternity and Lying-In at Swanley?'

'The Fever and Isolation. Life before death,' Etty tells him.

'Wait till we have the fever and need the isolation,' Charlie says, stooping to embrace her.

I see a bulky figure stooping over Isabella before he goes off with her father to golf (the old man was playing at the age of eighty-seven, 'determined,' as he put it, 'to outlive that bloody Nan'), kissing her not on the mouth but the top of her head, nestling his black moustache in her coppery hair, while Isabella's eyes, unfathomed, gaze at me: 'Will you be long?'

'Just give it a knock-about, Bella,' Corcoran says, calling, 'Are you ready, Father?' as Kells, dragging his bag ('That bloody woman's in the bathroom'), comes grumbling down the stairs.

'I liked him,' Etty says. 'Everything about Grandpa was larger than life, and therefore, of course,' she goes on, 'more real. Whatever we disliked about his views, unlike some he earned them.'

"You won't believe this, of course, as you float on your lilo (is it called?) and pedal your pedallo (is it called?) and drink in the sun (is it called?), along with the young men's looks (are they called?), but most evenings now I'm working on a novel – about a woman longing to escape from industrial confinement – a surrogate, no doubt, you'll say, for me. Since the house is crowded with brothers, parents and me, I write it on the toilet (the only place to sit in the bathroom, and the only place I can be alone). In addition, I am painting (when everyone has gone to bed) on pieces of tenting canvas purloined from Chamberlains. Everyone, of course, complains of the smell, just as they complain of the time I spend in the bathroom (of my giving up my 'career', of my consorting with 'riff-raff') – of, in short, as I'm told every day, 'ruining my life'.

P.S. I have forfeited a paragraph of *The Fox and the Hounds* to write all this – not, I'm sure, a promising title, but I'm sure you will appreciate how far, for you, I am prepared to go."

'I don't know what you've to complain about,' I tell her. 'He's on the Regional Health Board. He's Chairman of the Constituency Labour Party. He's on the parents' committee at Lottie's school, is about to become a governor, and has been asked to stand for parliament when the present member retires, or they've even offered to kick him out and put Charlie in at the next election.'

Her face is flushed: my presence in the house, where I notice so much, oppresses her. 'Get rid of me,' I tell her, 'in a book,' to which she replies, 'All it would do is tie me closer,' at which, to my surprise, she dashes from the room.

*

55

When I go to her room I find her lying on her bed (as I used to in the old days, after one of our 'discussions' to do with school or work or friends or, more potently – and acrimoniously – with 'ideas'): on this occasion, however, it's not face down.

'Would you like me to leave?' I ask, and when she doesn't reply, I add, 'I'd welcome going back. Taravara will be lost without me. The street's full of burglars, prostitutes and drug-dealers. As far as the council's concerned I'm the only one who gives it respectability.'

'You're not supposed,' she says, 'to live on your own.'

'Who says?'

'Bryan.'

'Who's Bryan?'

'Our G.P.' She turns, her red-flushed cheeks half-hidden by the bed. 'The doctor who examined you.'

'All he knows of me,' I tell her, 'is from the one examination.'

'He's been briefed on the phone. And Maidstone,' she says, 'has faxed him your notes.'

'I'm stronger,' I tell her, 'than Maidstone makes out. He's simply using comparable models. Such-and-such had symptoms like you and look what happened to him.'

'If you leave me alone,' she says, 'I'll be all right.'

'What about a book on Donatello? Viklund said your doctoral thesis was the best he'd ever read. Or Fra Angelico. Or della Francesca who, like Rossini several centuries later, inexplicably gave up at the height of his career. Or Domenchino, whose gentility aroused the wrath of everyone who knew him. Not unlike one or two I could mention today. Or the Perfect Draughtsman, Andrea del Sarto. Fra Lippo Lippi. Or Signorelli.'

To each, however, she shakes her head.

'I know what I can do, and I'm doing it to the best of my ability,' she says.

In this room lay Isabella, married for forty-five years to a man whom, though she loved, she considered a 'privateer' ('my brigadoon, my monster').

'Alternatively, your whole career leads up,' I tell her, 'to the illumination you can throw on your mercurial and much-gifted Dad.'

'If your work's failed,' she says, 'to achieve the recognition it deserved, what will mine be worth in fifty years?'

Sitting on the bed I say, 'You can't judge things like that.'

'You have in the past. You still do,' she tells me.

'Failure of that sort,' I tell her, 'doesn't count.'

We can hear Glenda and Lottie stir in their sleep, and the passing of a car in the road below the house. 'In those years,' I add, 'I was showing off. In the past five years,' I go on, 'I've had to pay the price.'

Something in my voice causes her, after a while, to turn her head: she looks at me directly. She wipes her wrist against her cheek and, reluctant to give her the handkerchief from my pocket, unwashed for several weeks, I pull out a corner of the sheet and give her that.

'Price?'

'There is no greater crime,' I tell her. 'All religions are based on it.'

She shakes her head, with the same dark, liquefacient eyes she had, as a child, when she listened to my stories.

'You children are the most positive thing that has happened in my life. I can't bear to see you unhappy,' I add.

She bites her lip – an habitual gesture – whitening the skin beneath her mouth.

'I'm not clinging on,' I tell her. 'I'm all for you standing on your own two feet. It's merely the impatience of the shipwright, wishing to see his vessel afloat. I was exactly the same with plays and novels, paintings and drawings. You've read the last poems of Buonarroti? "Evil has prevailed," he came to the conclusion, despite the Dying Slave, despite the Sistine Chapel. Despite the Dead Christ and His Mother.'

She lay back on the bed.

'That sounds very much,' she says, 'like God.'

'Freewill is a very big thing in my book, Etty. For years I went round as if the price exacted had been too much. "The train to Buchenwald," I said. Now, of course, I shake my head.'

An owl hoots from the Rectory roof (across the old wall against which, in the old days, peaches grew). Down in the village, at the Labour Club, Charlie, I presume, is chairing his meeting.

'I'm very proud of you,' I tell her. 'I'm very proud of Charlie.'

'He's everything, at one time, you used to despise,' she interrupts. ' "The socialiser," you described him.'

'The outsider,' I tell her, 'isn't outside by choice. He's longing, if not to be asked, to find a way back in. Because the everyday world was never for me, I could see the value it had for other people. Charlie is enhanced by fitting in. He brings an expansiveness to it which is normally associated only with those who don't, or can't fit in at all. He's unique. Just as,' I conclude, 'you used to think I was.'

"It's very cold, as a matter of fact," [Bea had written], "and I don't spend every day sitting on the beach. I'm doing, you'll be pleased to hear, a great deal of swotting. Father says I'm not here solely to enjoy myself – something with which, incidentally, I wholeheartedly agree. I've got reams and reams of schoolwork and am currently writing an essay entitled, 'The Starving Third of the World'. Plenty, or even a sufficiency, is not something I shall ever take for granted. I thought your description of sitting on the toilet, writing, was a form of childishness which characterises everything you've written. I hope the same quality is not evident in your novel. Don't you have a bedroom? Don't tell me you paint your pictures sitting there as well. The sun has *not* been hot. It has rained for several days, while the people with whom we are staying are often drunk (though Daddy, who gets drunk as well, merely describes them as 'merry'). They sit for hours at meal-times telling the most incomprehensible stories (in French) which Daddy pretends to understand (largely because he knows that Mummy does). Most of them are to do with the Second World War which, if you lived here, you'd think was still going on. Monsieur Duffon is Mayor of this village and it appears to give him rights to do almost anything he wants. I am longing to get back. Sally, my horse at the stables at Monk Bryston where I ride, has given birth to a foal. It's going to be named after me – Beattie – and apparently is most beautiful to look at. (Not like me, of course, at all.)

Mummy is having a wonderful time. The men ogle her, not least our host. Daddy says it's flattering and the way men are down here, which is where she came from, but if I were a man I wouldn't stand for my wife to be ogled at as brazenly as that. She says, of course, she doesn't notice. Isn't it awful? That men only see one thing in a woman. Despite Mummy's age she has, I can see, a wonderful figure. Her bosom, though not large, is very compact, her waist very slim, and her hips still slim enough to fit inside my costume. I've come to admire her very much, largely because she doesn't care what anyone says or thinks. She wears clothes, for instance, quite old and worn and, in one or two instances, belonging to my Aunt Veronica, her older sister, and Aunt Clare, her younger one, who *lent* them to her before we left.

I shall write again if I've time. Hope everything is well with you. Aren't you making too much of living on a council estate and being an 'artist'? Are you sure, in giving up your university career, and turning your back on 'society', you're not acting, to some extent, from spite? Since you see yourself as an artist and, as you put it, only concerned with the 'truth', I thought I ought to mention it.

Yours sincerely,
Beatrice Corcoran."

'What time is Charlie coming back?' I ask as, having antagonised Etty back to life, I help her out in the kitchen.

She wipes her wrist beneath each eye – onions: the only item that afternoon she hasn't troubled to prepare. 'Any time,' she says, and adds, 'I said we'd have a meal.'

'You don't have to be an outsider,' I tell her. ' "You can't all be like your father." ' I laugh, for this was Bea's most frequent complaint when, in their 'teens, the children 'revolted'.

'I am not,' she says. 'Nor was I ever.'

'Nor feel,' I go on, 'that my illness is infectious. There's no evidence of it in you, nor,' I go on, 'in any of the others.'

'Don't fight me back to life,' she says.

'You make me sound,' I say, 'quite healthy.'

'Only you can tell me that.' Standing at the stove she stirs a pan with a wooden spoon.

Isabella, with her capacity to absorb herself in tasks of little importance – sewing, gardening, playing with the children – the grass set out with cups and saucers, a jug of water standing in for tea – would often look the same: the same pose, and much the same expression.

'Charlie and I were thinking of having another child. One never seemed enough. Three has an imbalance which I prefer to the symmetry of two.'

'If it doesn't stop you writing.'

'I can hardly do research up here.'

Not for the first time I have the suspicion she has not invited me up here for my sake but to formulate something within herself. That, too, I reflect, is like the old days.

'Why not?'

'Your work,' she says, 'is out of fashion.'

'It was never in. I've never been an author in the way the middle class would understand, nor working-class in the way a popular audience would listen to. A humanist in an age of neurosis and romance is bound to go unnoticed.'

She laughs, turning from the pan and brushing back her hair. 'An author who writes books which no one reads, who produces plays which no one troubles to revive. A painter who paints pictures which are plagiarised by others.'

'Much of the work I did as a student became de rigueur with aficionados of the art world two decades after I was kicked out of the Drayburgh for doing it,' I tell her.

'Were you kicked out?'

'I was never invited back for my final year. When I enquired why not they said I had "matured beyond their expectations".'

"Dear Bea, I don't have a bedroom to work in because I share

60

it with my younger brother who, when I should be in there writing, is using it to study, or to sleep. Having explained to you why I've gone the way I have, and refused to be railroaded into a conventional life, I thought you at least would understand. It's easy to make fun of what I've done, particularly from the perspective of where you are at present, but I don't think you can be aware of what it feels like to have a father who works in the conditions that mine does throw his 'sacrifice' at you. Art is my life, whether you like it or not. I don't put any 'value' on it, no more than I would on the bloom of a rose, or the song of a bird. Because it has no political or commercial or, in this context, social worth, it's all the more valuable to me. Perhaps it's better we don't write. I have enough to put up with already. Furthermore, I don't believe the Riviera is as wet or as cold as you make out. As for your pony: I suggest you change its name, unless you wish to condemn it to a life of supercilious self-regard.

Yours,
R. Fenchurch."

'You must have been a handful,' she says, flinging over her shoulder another disparaging look.

The suggestion, I can see, has entered her head that by pretending to an interest in my work she'll be doing me a favour.

'A favour' is Maidstone's phrase – or so she tells me. Asking him, by telephone, if taking me back would be 'a positive step', he'd declared, 'It will do your father a favour. He will go to pieces living on his own, particularly in that house in Taravara Road. Isn't the place infested with drugs?'

She has taken me with her, whatever her other motives, out of love, and because, or so she says, she can't bear to see me 'a second time going mad'.

She is hoping to retrieve me single-handed: I can feel, already, a certain calm returning. I like, for instance, seeing her cook: I like seeing Charlie come in from work: I like his avuncular commitment to everything he does – big-hearted, generous, unthinking; I like seeing the children rush in from school – and rush out again to play with their friends – into the same garden that their mother rushed out to with her sister and brothers.

What I hate are the shadows I can't arrest and, where not the fear, the terror.

'I have always been in trouble,' I tell her. 'My damascene conversion to art at the age of fifteen not only made me enemies but lost me most of my friends. I felt indisposed to the world in which I found myself to a degree which, nowadays, it's impossible to describe. Particularly now the dangers we are faced with loom so large and safety, even in opposition, is only found in numbers. Being alone in opposition was, to me, a positive step. Because I was alone I knew I must be right. If someone, for instance, has to stick it out, it might as well be me.'

'Hubris.' Etty moves across the kitchen to collect a bowl, emptying the contents of the pan inside then turning off the gas.

'That wasn't freedom, of course,' I tell her, 'merely the use I made of it.'

'The renegade,' she says.

'The renegade,' I tell her, 'is all there is, for the world I would have wished to live in has now completely vanished.'

6

SHE IS standing in the evening light outside the Army and Navy stores, the shutters of which the proprietor – conscious of her standing there – is putting up: her coppery hair and her turquoise suit attract not only his but everyone's attention: the stockinged legs, the high-heeled shoes, the knee-length skirt.

'You're looking very well,' I tell her.

She smiles: her teeth, against the Riviera tan, are starkly white. 'So are you,' she says.

'You'd better ignore my letters,' I tell her. 'I had no one else to talk to.'

She laughs.

'It's too nice an evening,' I add, 'to spend inside.'

'Sure.' A handbag on her wrist, she places her hands in the pockets of her suit.

'You're more changed,' I tell her, 'than I'd expected.'

'So are you,' she says again. 'You've lost,' she goes on, 'the schoolboy look.'

'I'm beginning to feel,' I tell her, 'I shouldn't have come.'

'That's all right,' she says, and adds, 'My mind, I'm afraid, is somewhere else. I'm not really, mentally, here at all.' A moment later she goes on, 'I met someone on the Riviera. He's coming up to see me. He lives in Reading.' With the same aimlessness she continues, 'He has a car. What I told him about the place intrigued him. It doesn't stop me, of course, from seeing you,' and, since we are now strolling through the central streets of the town, she enquires, 'Have you decided where to go?'

'I've no idea,' I tell her. The cinema had been our intended goal.

'You're not despondent?'

'No.' I shake my head.

We walk towards the municipal park, away from the central hill of the town: the park where, over the years, I have met more girls than I remember: something of an earlier, carefree self returns. I talk of the past – anything, I reflect, to avoid the dilemma I am facing now.

'Is Otterton still around?' she asks.

'In the army.'

'And Jenny?'

'She went abroad.'

The treed slopes of the park's central, castle hill confront us.

'I'm back at school next week. I can't wait,' she says, 'to get it over. I can't wait,' she goes on, 'to get to college.'

'To do what?' I ask.

'Save life. My grandfather did the same when he was young. During the war he developed a food to supplement the diet.'

'Not Kell Cakes?' I enquire.

'They were named after him,' she says, and adds, 'He's living with us now. My mother's father.'

'They came out like rubber mats,' I tell her. ' "Any fool can make them," someone once wrote on the packet. "And most of the bloody idiots do." My father fried up thousands.'

'Did Mum react to your ideas of the renegade?' Etty asks.

'The first time I met her for a date I took her to Thrallstone Park. The sun was setting. She'd just come back from the Riviera. It was the first time she'd been courted by someone like me. We sat on the grass. Before us lay a view of the river, reflecting gold in the setting sun – not unlike the colour of her hair: so potent an image I fell in love. I wanted, in that instant, to paint a picture, to set her in it, behind her a blaze of red and gold. We talked – until, that is, the cold got to me. I'd put my jacket on the grass in order not to spoil her suit.

"Are you all right?" she said, and touched my arm. It wasn't until we'd left the park – by a hole in the wall I knew, for the gates were closed – that I kissed her – formally – as we waited for her bus. I was reluctant, for an instant, to let her go. "She'll be mobbed," I thought, "at the other end." I sat in the bathroom half the night, the only place in the house I could be alone, my mother saying, after I'd vacated it, "That seat is very hot," to which I replied, "I've got diarrhoea," to which, amazingly, she said, "Just like those Kell Cakes during the war," I unable, for reasons even now I don't wholly understand, to tell her that Kells and I were, that evening, through Bea, sensationally related.'

Do you remember that night lying on the hill in the Park with the strand of the river reflecting the setting sun – silhouetting, when it finally descended, the contour of the Pennine hills – while all around the trees grew dark, the rooks grew quiet, the grass grew damp and my excitement, as much as the chilling of the air, caused me, as you observed, to shiver?

I find – I'm not sure how it happens – I'm talking to myself, Etty in the dining-room, setting the table. When I go through and offer to lay out the knives and forks she says, not having listened to a word I've said, 'Eating so late will give you indigestion.'

'What about you?' I ask for she has, since my arrival, complained of the same.

'I'm used to it. Charlie and I often eat late,' she says, leaving me to arrange the table while she goes back to the kitchen, calling, 'What were you saying?'

'She didn't respond to what you'd describe as my bolshieness. She was all for the world as it might become. She never succumbed to my vision that progress is illusory. Our worst quarrels were to do with what she described as my "negative nature" and when I used to say, "But why do you think I paint these pictures, write these books, put on these plays if I didn't think at heart that life is worth it?" she'd cry, "It *has* to be improved!

We don't have any choice but to try and do it!" And I – I, in those days, would say, "That *is* genuine despair, my dear." '

'What did she say to you working as a labourer?' She brings into the room a bottle of wine – one of Charlie's exemptions from their otherwise ascetic life – the wood-panelled room in which, with 'Nan' and Grandfather Kells, and Bella and Freddie – and Bea – I have shared so many meals in the past.

'She refused to understand it.'

'But came to accept it.'

The room, too, in which the redoubtable Rose caught Isabella and I kissing beneath the mistletoe – with a recklessness that left all three of us embarrassed.

'We only met on one subsequent occasion after that evening in the park. For Kells,' I tell her, 'was taken ill and nearly died and the family was in turmoil for over a month, during which this youth in his motor-car came up – the son of a biscuit-manufacturer near Reading – and knowing they occasionally came to town, for we still communicated by telephone as well as letter, I hung around one evening at the cross-roads which, coming in from Ardsley, they would have to pass and, as if by telepathy, that Saturday night, this youth drove by, your mother beside him – looking more radiant, I thought, than ever – and, glancing out, though they didn't stop, she saw me. Years later she confided that that was the moment she fell in love. "Like," she said, "your conversion to art: the difference, I suppose, between 'want' and 'need'." '

'She fell in love from another man's car. Destiny was in it, after all,' she says.

'Like you and the book,' I tell her. '*The Fenchurch File.* Generations will be grateful for what you did.'

'Oh, that.'

'How could something,' I enquire, 'that began like that, end up in the way it did? The Parliamentary Private Secretary to the Minister of Health: that youth from Reading all over again. Class. Conformity. Wealth.'

'She's seen how,' Etty says, 'all you set out to do has ended.

In the psychiatric ward of the North London Royal, and in the long-term residential unit at Boady Hall.'

'I was driven there,' I tell her.

Having placed the food in the oven, she closes the door. 'Were you?' she enquires and, turning, declares, 'You drove yourself.'

I sleep little, if at all, that night: perhaps it's the food, however well prepared; or perhaps it is the house and the silence of the village, a place of perpetual noise in the time of Isabella; or perhaps it's the conversation which, at the end of the meal, concludes with Etty declaring, 'I'm not sure it's a good thing to start dragging up the past. What we must do is look to the future.'

'Not to acknowledge the past is not something,' I tell her, 'I can easily do. We go into the past, not to be detained, but to bring it into the present. It's only when it retrieves us, and not us it, that it's never any use. Moving forward in the way you've described is entirely out of the question.'

'You've got past loving Mother,' Etty says as she sees me up to bed, not sure, I suspect, whether her remark is a statement or a question.

When I say, 'Do you get "past" loving anyone?' she replies, 'I'd say so,' and adds, 'As soon as it becomes a habit, as it did with you and Mum.'

'Or a need,' I tell her, suspecting this idea comes not from her but Bea.

'We're all in need of love,' she says, 'but not in love with need,' and, intent on cheering me up, one platitude following another (one more liability of family life), she adds, 'It's what you saw in Mum. She saw her need in you, not, as you've been led to believe, the other way around.'

After she has gone I begin to fret that the pills I have brought with me are under lock and key in her and Charlie's bedroom.

Then, once more, the thought comes to me: they have brought me here to die.

7

'MY MOTHER would like to meet you,' Bea said at the end of our first encounter after the youth and his car had gone back to Reading.

'How about your father?' I asked.

'He leaves these things,' she said, 'to Mum. If she approves,' she added, 'he invariably approves as well.'

'Did they,' I enquired, 'approve of Keith?' (the name of the youth with the car).

'Father did. Mother thought him nice.'

'Nice?'

'She thinks he could do with growing-up.'

'What, in that case,' I said, 'is she going to think of me?'

'It's mandatory,' she said (a peremptoriness in her nature of which I was only slowly becoming aware: we were sitting in a café, eating food I couldn't afford, despite it being the cheapest on the menu: when I hesitated in replying she suddenly went on, 'They won't let me come again until you and she have met.').

I went the following Saturday. It was dusk: for the first time in my life I came through the garden door at which we'd dropped off Bea on the night of the Allgrave party.

We walked, at her prompting, hand in hand, the path flanked, beneath the trees, by knee-length grass amongst which grew cowslips, buttercups and daisies. The silence was intense and evoked in both of us a sudden apprehension.

We approached a flight of balustraded steps leading to a stone-built terrace: a path, dividing from our own, led to a wicket-gate: beyond lay an area of unmown grass across which were scattered several trees, their branches bowed – and in one or two instances broken – with unpicked fruit. Pears and apples, glowing, caught by the evening light, lay scattered in the grass.

Glancing back I saw how the place itself was like a wood: the garden door, the winding path and, beyond the trees, the lights of the village: the sound of the colliery dynamo was audible from below.

The house, a low, stone-built structure with a balustraded roof and tall, square chimneys, was visible beyond an intervening hedge, our path, consisting of irregular paving-stones, leading directly to a lawn into which had been set innumerable irregularly shaped beds of flowers: their scent was discernible in the darkening air along with the dampness of a suddenly descending dew.

One of several gravelled paths led to a pedimented porch, itself approached by a shallow flight of steps. A light shone in two of the downstairs windows, its beams illuminating, in two broad swatches, the ground immediately in front of the house and, attached to the dark façade, fronds of yellow roses.

I caught a glimpse, in the first of the windows, of a wood-panelled room and then, in the second, of a woman: she appeared to be sewing, her head bowed, her shoulders stooped. A needle came up, her head, in profile, drawn up as well. Magenta-coloured hair was secured in a coiled plait above her ear, her neck, arched forward, delicate and thin.

The light, suspended in a tasselled shade above her head, obscured her features until, hearing our steps on the gravel, she glanced up.

Her look was one of such benignity – green eyes made dark by the angle of the shade – that, caught by Bea's hand, I stood transfixed. I had never seen anything so beautiful: the slender boning of the face, the tautened cheeks, the broadening mouth: the gentleness, the candour.

'Come on.'

Bea's feet dragged at the gravel.

'There's Mum.'

69

The woman must have risen: as we approached the door it was unlocked inside and, a double-featured design, one half of it drawn open.

'You're late.' Her hand extended, Bea's mother came to greet us.

'The bus,' Bea said.

'Of course,' she said. 'You haven't the car.'

She took my arm and when she enquired, 'Are you all right?' glancing, as she did so, at my face, I found I couldn't speak.

I heard Bea exclaim, 'He's shy!' at which, leading us into the room in which we had glimpsed her, with a not dissimilar exclamation, her mother declared, 'But I wouldn't frighten anyone!'

'Mum's very *odd*,' Bea said later, as she walked me to the bus. 'It's to do with being foreign.'

'Foreign?' I said.

'Less Irish, of course, than Middle East. She doesn't know what effect she has.'

'Effect,' I said, less in enquiry than exclamation.

'She's oblivious of her beauty. Curious when, normally, she's so tuned in to men.'

'Is she beautiful?' I said.

'But you couldn't keep your eyes off her!' she said. 'And she, for entirely different reasons,' she went on, 'could scarcely keep her eyes off you. We shouldn't,' she concluded, 'have any trouble now.'

'I suppose,' I suggested, 'she's old.'

'Yes,' she said. 'But very handsome.'

'In you,' I said, 'it's something else.'

'What?'

We waited at the bus-stop, her arm in mine, a sudden and, on my part, a heartening confederacy between us.

'You're younger,' I said, 'and more unspoilt.'

'Am I unspoilt?' She paused. 'Keith said that.'

'He's right.'

I no longer felt challenged by the other youth: all I chose

70

to recall of the evening was the touch of her mother's hand when, on parting, she'd said, 'I hope we'll meet again.'

We had sat and talked in that lamp-shaded, wood-panelled room, and had had a meal. 'What do you mean by art?' she had said after listening to one of my self-proclamatory confessions and when, immediately, Bea had responded, her mother's look, turned from me to her, had calmly suggested, 'You don't have to impress me, my dear. I am impressed enough, as it is, already. If he has to be turned away it won't, I can assure you, be because of me.'

'How old do you think she is?' Bea said.

'I've no idea,' I said, her age, calculated in this fashion, of no interest to me, either then or later.

'She's fifty-two.'

'As old as that?'

'Lots of men still fall for her.'

'I see.'

'Lots.' The mystery of her mother endlessly eluded her: a lifelong antagonism, a lifelong complaint. 'I'm sure she'll speak glowingly to Dad.'

'You think so?'

'She told me as much before we came out, and you went into the hall to fetch your coat. She's not put off,' she added, 'by your being poor.'

'Am I poor?' I said.

'You will be!' She laughed, the bus plunging down the hill towards us and lighting up the queue, the majority of whom, I noticed for the first time, were, where not almost, completely drunk.

From the first-floor window I gaze out at the moonlit garden: many of the fruit trees, closer to the house, have been replaced, their staked stems invisible in the darkness – a darkness where, on summer evenings, Isabella and I would pick the fruit, careless or so it seemed, on her part, whether we could be seen from the house or not, giving vent to those feelings which, in me, had been provoked by the sight of her upward-straining figure – the tautness of her blouse, her skirt, the delicacy of her hand as, first, she fingered, then unloosed the fruit.

Bea's father, the redoubtable 'Freddie', I met on my second visit: a stocky, broad-shouldered, balding man, with dark, thick-set features, he reminded me of Harry Chamberlain, my equally redoubtable employer: as I came in the room he clasped my hand, enquiring, 'Are you the artist?' as if Bea's admirers were both too numerous and too confusing either to identify or to count.

In loving Isabella I came, of course, to love him, too: at a different time, and if not exactly in his prime, he also had fallen for this woman. I observed how, whenever he passed her in the house, he touched her hair – her arm, her hand, her back, her thigh – as a man, in passing, might make obeisance in church, a desire not only to express but to invoke a feeling which otherwise could not be conveyed.

'Come out to the yard,' he said on that first occasion, as much a desire for something to do as a wish to test or examine me, leading me to the, in those days, muddy enclosure at the side of the house where, for the better part of two hours, we hoisted hundredweight sacks of coal from the back of one lorry, which had broken down, onto the back of another.

'What about this art?' he said when we finished and he invited me into a shed he used as an office.

'What about it?' I asked, the invitation accompanied by a request I 'look at this'.

The 'this' he showed me – all the while examining me (something restricted on the back of the lorry) – was a picture he had bought – at, I discovered later, Bea's instigation – with a view to presenting it to Isabella on her birthday.

The colours, such as they were, had been put on with a palette knife, the overall effect, where not 'expressionistic', effusive: nothing in it, as I was quick to tell him, 'added up': the excrescences of paint, at a distance, suggested a line of orange rocks about to be engulfed by cream-topped waves (intimations, I suspected, of the 'Mediterranean'); recognising

72

a look, not unfamiliar where 'art' and 'artists' were concerned, if not of disappointment, outright rage ('short-changed' was the phrase he used when subsequently describing his 'final feelings' to Bea), I added, 'I'm sure Mrs Corcoran will agree, it'll add a touch of colour.'

'I can add a touch of colour mesen,' he said. 'And at a tenth the price of this,' adding, 'You go in for this art, then, do you?' sitting further back behind his desk, the shed, apart from a cabinet and a second chair, on which the picture was propped, furnished with little else: his 'work-office', apart from his 'yard-office', unknown to me at that point, was located in the house.

'It's like,' I told him, 'the calling of a priest.'

'A priest.' Pulling himself forward, he propped his elbows on the desk before him, his hands, clenched together, held in front of his mouth, a gesture – uncharacteristic of him, I was to discover – of uncertainty in anyone else. 'A priest is paid a salary. He has,' he paused before deploying the word, 'a job.'

'I don't mean painting pictures but anything creative,' I said.

'Creative.' The word roamed in his mouth, it seemed, for several seconds: not only tasteless but indigestible.

'Like writing.'

'Writing.' Another serving of the same.

'Or . . .' I might have added, 'Music,' realised, under his scrutiny – a darkening of his expression – I was steadily digging my grave and, unable to think of anything else, slowly waved my hand.

Black, I discovered, like his, with coal-dust (a smear across his mouth).

'We can all be creative,' he suddenly announced, 'if some other bastard pays for it,' adding, with an unconvincing hint of propriety, 'Excuse my language. You've heard worse, I'm sure, at Chamberlains.'

'Much,' I said in the hope that, like the unloading and re-loading of the lorries, this suggestion of confederacy might draw us closer together.

'I could give you a job in the yard.'

He indicated the black-painted lorries with their metal-lined insides ('Corcoran & Co. Contractors' inscribed in yellow paint above the cabs).

'You wouldn't be doing much different to what you're doing now.'

His hands, coal-black and massive, were lowered to the desk: there, fisted, they lay side by side as if, curiously, divested of his body. 'We each lay down our lives for you,' they appeared sensationally to announce – fingers, thumbs, knuckles – white-bared – prominent through the dust.

There was no intention, I realised, I should take the job, merely a desire to point out the incongruity of what I was doing – of his life and mine and, by inference, of my life and Bea's.

'I'm happy as I am,' I said.

'I know Harry Chamberlain. Funny firm to work for.'

'It is.'

His eyes examined mine.

'You won't have much time for painting pictures.'

'No.'

'Nor for writing books.'

'No.'

'He works them very hard.'

'He does.' I paused. 'I intend to find the time,' I added.

'He lays them off each winter. There's nought going on until the spring. Apart from his bunch of regulars. Not much to show for all those years at King Edward's.'

'No.'

'Beattie's going to college,' he suddenly declared. 'She wants to take up where her grandfather left off. You've heard of Kell Cakes? She wants,' he concluded, 'to save the world.'

He returned his hands to his chin.

'What do your parents think?' he enquired.

Later Bea told me he had been 'pumping' me to see if, as he'd expressed it, 'this boyfriend of yours is off his head.' 'He thought you might have been,' she said, 'because of something in your eye.' When I asked her, 'What?' she answered – her eyebrows lowered, her hands thrust up in front of her mouth (her father's expression transmogrified), 'He said, when you

74

talked about art, your eyelids never fluttered, something which he's read is an infallible sign of madness.'

'He thinks I'm after your money.'

'Not a bit of it.' She smiled. 'When he dies, he always says, his debts will equal his credit.'

'They're not very pleased,' I told him.

'I bet they're not,' he said. 'Your father, Bea tells me, is down the pit.'

'He has been,' I said, 'for thirty years.'

'Thirty years,' he said, 'is the time I've been in business. Me and commonsense. You've heard of commonsense? Commonsense is a gentleman few of us can do without.'

'I mentioned thirty years,' I said, 'to indicate he started work long before I gave up what you would describe as my education.'

Something in my expression – whether 'mad' or not – appeared to reassure him: in a curious voice – so inconsequential that, hadn't I been watching him, I might have assumed it to have come from someone else – he said, 'I'm not usually wrong about men. Women, of course, are a different matter,' a suggestion in it of a vulnerability both surprising and endearing.

I liked him; I liked him, above all, for loving Isabella, but also, I suspected, for his careless way with things: in his business, Bea once informed me, he was as likely to change his mind as hours in the day, being convinced he ought to sell in the morning, buy at midday, and do nothing by the evening. 'His evening thoughts,' she said, 'invariably prevail.'

From that first interview onwards he paid me little if any attention. I visited the Old Hall from time to time but principally Bea came to town for our weekend meetings. 'Daddy says I ought to be meeting other boys,' she said on one occasion. 'Of course,' she added, 'there's always Keith. And once I get to college,' she concluded, 'there's bound to be lots of others.'

Whenever I dream of the Hall and Ardsley it is Isabella, however, not Bea, who comes to mind: I see her stooping in

75

the garden, her figure poised, half-balanced, leaning to a plant – her arm outstretched, her head half-bowed: the straightening of her back as, conscious of my approach, she finally turns: the smiling, green, half-questioning eyes – and my enquiry, misleadingly uninvolved, 'Is Bea around?'

'She's in the house. Give a shout. I'm sure she's there,' Bea observing us on one occasion and afterwards remarking, 'You go together, in a curious way: the way your heads come down when you're not quite sure what the other one has said. As if,' she paused, 'you've known her,' she paused again, 'longer even than I have.'

I spent most of my time, when not at Chamberlains, writing and painting, the former in an exercise book (one of several which, on leaving, I'd stolen from school), the latter on pieces of Chamberlain canvas subtracted from the sheds. 'You mean you'll earn a living painting fucking pictures?' a fellow-employee asked me returning one evening to Linfield on the back of a Chamberlain truck.

'I don't have to, necessarily,' I said. 'I can carry on doing this.'

'And write a fucking book?'

'Why not?'

'About this place!' He gestured round: the pits, the slag-heaps, the terrace streets, the railway arches, the advertising hoardings, and the barge-laden canal by which, at that moment, we happened to be passing. 'I can't see anybody buying a fucking picture or reading a fucking book based on a dump like this!'

He laughed, encouraging our comrades to join him.

'Shouldn't it be about London?'

'London?'

'Or some fucking place like that!'

It was but one of several low-key exchanges which character-ised the summer. My only response was to re-apply myself to writing, to painting – and to seeing or visiting Bea (the last a pretext, carefully disguised, for seeing Isabella: her smile, the

76

inconsequential touch, the drawing of my arm to hers as she pointed out her roses).

The summer shows – agricultural, horticultural, industrial – were coming to an end as, with the first signs of autumn, were most of the weddings. The summer 'casuals', amongst whom, initially, I'd counted myself, began, one by one, and then in groups, to disappear: we'd see them, as we went off on the backs of the Chamberlain lorries to the last of the jobs, drifting aimlessly around the centre of the town: we'd wave: they'd wave in return, at first cheerily, than, later, offering scarcely any acknowledgement at all. Between Bea and I something, too, began to fade: her schoolwork now was making demands and, as my first rejecting notices began to arrive, a certain disillusion-ment was evident in me: was the species of self-expression I was involved with worth the isolation that, I could see now, inevitably came with it? In addition to which, Bea was being courted – 'passionately', as she described it – by the Head Boy at King Edward's: a boarder (one of a privileged group of twenty-three) and always on hand (much fancied – she much envied by her friends). He had a car; his father arrived to watch him play in the First Fifteen and the First Eleven, and compete in the Athletics Team, in a chauffeur-driven limousine, with a fur-clad wife who led, in turn, a coiffeured poodle on a jewelled lead – Bea much flattered by their and the boy's attention.

It was against this background that the turning-point came in my relationship with Isabella ('Of your life,' Maidstone remarked when I first described it). She and Freddie were dressed up one evening to go out to a dinner of the Inner Wheel at which Freddie, who was visibly nervous, was to give a speech. Uneasy at the prospect of Bea and I spending the whole of the evening in the house together, he had suggested that Rose might be asked to stay behind, 'In case there was anything you might need,' and when the absurdity of this was pointed out by Bea ('I can easily make a cup of tea') he offered, uniquely, to pay for us to go to the Ardsley Essoldo, a flea-pit of a cinema in the terminal stages of decay – and to which he had forbidden her to go on every previous occasion.

It was at this point ('smiling her Gioconda smile,' as Bea put it) that Isabella declared, 'Surely, Freddie, we can trust the two of them together,' stooping, as she did so, to kiss Bea on the cheek and, crossing directly to the chair, beside the fire, where I was sitting, stooping to kiss my cheek as well.

I saw her shoulders, bare within the low-cut velvet collar; I felt her lips: I watched her turn across the room – joining Corcoran at the door where, her arm on his, she called good-night. I watched her hips, I watched her thighs, I watched her ankles: I watched the high-heeled shoes which gave so much shape to her calves. I trembled. Years later, when I asked her if she had been aware of the effect she had had that evening – I had, for instance, never seen her dressed formally before, her shoulders bare, her breasts – fuller than I had imagined – visible, sensationally, as she stooped, within the looseness of her collar – she was, astonishingly, offended: 'You don't honestly think I'd lead you on?' her displeasure at the interpre-tation I'd put on the incident so profound that it blighted our relationship for months. Long afterwards she would bring it up and when I sullenly enquired, 'What distresses you so much?' she'd cry, obscurely, 'You seeing me like that!'

'But I loved that moment more,' I often told her, 'than life itself. You don't realise,' I'd go on, 'how beautiful you are. More beautiful than anyone I've ever known. Sensationally, organically, ethereally,' brought to tears on more than one occasion when, unbeknown to her, I'd glimpsed her in the street, or across a room, or, at one of our later rendezvous, standing at a window. 'Those are the most important moments of my life when I'm aware how much I love you.'

'I hate it,' she'd say. 'It's voyeuristic. I wish that evening had never happened.'

'To me,' I told her on one occasion, 'there's never been another like it.'

'Not even,' she paused, 'when you first made love to B.'

I may have misheard her: conversely, she may have intended to say 'me' but, during that pause, retracted.

'Not even then,' I told her.

'When was that moment?' she asked.

'That's something,' I said, 'between Bea and I.'

'Why?' she said, increasingly obtuse.

'Just as it is between you and Freddie.'

'Freddie is my husband.'

'Bea is my wife.'

The irony struck her, too – not to say, the wickedness and, as at all such moments, faced incontrovertibly with what we'd done, we instinctively retreated.

'Bella sees you as her son,' Freddie said on more than one occasion, seeking to explain, if only to himself, what, if he didn't suspect, he might, if a more imaginative man, have sensed was going on. He liked, perhaps because of this explanation, to see the two of us together. 'Freddie doesn't mind!' she said on one occasion, laughing, when she'd pointed out Freddie watching us from the living-room window. 'He likes to see us holding hands!' – something she did, and not only with me, without a second thought, as impetuous in this respect as she was in so much else. 'Tell me how much you love me,' she would say in later years when Bea and I came up with the children, adding, in the same loud voice, 'I'm taking Richard for a walk. He looks so pale. The air up here will do him good. It's what, after all, he's used to.'

It had not been long after that 'memorable' evening that the second incident occurred that drew us, in retrospect, if not closer, irretrievably together.

I had gone over to the house one afternoon to find Bea swotting for an examination: Isabella, who was busy in the kitchen, and hating to see anyone idle, said, 'Come and look at our new neighbour. It's in the *Ardsley Express*,' adding, as she got on her coat and put on a woolly hat (it was autumn), 'As an artist you can tell me what you think!'

She called to Bea, 'I'm taking Richard to look at the Swansons',' closing the back door and leading the way across the yard. A backward glance revealed Bea at her bedroom window, waving and, assured of my attention, levelling her palm and blowing me a kiss.

79

We passed along a footpath enclosed on one side by a hedge and on the other by a quarry. Holding back the branches, I went ahead. At one point, where the path divided, I took the broader of the two and heard her call, 'This one, Richard!' turning to find her close behind me, her cheeks aflame, her eyes alight (our breaths rising in the chilly air). With the same impetuosity which characterised so many of her actions, she took my hand – at one point, pretending an obstruction, I grasping hers more firmly.

With the subtlest – and, because the subtlest, the most sensual pressure, she responded, our bodies stooped, our heads bowed and, because of the encroaching branches, almost touching.

We emerged, finally, at the foot of a steep embankment. The soil was loose, its surface pitted with rabbit holes: I scrambled up, reached the summit and, as she followed, took both her hands.

I drew her to me.

How long we stood there I've no idea, our arms around each other's waists.

'Are you all right?' she finally enquired.

'I'm fine,' I said. 'And you?'

'I wouldn't have got here,' she said, 'without your help. It's just as well you came.'

We drew apart.

'That's the Swansons' house,' she added.

Almost as an afterthought, or so it seemed, her hand slipped back in mine.

Immediately below us, at the foot of the slope, a concrete structure had been erected, into the sides of which had been inserted several rectangular and oval holes intended, I assumed, to serve as windows: the site was encroached upon by builders' debris – stacks of bricks and piles of sand and mounds of ochre-coloured timber – themselves encroached upon by the woods which came up the slope from the back of the Hall and over the crest of the embankment on which we

80

were standing. A brick wall was in the process of construction to separate the two.

Hand in hand, her head imperceptibly but, as far as I was concerned, unmistakably inclined to mine, we stood side by side discussing the impropriety of someone building a concrete edifice in a landscape which, where it was not characterised by woods and fields and hedges, was only distantly encroached upon by the encircling pits.

The coat she wore had a brown fur collar, the coat itself a bottle green – one she invariably slipped on when she went to the village, shopping: the texture of the fur (I allowed her remarks to turn her to me) highlighted the colour of her cheek – a pinkness which extended to her brow where, deepening, it was absorbed within the magenta of her hair.

'He's an architect,' she suddenly declared. 'It's been in all the papers. Though which ones, apart from the *Express*, I can't recall.'

She turned.

'Are you all right?' she added.

'I feel,' I said, 'a little dizzy.'

'I thought you were,' she said. 'It's to do with all that bending.'

'I'll be all right,' I said, 'in a minute.'

'Have you had these spells before?' she asked.

'I have,' I said, 'since adolescence. They very soon pass,' on the verge of confessing to something else entirely, and hastily concluding, 'I feel much better already.'

'What do you think to the house?' she said, intending to distract me.

'It looks more like an office,' I said.

'That's what I thought!' The exclamation drew us closer: linking her arm in mine, she added, 'The view, I suppose, will be nice.'

'It will,' I said.

'Looking the other way!' She laughed: the purpose of the brick wall – to prevent the house from being overlooked from the grounds of the Hall – was obvious to both of us. 'In addition to which,' she went on, 'he's installing central-heating.' (An unheard-of luxury in Ardsley at that time.) 'By oil.'

The logistics of this enterprise – quantities of oil transported to a private dwelling at least twelve miles distant from the nearest town – provoked a second burst of laughter.

As far as I was concerned, the conversation, as, indeed, the view of the concrete house itself, was merely a distraction from what Maidstone was to describe, years later, as my 'principal perception': the realisation I had fallen in love with a woman thirty-four years older than myself.

The first time I described this incident to him I had produced a photograph, creased, from an inside pocket – over which he had stooped, frowning, for several minutes, the photograph itself (he invariably sat in a chair set, incongruously, in the corner of the room, between a filing cabinet and his desk) laid on my file which, in turn, was propped on his crossed legs. 'She is,' he said, after a while, 'a beautiful woman,' a clinical assessment, or so it seemed, to which he appended, glancing up, 'What would you say were her imperfections?'

'It was, incongruously,' I said, 'the accumulation of imperfections that rendered in her, uniquely, the possibility of perfection. In his *Journal*, Delacroix observes that it is the imperfections of a work of art which give it its vitality. Poe, echoing Byron, says much the same about men and women.'

After the second burst of laughter, for several seconds, neither of us spoke, gazing down at the windowless hulk: it was as if that side of my body had been ignited, her cheek so close to mine I could feel its heat.

I moved.

'Looking out, from the inside, you won't be able to see the house at all,' she added, 'and, if the wall weren't too high, you could see up to our wood.'

She indicated, with her head, the trees below.

'But if the wall is too high,' she went on, 'you'll have the view the other side, of Fernley Pit.'

As I listened to her laughing she took my hand, her fingers enclosing mine without, it seemed, a second thought; perhaps,

I reflected, she was used to the importuning demands of men other than her husband, accommodating them in such a manner that it seemed, to the importuning agent, she had scarcely noticed them at all: a graciousness, I further reflected, that only added to her charm.

'We ought, I suppose,' she continued, 'to be getting back,' as if the propriety of our coming here had not yet been settled in her mind and the immediacy of returning, therefore, still in doubt.

She drew her coat about her.

'At least you've seen it now. And your opinion, I can see,' she concluded, 'agrees with mine.'

Her hand now clenched in mine, she began to descend the slope behind us.

Our return along the path was conducted in silence. I watched her back, her feet, her calves (the woollen hat which covered scarcely half her head and from beneath which her hair, unplaited, tumbled out), her head, her hands (her delicate neck): 'Are you all right?' she asked as we reached the yard, using this enquiry to release my hand yet, moments later, when, having turned to me, she had watched me nod my head, she took my arm and led me to the porch where, with a peculiar excitement, she suddenly exclaimed, 'That was a grand adventure!'

A moment later, her coat off, she had returned to her chores in the kitchen – her hat, forgotten, still on her head – while, from overhead, came Bea's shout, 'I shan't be long!' to which Isabella, absorbed already in her tasks, called, 'Don't rush that work, young woman!' glancing up, abstracted, to where, half-stunned, I stood against the wall and, with a smile, announcing, 'Richard and I can wait!'

"Dear Bea, my mind wanders these days from the subject in hand; in hand, literally, on this occasion as I held your mother's on Sugden's Bank (as I later came to know it), my arm, folded in hers, cushioned, moments later, against her breast – the breast which, as she turned to make a remark, moved from me and then, as she listened to my response, came softly back; the breast which, months later, I enclosed within my hand as we sheltered one evening beneath a tree – hidden by its shadow – in the cul-de-sac at the back of your school. I'd met her from a meeting in town – 'by accident,' I told her. 'I happened to be passing,' offering to walk her to her stop (it was before she acquired a licence to drive your father's car and, later, the absurd sports model he went and bought her: he enjoyed seeing her as a flighty figure, seeing it, I suppose, as flattering him). I said I wanted to talk about you and we strolled, not in the direction of the stop, in the centre of town, but up the footpaths that led to your school: a married woman (someone who, in the ensuing years, was not infrequently mistaken for my mother). I can't, no matter how hard I try, remember how 'the moment', as I described it to Maidstone, came about. 'I am a perverse and wicked fellow,' I said. 'I am devious in all things and seldom to be trusted.' Yet I remember Sugden's Bank so clearly – my arm enclosed within your mother's, the turning of her face to mine, our returning to the house, the descent of the bank, our going indoors, your call from the stairs and, 'What did you think to the Swansons'?' when you finally came down. And what I recall most clearly is her face as, once in the kitchen, removing her coat, she turned to me and, for an instant, as I held its collar and helped her to withdraw her arms, I felt convinced, if I had lowered my head, she would, sensationally, have raised hers – as involuntarily as, finally, she did on the evening I met her and we strolled up the cul-de-sac at the back of your school – discussing you (initially) and then, absurdly, prompted by the darkness, her. I say 'involuntarily' for I don't recall any precipitating gesture, merely passing into the shadows between the lamps until, in the midst of one such shadow (the quietness of the evening, the singing of a bird), I turned – as fortuitously, it must have seemed, as she to me and, for reasons neither of us, either at that moment or later, could understand, she raised her face to mine and when, after the closest scrutiny, she closed her eyes, I took that as her signal . . .

Why I did what I did I can't make out. Something indecent
– against a brick wall – white with salt and bevelled from age
– shaking so violently I could scarcely stand . . ."

The moon shines in the garden below: the garden in which
the ghost of Isabella wanders, tending her roses (waiting for
me): the garden in which the four of us – Bea and I, Corcoran
and Isabella – would, in the summer months, often talk for
hours: art as opposed to business, pragmatism and empiricism
(the meaning of love), Corcoran bored by such discussions but
bemused by the animation they aroused in his daughter and
his wife, a broad, phlegmatic smile on his otherwise sombre
features: 'What does it add up to? You end with what you
began!'

'What's that?' (from a sulky Bea).

'Work!' (inexplicably) 'is the only thing that counts!'

The garden is much neglected – by comparison with the care
lavished on it by Isabella. She had, in those days, the assistance
of a man who came in several days a week, an enthusiast, if
not an eccentric, known both for his gardening skills and an
idiosyncratic selection of gardens in which he chose to work:
Isabella, not the garden – its soil or the disposition of its
vegetation – was the principal influence in his choice of the
Hall. He loved, like I did – he covertly – to see her red-haired
figure move amongst the flowers, raising his head from his
digging or raking, his weeding or pruning, his tying back or
staking, to watch the juxtaposition of coppery red, or fiery
magenta, with lilac, lemon, a reciprocal red, a glowing purple
– with the crimson and pink, the yellow and orange of the
climbing roses which hung in festoons across the front of
the house (drowning the windows, drenching the porch).
Once, coming upon Isabella and myself in the garden shed at
the back where, our heads together, we were examining the
dahlia roots, wrapped in newspaper, stored for the winter, he
had hastily stepped outside, aware – despite the fact that no
intimacy was taking place – that there was an unseen quality –
an unseen presence – which, while not evoked separately by

85

either one of us, was immediately apparent the moment the two of us came together – a vibrancy which he, Mr Rawlston, was by no means the only one to notice and which, over the years, was commented upon openly by Bea as much as by Corcoran himself – a 'peculiarity', as the latter described it, 'as if you were Bella's child.'

I've a feeling Etty looks after the garden herself, with the help of a man who, as the mood takes him (a retired miner), comes in once a week: periodically a firm of contractors appears and lops the trees and cuts back the hedges and gives a perfunctory mowing to the lawns, and hoes the more accessible beds, but, as her grandmother did before her, Etty, at odd moments, dressed in a smock, cuts at the plants and ties back the branches and, whenever they accompany her, allows the children to dig and run about almost anywhere.

It's cold; I'm cold, yet disinclined to return to bed: a cry, from the back of the house, echoing along the landing, comes from one of the children: each night one, or perhaps both of them, calls out, disturbed by dreams which, evidently, never wake them. Once I went along to their room, startled by the sound, but both dark-haired figures were asleep, Glenda snorting (like Etty) with her thumb stuck in her mouth. As with her mother, when I drew it out, it immediately went back in.

I take a chair; I pull a blanket around myself – drawn, after much exertion, from under the heavy quilted cover of the bed – and sit in the window: the lights of the village show beyond the trees and I half-envisage in the darkness the contours of the pit – the steam, the crepitation of distant feet, the whistle, the occasional siren, the murmur of a forgotten village life.

'You hated the place,' Maidstone would tell me, at which I would explain, 'It's in my blood. It's part of me. It's not merely a perversion that impels me to love it. It's the way – perhaps the only way – I can come to love myself.'

At which our talk of Ardsley would deteriorate into one of our endless discussions about 'reclamation': was it, as I frequently declared, a hubristic impulse and therefore self-defeating, or was the desire to retrieve the past and bring it into the present a 'condition for living' – living, as opposed to the 'morassic ingenitive' which was how Maidstone identified existence for the majority today. When, after his third or fourth use of the phrase, I informed him that it was taken from *To Die with the Philistines* (the first play I'd written), and much bandied about in the press at the time, our relationship took on a new dimension ('I thought I'd heard it somewhere': he was, after all, he confided, writing a book himself, of which the provisional title was, indeed, *The Morassic Ingenitive: the inevitable dissolution of the human race*) and, for the better part of a year, if I recall, we talked of little else.

8

"I HAVE A problem. From time to time I am engulfed by terror . . ."

I have picked up a school exercise book ("King Edward VI Grammar School for Boys" imprinted on the cover) which is lying on the window ledge, and which I must have placed there with a view to showing Etty. Numbed, if not bemused by re-invoking the colliery scene outside – all that is actually visible, beyond the trees, are rows of lights, irregular and inter-laced, marking the roads of the commuter estates – I turn on the lamp which stands on the nearby table (the one on which Etty is convinced I should do some work) and read the entry, written in a post-schoolboy scrawl (I was, after all, writing a novel at the time).

" . . . or something akin to terror which not only I can't describe but am driven to hide. Am I alone in this, or is it something that goes on and, by a hidden or implicit imperative – conceivably a subliminal understanding – no one mentions? In which case, to have mentioned it, if only here, makes me a coward . . ."

I re-align the book.

"Where it comes from I've no idea. I thought, at first, it was induced by things I saw. Now I've discovered that what I see is merely coincidental with what I feel (but afterwards becomes irredeemably associated with it: a face, a person, a place: a tree, the shape of a leaf, a branch). The attacks come most fre-quently when I am on my own, or away from familiar surroundings; but they also come in the night – and, most violently of all, when I wake in the morning. Nothing specifically appears to arouse them – the unfamiliarity of a place, for instance, can often raise my spirits – as can the sight of a tree, or a face, or a person, or a place not associated with a previous attack. I am afraid. What I am afraid of I have no idea. As a test of my courage I force myself into situations where the fear is bound to erupt – such a test, of course, is Chamberlains, but the greatest test of all ..."

I pause: after all these years I recall the reluctance to write it down – not simply fear, but prudence. Below, in a formal script, is inscribed, "The Linfield College of Art" and, at the foot of the page, as if in code, "is a bell a challenge superseding all."

The art school stood near the centre of the town, separated from the High School (and King Edward's) by an area of unpaved private lanes flanked by large, detached, brick-built houses, the lanes interspersed with cul-de-sacs and narrow, gas-lit alleys. I would meet Bea here, occasionally, from school for, the summer over at Chamberlains, I had saved enough money to take time off to write and paint and, over the autumn, attend classes at the college.

The place had been constructed in the previous century – from funds raised by an 'industry and crafts' exhibition when the town – a former river port, trading with Russia (the Czar's armies clad in Linfield worsted) – was at the height of its prosperity. The school reflected the aspirations of the local burghers: two large rooms on the first floor, with windows looking to the north, provided the facilities for, in one room, drawing and painting from the model, in the other for drawing from the antique. Smaller rooms provided facilities for lithography, etching, pottery and printing, and what was euphemistically described as 'industrial design': there was a section for carving in wood and casting in metal, for dyeing cloth, and for baking pots. Over the years, at the rear of the premises, a technical college had been constructed – not in the original stone, but brick – its function gradually superseding that of the original college: its students, on most days (the majority on day-release from local industry) would pass through the original, sienna-tiled entrance hall – flanked by Greek caryatids and figures symbolising the ascendancy of arts and crafts – to the classrooms and workshops at the rear from where, throughout the remainder of the day, came the whine of machinery and the banging of metal.

The art-students, conspicuous by their appearance if nothing else (a raffish bohemianism as parochial as it was absurd) slunk in and out of the building, subdued by the more numerous and invariably younger students who, demonstrably, had a purpose to their labour: out of their studies would come the electricians, the engineers, the mechanics, the plumbers, the carpenters, the machine-operators, the miners, the factory technicians – the inheritors, in short, of a post-nineteenth-century ideal: out of the art school came nothing but art; or, at least, the provincial, twentieth-century substitute for it. Painting and sculpture were largely 'out' – adjunct studies to the more relevant pursuit (cf. the technical college) of industrial design: posters, record-sleeves and advertising were much discussed, along with the prospect of teaching teachers to teach prospective teachers like those teaching there themselves.

Into this atmosphere of purposive endeavour stepped – or latterly intruded – Richard Fenchurch, a self-confessed apostle of non-purposive creativity – a youth who, on his road to Damascus, had seen art as the salvation not only of his own but of 'purposive' existence in general: this mentor of his own and other people's ills – the involuntary offspring of mines and mills, of factories, of waste-heaps – polluted streams, pestilential rivers, odorous lakes and ponds and becks – stepped through the door of the Linfield College of Arts and Crafts and proceeded to lay about him with a spiritual stick – a stick which, if it didn't break (hardened on Keats, Dostoyevsky, Tolstoy, Flaubert, Wordsworth, Dickens – Van Gogh, Mendelssohn, Sibelius, Prokofiev – Beethoven, Shakespeare, Kafka, Lawrence) became, nevertheless, a little twisted – opposed by sticks hardened by more accessible (and immediate) fervours (like

90

earning a living, supporting a wife, educating children, financing a house). 'So what are you going to do in your attic,' Wormald, the teacher of industrial design (record-sleeve covers, food packages, saloon motor-cars and domestic irons) would ingenuously enquire, 'while others labour in coal-mines, mills and factories to supply you with heat and food and light – direct or indirect, I have to add – not to mention adequate transport, armed services to defend your freedom to express yourself in any way you like, and one or two other irrelevances, like a health and dental service, which you may have over-looked? While we all work, what value, *Harry*,' (a nickname he bestowed on me to indicate the fly nature of my enterprise) 'would you bestow on the products of your labour? You're not' (gesturing to the guffawing room in general) 'suggesting you're a *genius*!'

'Yes,' – to more guffaws, for who is the first to know of genius but the genius himself – the first mark of paint, the first paragraph, the first sentence: the sensational effect of the unpredictable coming from nowhere but within oneself?

'Harry,' was Wormald's only response (a provincial boor, a provincial berk, apotheosised as provincial jerk).

Wormald, poor Wormald, was not alone: Bairstow, the Principal, Dawlish, his acolyte, a phalanx of subsidiary teachers (Cass, who taught drawing from life and modelling in clay, whose metropolitan artistic ambitions had foundered in the inertia of the Linfield College of Art – ambitions bred in a similarly shallow stream whose water ran away as soon as not, disappearing into God knows where but, most probably, a hole in the ground) – and not least of all the students themselves – guffawers to a man (and woman) – proclaiming that 'Harry' was, to say the least, an affected fellow – proclaiming 'art' and 'self-expression', not to mention 'spirituality', have precedence over, if not industry, commerce and doing-what-you-can, life itself.

'Have you slept, Father?' Etty coming in the door, having knocked and entered with scarcely a pause between. 'I didn't hear you moving about,' (suspecting, no doubt, I'd died in the night).

The light has come up behind the trees – as on the morning Bea came in the room – this selfsame room – and said she'd been to bed with a fellow student. The news, at the time, had cut me in two: we'd gone into the wood: I'd lit a fire: over the smouldering flames she told me, at my insistence, the details of the incident (the ejaculation which, I could sense, had caught her by surprise, the swallowing of his semen): the sickness that came to me as I rose from the fire (the wood was wet, the fire half out, the drift of its odorous smoke amongst the trees: the distant glimpse of Ardsley Dam). 'Didn't I deserve it?' I asked myself, yet all I felt was – how should I describe it? – a spread of blood from a wound which, after all this time, has never healed.

'I was awake,' I tell her yet realise, from my dishevelment, and the unobserved intrusion of the light in the room, I must have been sitting here for hours. 'It was the most terrible moment of my life,' I add, and when, perplexed, Etty enquires (her housecoat loosely wrapped around her, a cup of tea, I notice, in her hand), 'What was?' I merely shake my head and remark, 'The day your mother came in here, when we were up, as students, one Easter break and confessed something which even now I can't acknowledge,' covering my face and, to my surprise, involuntarily weeping.

'You've been sitting there too long,' she says. 'You've been told,' she goes on, 'not to dwell on the past.'

'How can I fail to,' I tell her, 'in a place like this? It comes back without any warning.'

'I thought you'd got over Bea,' she says, identifying her less as her mother than my wife.

'Long ago,' I tell her. 'But how do you get over so much pain?'

'What did she tell you?' she enquires.

'Nothing,' I tell her behind my hands: tears – at least, the coldness from them – fall from my cheeks and dampen my chest.

'You're cold,' she said. 'You ought to be in bed,' and then, 'At least you've started writing,' for, on the table, before me, in front of the window, and only inches from where I'm sitting, are my glasses and my fountain pen and the sheets of paper which Etty, thoughtfully, had provided, and, written on the topmost sheet, a blur which I assume to be the beginning of a sentence.

'I can't remember writing anything,' I tell her and, instinctively, cover it up; then, confused – realising this has been a device merely to get me to lower my hands – I add, 'It's how I started my first novel, the first, at least, to get into print, sitting at a table, like this, in my student lodgings in London, a fountain pen – no glasses – an old school exercise book, its pages numbered,' while, in the process of telling Etty this, I put on my glasses and to my surprise discover I have written, "His mind was in pieces: the normal flow of associations was no longer available to him."

That's all there is left to write: the process of the mind, for the cinema and television have taken over the province of appearance. Actuality is the beginning of appearance, and appearance stands merely on the threshold of reality – the threshold, without the capacity to look inside. 'If Bea were here she'd despise me,' I tell her, rising, taking off my glasses – and, to my dismay, in putting them on the table, placing them in the space beside it and dropping them on the floor.

Etty stoops to pick them up; fresh tears obscure my vision.

'If only you knew how often, and not only in dreams, Bea has come to me in this room,' I tell her. 'Slim, as when I first knew her, dressed in her blue dress with its turned-down, round-winged collar, a rim of white against her neck, the buttons down the front, the line of which, in the most erotic way imaginable, divided her breasts, a thin blue belt outlining her waist. Gone. Without the least compunction. Innocence,' I pause, 'destroyed,' and add, 'Nothing to replace it.'

I am sitting sideways on the bed, reluctant to get in or be put inside.

'This room,' I tell her, 'is like a coffin. Once in, I fear, I'll never be let out.'

'You're free to go wherever you like,' she says, endeavouring to lift my legs (clearly beyond her) at which I get into bed without her assistance.

'Back to London?' I enquire.

'Raynor doesn't advise it. Neither,' she goes on, 'does Maidstone.'

'Maidstone's retired. To write the definitive life of Rossini. Have you,' I enquire, 'heard anything more ridiculous?' aware, once inside the blankets and covered by their weight, how cold I really am. I immediately begin to shiver. 'Why he gave up at the height of his career. Piero della Francesco, of course, was the same. Rimbaud, too, another,' and, anticipating her look of boredom (the children, I can hear, are stirring – with one or two yells – at the back of the house), I add, 'In your case it would have a definitive edge. I'm prepared to spill the beans on everything.'

'Everything?' she asks, more in provocation than with interest, I conclude, for she knows how notorious I am for covering my tracks, or, more nearly, leaving totally misleading signals.

'After all, what have I to hide?' I tell her.

'A great deal, I would have thought,' she says, and adds, 'A child, after all, shouldn't know everything about its parents.'

'Even when it's grown?' I ask.

'Are we ever grown?' she says, with a look in my direction: she is tucking in the blankets and the sheet. Before I can respond, she adds, 'What is knowledge but a half-truth, and often, at best, not even that?'

'If I don't talk, and you don't write, how will we know anything?' I ask. 'Isn't knowing something better than knowing a little?'

'It depends what you mean by "know",' she says. 'Knowledge is rarely matched by a facility for expression.'

Sullen with early waking, her face, her eyes half-closed, her cheeks bloated, is turned away: she is anxious, after all, to see what I have written (it's five years since I wrote anything at all). Moving across the foot of the bed, she tucks in the blankets on the other side, passing closer by the table.

'I could write a great deal,' I tell her, 'if I had an inducement.'

'What?'

'An audience.'

'You have.'

'Inattentive.'

'Not at all.'

'Not always applauding, either,' I go on. 'Nor necessarily appreciative. All I want, after all,' I conclude, 'is to turn subject into object.'

'Those whom we love remain subjects for as long as we are here to love them,' she says.

'And be loved by them.'

'And be loved by them,' she says. 'Though that, in the past, has often been difficult to detect.'

'Did Boswell love his subject less for turning him into the subject that we know today?' I ask.

She hasn't glanced at the paper for, turning to the table, she picks up the cup of tea she's brought.

'Do you want this, Dad?' she says, so unaffectedly that, to hide my distress, I turn away.

'You can put it by the bed,' I tell her, not wishing to be left alone and, as she re-approaches the bedside table on which she has already placed my glasses, I add, 'The past isn't that bad. Think of the illustrations, the paintings and drawings, the shots from films and plays. None of the trivia of domestic life,' at which, unexpectedly, she laughs and, lightened by her mood, I enquire, 'Did you say I could go to London?'

'There's nothing to stop you,' she says. 'Charlie isn't inclined to, and Raynor is unlikely to section you in the way that Maidstone did.'

'What can be disposed of so easily by someone like that leaves a great deal to be questioned,' I tell her, 'regarding his judgement.'

'Maidstone wasn't a fool,' she says and, having placed the tea beside me, retreats to the door.

'He was tired,' I tell her, 'and overworked. The psychiatric department of a National Health hospital is not the best place,' I add, 'to form definitive judgements. No wonder,' I go on, 'he took early retirement. No doubt he's sitting on a terrace in Majorca writing something to the effect that it was depression conjoined with anxiety neurosis that obliged the greatest composer of his age – renowned above Beethoven, in his time – to give up his extraordinary creativity at the height of his career, whereas, as I told him, it was nothing of the kind. He was granted a bursary by the French Government on the sole proviso he spent a certain part of each year in Paris. Money, Etty. Money.'

'Is that,' she says, 'the same with you?' while, 'Mummy! Mummy!' comes from the landing from where Lottie and Glenda have heard her as they dash to the bathroom.

'Hello, Grandpa!' they exclaim as, round-eyed, they cling to her housecoat.

'Money was not my downfall,' I tell her. 'Even though I earned a lot. After all,' I go on, 'there was no one who wasn't, to some degree, rewarded. There are painters in London who never earned a penny to whom I handed cash I never even had. As for the family . . .'

She is, however, already outside the door: 'Grandpa is resting. Now go to your room.'

She has, before departing, drawn the curtains and now, with a perfunctory, 'I'll see you later, Father,' from beyond the door, she closes it behind her: her voice and those of the children, still clamouring, fade to the back of the house.

The moment they have gone I get out of bed and stare at the sheet of paper and, beside it, the school exercise book. "What am I? Who am I?" I have written in the latter. "Isn't what I am doing counter-productive to what I intend to be? Sometimes, walking from Onasett to the art school – a distance of two miles – I pretend to be blind, stepping along the pavement, panicking after a while, glancing down, continuing again, my ears attuned to the traffic, to the sound of approaching feet, inducing – my head bowed, seemingly downcast – a state of mind from which, in a curious way, I feel I'll never be released . . ."

I am standing by the window, looking down the slope, beyond the garden, the trees, the intervening wall, to the village – a smear in the morning light against the mist-drenched hills – and recall Etty remarking on the morning after my arrival, 'The past, I'm afraid, didn't do you any good.'

'Yet we're standing here,' I'd told her.

'We are,' she'd said, without expression.

'What I'm looking for,' I'd said, 'is a way to carry on. To disinter the past has become less of a prerequisite,' I'd added.

'Look at the way,' she'd said, 'your work is written off, or, worse,' she had gone on, 'not even mentioned,' and, suspecting she might have gone too far, she added, 'It should be enough to rouse you to composing something else,' and then, her gaze returning to the window, 'I envisaged you going out with easel and paints and starting again from scratch.'

'The peculiar thing,' I told her, 'about the village is I drew it very often. The number of paintings I have of the pit. Not to mention sketches. Of a place,' I continued, 'that doesn't exist. I put it into novels, descriptions of the streets, the houses, the appearance of the people, the twin winding-gears above the roofs, the colliery engine hauling trucks, the engine hidden in the cutting, visible only as a cloud of smoke, of steam . . .'

And am sitting in Maidstone's room at the North London Royal, he confiding, 'You're written out. It's better to acknowledge that than go on tormenting yourself with dreams that in the future your material and gift will come flooding back. Why don't you teach? It's better than sitting on your own, with or without Vivienne, endeavouring to recapture a fame and a fortune which, let's face it, have gone for good.'

'I don't believe,' I'd told him, 'I've even touched on the things I intended to touch on when I first set out,' and when he enquired, half-smiling, 'What are those?' I replied, 'The malevolence of the family I came from, not to mention, of course, the world around,' and, in that instant, recall walking the lanes and alleyways at the back of Bea's school, her summer dress, her sun-flecked features, the patches of shadow beneath the copper beeches (each garden of each house possessing at least one), the entanglement of their coiling branches, smooth, grey-sheened, flecked with cicatricial scars of rotting wood: the dust stirs at her heels – her white-socked ankles, her thin-strapped, low-heeled shoes which nevertheless enhance the slimness of her calves. Tall, she has her mother's grace but not the fulness of her figure (the same porcelain-delicacy around her cheeks – her eyes, her nose): much of our time we spend avoiding teachers from her school: 'That boy isn't doing you any good,' which, years later, she pointed out, came close to coinciding with the truth: 'A girl's education is more important than a boy's, for he acquires his by the volition of his sex whereas a girl's, in those days, at least, had to be prescribed.'

We are walking, hand in hand, along Cliff Lane, a winding, narrow track, formerly a drovers' back-route into town, above us the sooted sandstone of the town's principal buildings – towered, steepled, domed, irregular and daunting – and come to a gap in a tall brick wall which allows us a glimpse of the hill below the town on which I have lived the previous eighteen years, a scree, as it appears, of red-tiled roofs. 'That, at least,' I announce, 'will soon be gone.' It is the summer of our escape to London, she to college, I to the Drayburgh: applications have gone in the previous spring and, in both our cases, been accepted, she to a college in Regent's Park, I to one off the Euston Road . . .

'You haven't got dressed.' Moving from the door, Etty pulls back the covers from the bed. 'What's that you're writing?' plumping up the pillows, constraining herself from looking, while, seated at the table, the pen falls from my hand.

'I can't cope,' I tell her, 'with interruptions,' and add, 'I thought I'd take a trip.'

'Where?'

'Onasett.'

'Why?'

'See how the old place is.'

'Do you want a lift?' (more alarmed by this, I believe, than anything previously I might have said).

'I'll go on the bus. I haven't been back for years. I wonder if it's changed.'

An ache, beginning in the region of my stomach, rises, like an outstretched hand, to grip my heart – to squeeze then wrench it from its vascular mountings.

'For the worse.' Etty pounds the pillow. 'We passed by it, not long ago. It looks run down. The motorway comes out above it. It's not like it was in the old days.'

'You didn't know it in its prime,' I tell her – and am back inside this house with the rattle of carts and wagons and the revving of trucks from the yard next door, and Corcoran calling from the hall, 'I'll be over in the office, Bella,' she, moments later, appearing in the door, a cup of tea or coffee in her hand, her ingenuous, 'I thought you were going out to paint . . .'

'In those days,' I tell her, 'it was full of life,' yet wonder if, in reality, it was or, retrospectively, I am provisioning it with certainties which were lacking at the time – and which, in reality, are lacking now. 'The people, of course, were innocent. They'd come up from the river – the streets and alleyways around the docks, with the outside toilets, the periodic floodings when the polluted water came over the banks, the stench from the malt-kilns. You've no idea how oppressive a smell like that can be. The odour, too, from the mills, the effluent from the factories,' and, before I know what I'm doing, I'm standing in the door, forbidding her departure, declaring, 'Onasett was freshly built, the contractors' lorries still moving up the slope, the piles of bricks and the stacks of timber, the lorry loads of tiles, the houses interspersed amongst the grey ash spoil-heaps of the ancient pits – gin-pits, themselves overgrown with silver birch and occasional sycamore and alder, like tumuli scattered up the steepening slope, strewn with its coiling crescents, avenues and roads, the brick-built school and the stone-built church bastions at its summit,' breathless, 'to the south, the

99

river, coiling across its formerly lake-bedded valley floor, the gorge to the west silhouetted, at sunset, like a cavernous eye. The great days, Ett, the people stunted dwarfs creeping from the alleys, the mud-flats and wasteland by the river, breathing, reaching out – in effect, new people entirely, the residue of the industrial revolution re-born. At one time I had a photograph: my father, in waistcoat, shirt-sleeves and trousers, in the field at the back of the house – the houses behind him half-completed – Raymond, my eldest brother, in his arms, the gardens unfenced, the moorland, long-grassed and criss-crossed by the tracks of the builders' lorries, running to the back doors and low living-room windows . . .'

'Shouldn't I come with you?' Etty shoulders past. 'We could drive there and back within the hour. Give it two,' she says, 'to look around. The bus,' she is about to go on, 'isn't regular,' but when I declare, 'It wouldn't be the same with another person (no matter,' I add, in parenthesis, 'how loving and caring, and even indulgent she may be'), she slips out to the landing and without a word (other than, 'Your breakfast's been ready for over an hour'), descends to the hall from where comes the sound of Mrs Otterman singing (having foolishly been persuaded by Etty she has a pleasant voice: 'I like to hear *something* going on in the house' – in this instance a song recently made popular, on television, by an (alleged) castrato, and improved in no discernible way by Mrs Otterman's interpretation) – an indication that, in her irredeemably casual way, she has started 'dusting'. 'He'll be down in a minute,' I hear Etty call out (everyone, of course, equal in this house: formal address always in front of the servants – except, curiously, where I am concerned, 'Richard' and 'Grandpa' disseminated like the name of a dog), '*Mrs Otterman.*'

'What I don't understand,' I tell her when I finally get down, 'is where the miners have got to. Some, I know, are in the new drift mine at Wharnley, and some have gone east to the deep mine at Thornton, but where are those who sat on their haunches in front of the Miners' Welfare, and the Labour Club and the Ardsley bus-stop waiting to go out to that ghastly estate they built at Ashworth? They were the salt of the earth. At least, at the very least, the grit in the oyster from which the pearl of enlightenment was supposed to come – the enlightenment, I might add, of industrial progress,' only, of course, she doesn't answer for, moments before, I have heard her call Raynor (and having difficulty locating or being allowed to speak to him), enquiring, finally, 'Is it safe to allow him out alone?'

'Not to mention,' I tell her, 'social justice, for the fact of the matter is the third Industrial Revolution took place without our being aware of it, except, of course, by omission,' (she is peeling potatoes at the sink when, in reality, she ought to be in her study preparing notes for *The Life and Times of Richard Fenchurch*, the life and times of a modern saint). 'Places, not only pits, are disappearing, their entire surface workings with them, so that all we are left with is the residue of a pre-industrial landscape across which is scattered a post-industrial fenestration of streets and houses which have, apparently, no industrial, commercial or – how should I describe it? – onto-logical support. The landscape is bereft – bereft of all but the people living on it. No one,' I go on, 'appears to work.'

'Are you going to Onasett?' she asks and when I enquire, 'What did Raynor say?' she replies, 'He insists I go with you.'

'In that case,' I tell her, 'there's no point in going. It begins to sound as if he's inclined to section me already.'

'Nothing of the sort!' she cries and turns to add, 'Why do you look for the worst interpretation? The best is close enough!'

Tears, and not only recently, I can see, have sprung to her eyes.

'I'm not sure why I'm here,' I tell her. 'Is it because I should have been locked up and it's something Bea couldn't bear to see? Am I to be treated as a prisoner, not for my sake, but the benefit of others? After all,' I tell her, 'I'm not quite mad. I never was, despite what Bea and others might have said. It's the world out there that has gone quite wrong while I, a freak of nature, have remained, throughout this maelstrom, Bea, untouched.'

'My name isn't Bea,' she says.

101

'Etty.'

'Doesn't it come to something,' she goes on, 'when you confuse me with your former wife?'

She isn't, after all, peeling vegetables but potting plants: something with which she has become increasingly preoccupied, according to Charlie, since I arrived in the house: they stand, their stems green-leafed and largely flowerless, in tiny plastic bowls and urns along the window ledge before her, on the draining-board and, I further notice, the kitchen table. 'They remind me of your mother. It must,' I tell her, 'have confused me. She was always preoccupied with plants.'

'Instead of you.' Back stooped, head bowed, fingers blackened to the knuckles. 'I don't think you're even half-aware of how much concern has gone into looking after you. Raynor says Maidstone gave you priority over all his other patients, and Raynor, no doubt, will do the same.'

'I don't believe he did,' I tell her. 'On one occasion, when I arrived, as per appointment, he was nowhere to be found. I was at the time, in an abject state. You've no idea . . .'

'And Mum.'

'Mum?'

She transfers several potted seedlings to a fibre tray.

'All the care she gave you.'

'Was directed to her leeches. Have you seen her in her lab?'

'Often.'

'You never told me.'

'You never asked. I've seen a great deal of her the last two years.' Her next words are obscured by the sound of running water.

'While all the while I was going mad.'

'You've been recovering the past two years,' she says.

'Maidstone wrote me off completely.'

'He did not.'

' "Lithium, Fenchurch," he said, "or nothing." I refused to take it. What you see behind you, for you refuse to look me in the face, is someone who defies, and has defied, the laws of science. Defined, I might add, by medical knowledge which sees chemicals as the solution to all our ills.'

'As it happens,' her back still to me, 'the subject doesn't seem half as important to me as it did before.'

'Why come and rescue me?' I ask.

A feeling of lightness – invariably preceding a delirious attack – absorbs me entirely: instead of sitting down I stand by the sink, gaze into the discoloured water collected there, and at the welter of uprooted, thread-like seedlings – like the whitened nerve-endings of the mind itself – and add, 'Or were you worried about the money?'

'Money?'

'Mine.'

'You gave it all away, you said.'

'Which didn't stop Bea from asking for half. She has a hare-brained scheme, when her Medical Research Council grant runs out, of financing her own laboratory. "The proceeds from one of your plays," she said, "will be enough. All the equipment I need I can get into a shed." "What shed?" I asked. "The one on the farm I intend to buy. Didn't Etty tell you? I've thought of a scheme for marketing leeches. Apart from the research demand, they're back in fashion." When I made the inevitable response, "Leeches are the one thing you and I have in common," she threw the electric fire at me.'

'Fire?'

'I'm surprised she didn't tell you. It cut my head from above one eye to behind my ear. I had to have thirteen stitches.'

'Liar.'

She lays down a potting-tool – a wooden spatula – and kneads in the soil around a root.

'What are these going to be?' I ask.

'Sunflowers.'

'From seed.'

'What alternative is there?' she enquires, brushing, as she does so, the back of her wrist against her brow – ironically, in the same spot that the first of the thirteen stitches was inserted

103

when I ducked into the fire which, rather than hurled, was tossed at me by Bea.

'I'm surprised she hasn't told you. On the many occasions,' I go on, 'you've been to see her.'

'She's been up here more often,' she says.

'She doesn't like the place,' I tell her.

'She's getting to hate it less now that she and Albert are married,' she says.

'You can imagine the field-day the cartoonists had with a wife who grew leeches. "Political Leech" was hardly in it.'

The fibre tray, beside the sink, is full: she carries it to the door and, moments later, is visible in the yard, crossing to the recently-constructed greenhouse – erected on what, in the old days, was the tennis-court and is now an area of tussocky grass. I follow – seeing not Etty but Isabella striding there: her tennis dress and tennis hat (she discoloured disagreeably in the sun), standing with Corcoran on their side of the net (he in white flannels and a short-sleeved shirt) while Kells, like an emaciated stick, sat by the net on a chair to keep the score, Bea and I – she attired in a pleated skirt, I in my paint-stained trousers – knocking the ball back with the sole intention of not, by winning, driving Corcoran to distraction.

'Is that the reason she suggested I come here? To get to hate my past?'

'It was one idea,' she says.

The musty air of the greenhouse has a deleterious effect: seeing an upturned box, I remove a pair of gloves and sit – more heavily than I intended.

'Are you all right?' she asks.

'Perfectly,' I tell her, and add, 'As for the care expended on me, I don't suppose you've seen her staining her leeches, her eyes pressed to her microscope more intently than they were ever focused on me. Did she *tell* you about the times we spent up here?'

She is running water from a tap into a watering-can with a preternaturally long spout to which is attached a, proportionately, even larger rose.

'What she didn't tell me, you have,' she says, and adds, 'Apart from your relationship with Gran.'

'Oh, Gran.' I dismiss it with a wave of my hand. 'In the last years of our relationship the whole of her time and energy were spent in re-learning the art of staining cells. Cancer cure or not – and I have my doubts – there was more in her absorption than meets the eye. To have been fifteen years away from research and to go back in with, as she described it, an open mind and a facility she inherited from Kells – his cakes aside – to discover what she has, reputedly, discovered, speaks for itself. She had no time for anything else. Not even Albert when he arrived. She only got her hooks on him when she thought her grant might be running out and the publicity and celebration went to her head.'

'Mother is a remarkable woman,' Etty says and, if briefly, I glimpse something of her own discontent: 'If my mother can achieve all this, what challenge is there left for me?' she must have asked. 'Another treatise on Renaissance art transposed, let's say, to an artist of today? Even with two children, and Charlie as a husband, how does that compare with the achievements of my mother, with her menopausal research, her ten years' younger lover and a husband who, if divorced, was once described as the leading writer of his generation?'

'She's one of a team,' I tell her, reading – or so I think – her mind, but she adds, 'I've been growing these all winter, but the heating went for a time and I doubt if they'll recover,' pouring the water from the can over a row of withered stems which, alone amongst the trays and boxes, appear in need of her attention.

Try as I may, however, I can't keep the objects near me in focus: I look through the distorting panes of glass and see Mrs Otterman hoovering in the children's bedroom, passing to and fro, her head stooped, her arm thrust at an angle, and am reminded again of Isabella, for there is scarcely a door or a window of this house in which I can't or haven't pictured her – as I was, for instance, moments before, watching her agile figure alongside Corcoran's immobile one: her excited laugh as, running in front of her stationary husband, she flicks the ball past Bea and calls, 'Our game, darling!'

The water hisses against the plants, drums on the wood planking of the shelves and on the plastic rims of the pots.

'What has she done when she's been here?' I ask.

'Walked. Gone into the village.'

'To do what?'

'See people.'

'Who?'

'From the old days. There are still one or two. She brought a few back for tea, one day. Rose, who used to clean and who, when I was here, looked after me.'

'Did she bring Albert?'

'Once or twice. She wanted him to see it. "The place," she told him, "where I grew up." '

'And fell in love.'

'With a man from Reading whose parents manufactured biscuits.'

'Boasting.'

'She said she gave him up, not because she didn't love him, but because she thought you needed her more.'

In endeavouring to rise I miss my step, clutch at a seed-tray (intending to clutch at the plank shelf itself) and find myself a moment later lying on the brick-lined floor; more pertinently, with my head immersed in a mound of compost: "potting compost" – the words on a plastic bag pass, in a series of horizontal hieroglyphics, in front of my eyes.

'You seemed to do it,' she says, 'on purpose,' but I realise this is a response she conjures up whenever she foresees an incident occurring, involving the two of us, over which she suspects she will exercise little if any control.

'You don't think I'm lying here for fun?' I ask her and, without her assistance, attempt to rise. My head falls back against an unseen wooden batten holding up the banks of plants.

'Are you all right?' her figure stooping by me, the pressure of her hand beneath my arm.

'Ever since I got up I've felt a little strange,' I tell her.

'Not your tachycardia?' she says. 'You haven't taken any of the pills since you arrived.'

'My blood pressure, by all accounts,' I tell her, 'is coming down. I don't need medication for anything.'

I am – should anyone come upon us – on my knees in a position not altogther indistinguishable from that of praying, my hands together, my fingers intertwined: a feeling of alarming despondency overwhelms me: is this, I mentally enquire, how Richard Fenchurch is going to end?

'I swam, you know, each morning, at the Kentish Town baths, eight o'clock, a dozen lengths, which isn't bad for someone who, unlike you, the family swimmer, sinks like a brick unless he's lifted out. I *struggled*, Etty, for every stroke.' Invigorated by this thought I add, getting to my feet, 'Why your mother should say that I've no idea. She idolised me in those early years, if not for a few years after.'

I am standing in a sea of glass: a greenish haze intercedes between me and everything around.

'It's not the past she came here to hate,' I suddenly conclude. 'But me.'

'I'm sure you were included,' Etty says, leading me, within the confines of the greenhouse, to the door.

'You don't accommodate the past by attempting to re-write it. The only past you have is the present,' I announce. 'Though syllogistic exercises of that nature,' I further pronounce, 'are quite beyond her,' she leading me, my hands still clenched, to the yard outside. 'It was the smell of that manure,' I tell her. 'I'm not very good at confined spaces. I recall flying to Los Angeles for the first time – a mad scheme by a producer to film one of my books – and they had to carry me from the aircraft. The moment it moved at Heathrow, knowing I was to be enclosed inside it for the next thirteen hours, I had the most appalling attack of nerves, something which, until that time – I was twenty-seven – I had never had before. Not precisely in those terms. Something no doubt was telling me that a journey of that length, with a purpose of the sort I have just described, represented an unacceptable compromise with the standards I'd pursued with such integrity throughout my life. "This is wrong", my mind announced, and endeavoured, in the most sensational manner, to take leave of the issue in the only way it could. I feel that now, or, rather,' breathing in more deeply, 'did until a moment ago,' at which Etty says, 'These attacks of verbiage are part of the pattern, I take it?'

We are standing, her arm around me, in the yard while, from overhead, I have no doubt, Mrs Otterman is gazing down, the vacuum cleaner still in her hand (more refuse to dispose of).

'This compulsive talking. I've noticed, and so has Charlie, you do it increasingly. Even Lottie and Glenda have mentioned it.'

"Dear Bea, how could I describe those moments when I met you after school without re-writing the past and bringing it into the present with the most disreputable credentials?"

'It's something to do,' I tell her, 'with being on my own. All my previous associates, for whom, in one way or another, I did so much, where not dead, will have nothing to do with me. "Failure", after all, is the most frightful thing to happen to someone who is geared, as I was, to "success". Of a kind, I might add, I prayed for, for, in all those early years, when your mother was living here and I at Onasett, I prayed each night, "Dear God, may it be Thy will I become an artist, for what is the purpose of suffering to leave even part of it unexpressed?" to which I had an immediate response: "You are an artist. Isn't it evident in your susceptibility to love?" I watched my hand acquire a skill in drawing – something which, until that moment, I'd scarcely had at all.'

'You talk as if your life is over,' she says, leading me to the house but, disengaging myself, I announce, 'I've had that impressed upon me in no uncertain manner. *She* says it is, she with her much publicised research and even more publicised – if I have anything to do with it – lover. It's far from true she loved that youth from Reading. It was me – me alone. She told me at the time.'

We are standing face to face: what anyone, observing us, might have assumed we were discussing, is beyond my imagination: the state of the nation, the merits of one plant food over another: compost is scattered about my clothes and, in an aimless manner, she begins to brush me down.

'I'll walk about the grounds,' I tell her. 'I feel much better for saying that.'

'You've only got your slippers on,' she says.

'You water your geraniums,' I tell her. 'I'll get my shoes.'

'And put on a coat.'

'I'll put on a coat,' I tell her. 'You unwrap your dahlias. They ought to be planted by now.'

9

I LOVE THIS house: it stretches forty-five feet exactly from its
front façade, forming, at the rear, a kitchen/scullery wing –
enclosing, in the process, the stone-flagged yard. In its sunny
half, secluded by a privet hedge – one of the few vegetal
survivors from the old days – stands the greenhouse on the
remnants of the tennis lawn – catching the morning and, in
the summer, the midday as well as afternoon sun, a bank of
baize-like calmness against the darkness of the stone.

The back of the house is stained where the drainpipes and
the guttering in recent years have leaked (the place, for two
decades, let to – on the whole – uncaring tenants); and where
the accretion of soot was unchecked by the prevailing wind
and rain, the yellow sandstone acquiring a greenish tinge. The
windows are mis-aligned, the subsidence irregular: one end of
the L-shaped façade – that furthest from the scullery wing –
declines towards that side of the garden where the old stone
arch, with its pitted keystone, surmounted by a painted stork,
opens into what, in the old days, was the stable yard and, later,
the parking bays for Corcoran's lorries. In the days before I
knew him he kept horses here for hauling carts – square, high-
sided, two-wheeled creations, as well as low-sided, rectangular,
four-wheeled ones – the teams of horses hauling, not in pairs,
but single file. The old harnesses, when I first knew Bea, were
still hanging in one of the mouldering buildings, and several
of the old two-wheeled and several of the four- (and one curious
six-) wheeled ones were parked, rotting, in the field, and
former grazing pasture, behind the stable wing itself. Now

houses occupy 'Ardsley Close', small, three-bedroomed terrace dwellings bought by professional couples whose children often come into the grounds to play with Lottie and Glenda, but whose school, a private one, in Linfield, they don't attend.

The sale of the stable wing and the construction of the houses was one of Corcoran's final 'investments': not many years after Bea and I were married he re-leased the Hall, sold off his business and – in the manner he had foreseen, and prepared for, the nationalisation of coal and its transport – moved his capital into land. On most of it he built 'executive' dwellings: having started off as a colliery stable-lad, his final creation, via horse-drawn transport, motor transport, property and land (he was, for a while, in the insurance business), was the industrial estate which, hidden from Ardsley, dominates the vista of rolling fields and woods that lie between the village and Linfield. 'I've come,' he told me, 'a full revolution. From towing up muck from a hole in the ground I've filled it up and levelled it off and put buildings o'er the top of it. Now, that's what I call *creative*,' (a glint in the eye which as much as said, 'I don't know what an *artist* would think of it,' not much caring, with this as with other things, whether I responded).

The grounds at the back of the house are much overgrown: the old tennis-court apart, the once meticulously maintained woodland, with its ancient quarry – shaped over the years into a smooth-lawned, shrubby dell (a rock-strewn pool, festooned with lily-pads, at its centre) – is indistinguishable from the woodland which, owned by a neighbouring farmer, and much neglected, adjoins it further along the slope. As for the Swansons' flat-roofed house (known as 'The Pillbox' to the villagers), it has been joined, beyond the summit of the slope, by a number of imitations, none of them as austere, and the majority built in brick and stone, or an injudicious blend of both, a string of such creations, each tree-enclosed and garden-walled, standing on the edge of a recently broadened road and acquiring, because of their common size and close location, the district name of 'Ardsley End' – a southern sobriquet which is echoed, perhaps evoked, by their suburbanised appearance.

The grounds I walk in, therefore, are somewhat circumscribed and the route through them obscured, where not by fallen trees or untrained hedges, by weeds and grasses and occasional mounds of refuse – most of it of domestic origin – carried here at night and dumped by trespassers from the village: probably, Charlie has declared, relatives of those miners whom he allowed into 'The Wood' to cut timber for burning during the final miners' strike and most of which was used not by the wives for cooking but burning in the braziers at the colliery gates. 'I may have been mistaken, but one lorryload was used to block a lane at Winnington Pit when half a dozen scabs went back to work. The police came here to check it. Contrary to popular belief an "evolutionist's" life is not a simple one.'

It was here that I often wandered with Bea – and, more often still, with Isabella; for it was easier – it appeared a natural and casual extension of domestic life – while I waited for Bea to complete her 'prep', as Corcoran called it, for her to offer to show me a recently discovered nest (she was uniquely fond of birds), a hitherto unknown flower (we bought a book to discover their names), or the latest change to the 'choreography' of the wood or garden – achieved with the help of the gardener, but more often on her own, by cutting back a hedge, removing a bush, or planting something new and, invariably, exotic. Little evidence of her efforts remains: here and there I recognise a shrub, a hedge, a declivity or hollow (the site of an ambitious excavation to uproot a tree), but most, if not all, are overgrown: animals – rats – scurry away in the undergrowth, and in one particular spot where we often embraced – a patch of grass screened by rhododendron – someone, recently, has lit a fire: smoke from a clump of ashy twigs, and, on the flattened ground, the ends of several cigarettes, drifts among the trees.

It was Isabella, after all, I loved: a woman turned fifty – a woman reconciled (it seemed, at the time, supremely) to the kind of life she led: the kind of life she had always led. Much to my surprise, years later, I discovered that what she had told me at the beginning – that this was the only infidelity, on her part, in her marriage – happened to be true: what, I asked myself, ecstatically, each night, could a woman of her age – almost three times my own – want with someone like myself; someone who, uniquely, presented so much danger and could offer her so little, unless our short embraces, our hurried kisses, the frenetic caressing that took place not only in this wood but in alleyways and shop doorways and at street corners in town could be described as 'wanted' – tokens of a love which, at that time, and often later, I told her went deeper than anything I had ever known.

When she complained of being old – 'So old, at times, I daren't think,' – I would cry, 'I love you old! I like you old!' and, 'I wouldn't have you any other way! You're sacred to me: when I'm on my own and think of you my hands, would you believe it, begin to shake. My legs, at times, won't hold me up,' for, on occasion, when we met – particularly after an interval of several days (and once, torturedly, after she'd been abroad, on holiday, with Corcoran, after an interval of several weeks) – I would shake so violently she would grow afraid, holding me at arm's length, while I – I struggled only to draw her to me.

Everything about her – her clothes, her hair, her gestures, her expressions, her appearance – her voice, her manners – entranced me: 'It's not me at all you love,' she would say – she did say – lying on the ground on which I'm standing now: a fifty-four-year-old woman and a twenty-year-old youth. 'It's a fantasy you have of me. And I, of course,' she had gone on, 'must have about you.'

'Is that different,' I'd asked, 'from anyone else?' adding, '*Anyone* else,' caressing her intently. 'What do we have, after all, but projections – *elucidations* of how we feel which we see reflected in other people, and which, in my case, I see so deeply and profoundly reflected in you?'

'But what *am* I?' she would ask, her eyes darkened by a fear I seldom saw on any other occasion. 'A wife, a mother, a woman old enough to have given birth to you – a woman who has given birth to a girl you say you love and who, I haven't any

113

doubt, is in love with you. This would *shatter* Bea if she knew. It would shatter me. It would shatter all of us, even an inkling of what was going on.'

Her stupefaction would drive her to despair – and to almost unapproachable silences: we got in touch, for instance, by the most tortuous arrangement. I would ring Ardsley at a particular time – one she had chosen when, she assumed, Corcoran and Rosie (Mrs Hopkins) would be out, Kells and Nan otherwise engaged. Sometimes – more often than not – it didn't work, so that I would find myself holding a conversation with Mrs Hopkins or, disengagingly, with Nan, or, confusedly, with Kells – or even Corcoran himself, enquiring about a pen or a book or a drawing I may (deliberately) have left behind, Isabella summoned finally to offer her suggestions – a whispered time and place between more loudly-offered phrases, or a vehement, but still whispered (and frightening) 'No!'

I never lost my nerve: not even when Corcoran, on one occasion, in the darkness, came blundering down the garden path and Isabella, whom I had met, moments before, by arrangement, by the garden gate, was caught in my embrace, the shadow of the hedge alone concealing us.

Oh, Bella!

10

SHE WORE a flowered dress: blue-patterned, the flowers, broad-petalled, within a green enclosure; white buttons secured the lapelled collar, the declivity between her breasts incisively pronounced. Her legs bare, she lay back in the grass, the skirt of the dress unbuttoned, the petticoat beneath it raised above her thighs. We had spent the afternoon by the side of Winnington Pond, a reservoir, enclosed by woods, from which a stream wound down, through a rock-strewn, narrow valley, to a smaller, shallower pond beneath. Children – we could hear their voices – played in the stream while on the pond itself a man, throughout the afternoon, motionless, had sat in a boat, fishing, glancing – as far as we were aware – only once in our direction. The bed of the pond was muddied, laced through by a network of weeds and grasses amongst which shoals of tiny, silver-coloured fish darted to and fro. Isabella, allegedly, had been in Linfield, shopping and now, having followed the path down by the playing children, we were lying on a bank beside the lower, deserted pond. A mist, as the afternoon passed and the first chill of the evening came across the unruffled water, caused her to shiver and, as I drew out her dress, to push down her hand and fasten it.

'Let me do it for you,' I said.

I slid each button into its hole more slowly than I had, earlier that afternoon, removed it.

'We can't go on like this,' she said, I, ignoring this threat, as I always did, proceeding with my task.

'How much I love you,' I said, lowering my head to kiss her.

115

She presented me her cheek.

'Ever since I've met you,' she said as, after several seconds, I withdrew, 'I've lived in two worlds. Heaven, like this afternoon, and misery the rest of the time. My hair is grey, my figure unattractive, my skin has "gone", my breasts have sunk, my thighs, I know, are flecked with veins. When you aren't there, I long – I can't tell you how much I long – for you to touch me. And when you do, I go to pieces. I cry – sometimes when I'm on my own, sometimes with other people. I don't know why. Like this afternoon, you lying there, asleep, so peaceful. It's as if I didn't mind that anyone might see. You know how weak I am, how naive in many ways. No woman I know would have responded in the way I did when I first saw you. I didn't even know myself until long after it was over.'

'I don't think you're like you describe at all,' I said. 'There's not a day goes by when I don't set off for college, walking, without an image of you in mind. I love your breasts, your face, your thighs. There's nothing about you I don't love to touch. Like now. Like this,' until, with a sigh, she arrests my hand. 'You shouldn't diminish yourself in the way you do. My whole life,' I tell her, 'is geared towards you . . .' repeating these words as, walking in the wood at the back of Ardsley Hall, I look up at the spring-bared starkness of the trees, reminded of the times, at dusk, or on a summer afternoon, on the pretext of there being something, to do with her gardening, I ought to see, we embraced beneath these trees, on this now litter-strewn slope, her head couched against the grass, her hand arresting mine before, with a groan, often with a cry, she solemnly yielded (her dark eyes watching mine as, in the depths, she imagined – preternaturally evoked – what, in the next few moments, was going to happen).

The afternoon by Winnington Pond and, later, by the lower pond, was something of a revelation: we stayed until dark; then, in the dusk, as we undressed and, having undressed, slid in the water – swimming out to a raft, made of metal, moored at the centre – we talked, peculiarly, of getting married, me insisting, she, with a tearful vehemence, declining; and then, having reached the raft, and hoisting her beside me, her nakedness gleaming in the light of a newly-risen moon, I suggested we ran away; that we didn't go back – she to Ardsley, I to Onasett; with whatever money we had, with whatever clothes we had, we set off 'hitching' to the south. 'The south, full,' I misquoted, 'of the blissful sun. We'll find a cottage. You can grow plants. I'll paint. I'll write. Pictures no one's dreamed of. Novels no one has even imagined . . .' lying there for hours until, shivering, the moon, like a baleful presence, reflected in the surface of the pond, we slid back in the water and returned to the bank.

I dressed her; I dried her – I consumed her in that following hour, and yet, towards midnight, as we stumbled through the moonlit wood, she cried, leaning against a tree, her head cradled in her hand. 'How could this have happened?' she said. 'I was a happily married woman. I was,' she told me, 'so content. I loved my husband. I loved my child. I feel like a killer of both of them.'

Later, she described that day as 'our honeymoon'. It was the early hours of the morning when she got home; strangely, I never asked her what she'd told Corcoran, or Bea, to explain her absence. It was in reference to an altogether different incident that Bea mentioned 'the night my mother came home delirious. My father said drunk. He'd phoned the police twice before going to bed, and had driven round the village more times than I remember and even, would you believe it, to Linfield and back, the buses having, by that time, finished running, then to the railway station thinking she'd be waiting there. Then, singing to herself, he said, she came up the garden. She'd met a friend, she told him, in Linfield, whom she hadn't seen for years. "Not since school," she told him. They'd talked, of course, forgotten the time, and when they remembered the friend had driven her back. As I saw when I got up, she was deliriously happy, and when I suggested she'd been out with a man, Daddy laughed. "You don't know much about women," he said. "Which is just as well. As for your mother," – she'd kissed him quite passionately on the lips as he told me – with a directness I'd never seen before, and which, I have to confess, I've never seen since, "she'd be behaving quite differently if she had." '

'The Harem?' I couldn't help reflecting at the time: the legacy, not so much of Connemara as the Lebanon, the Sardinic fringe. For it was true, because of the irregular and vehement nature of our love-making, it affected, in a positive and, to her, bewildering way, Isabella's relationship with Corcoran, he overwhelmed by the passion which, he assumed, he had aroused in her himself. 'Mummy,' Bea told me on one occasion, 'for the past few weeks, has been hanging round Daddy's neck. He gets irritated by her stroking his hair, particularly in the evening when he sits by the fire and smokes a cigarette and tries to listen to the wireless or read a paper. And I get embarrassed, I can tell you, by the number of times she goes up to him, even when Mrs Hopkins is present, let alone me, and says, brazenly, "I love you!" or, "Darling Freddie!" looking into his eyes like those awful girls at the back wall at school look over at the boys from King Edward's.'

When I mentioned this to Isabella she said, smiling, 'How can I help the way I am?' and then, 'I have duties as a wife. They preceded the feelings – which don't amount to duties – that I have for you.'

'How can you love two people at once?' I asked, and when she said, 'Isn't it the same as you and Bea?' I added, 'Physically. How can you allow him in you?'

She cried (allowing me, after that, intimacies in places which, previously, she had proscribed: in trains, in doorways, in buses, even in cafés: I became exacting about the way she sat, her legs, whether stockinged or bare, displaced towards me, allowing, with as little impediment as possible, access to my hand – recalling an occasion, even, when I required her to wear a particular dress – fastened at the side and providing entry to her underclothes and breast).

She grew disturbed at my audacity. 'Aren't you putting your mark on me?' she said after one disagreeable incident on the back seat of a bus, and when I asked her to explain, she added,

'Making me submit to indecencies in places where genuine intimacy is out of the question. I don't like that side of it. It's brought out something cruel.'

'Because,' I said, 'you wouldn't go away with me?' at which, to my surprise (we were standing in a bus queue), she slapped my face – so hard I felt the force of it long after the bus itself (she on it) had departed and I was walking home.

Late teens, approaching twenty, childish in thought as well as need: it was shortly after this I suggested she allow me to draw her ('for posterity,' I reasoned, 'if nothing else'), and hired a 'studio' – a room above a barber's, near the centre of the town, full of discarded boxes – an attic used by a fellow-student who had ambitions, misplaced, to be a painter. One afternoon a week I absconded from college and drew her – first in the dresses that she chose then, after much persuasion, without them. I'm not sure why none of these drawings – and, with one exception, paintings – succeeded: the intention was to use them in my application to the Drayburgh, which had a reputation for drawing and painting from life – even (an unspoken codicil) it would provide the means by which I could give full expression – not to my love (on that, to say the least, both of us could count) – but to a talent, if not a genius which hitherto had been proscribed by the regime of the college. She would lie – at first with decorum – on a mattress on the floor; at an intermediate stage with her dress and perhaps one under-garment removed (her beautiful stockinged thighs), but finally, after infinite persuasion, with nothing on.

She would turn her head and watch, anxious at being exposed, the ambiguity of her purpose affecting, or so it seemed, the movement of my pen (later on, my brush): need-less to say, at some point, I would divest myself of my own clothes and, drawing down the blind (for, though in the corner where she posed she couldn't be seen, the room was overlooked by a departmental store across the road) I would cross to the mattress and lie beside her – or beneath her as, by her choice, was frequently the case.

*

119

A bird flies from the shrub ahead: I recognise a chaffinch (another debt unpaid). 'Chaffinches,' Bea once told me – she, too, indebted to Isabella for her fascination with birds – 'acquire a regional accent, so much so that one taken, as an egg, from the Orkneys, sings a different tune when it's hatched in Essex. Like you and me,' she concluded, 'are children of the north, and Mum,' she'd paused, 'the child of somewhere else,' my interest in the bird re-igniting my memory of standing at the window of our house in Belsize Park and watching a firecrest which I had never seen before darting around the root of a rhododendron bush, a minuscule bird, mistaken for a wren (and then a goldcrest) until I identified the strand of orange dashed along its head.

It was the window at which I would stand when I couldn't work, gazing at the old-world garden – the buttressed wall, an ancient fig tree coiled against it, its sinuous, light grey branches masked by the dark green plates of its leaves, the grey-green fronds of the buddleia with its tentacles of purple flowers in June, the roses – ancient and modern – variegatedly coloured against the darkness of the creepers (the numerous shrubs and plants whose names – despite Isabella's teaching – I never retained), the japonica in spring, the lilac in the summer, the 'chrysanthemum shrub' in autumn – and the birds (my bird-book and binoculars – presents from Isabella – by the window), the rare glimpses of a fieldfare (twice), the firecrest (once), a spotted woodpecker (three times), the finches, redpolls, siskins and linnets; the flycatchers, nesting by that selfsame window, the chiffchaffs (perhaps, more nearly, chiff-willows), the tits (willow, blue, great, coal, long-tailed and – once – bearded), the magpies, rooks, the perpetual pigeons, the dunnocks, wrens and starlings; the house-martins, swifts and swallows; the wagtails, blackcaps and the regular winter redwing – the tawny owl – the thrushes (song and mistle), the blackbirds and, throughout one summer, the (presumably escaped) perpetually mimicking myna bird that perched on the chimney and whistled alternately like a blackbird and a telephone bell.

'Birds are my recreation,' I would say – without conviction –

to Bea; and when, years later, I would, in parenthesis, add, 'Like leeches are with you,' she would laugh, eyes querulous (startled, too, at times), her mouth flung open as if, even in the middle of her laugh, she still held back, half-confused by her own amusement. 'Leeches are my work, like writing is with you. Is recreation quite the word?' she'd ask and, if I were in the mood (which, in truth, I seldom was) to pursue the subject, her penultimate response would be, 'It's more a reaction, wouldn't you say ('to Mum', I was always tempted to say) to life,' her ultimate and invariably unanswered rejoinder, 'Birds, when they're frightened, fly away.'

It was the beginning of my 'loneliness', as Etty once described it. 'I've never seen anyone so lonely,' she said at one of my first nights – she in her 'teens. 'The author of the piece, and no one speaks to you, nor you to them. It's to Liam,' (the director), 'that they flock. Haven't you anything to tell them?' While others, too, would come up and complain, Vivienne – the turbulent Vivienne – at the height of her fame, too, at that time, her dyed hair blended seamlessly with that of her cascading wig (bedecked with ribbon and tiny flowers), announcing, in her dressing-room, backstage at the Globe (champagne glass in one hand, bottle in the other), 'I've never seen a sadder man,' leaning forward, her tempestuous, tortured, turbulent blue eyes narrowed with their particular pain, 'What are you *afraid* of?'

It's true: more afraid than I dare express: the wringing of hands, the endless weeping (the cowering on the floor, the involuntary spasms).

Vivienne terrified me more than any person – let alone woman – I had ever known: fiendish, electric – sensational when (as was not unusual) treated with contempt. A robust, venal, undiscriminating woman, besotted by her love for Melvyn, the neophyte actor who rose to stardom, so she alleged, while in her hands, Melvyn Zygorski, an out of work (out of trousers) hustler she seduced into notoriety – one which, to her chagrin, outshone her own (a pedlar of drugs on his way

121

to the top, a free dispenser – tragically, for Vivienne – when he finally got there).

Smaller in stature though larger in presence than Bea (or Isabella), with a peculiar skin which varied, alarmingly, according to her mood (foul-mouthed, loose-tongued), the daughter of a minister of the Scottish Free Presbyterian Church, she might, had she stayed in Glasgow, have survived the vicissitudes of her middle life ('my beauty and my lovers gone, what else is there to live for?') holding up the bottle (of her native drink) that played as much a part in her decline as her 'Hollywood diets', her mystic chums, her free-loading psychiatrist: 'Now there is a man, if you want one, Richard: a genius from the Gorbals,' a fellow-Scot and alcoholic.

The path winds off to the left: I recognise the contour of the land – the layout of the bushes, much overgrown, and crushed, dramatically, close to the summit of the slope, by a fallen tree. An attempt has been made to saw off its branches: scatterings of white dust lie at intervals beside the trunk: no doubt the work of intruders. Skirting it, along a track recently worn, I come to the foot of Sugden's Bank up which, over forty years ago, I scrambled on that memorable day with Isabella.

On all fours, I scramble up again: the rabbit holes, the tufts of grass, the decimated shrubs and bushes. A wire fence, just beyond its summit, divides the grounds of 'The People's Palace' from the still-cultivated farmer's field beyond. The slope, at the foot of the field, is lined by the recently-constructed houses which form the self-enclosed enclave of Ardsley End, the Swansons' original concrete structure obscured not only by the tall brick wall but by trees: the severity of its façade, overlooking a flourishing garden, has been ameliorated by covering it with, if not synthetic, symmetrically-featured stone.

'I am here to make amends. Not,' I add the codicil, 'to hate the past (to bring that hatred into the present).' Amends for what? Being what I was: what biological determinism has made me (demonstrated, alas, for all to see)? To make amends with Etty – the child who, in a sense, is older than myself (wiser, more contained), the last love of my life, perhaps – the inspiration, conceivably essential, to make me move again.

11

HAND IN HAND, walking, finally, past Thrallstone Park – the Chamberlain tents put up for a summer feast – passing beneath a railway bridge, over the canal (a barge locked in the basin beneath, smoke rising from its metal chimney, a line of washing from stem to stern) and over the adjoining river. Beside this second, larger bridge lay a crumbling, cliff-like excrescence, covered in shrubs and, where its grey surface was not exposed, by a smooth, round-bladed moorland grass: the waste-heap, not from a local pit but a soapworks. Perhaps it had been the prospect of London – departure, new worlds, destiny – which induced her to 'vouchsafe' me – as, once, Isabella described a similar if not identical occasion ('the final sacrifice a woman can give': in reality, of course, the first): the warmth of the day, the softness of the grass, the enclosure of the artificially-constructed, crag-like slopes, the shelter of the shrubs, the murmur of insects on the clover and daisies by our heads: the feeling we were embarked on a course from which, foreseeably, there was no return: those physical, moral, if not artistic considerations (not to mention psychological) induced by a recklessness which nothing in our natures, at that juncture of our lives, was in the least way inclined to discourage. Perhaps the precedent set by her mother persuaded me to pursue a course with Bea which had already been prescribed – she, her mother, an experienced woman: physically, the demands made on her, she told me on one occasion, had been extreme: 'Three times a night he would climb on top,' (weeping into her hand and adding, 'I don't know why I tell you this,') – my own efforts, on more than one occasion, having been greeted with a laugh – unique for her at such a delicate moment: 'You don't know much about it, love,' guiding my hand to a particular spot where, teeth bared, eyes fluttering, she carefully deployed it.

With Bea it was my first experience of – as I tentatively explained it – 'God': the greenness of the grass (the blueness of the sky): the bees, the roar – over a shoal of rocks – of the hidden river (the unblemished thigh, the pubescent breast).

'I had a feeling,' I said, 'of Christ.'

'Christ?' (her dress drawn up above her thigh).

'For the first time in my life,' I said, 'I feel in touch with God.'

'I didn't feel that at all,' she said, and added, 'I'm so glad you enjoyed it.'

With Isabella it happened, invariably, at night – and, on one of the earliest occasions, beneath the trees at the back of the house. Which trees, and precisely in which spot I never found out: we had gone, absurdly, to look for an owl – heard hooting from the wood and since, I declared, I'd never seen one, she had said, 'I must show you, Richard. We see it here quite often,' pulling on her coat, Bea – and Corcoran – if not contemptuous, disinclined to join us. 'Off you go, Bell,' Corcoran had said. 'If *we* come out we'll frighten it,' adding, 'Once you've seen one you've seen them all.'

We had stumbled in the dark, she finding my hand, a peculiar perversity gripping both of us. Without a word she lowered me to the ground and moments later allowed what she described as 'our vouchsafing': the pallor of her face against the grass – featureless, alarmingly, in the dark – the enclosure of her arms – the guidance as her hand reached down – the speed, the brevity: moments later we were returning down the slope, she dusting down her coat, I, bemused, some distance behind (not only bemused, I thought, but mad) – sceptical that Corcoran wouldn't deduce what, in the darkness, had taken place (three times a night, I thought, for him) – he, as it was, glancing up (smoking his pipe beside the fire), enquiring, 'Did you see it?' to which Isabella, shaking out her hair from a headscarf, had said, lightly, 'For a second, Freddie. Nothing else.'

With Bea, paradise, or so it seemed, was in the grass, in the murmur of the insects, in the sheltering shrubs (in the warmth of the sun), in the enclosure of the cliff-like crag, in the roar of the river, in the depths of the sky – in the peculiar opacity of the blue itself.

With Isabella, that summer, it happened most frequently in the wood behind the house where, 'for peace of mind', as she told Corcoran at the time, she strolled each evening, the 'reflection', she assured him, 'did her good', while he, after several weeks, according to Bea, had enquired, jokingly, one evening, 'You're not meeting a lover, Bell?' and had even, still jokingly, offered to accompany her. 'I should meet him,' he told her. 'We might have a lot in common.'

'What do you do out there, Mummy?' Bea had asked.

'Think my thoughts, dear,' her mother replied.

We moved, on some occasions, further afield, meeting on afternoons I took off from college, discovering a wood on the bus route between Ardsley and Linfield where, in the fields fringing it, we would lie with my paint-flecked raincoat beneath us. There was a perfunctory quality to these, as to all our encounters, not least on account of my 'inexperience', as she described it (ejaculating, on one occasion, merely at the sight of her waiting at the stop, I subsequently to be coaxed by the – then unique – deployment of her mouth. When I enquired, 'Do you do that with Freddie?' she had cried, 'Don't ask me anything about him again!').

She was, as she told me frequently – and sincerely believed – 'happily married'. 'I wouldn't change Freddie for anyone,' she often announced. 'Not even for me?' I finally enquired. 'Not even you,' she said, 'for you'll leave me in the end.'

'Never,' I said.

'My dear,' she said. 'You know nothing.'

'Why don't you take a sketchbook?' Etty had said as I came out of the house and, standing on the embankment, I find it and a pencil in my hand. I sit by a rabbit hole and, opening the book, begin to draw. My nerve, over the past five years, has gone, the feeling for line, the feeling for feeling, disappeared: there is nothing but dizziness, palpitation, dispiritation – and, worse than all these combined, dread.

'What is dread?' Maidstone would enquire.

'Fear and dispiritation,' I'd tell him, 'combined.'

'Where do you feel it?' (without a smile).

'In the heart,' I'd tell him.

'The heart, dear boy,' he'd tell me, 'is in the head, and – the great discovery of the century – the head is merely a physiological entity. Which is why lithium, in your case, is indispensable. If you don't agree to it now you'll be obliged to do so later. When,' he'd pause, his features quizzically distorted, 'you'll be much worse. Much, much,' he'd pause again, growing paler, continuing, finally, with the softest exhalation, '*worse.*'

The houses take shape: the line of the field; the trees which have much engulfed the scene in the past ten years, the saplings in the gardens tinged with buds, if not with blossom. Beyond: the pattern of fields and copses and, like Giza without the pyramids, Aswan without the temple, those quaint omissions where the collieries stood – and can see, in the distance, the declivity of Winnington Pond, though not the pale disc of its water, lost in the darkness of the woods where, on alternate evenings, hand in hand, I had walked with Bea and her mother.

I queried five years ago why I drew or wrote: the pictures (even the sculptures), the books, the plays (the poems, the novels), the notes, the diary – 'why?' displaced by the question 'how?' (What was the point in going on?). 'Would you be happy,' Maidstone had ingenuously enquired, 'doing anything else?'

'I'd be happy doing anything,' I equally ingenuously responded, 'that made me happy.'

'A mechanical job?'

'Anything which, at the end of the day, left me with myself.'

A quiet afternoon – an interregnum between visits to the

wards or the demands – announced directly by a hammering on the door: 'Are you in there, Professor?'

'Go away. I'm busy.'

'I want to ask you one thing!'

'Go away!'

'*One thing!*'

'*Go away!*'

The pin-striped suit (creased at the back from hours of sitting), the starched shirt collar, the college tie (Balliol: a likeable conceit), the small, square, short-fingered hands, the fountain pen held quaintly between his middle fingers: the 'thousands and thousands of pictures and millions and millions of books' to which I was adding. 'For what? What,' I enquired, 'is the point of it all?'

'Isn't the point of the point,' he ingenuously persisted, 'that the point of the point is a circle?'

Diagonal strokes of the carbon from top right-hand to bottom left: with parallel lines of varying length I shade in the woods and Winnerton Pond (shade in Bea and Isabella); shade in where Fernley and Dorrington collieries stood; shade in the furthest line of hills which, beneath a grey-hulked sky, loom above the streets, the yellow sandstone buildings – the towers, the domes, the steeples (the housing blocks, the polluted Lin) – of the invisible city of Linfield – its presence suggested by a drift of smoke from its soon-to-be-disassembled coal-fired power-station.

'An abundance of riches. Gifted,' Maidstone says, 'in so many ways. Yet all it amounts to is self-referral.'

'A romanticist,' I tell him. 'A layman. Can't you see that art has led me to the psychiatric department of the North London Royal and the delusion to which I wake each morning that I am about, not to be sentenced, but executed for a crime I didn't commit or which, even though I don't know what it is, I know I have committed?'

'Art is a physiological phenomenon, too,' Maidstone says.

'Perhaps you ought to see your friend, the maverick Mack-endrick.'

'The two great M's in my life,' I declare.

'How about a third?' he says. 'How about your mother?'

'Mother's been very odd,' Bea says.

We are walking, hand in hand, down through the town, from school, to the station.

'In what way?' I ask.

'Oh,' she tells me, 'very *strange*. She says I need a holiday.'

'Perhaps you do,' I tell her.

'Not just me but her. She's invited Veronica and Clare, her two incredible sisters.' (Both widowed, one with a son, the other a daughter – both married – living overseas.)

She paused.

'She's invited you as well.'

'Me?'

'Daddy isn't going.'

'Why?'

'He says he's too much work.' She clasped my hand more firmly. 'In the old days, when Daddy was very busy, particularly during the war, we often went away – Veronica and Clare and my two cousins. Their husbands, during the war, were both called up. It'll be like the old days. It was always jolly. On holiday,' she concluded, 'Mum is such a wheeze.'

I am drawing a copper beech. Where? Not on the slope above the house. I have vacated the spot on Sugden's Bank (Swanson, Etty has told me, after being imprisoned for corruption – paying backhanders to Council officials for municipal contracts – is currently out on parole) and must, I conclude, be at the far corner of Charlie's and Etty's 'kingdom': a gate, behind my back, leads between familiar old stone buildings, the one-time yard of Oldroyd's farm (from where Etty, in the old days, when we were up here on a visit, used to go round with old Oldroyd's father, delivering milk): an architect, however, has transformed the yard (but for the buildings themselves) out of recognition: a Mercedes shooting-brake stands there now and, beside it, a sports car whose make, like most makes nowadays, I fail to recognise – me a one-time Mercedes-Jaguar-Alvis owner – all sold, as a (failed) means of enticing Bea (back) with the prospect of a laboratory at the bottom of our Belsize Park garden. The grey, coiling branches of the copper beech are not unlike those of the fig tree – statelier, stiffer – an arthritic articulation of ageing wood, bowed where the weight of a branch and the swaying of the equinoctial winds have brought the branch itself against the ground: pale filigrees of lemon mark the beginning of the early leaves, spiked, irregular, pointing into and outwards from the dome-like head.

'I am visited by a vacuity of mind,' I explain to Maidstone, 'which I can never explain nor wholly describe. The whole self-system comes apart and in its place a vacuum conveys its presence by a feeling I can only describe as terror. Indefinitely prolonged, it creases the body – the victim stoops, his arms across his stomach, and bows to ease the pain. Your other patients, though less articulate, must surely describe identical symptoms. It gives an insight, on the other hand, into the structure of the mind. How, under stress, it comes apart. *The Quinary or Pentadic Theory*. When I've written the book I'll ask you to check it. Once published, assimilated, and understood, it will revolutionise psychiatry.'

Two evenings before Bea had told me of her mother's invitation I had come out of the art school to find Isabella waiting in much the same fashion as I had waited for her outside the City Women's Institute on the evening of our first intimate embrace. Her face was tense, her habitual tenderness displaced by apprehension, a look which announced, 'There's nothing left for either of us if you don't give me what I want.' 'I had a meeting in town. I happened to be passing. Perhaps,' she said, 'you could come to the house.'

A luminous light in the windows of the offices and shops, and the less prepossessing windows of the college, etherealised, or so it seemed, the street – less a place, I thought, than a vision.

130

'When?'

'Tomorrow.'

'I'll be at college.'

'Take the afternoon off.' She added, 'You've done it often before.'

'They're beginning to notice,' I said, and asked, 'What's it about?'

'Bea will be at school. Freddie away. Rose I've given the afternoon off. I'd like,' she said, 'to see you in private. Not,' she went on, 'a place like this.'

'Why?'

'There's something,' she said, 'I'd like to ask.' She paused, her look more direct – and curious – than on any previous occasion. 'You're not afraid of coming?'

More than a challenge, I reflected, was implicit in her look: a right was being asserted – one she had earned and to which I'd acceded. 'I'll take the afternoon off,' I said.

I am standing at the Linfield stop: one or two people are waiting with me: it is the middle, I assess, of the afternoon, and realise I have eaten nothing since breakfast (hadn't Etty, moments before, been standing at the sink, peeling potatoes, potting plants?) and concluded it must have been mid-morning. It is warm: traffic comes down the steep slope of the hill, past the church, to the cross-roads at the bottom: here five roads meet around what, at one time, would have been the village green, a rectangular tarmacked area dominated by the employment exchange (housed in a former primary school building) and a piece of cultivated ground equally divided between grass (denuded) and flowerbeds. Here Bea and I have met on numerous occasions, getting off buses, getting on; here, in the past, Etty, her sister and her brothers, have bought ice-creams; here, in the dark I have quarrelled with and subsequently consoled Isabella. Immediately ahead is the principal road leading through the village – and the declivity, some distance away, where the railway crossed from the colliery yard: the ghosts of steam engines whistle in my ear

131

and, in my otherwise vacuous head, the winding gear and slag heap rise, once more, above the roofs: boots shuffle in a cobbled yard; carts, pulled by horses ('Corcoran & Co Contractors' inscribed, yellow paint on black, along the side), come groaning down the hill, the ejaculations of the drivers, the cracking of a whip, the steam from the horses' backs and mouths, the rasp of the metal-rimmed wheels against the tarmac, of the brake blocks against the wheels themselves (the rattle of chains as the blocks are deployed). 'Her father, they say, went off his head.' I hear the words quite clearly. 'He was certified for over a year, believed he'd been condemned to death and woke each morning expecting the sentence to be carried out. Nothing would console him.'

'If I have gone out of my mind it's quite all right by me,' I said. 'Who wouldn't go nuts in a place like this?' to which a woman beside me says, 'It's alus late.'

'Late?'

'The bus to Linfield.'

'Linfield.'

'Aren't you Mrs Stott's father?' she suddenly enquires.

'I was,' I tell her, 'but left, in fact, some time ago.'

'I've seen you on television.'

'Television?'

'Years ago. I don't get much time,' she adds, 'for reading. I go to my daughter's to look after the children. She works. Her husband,' she goes on, 'is unemployed but has no flair with the kiddies. Sits and mopes, when he's not on drugs. Ten years ago he was down the pit, drunk each night and happy as a lord.'

'Not much to choose between the two,' I tell her.

'Give me drunk every time,' she says. 'At least when he was he wa're alus singing.'

The woman is old: her hair, beneath a headscarf, is fastened in pins: a scarf wrapped beneath a bright check coat: stout, double-chinned, rouged cheeks: between two vivid streaks of lipstick she smiles: teeth more vivid than the lipstick itself, eyes brighter, more vivid than the teeth.

'Children keep you going,' to the others in the queue beyond her.

I am on my way to Onasett (via Linfield): o happy land!

Lunch is laid on the table when I arrive; and has been waiting I assume, for several hours (I'm late) – a table at which I've eaten with her husband and her daughter, talking of war, politics, art and religion, on none of which Corcoran has any views other than those conjured up in opposition to Isabella's (and Bea's): called up during the war he was offered an immediate commission, because of his 'transport experience', in the Army Ordnance Corps.

The day is chill (it is raining as I walk from the bus to the house): she wears a suit – a loosely-cut jacket and a pleated skirt: dove grey, it is relieved at the throat by the lace collar of a high-necked blouse: I have never seen her look more lovely. Her colour is high.

I have seen her setting and re-setting the table as I've come up the path through the garden: the neatness of her hair, the squareness of her shoulders, the trimmed-in waist, the flaring hips. 'I don't feel hungry,' I tell her, she, having departed to the kitchen, returning with food she's kept hot in the oven.

'I thought you'd have an appetite,' she says. 'Working,' she goes on, 'all morning.'

'I don't feel hungry,' I tell her again, not sure that my arrival has gone unnoticed: from the yard, through the archway, it's possible to see the house and the garden: any amount of men are working there, lorries being backed, loaded, fuelled.

She shrugs: her hair is brightly ribboned: it has, as on most occasions when I see her, been fastened in a bun (she intoxicates me with her dress, her make-up, her preparation – above all, with her circumspection: so she might prepare, a headmistress, to interview a parent about a child).

'I thought it was better,' she says, 'to talk like this, not like we always do, in a side-street doorway, or on the back seat of a bus, or in a café, or beneath a hedge.'

'I like those places,' I tell her. 'I can't tell you how much

133

those doorways and buses and cafés and hedges mean. I some-times go by them and, prompted by what went on there, think of you all day.'

'At no expense,' she says, 'to yourself,' and adds, before I can respond, 'At least, in here, we're not overlooked. At least,' she goes on, 'we can talk in private,' (gesturing to the window – the murmur of engines, the cawing of rooks, the panting of the pit, the rattle of the sorting plant, the whistle of the engine – the shuffle – the shuffle of thousands of feet).

She smiles (sitting sideways at the table herself).

'Won't you sit down?'

Fenchurch is what people assume he isn't: malevolent, uncaring, demonic, unkind: the graffitist of the notorious Benedict Ward at the North London Royal, named after a benefactor who came to no good (not unlike the clothing manufacturer who gave his name to Boady Hall, the even more notorious rehabilitation centre in North London).

I, too, sit sideways at the table: hungry I might have been – it is three-quarters of an hour by bus from Linfield – but apprehension – an awful apprehension – grips not only my stomach but my intestines; and not only my intestines but, finally, my heart: I am here, I have concluded on my three-quarters of an hour journey on the bus, to be cast off.

'In many respects, all I want to do,' she says, suddenly, 'is to see you sitting there.' (I can gaze at her for hours, entranced, besotted, entwined.) 'Like an artist,' she continues, 'sits for an indefinite time, or so you tell me, before his subject. I imagine,' she goes on, gazing at me with glistening eyes – enigmatic, in the extreme, 'you've done that lots of times yourself.'

'A few.'

'You're my model.' She smiles again. 'But,' she continues, 'in a different art entirely.'

'Which art is that?' my voice disappearing, huskily, halfway down my throat.

'The art – would you call it? – of growing old.'

'You don't look old, in the least,' I tell her.

'I'm sure.' She laughs. 'Which is why I've spent the best part

134

of the morning getting ready.' She glances at the food, her arm laid on the table beside her: my gaze – her fingers, slightly raised, are tapping at the cloth – is directed to her ring.

Her knee, her legs crossed, gleams beneath the hem of her pleated skirt: her foremost shoe, high-heeled, has drifted from her foot.

'I've given you,' she adds, 'a terrible weapon.'

'How?'

We sit at adjacent sides of the table: by reaching out, I speculate, I could touch her hand.

'By competing with my daughter. You could destroy both of us,' she adds.

'I love you both,' I tell her.

'Do you?'

She waits to be convinced.

'I love you more than Bea.'

'More?'

'Much.'

'How much?'

'In ways I can't express.'

'It's those ways I'd like to hear about,' she says, revealing a ruthlessness which, until this moment, I have scarcely if ever glimpsed. She sees me as an opportunist, I suddenly reflect, dissuaded only from this view by what she suspects may be my talent.

'If I can't express them I don't see how I can describe them,' I tell her. 'I like to love you in ways that neither you nor I can understand. That,' I pause, 'is the heart of it.'

The colour deepens round her eyes – around her eyes and despite her make-up.

'I was never aware of anything,' she repeats '*anything!* – until I touched your hand.'

'When?'

'When you went the wrong way up Sugden's Bank.' Gesturing to the grounds at the back of the house, she adds, 'It was all so wrong.'

'Wrong?'

'Terribly.'

The word, used in isolation, brings out a smile.

The ring: nothing entrances me so much as when – its thin gold strand – I persuade her (refusing to touch it myself) to take it off: more erotic, for instance, than her removing her clothes (the mechanical way she draws off her blouse, or, half-twisting, first unfastens then lowers her skirt, unclips her stockings, releases her breasts: the nonchalant way she introduces, with a casual raising of her hips, the 'vouchsafing' which, after-wards, she confesses means more to her than she suspects (incorrectly) it does to me. 'There is,' I always tell her, 'no condescension in it. I'm sure not on your part and certainly not on mine.').

Re-crossing her legs, she says, 'I don't know where we go from here,' while, her own gaze fixed on mine, mine seeks the wall behind her back (a photograph of Kells standing beside a war-time bomber: a visit to a nearby aerodrome arranged by a colleague engaged, he subsequently told me, on radar research).

'Unless,' I tell her, 'we call a halt.'

'A woman old enough,' she smiles (a familiar refrain), 'to be your mother. Certainly,' she continues, 'twice your age.' Her hand reaches out and covers mine. 'And yet,' she smiles again, 'a whole day goes by and, at the end of it, all I have thought about is you.'

She stands.

'Don't you ever wear a hat?'

'Never.'

'I suppose you did at school.'

'A cap.'

'A cap.' She caresses my head. I smell her scent. 'The whole thing,' she says, 'is quite ridiculous.'

'My ring as well?' she says. 'I feel quite naked already,' retaining her skirt as well as her stockings until unbuttoning her blouse ('I chose high-necked, my dear, on purpose') I persuade her to remove them. 'I'll take off what you like. All I wanted,' she goes on, 'is just one time in bed,' recalling each incident as I return home on the bus. 'A betrayal of Bea as well as Corcoran,' I announce. 'Not to mention Kells and Nan.'

'I beg your pardon?' the man beside me says and I am gazing at the curve of a hedge, the shape of a tree familiar from almost forty years before – glimpsed like this, fleetingly, from the window of a passing bus.

'Not at all.' I ease my feet – absurdly, I discover, in my slippers – aware of the draught from the bus's open door.

The hulk of Ardsley Priory appears – a black, stone building, tall and square, and surmounted by a balustrade whose silhouette is pierced by chimneys: beyond a battlemented gatehouse a drive winds off across a tree-strewn park. A wall, bowed and buttressed, its brickwork less dark than the house itself, obliterates the view: we cross a hump-backed bridge: a lake, enclosed by trees, appears.

Lying on her bed, her ring removed, the curtains drawn: 'O, my dearest love,' she said.

I walked this road – the familiar fields, the familiar hedges, the hidden declivities, the sudden promontories – grey-heaped and silver-birched – that marked the medieval gin-pits: walked the twelve miles from Onasett to Ardsley (I was running out of money, that summer before our move to London). At the end of the journey I limped to the door and spent the best part of the following hour sitting in the kitchen, talking to Isabella (occasionally to Bea as she darted to her room, to study, and darted back), my foot in a bucket of water. Periodically Isabella would take the foot and massage the swollen ankle (her ringed finger passing to and fro across the tendon). 'You do too much,' she said. 'That's half your trouble.'

'I need experience,' I told her.

'Of what?'

'All sorts of things you can't imagine.'

'Such as?'

'Love. Hatred. A tent erector,' I told her, 'is nothing to be sneezed at.'

'You and your tents!' (in much the same manner as she might have said, 'You and your kisses!').

'Are you two fraternising?' Bea said, coming in, unaware, as always, of what, in reality, was going on.

'If I am going mad,' I said, 'at least I am going mad in style,' at which the man beside me, turning further round, enquires again, 'I beg your pardon?'

'I spend my days and nights in what I can only describe,' I tell him, 'as a maelstrom of despair,' while at the art school, leaning over my design for a record sleeve for Haydn's 'Creation', the graphics teacher and vintage car enthusiast observes, 'It's too much like a painting.'

'That's what I like,' (a vortex of swirls and whirls in variegated colours).

'This is graphics,' Wormald declares. 'Painting is finished,' he goes on. 'I had a friend at college who now earns his living like everyone else, and who, whenever he wanted to paint a picture, closed his eyes and painted it in his head. Not only does it save money and paint and canvas but time.' He waves his leather-elbowed, tweed-jacketed arm.

But what, after all, I mentally enquire, drew me to self-expression? A feeling – as grave, as inspiriting, as falling in love: as predictable – and as simple – as reading aloud, 'Who is the happy warrior, who is he, whom every man in arms would wish to be?' gained momentum with, 'How oft, on moonlit nights,' and reached a climax with, 'The violin sobs of the autumn wound my heart with a monotonous languor . . .'

Or wasn't it, I reflected (sitting upstairs on the bus on which, downstairs, I am sitting now), my gazing at the familiar landscape of field and wood and hill and dell – the rolling countryside between Ardsley and Linfield – and specifically at the colliery tracks leading from the massive Culloden Pit (a phalanx of coke ovens along one side) endeavouring, beneath the industrial dereliction, to identify the contour of the original fields; or those early mornings in camp at Broughton Woods, looking out from our tree-enclosed clearing (approached, up the slope, like a castle mound) with its view of the iron-workings of the medieval monks on the opposite valley side, and the mounds of the more recent gin-pits covered in moor grass and silver birch; the grandeur of that mist-strewn valley that formed a boundary to Broughton Springs (the sun gilding the trees still wet with dew and, in the furthest distance, the Pennine hills: where the limestone uplands meet the sandstone valleys), the wood-smoke rising from the roped-off fire, the smell of bacon and mushroom frying, the sound of the earliest risers washing in the stream below, the towel-draped figures emerging from the game keeper's cottage which, ruined, provided us with our alternative earth-closet?

Or singing round the fire at night, the moon pinioned to the branches overhead; or those afternoons when, shrieking, we mounted the truck on the tiny, narrow-gauged timber-merchant's rails and rattled and swayed to the wood-shed below (the draped shape of the circular saw: the scoured texture of its metal sides, the angularity of its savage teeth: the smell of wood and the sensuous mounds of resinous dust): that sensation of release, evoked in the bowels, that came with those feelings of beauty and peace?

'Aren't you a romantic?' Wormald enquires, leaning over my 'Creation' design – the lettering of 'Haydn' not all that grand: couldn't I have chosen an orchestra shorter than the 'Philharmonic'?

'What's romantic?' I enquire.

'Do you mean, what is the romantic comprised of, *Harry*, or what is romantic in you?'

'In me.'

'By definition,' he says, 'they're both the same. Take, for instance, your addiction to *art*,' (pronounced with a scarcely silent prefix 'f' and an indefinite extension of the vowel). '*Aaaart* has been superseded by life. Who, for instance, is the most significant painter of our time?' voice raised to reach my fellow students scattered, on stools, around the design-room tables, each listening with an interest verging on obsession to this putting down of 'Harry': 'Picasso!' comes up their single cry.

'Who is a parodist,' Wormald says. 'Who, half a century before you did, Harry, got the message. When the philistine public – condemned by people like yourself – say that modern art is rubbish, they are, in reality, speaking the truth. Why paint a landscape or a figure when a camera can do it for you, in a matter of seconds, and, further, if required, can make it *move*?'

Discussions of this nature are 'rationalisations', as Maidstone would put it, of Wormald's antipathy to me as a person, viz: 'Your determination to turn every student exercise into a work of art, to eschew not only propriety but common sense, will condemn you to obscurity for the rest of your life. Or do you extol the virtue of living in a garret? Have you ever *known* an artist in a garret? I knew one in London who used to speak like you – until he ended up having to eat his candle.'

Wormald is my antagonist: blue-eyed, fair-haired, axe-wielding (philistine): a Saxon type. His attitude, if more perniciously expressed, is endorsed by the pipe-toting Principal, Bairstow, who not only talks but looks like a miner: short, stocky, with bowed legs. 'What dost think thy's doing, Pisschapel?' on a painting I've stuck on a wall. 'Thy's only here to study,' (not, he was about to go on, to paint bloody pictures).

'My name's Fenchurch,' I tell him.

'Fenchurch, Pisschapel, thy's only here for one thing,' adding to Dawlish, his second-in-command, 'They all look alike to me.' Balding, with a head like a boulder lying, centuries-smoothed, in a Pennine stream, he stalks the rooms of his cultural outpost as might a Roman his beleaguered fort on the outermost fringes of his northern empire: the barbarian hosts have worn him down (assimilated him into their barbarian culture – 'culture', as he might otherwise have known it, a pernicious reminder of all he has left behind in the sun-drenched streets of Rome: days of love and wine and roses – refinement, taste, and self-expression). Much of the beleaguered man of action is evident in his attitude to me: the look which declares, 'You think you're destined for the capital, do you? (Afternoons in the Colosseum, nights at the Baths of Caracalla). I'll be buggered if you'll get away, my friend

(Pisschapel or Fenchurch), while I'm condemned to stay in this benighted fucking hole. You'll stick it out like I do. As for *art*...'). He comes into the design-room and, reminded of who I am, remarks, 'You're the artist, are you?' adding to the much-tried Dawlish as he walks away, 'We'll knock that bloody nonsense out. We don't want a place of pussy-footing pansies here.'

My philosophy takes root in opposition.

'I beg your pardon?' the man beside me says again.

I find relief in Isabella: I meet her sometimes once a week: the cost of the 'studio', when it becomes too much (refusing her offer to finance it), obliges us, once more, to resort to a field outside the town – lying beside the road along which the Linfield–Ardsley bus comes twice within the hour: we meet in wind and sun and rain, something monstrous – insatiable, demonic, malign – in everything we do.

'I'm not sure,' she had said on the day I had visited her at Ardsley, 'that it means as much to me as it does to you. That is to say,' she suddenly declared, lying against the pillow as she watched me dress, 'I could go on seeing you without this happening. I do it,' she went on, 'because it means so much to you. To see you so moved and raptured, raptures and moves me, too.'

We are, as it happens, mistaken more and more often for mother and son ('Would your son like another cup of tea?' in the café: 'Your son got your ticket for you, missis,' if we are separated on the bus). She is terrified of being recognised by one of Corcoran's drivers (or, indeed, by anyone from the village: 'I'd like to tell everyone how I feel. There's so much I'd like to confess. But there is, of course,' she'd go on, 'no one.').

On one occasion she didn't turn up.

'Has your mother been ill?' I asked Bea the next time we met.

She shook her head. 'She's been quite perky recently,' she said. 'Over and above her usual self. I've never seen her quite so loud. I suppose,' she went on, 'it's the middle-age crisis, but she's happier than I've known her all my life. She's always asking, of course, after you. "You must look after Richard," she says. As if you were an invalid. "He has," she often says, "a very hard life." '

'She's not been ill?'

'Far from it.'

'I thought I saw her in town the other day. It must,' I tell her, 'have been someone else.'

'If she was looking ill,' she smiles, 'it must have been someone else.'

'In any case,' I tell her, 'you must give her my love.'

'Oh, I shall,' she says. 'She knows how much you admire her.'

'How?' I ask.

'A woman's instinct, Richard!' She laughs. 'As for she and I,' she laughs again, 'one woman to another.'

I didn't see her, nor did I hear from her for several days: I kept away from Ardsley, meeting Bea at the weekend and most schooldays in town. I felt, alternately, relief and alarm – relief that, at last, the relationship was coming to an end (had conceivably, already ended), alarm that, if not the whole of it, something of what had been going on had been discovered – and if not by Corcoran, someone else (Bea still in the dark). It was, I reflected, so unlike her not to keep in touch; although I wrote to her each day – 'I miss you' (platitudinously) 'more than I can say' – re-discovering, in her absence, she meant more to me than often she did when the two of us were together – I tore each letter up. I wrote appraisals of her figure – her eyes, her nose her mouth: her waist, her hips: I imagined her, as Wormald would have recommended, in my head, then drew her naked as I had many times before (several of which drawings I placed in my folder to take to the Drayburgh). 'If I've nothing else to show for it, I might as well,' I thought, 'keep these.'

Then came Bea's message, as I saw her off to Ardsley one evening, 'Mummy leaves for Clare's and Veronica's tomorrow,' (the two widows living together). 'I'm to follow at the weekend.

142

So are you. She's already bought, she says, the tickets'. I astonished the following day to find a message at the college, a
ticket attached, 'I've gone ahead with Mummy. Come as soon
as you can. I'm sure we'll have a wonderful time, all five of us
together. I'll meet you if you ring,' a telephone number and
an address scrawled beneath with, 'Mummy sends her love.' In
brackets: 'Not as much as I.'

12

THE TRAIN moves steadily to the south: I sit by a window, hemmed in by a boisterous family, their suitcases piled with my hold-all in the rack above my head. A sense of desolation (arguments at home about my leaving, arguments about the cost, set against my Chamberlains earnings) is lightened by the prospect of meeting Bea but, more potently, being reunited with Isabella (what, I am endlessly reflecting, is she up to: are we, in future, only to meet in the company of other people?). A branch line (the sun is setting); shadows come down from a range of unfamiliar hills (a chilling of the air inside the carriage). I imagine, as the shadows lengthen – coalesce and deepen – I am going beyond the unknown village where Bea and her mother and her aunts are waiting – beyond the south coast where (evidently) our holiday is booked, beyond the English Channel, beyond the coast of France – to a world of art and self-expression.

'I beg your pardon?' the man beside me says again and, shuffling my feet inside my slippers, I gaze at a landscape of ploughed fields and copses, and the unreclaimed, perpetual gin-pits standing up like tumuli from the cultivated ground: we breast a rise: overhung by cloud are the steeples, the domes and the towers of Linfield – in silhouette, not unlike the profile of a castle.

'I was recalling,' I tell him, 'the time I came this way before and saw, as I'm seeing now, the town of Linfield, laid out like a ghost.'

'A ghost?' The man has a pouting lower lip: saliva occupies

each corner of his mouth. His nose is long, his eyes – how much, I idly reflect, have I told him? – inquisitive and strong: his nails – his adjacent hand gripping the seat in front, the barrier of his arm between us – need cleaning.

'Visited by Defoe, Doctor Johnson and – when he caught the wrong train from London – Wordsworth,' the buildings caught in the midday light with, on the slope beyond them, the dull, red glow of Onasett (tiled roofs, brick and pebble-dashed walls) with, at the summit, the short, square tower of Onasett church, the pyramidal roof of the church hall beside it, the long, low structure of Onasett school and, at the highest point of all, the forbidding walls and block-like structures of the isolation hospital. (O happy land!)

'I lived there as a child, a youth.' Beyond the cathedral spire, the County Hall dome, the Town Hall tower – in the shadow of which resided the Linfield College of Art (now closed, its site occupied by a college of technology) – beyond, too, the gothic turrets that marked the site of the former Parochial School and which is now occupied by the renowned King Edward's. 'I am an Old Edwardian, of course, myself and yearly receive the *Edwardian* magazine in which some of my more celebrated feats have been set down, amongst the other sensations of Edwardian life, like the redoubtable feat, last season, of the First Fifteen and the First Eleven having never lost a match – a precedent which was created when I played in the First Fifteen myself. It's not for nothing that my name is Fenchurch, though my books are never on sale in the town, nor have my plays been performed in the theatre, nor my paintings exhibited in the gallery. I have often reflected that a Freeman of Linfield is the very least I might have expected – a golden key to a golden city – but, I'm afraid, apart from an occasional demand for money on behalf of a charity, not a tinkle. I was telling Maidstone, a man of not immodest achievement himself, Sub-Dean of the medical school and Professor of Psychiatry at the North London Royal – the largest teaching hospital in Europe, second only to the Konecki Foundation in New York for the progressive treatment of, amongst many other animadversions, anxiety neurosis conjoined with clinical depression – that, despite a lifetime of artistic endeavour, most of it centred on, if not inspired by this very town and my experiences in it, it has failed to raise a cloud in anything that might be discerned as my direction: not one hand raised to a furrowed brow to give this returning son of home a signal of approbation.'

'Are you,' the man asks me, 'mad?' (more statement, I reflect, than speculation).

'No,' I tell him. 'I am going to Linfield.'

For there, not one hundred yards from the side of the road, where the bus has pulled up to allow a figure not unlike Isabella to ascend, is the wood – or remains of it – where, on many a weekday afternoon and on an occasional summer evening, she and I – hidden from the road yet able to see, through a barricade of leaves, the approach of this, the Ardsley bus – had lain, if not on my familiar, paint-flecked raincoat, on a bed of cushioning leaves. By a curious coincidence the woman coming into the bus – easing her way between the seats – is of the same age as Isabella (of those days): greying at the temples, her face lined, her hands (the backs) marked by tiny blotches, her breasts subsiding above the belted waist of her coat (her abdomen no doubt flecked with post-natal creases, her legs with varicose veins – scarcely, of course, like Bella at all), she takes her seat, as the bus moves off, diagonally across from where I am sitting and, prompted by a desire to re-acquaint myself with those distant times, I smile, and feel an involuntary lurch (an alarming spasm as, without any prevarication, she smiles directly back): a pleasant, rotund face, unlike the austere sanguinity of Bella's, but nevertheless, in that instance, the embodiment of a love that, no sooner had I won, I lost. By the same extraordinary coincidence, outside, on the road, stands a youth – of nineteen, perhaps twenty years – who waves and she, as the bus departs, having acknowledged me, waves back, her head ducked down in that inimitable fashion (love! love!). 'Linfield,' the man beside me says.

'Not much to write home about,' I tell him, for the familiar headgears, waste-heaps and coal-black ponds which stood like sentinels on either side of the road have been displaced by uniformly cambered slopes on which, asymmetrically (deceiving no one as to their spontaneity), have been planted tiny, posted trees and shrubs, the equally anonymously distributed grass sprinkled with daffodils and tulips.

'It's not a bad place,' the man replies, and adds, 'Particularly the market,' I distracted by the woman, her body (her body!) twisted to wave to the youth in the road behind (no doubt, her son) – reminding me less and less of Isabella than of the feelings she inspired.

The station is lit by a single lamp: I take down my hold-all and clamber out – stiff, aching (the confinement of the carriage), scarcely able to stand. In the shadow of a hut, beyond a tiny barrier – the shadow cast by the single lamp – not Isabella but Bea is waiting: a summer dress, a summer coat: white ankle socks and flat-heeled shoes.

We kiss.

'Are you all right?' She takes my hand (my hold-all in the other).

'How far do we have to go?'

'Not far,' darkness all around, the train, a string of lights, tracing its course along, it appears, the bed of a valley. Disparate lights, scattered across a slope, blend, imperceptibly, into the darkness overhead. 'Are you all right?' she says again.

'I think so.'

A country lane gives way to a residential road: as if on stilts, the tallness of the houses heightens the effect of the steepness of the climb: driveways run up past terraced lawns: flowerbeds cascade with shadowed blooms.

Her aunts – one small and slender (Clare), the other short and stout ('Venny') – are waiting at the door.

'How are you, Richard?' Each shakes my hand.

Bea's mother comes out from a room at the rear (a coal-lit fire, a shaded lamp). 'We wondered where you'd got to.'

'The train was late,' Bea tells them.

'Full of holiday crowds,' I add, Isabella clad not in a summer but a woollen dress: sweetness, as I kiss her cheek, is in her breath (restraint, however, in her manner).

A tray of food is laid by the hearth.

'We've got your supper ready.'

We sit by the fire: a slender woman, a less slender one, a less slender one still – and Bea. We talk about the journey ('longer than I expected': we are in the Derbyshire hills) and move on to the arrangements the two aunts and Isabella have made for the following day: a taxi has been booked: breakfast will be early: chores are assigned for making beds, preparing breakfast, washing-up: the room grows warm after the relative chill outside: four women all of whom, because of their inter-action with the one, I love.

I am shown upstairs: an attic window looks out to the roof and the unlit windows of an adjoining house (to a starlit sky, to the flank of a hill, to the silhouette of trees ascending precipitously a steepening slope). I fall asleep, tossed, at intervals, into wakefulness by the strangeness of the bed. I am wakened finally by Bea ('Don't stay in the bedroom, pet,' from one of the aunts on the landing outside): she has brought me a cup of tea and, with a kiss to my cheek, departs.

The taxi arrives: having made the beds, breakfasted, cleaned the house, I carry the cases out with Bea. Her mother (I have never seen Isabella so early in the day – as, on the previous evening, rarely seen her so late at night) is radiant beyond belief (what, I reflect, has she in mind?). My heart leaps as she hands me her case (the softness of her fingers, the harshness of her ring) and, with an impetuosity comprised of foolishness as much as love, I kiss her cheek, she drawing back and saying, 'We'll still be together this evening, dear,' as much bewildered as startled by the gesture.

A genial companionship continues throughout the day, Bea and I opposite each other beside the window, the three women chatting to one another across the carriage, I in love (in love!) with two of them, enamoured of the third (the doe-eyed Clare), infatuated with the fourth (the placid if curious

Veronica: what on earth, her look suggests, does she suspect is going on?).

We reach the coast: a taxi takes us to our two hotels – one earmarked for me (modest), the other (family Edwardian) for the rest. My room is small, filled day and night by the sound of running water. I move the following day, at Bea's suggestion, to one around the corner ('Mummy will pay the difference,' which I refuse): a view of the sea, the fold of a cliff, a clump of pine, the room adjacent occupied by a honeymoon couple, their activities, and conversation, scarcely filtered by a thin partition.

We venture, one morning, into the sea: the sky is clear, the breeze warm: a ball is thrown: much spray and screaming: my arm on Bella's: 'Are you all right?' 'Much, Richard, thank you,' while, from Venny, 'Leave that man alone!'

Evenings walking on the front, trips along the coast in the afternoons (mornings on the beach): breakfasts alone (watching the honeymoon couple kiss, hold hands beneath the table, whisper, head to head, over a newspaper or the menu): dinner (my solitary table immediately beside the dining-room door), a copy of *Don Quixote* propped on the salt cellar before me (six hundred and sixty-eight pages still to go), the problems of the amorous knight infinitesimal beside my own: nights spent listening to the sounds – much laughter – and attempting not to imagine the activities of the honeymoon couple next door: 'You haven't tried it!' 'When?' ('What?') 'Is it bigger than you thought?'

And evenings ('Back at nine, Bea,' Bella. 'I don't want you starting any habits,' and, 'We've been in love, you know, before,' her aunts), lying on a pine-strewn slope, the sea below us, rising and falling: 'What does it matter? I can't stand life being so prescribed. (We'll go to Paris. I'll become an artist.)'

We picnic on the sand, play croquet on the Edwardian lawn (waiters in the hall and on the terrace, squirrels in the pine trees, parasols and tennis, shaded tables: teas carried out on white-linened trays): 'We've got to know one another, Richard, on this holiday, so well,' (Venny). 'It's been, apart from one or two anxieties which, I'm sure, when you grow older, you'll understand, an enormous pleasure to have you with us,' (Clare).

'Perhaps I will see you later?' (Isabella).

'Where?' (as I am leaving).

'The gate of our hotel.'

'When?'

'Say, ten?'

She comes down the driveway between the rhododendrons and the pine trees and takes my hand: I've been gazing up for half an hour at the lighted windows, endeavouring, in the darkness, to work out which is her room and which the aunts'.

'There you are,' she says, and adds, 'I hope you've missed me,' her look both matter-of-fact and full of mischief.

'I've waited for this moment,' I tell her, 'since we arrived.'

'And all those afternoons and evenings with Bea.'

'Only,' I lie, 'as a substitute for you.'

'I've seen how much you look at her. So have Venny and Clare,' she adds.

We walk along the chine: the trees, from the moon above the sea, throw shadows up the slope.

'Why haven't you been in touch?' I ask.

She waves her arm. 'It had to come to an end,' she says. 'The whole thing,' she goes on, 'was quite absurd.'

'I don't see why.' She is, I see now, throwing me at Bea, the whole thing – the holiday, the aunts – a device.

'Divesting me,' I say aloud, and as she adds, 'Of what?' I announce, 'There's not one day gone by when I haven't been tempted to get on a bus and come and see you, Freddie or no Freddie, Bea or not.'

'Oh, that.' She waves her arm again. 'It wasn't real. Coming here, with Clare and Venny, seeing me with women as old or older than myself, I thought, at the very least, would help. That's why,' she adds, 'I had to see you. To make it clear it's at

150

an end. Given time, we'll both relate to one another,' she concludes, 'as we should have done from the start.'

At the summit of the chine I turn her to me: I trace the contour of her cheek, her nose: I press my hand against her mouth.

It must have been midnight when I took her back: after ringing the night porter's bell, I stepped back in the shadows and watched her let into the lighted hall: her legs were bare, her coat, I could see now, stained with grass: a last look round, followed by a smile, blinded by the light.

13

'I WORKED AT that pit' the man declares.

'So did my father.'

'What years were that?' The saliva re-appears at the corner of his mouth: coal-dust darkens the tissue above each eye: like the bark of a silver birch, scars, horizontally, cross his brow.

'Until,' I tell him, 'the end of the Second World War. After that he taught D.P.s – Estonians, Latvians, Lithuanians, Poles. Then he came home and got a job at Onasett.'

'Fenchurch?'

'Right.'

'I never knew him.' Shakes his head. 'That hill they have yonder wa're a pit heap ten year ago. That little lake you see down theer, wi' boats on, were the pithead baths.'

'Vivienne, of course, when I brought her here, enthused about the place,' I tell him, 'no end. As for my father – he was still alive and living in a house at Notton End – he couldn't understand a word she said. She had this accent which came out in private whenever she wished to make an impression. On stage, however, as clear as a bell. "What the bloody hell is she talking about?" he said. "I thought you were married to somebody called Bea." '

'Bea?' the man says.

'I said, "This is Vivienne Wylder, the actress that I wrote you about and, if all goes well, I hope to marry. The second," I told him, "Mrs Fenchurch." '

' "Mrs Fenchurch," my father says, "is dead," adding to the putative Mrs Fenchurch, "She died before I did." '

' "He's talking about my mother," I said.

' "The finest woman that ever lived!" '

The finest woman, I might have concurred, had it been a mother I could write home about. She took him to live in the south of England, away from the millstone grit and the pits and the valleys and he faded like a flower. You wouldn't think of this place as light, but in his case the light up here was the light he was used to. Today, with the coal-dust gone, the manufactories reduced to rubble, with service facilities littering the place, there's nothing to come back to. Except a present-iment of what this place was like.'

'Like,' says the man, the bus cresting a rise at the top of the Common, before us, on an opposing hill, a view which, from a different direction, I knew as a child, coming down the hill from church (on Sundays), school (on weekdays): a rampart of buildings, black with soot: the dog-toothed spire of All Saints church, the chisel-shaped profile of the Town Hall tower, the rotundity of the County Hall dome – a cornucopia of cornices and pediments, friezes and roofs – as, for instance, we see them now, from a different perspective though a similar distance: 'A softer profile, I have always thought, when viewed,' I tell him, 'from the top of the Common,' the bus speedily descending. 'Nevertheless, one which, at this late stage in my career, returning as an Old Linfieldian ("Floreat Linfieldia! Floreat Edwardia!"), a proselytiser of this indentured place, I very much appreciate. To the extent, as you can see, that this view of my native heath – this Common on which I have won and lost (if only at the Easter Feast) much of what I cherish most in life – brings tears to my eyes. Tears that remind me not only of the women I have loved, the men I most admired, the parents who, having borne me, tore me apart, but, specifically, of my wife, of Isabella, who was not my wife, of Vivienne who, to put it mildly, was the revelation of my later years, an amalgam of Bea and Isabella whom if I'd met – for these things do occasionally happen – as a younger man I would have married, if only to my cost, unable to accommodate her ferocities which,

153

unique to her, were antagonistic to my own. I loved and lost –
and lost. And lost.'

'Are you all right?' the man enquires.

'Perfectly,' I tell him, for my voice has carried to the front
of the bus (we are sitting – a precaution one always takes on
public transport these days – at the rear) and heads have turned
(shoulders raised, I further notice, to the conductor). 'I have
never felt better,' I go on, 'even if, between ourselves, if the
truth were known,' I lower my voice, 'I have been in and out
of a certain institution which – again, between ourselves – I
wouldn't recommend to anyone. Boady Hall,' I breathe the
name, 'is not a place to write home about. It contains people
who destroy themselves, and though Vivienne and I had that
in common – she a genius of gigantic proportions (the greatest
Mrs Macbeth in years), with flaming hair – admittedly, the
effect of dye – and ludicrous make-up – though scarcely any in
later years – we struggled – separately as well as jointly – to
overcome the ravages wreaked upon those who travel, whether
by vocation or not, across what is euphemistically referred to
as "inner space" – a maelstrom of a place, without form or
purpose, the black hole into which the mind descends, transcending all laws and known experience, superseding hope
(and joy and love), and for which the human imagination has
yet to provide a word. I've been there, pal!' I slap his arm. 'I've
got to admit that Vi – Vivienne, as I previously described her
– got to me in ways that no one else quite has. She – like I was
– should have been confined. She went to a private clinic in
the south of London, visited, fatefully, a similar place outside
New York, a third in the suburbs of Los Angeles, a fourth in
San Francisco, and came here, finally, would you believe it, and
begged me to minister to her myself. I – like Our Lord – who
could not save himself. One evening, returning to the house,
I found her gone. Along with her luggage and a bottle of
bleach. An innocuous-looking liquid which I didn't miss for
days. Until, one morning, I went out to the yard. Stoned, she
might have been, before she took it. "How," you are beginning
to ask, "could a man, nurtured in these parts, loved by the

154

mother, as it happened, of his future wife, who made his fortune from books and plays, and, latterly, pictures, incur the hatred of his children and the contempt of his wife?" Reason is one thing, existence another. In reality, of course, they are both the same. You have, without your being aware of it, been sitting next to a man who, in the halls of misfortune, is virtually unique.'

'Are you going to Linfield?' the man enquires and, by way of answering, I reply, 'So you worked at that pit?'

'For twenty-five years.'

'Twenty-five.'

'Fifteen afore that at New Rawlston.'

'Weren't twenty-five men killed there in the nineteen-fifties?'

'Eighteen.'

'Eighteen.'

'My cousin, by marriage, was one of them.'

'My uncle, on my father's side, the youngest one I had, was killed at Arnhem. The largest parachute drop in recorded history. I had a photograph of him, years ago, on Linfield Station, standing with a group of men who were painting the wrought ironwork above the platform. A doughty, good-natured, adventurous fellow who was turned into something little short of a bandit. Times, of course, have changed since then. Qualities like those are not required. His nephew, who inherited from him, if you like, his appetite for painting – not railway stations, I might add, but pictures – for not dissimilar reasons, acquired not dissimilar characteristics. In struggling against, if you like, a not dissimilar opposition he became something of a *bandito* himself, dropping out of the skies onto something little short of a cultural desert, a plain of middle-class sentiment, virtue and ambition. My uncle did it as one of ten thousand, I as one of four or five, most of whom expired on landing or, if not on landing, shortly after. The heat and dryness burnt them up, the peculiar desolation, not to mention isolation, in which, surrounded by good intentions, they found themselves. Unlike them, however, or even my uncle, I had a more peculiar training. Enigmatic . . .'

'Linfield,' the man says as we pass over the river, visible above the parapet of the concrete bridge: barges were once drawn up above the concrete weir, moored in ranks, the river front, with its cobbled wharf, overlooked by warehouse buildings, malt kilns, cranes and derricks, dockside offices and chandlers' stores (boat-builders' yards and the hulks of barges). The shiny black coal slip and the rusted metal gantries on the coal-wharf, which stood closest to the bridge (on the site of Much the Miller's mill in the legendary accounts of Robin Hood), have gone: a tree-lined walk, relieved by rockeries and stone embankments (a children's playground) and by stone-paved footpaths, following the contour of the river, winds off in the direction of the one remaining mill. The tang of the river is still the same, as is the view on the opposite side of the bridge: an expanse of sky where the valley of the Lin, taking leave of its stone embankments and its gorge-like exit below the town, winds across the shoals of Ferry Ford where the Romans made their earliest crossing.

Beyond the bridge, the bus enters the narrowing streets of the town.

'I get off here.' The man gets up beside me (I feel the warmth of his body). 'Is anybody looking after you?' he adds.

'Lots,' I tell him. 'There'll be a queue.'

'You're going to the bus station, are you?' signalling to the conductor.

'If I don't get off before.'

The bus pulls up: several passengers, preceding the man, descend.

'He's getting off at the bus station,' he says to the conductor. 'You may need the help of a bobby.'

He disappears; at least, I lose sight of him as he steps down to the pavement: more people than I might reasonably have anticipated are milling about outside.

I nod at the woman across the aisle. 'A friend of mine. He worked,' I tell her, 'at New Rawlston, but is presently unemployed.'

'He looks old enough to be retired,' she says.

'That as well,' I tell her, and add, 'Your name isn't Isabella, by any chance?'

'It isn't,' she says, refraining from informing me what it is.

'You look like a Mrs Corcoran,' I tell her, 'whose maiden name was Kells.'

'Not me.' She smiles.

'You have the same eyes, if not the same mouth. Your hair,' I go on, 'is different. Hers was red, or, to be precise, a curious magenta, a mixture of the celt and the latin. She had, when I knew her, a striking warmth, of personality, that is, as well as manner, which your eyes and your mouth remind me of. In addition,' I indicate these features by pointing at a spot beneath my eye, 'a high, arched nose and glancing cheekbones which, in her daughter's face, was characterised by convergent brows, indicating, in their obtrusiveness, a predisposition, I've been told, to paranoia. That wasn't your son, by any chance, who saw you off at the bus-stop?'

'My nephew.'

'Nephew.'

I am about to add, 'A new one on me,' when she continues, 'My sister's son. They live at Wrainthorpe,' (a village close to the stop where the bus picked her up: how often had Isabella said, 'The Wrainthorpe stop,' on her journeys from Ardsley to me).

'Linfield,' I tell her, 'is a curious place. On the site of the cathedral, for instance, which we're passing now,' (its cleaned sandstone façade visible through the windows on her side of the bus), 'was a sacred grove, in pre-historic times, and, subsequent to that, in Roman times, a temple to Diana. That wouldn't, by any chance, be your name?'

The woman has dark hair: it obtrudes upon her collar in a way which, once I had released it, Isabella's did, cascading down in shiny bright waves; her features, like Bella's, are set widely apart (she may, in effect, be not much older than myself), creating an impression of openness and candour, and – not to be sneezed at in a woman – humour.

'No,' she says.

'And it isn't Isabella.'

'I'm a housewife,' she says (the bus coming to a halt, passengers, with glances in our direction, getting off).

'That's the greatest calling on earth,' I tell her. 'Like "miner" is for men. Where would we be,' I go on, 'without you?' she, however, already rising (the bus in the Bull Ring and, having circuited Queen Victoria's statue on its central island, entering the bus station). 'My friend, the one I mentioned, Isabella, and I haunted this place. A veritable companion,' I tell her, 'in my hour of need. There were thirty years or more between us,' calling over the shoulders of the passengers between us, she already some distance down the aisle. 'More an obstacle in her eyes than it was, of course, in mine, age, inevitably, a preoccupation when appearances are all that count. Yet age, in her case,' raising my voice, 'was her one credential. It informed not only her appearance but her thoughts. Everything she said was imbued with grandeur, with the ineffable mystery of – how otherwise could I describe it – *being in love*.'

I am talking – as far as I can discern – to the concrete pavement onto which – the final passenger to leave the bus – I have now descended. Only the conductor – and, with the conductor, his attention having been attracted, the driver – contemplate my struggle for, in descending, having lost one slipper, I am searching for it in the gutter between the side of the bus and the exceptionally high kerb of the bus station's pavement.

'Perhaps,' I tell the conductor, 'I have lost it inside,' and having re-entered the vehicle, discover it, as I'd anticipated, beneath my seat (so anxious to engage my fellow-passenger's interest: what more, I reflect, have I to lose?). On the seat itself are my sketchbook and pencil. 'Good job I came back,' I add. 'Bringing the great indoors outdoors is invariably, I've discovered, the corollary of wearing one's indoor footwear in the street. Normally, to move at all, I require a stick. As it is, from the moment I got up this morning I felt my hour had come. I must do today what I cannot put off any longer. "I will go outside," I said, "and draw a tree." '

Across the bus station I see the woman.

'That's not the Onasett stop she's waiting at?' I ask, to which the conductor replies, 'The opposite end,' and then, 'Do you want me to put you back on the one to Ardsley?'

'My family live at Onasett,' I tell him. 'Or did. Previous to that, of course, myself.'

The bus doors hiss to behind my back.

I cross to the queue where the woman is waiting and, with a geniality which had, I assume, characterised my previous remarks, enquire, 'Would you like a cup of tea?'

'No, thank you,' she says.

'Coffee?'

'No, thank you.'

'I have the money.'

'So have I,' she says, 'but my bus will be here any minute.'

'The cafeteria,' I tell her, 'is directly opposite the bus station entrance. We can, once we spot it, be back in no time at all.'

'No, thank you,' she says a third time at which a man standing in the queue beside her enquires, 'Is this man bothering you in any way?'

'He is,' she says, 'as a matter of fact,' to which I reply, 'She is like a very old friend of mine. Someone to whom I was devoted. A woman of infinite charm,' to which the man – of no great height – responds by placing himself between the two of us. 'I'd advise you to clear off before I have you taken off,' he says.

'She spoke to me on the bus,' I tell him, 'and smiled at me in a way which, if it hadn't been broken already, would have seriously incommoded my heart. She doesn't know what power she's got. What wonder. What grace. Like Isabella. Like Bea. (Bea stands for Beatrice, by the way),' I add. 'If only you knew how hard it is, not only to focus my thoughts on what, specifically, is happening now, but, out of the memories and feelings associated with this place – the majority to do, if not with love, a state of mind conducive to it – to extract a phrase, an appropriate noun, an adjective which describes what it is I would wish to say, you wouldn't feel obliged, as, evidently, from

159

the pressure of your hand against my chest, you are feeling now, to disengage me from this woman,' peering round to find a woman, not unlike her, standing in her place. 'All I wish to confess,' I confirm to this second figure, 'is that, while I may not be compos mentis, I am nevertheless mentis par dessous, which is another way of announcing that Maidstone and the present Raynor and, before that, the renowned Mackendrick, the transcendentalist Russo-Scottish psychoanalyst whose mother and father were born in the Ukraine, pronounced me "rational", in the latter's phrase, "this side of God", the line a quotation from one of my plays, for want of a better appellation, *A Better Man*, which drew Mackendrick's attention to me in the first place,' concluding, 'Could you direct me to the Onasett stop? I merely wished to ask.'

'This, with one or two exceptions, is the most familiar place on earth,' I tell the man who is waiting there. 'I have endured more, waiting on this spot, than I have on any other. I know this place like the back of my hand. Or, better still, the palm.'

I hold it out.

'A simian line, the heart and head line combined in a single furrow, not unlike an ape's. A sign,' I add, 'of criminality – two out of three condemnees, in a famous survey, possessed this characteristic – or of high, exceptionally high artistic endeavour. Michelangelo, Leonardo, as well as Shakespeare, are often quoted as examples. Which latter case applies to me, the line between crime and art, as that between sadness and madness, not to mention badness, being very thin indeed.'

Bowed down by a bag of shopping, after glancing at my hand, the man announces, 'Mad!' to a figure standing on his other side (a woman) who, in turn, stands at the head of a very large queue.

'It is the Onasett stop,' the woman says, 'but you have to join the other end.'

'I shall,' I tell her and peruse the faces as I move along the line: not once, in my youth, could I have walked along this queue and not seen a dozen, if not half a dozen, if not two or three familiar faces: here Bea would queue (to come and see

160

me); here I would queue after seeing her off; here my mother waited with a weekend's shopping; here my brothers and I on our way from school (the redoubtable King Edward's); here our father on his trips from town; our neighbours, now deceased, from a multitude of errands.

'It's all too much,' I tell a child, the last figure in the queue – and who, with a violent tug, is propelled towards its mother – as I, with similar alacrity (if by invisible strands), was propelled to mine. 'Is this the Onasett stop?' I ask her.

'It is,' she says, and turns aside.

'I too stood here,' I tell her, 'as a child,' and add, 'Or, rather, in the Bull Ring. This place wasn't built until after the Second World War, an area of derelict streets and houses which were bulldozed to the ground before the war began and remained like that until five years after when pre-stressed concrete came to the fore. It's why,' I add, 'it's dropping to pieces. How is Onasett?' I enquire.

Her head turned from me, she remarks, 'Not bad,' as she might, I reflect, of a dog or a husband.

'Not good,' I might have said, but respond, 'That place was paradise on earth. Bricks from Chalkley's Quarry. I suppose that's gone as well. A hole in the ground directly opposite the first road they cut across Onasett Common, a buttress of land, crossed and criss-crossed by dry stone walls, rising to the peak of Onasett Moor, in turn looking out to the Pennine uplands where we, the Onasettians, camped as boys, leaders of the tribe, despatched, in later years, to the four corners of the earth.'

The war went on for a very long time: in some instances, my dear, it never stopped; stepping, as I did, at the age of six, into the field at the back of the house to see reality re-valued: overhead the enemy lurked (about to descend at any moment): nothing after that could be the same, the brick no longer brick, the grass no longer grass, the sky no longer sky, embodiments, merely, of a soon-to-be-unleashed propensity for destruction.

And, secondly, of course, the films of Buchenwald, Auschwitz, Dachau and Belsen: figures that walked into and out of the mind, their ingress and egress continuing for ever.

'That man,' the child says, 'is wearing his slippers.'

'Don't point.' The mother draws the child's arm in the opposite direction. 'It's crude.'

Conversely, would I recognise the youth who, thirty-five years ago, came to this stop: the dark-eyed look, the shadowed frown (two vertical creases incising his brow), the drawn-in cheeks – robosity itself, and yet constrained: braced like an animal before a jump which it, and it alone can see (the impediment of his years ahead, the liabilities of temperament)? I doubt, looking round, I would know him at all. Would he, for instance, be disguised as that long-haired, broad-shouldered figure over there who, while maintaining the appearance of having succumbed to the proprieties of everyday life (job, home, wife, car), has preserved a sense of indecorum: the wide-legged stance, the unshaven jaw, a wild-eyed look beneath a furrowed brow? Or – council house, unemployment cheque (disassociation) – is he a plumber on his way from one job to another, the bag at his feet containing, if not his tools, his week-long washing? Or the youth over there with a close-cropped head, jeaned and denim-jacketed (arms thrust to his elbows in his pouch-like pockets), he the embodiment of what I, dark-eyed and shadow-browed, embodied then: an indisposition to take yes or no for an answer, recalcitrant, obtuse, inapposite, grand?

'I lived at Onasett for twenty years,' I tell the mother. 'The first twenty years, of course, are supposed to be the best, the first five being the most important. Quite a sentence when, at that age, there is no redress. Sentenced, I'd say, without a hearing. It was only when I published my own *Theory of the Mind* that this scheme of things had to be revised. You must have heard of *New Mind Theory*, or *The Narrative or Pentadic Theory of the Mind* (attributed exclusively,' I tell her, 'to myself).'

By 'mind', of course, I mean the psyche.

'It may not be commonly known, for instance, that I made much of my recent reputation by re-writing a tripartite theory of the same, replacing it with a more clinically exact one of five recognisable selves.'

162

Viz:

the primal self,

common to us all, described as the reservoir of primal appetites;

the intrinsic self,

the unique conjunction of two equally unique parental systems;

the construct self,

the interaction of the primal and the intrinsic selves with everything around them;

and the preceptorial self,

which was the validating system that emerged from the conjunction of the previous three.

'My extra-curricular discovery was of the fifth self, a super-authorial presence which, while independent of the previous four, was nevertheless integral to them. The impersonal element we become aware of when we sleep, the still, small voice of poetical inspiration – '

'Are you all right?'

'A totality I named "the composite self".'

A policeman – I am aware, merely, of the darkness of his sleeve, and of a silver button which secures a flap (of his pocket) above his heart – and of his finger and his thumb as he takes (perhaps has taken now for quite some time) my elbow.

'Perfectly,' I tell him.

'Where are you going?' (he enquires).

'Onasett,' I tell him.

'The bus,' he says, 'has left.'

He is – I glance up at his face – younger than his voice suggests: a moustache – a low, triangular shape, bifurcated, curiously, by a bare, scar-like patch – lies above a juvenile and singularly ill-formed mouth: sallow cheeks but not unfriendly eyes – immaturity bolstered by authority (constrained, temperamentally, by a lack of style).

He might, on the other hand – not unusual in his profession – have been in an accident.

'I am,' I tell him, 'waiting for the next.'

163

'You live at Onasett?' (Definitely an impediment in speaking, brevity a tool).

'I did. Presently,' I add, 'I live in London. Are you an inspector?'

'No, sir.'

'Nor, I suspect, an Old Edwardian.'

'No, sir.'

'You have a ring of the comprehensive.'

'Yes, sir.'

'All my children went to comprehensive. On principle. It did none of them more than adequate harm. "Education is a right, not a privilege," I told them. "Not a commodity," I expanded, "to be bought. Anyone who thinks it is confounds the first principle of a democracy. No democracy can exist that compounds within its system private education. Privilege abrogates demos." '

'Do you need any help?' he enquires.

'None,' I tell him, 'I can think of. Unless you have, secreted upon your person, a means of redressing pain.'

'Pain, sir?'

'Synonymous with "mind", a physiological phenomenon not contingent upon environment. Indeed, not contingent on anything discernible at all. Were you aware, for instance, that the incidence of psychosis in the rural communities of East Africa – a region beset by natural disasters of every type – is precisely the same as it is in the English home counties? It makes a nonsense of the current superstition that form determines content, or, indeed, determines anything at all. Whereas odium theologicum characterised the previous century, odium psychologicum characterises the present. Odium politicum, I haven't a doubt, will follow.'

'Are you a school teacher?' An impulse to take out a notebook is replaced by a gesture which involves the unhitching of a two-way radio from the region of his waist.

'I was. In some of the worst schools in the United Kingdom. Whitechapel, Dalston, Islington, Hackney. Seventeen, three of them described at the time, in a report from Her Majesty's

Inspectorate, as amongst the four worst schools in Great Britain. You name it: I've seen it. Latterly, I have decided art and didacticism do not mix, unlike sentiment and religion, lunacy and charm, except, of course, in the subtlest sense, that the former may serve a moral purpose. For instance – '

'Are you staying in town?'

'With my daughter. Her husband, Charles, is the principal partner in Stott, Stevens and Hopcroft, barristers at large. The final epithet, of course, applying to their fees. Though Charlie, to be fair, is the chairman of the local constituency Labour Party which returns a member to parliament at each election with the second largest majority in the United Kingdom. Or did until the pit was closed.'

'Ardsley?' he enquires.

'Fenchurch is her maiden name, which happens to be mine. Perhaps you've heard of it?'

He shakes his head.

'What sort of education did you have? Apart from one who died a hundred years ago, I'm the only author – not to mention artist – this town has ever had.'

'My father was a policeman and couldn't afford to keep me in school,' he says.

'Mine was a miner and thought he could. First at Callwood Pit and then at Onasett. Both gone. I passed the former, coming into town. Not a sign it ever existed. Ground smooth as silk stretching to the summit of a slope which, in the old days, was decorated solely by a gantry from which the waste-trucks used to tip their load, leaving a plume, on windy days, blowing across the fields, invariably in the direction of Ardsley. I suppose he's still alive.'

'Alive?' He shifts his weight from one foot to the other.

'Your father.'

'Retired.'

'Not much older than I am.'

'No, sir,' he says, and adds, 'younger, I should think.'

At which a shadow falls upon us. 'Onasett,' I tell him, as a bus pulls up by the kerb. 'I might see you,' I go on, 'when I return,' clambering inside – at the head of a queue, formed behind my back, unnoticed.

He watches me take my seat inside (to one side of the driver, anxious, in this instance, to see ahead). I nod my head, point at the sky, mouth, 'Fair,' and nod again. The vehicle sways: people clamber overhead: with one or two groans the vehicle subsides. 'No standing,' I announce, 'on the upper deck. No smoking on the lower. No spitting, of course, on upper or lower!'

The policeman's head appears at the door.

'All right, conductor?' addressing the man who, with something of a smile, has listened to my comments.

'It's all right by me, officer,' the man declares.

'Something of a comic,' the policeman says.

'So I see,' the conductor replies.

Soon to be made redundant (I have heard from Etty): driver-only buses, abandoned because of vandalism, about to be reprieved.

The bus drives out: I see a perspective of the cathedral above the roofs of the nearby shops, the pilastered, tall-windowed façade of the old Mechanics' Institute, subsequently the Music Saloon and now the City Museum, the Town Hall tower – the municipal proponents of a bygone age, the bus passing the end of North Parade so quickly that this vista is curtailed, allowing a glimpse only of the placarded site of the ancient Butter Cross in Cross Square before, with an accelerating roar, we reach the broader expanse of once tree-lined Westgate.

Directly ahead, beyond the driver's bulky figure, across, at the foot of our descending slope, a shallow valley, lies the more precipitous hill at Onasett – framed, in this instance, by the distant, smooth-featured profile of the misted Pennine hills.

'I used to be a Peewit, a jolly Peewit, too, but now I've given up Pee-witting I don't know what to do, I'm growing old and weary and I can Peewit no more, so I'm going to work my passage if I can. Back to Ona-sett, happy land! I'm going to work my passage if I can!'

*

Within himself the putative Richard Fenchurch feels diminished (indisposed, withdrawn) out of his depth, bewildered by his situation – the circumstances which enclose him on every side (and the feelings they evoke). He considers the part of him he and his parents haven't spent, writes (somewhere in his diary – 'Any more fares?' the conductor enquires), "What I am attempting to do appears impossible, reconciling a reflective life with one which is active. There is something in the atmosphere which inhibits me from making contact – unless the willingness to listen is all the contact I require. My invalidity is as absurd as it is oppressive. ('Who wants to be an artist? Our budding Fenchurch here!')"

Fenchurch, the indomitable Fenchurch, his feet, divested of his slippers, shuffling in the debris on the floor of the bus, consults his parents: 'Which stop do you want?' the conductor enquires.

'Is Spinney Moor still there?'

'It is.'

'Spinney Moor,' I tell him, across a gap of forty years. He slides the ticket out, hands me the change.

'Soon to be dispensed with, conductors and the like.'

'They are.'

'Me, too,' I am about to tell him.

'Any more?' without listening: sets off to the stairs.

Onasett, a phalanx of red-tiled houses, rises up ahead.

'On the other hand,' I tell the woman beside me, 'I have, subsequent to the experiences of the past few months, if not the past five years, acquired a tendency to fall in love with every woman I meet.'

She smiles, loaded down with shopping (no view of the way ahead).

'Her physical appearance, for instance, is infused with what I can only describe as the elemental, something little short, I would say, of the irresistibly divine, a quality unimpeded by what, normally, where female beauty is concerned, might be considered a liability, age. Or even insanity, in one or two instances, hence my preoccupation, verging on obsession, with Vi.'

Such a woman is seated by me now: middle-aged, wearied (by circumstance – class, temperament, geographical location – as well as shopping): dark eyes, with folded skin beneath each one, the cheeks drawn in, the mouth crudely fashioned by the indelicate use of make-up: yet, despite the corrugation of skin beneath her chin, despite the amplitude of her waist and bosom – exceeding the demands, the latter, of any reasonable requirement – despite her smile (as much an expression of pain as pleasure) she is everything I love: 'I am,' I tell her, 'from Onasett myself, eulogised by the Reverend Swanson in his memorable creation, "Happy Land!", the first vicar of St Michael's, a song we sang, invariably, on the backs of lorries when returning home from camp. *O happy land!*'

Teeth regular and artificial: she smiles again – I recalling, in that instant, Bella's habit, while talking by the fire, seated across the hearth from Corcoran, of tracing then arranging then re-arranging, the folds of her skirt across her lap – revealing, inadvertently, her stockinged thighs – and further recall the way she lowers her voice – then lightens it – recounting, first with censure, then with humour, an incident witnessed in the village.

She laughed, with me, like a woman who had been restrained from laughing all her life – revealing, in the process, something of the girl she might have been (she *was*, years later showing me – our children, her grandchildren (Etty on her knee) – photographs taken by Kells shortly after the First World War, she in a long skirt and (for those days, I suspected) provocative blouse standing amidst a group of chums: the lean-back of her body – her hands on her hips, her fingers spread-eagled across her stomach – laughing at the father who was taking the picture, her sisters, Venny and Clare, beside her).

I hear a piece of music (played, in reality, at the back of the bus), and am standing at the window of our house in Belsize Park – the fourteen-roomed mansion bought at the height of my career – our youngest daughter, Rebecca, in my arms: I

168

have been living alone in the house for the previous year: Bea, on this particular occasion – a weekend – is in a hotel, in Brighton, with her lover, Albert. Normally, she and Rebecca live in their flat, close to the Medical Research Centre at Barnet. An airship is passing overhead – an aluminium-coloured capsule with the name of a beverage inscribed along one side: a tiny sliver of rope dangles from its prow (a low murmur, its engines, like a vacuum cleaner being pushed across the sky).

A constant occupation of mine over the previous year, I am standing at the window, looking out: a tiny cabin is slung beneath the vehicle overhead (swaying and rearing, ducking and bowing) and behind its square-shaped windows we imagine we can see pale faces gazing down. Five hundred feet, perhaps, above our heads, the airship gives the impression (Beckie flinching unconsciously, as she glances up) of being close enough to step inside (an involuntary lurch, we might find it dangling in the garden). Below us, in the street a cyclist slows and raises his head: arrested, one foot on the ground, he shields his eyes. Clouds unsheathe the sun.

'I'd like to be up there,' Rebecca says.

She grasps my arm more tightly (forty feet above the ground ourselves: the upstairs front bedroom that, years ago, was occupied by Etty).

Meanwhile, to the south, in a hotel bedroom, at Brighton, her mother: the airship is proceeding in that direction.

'Will it crash?'

I shake my head.

'I think it will.'

'I doubt it.' (She flinches once again.)

'Is Benjie coming?' (our youngest son).

'I shouldn't think so, Beckie.' (Arm aching at her weight.)

'Kenneth?' (our other son).

'Kenneth is abroad,' I tell her.

'Where is that?' (head ducked again).

'The United States. Studying,' I tell her, 'the philosophy of science.' ('Has science a philosophy?' his mother ingenuously enquired when, bright-eyed, dark-haired – her colouring, my features – our eldest son declared his intention of studying at Berkeley. 'Hasn't it, Mum?' he asked, wise, at this stage of her life, to, if not her malignancy, her mischief).

Beckie, as it is, more nearly sees her brothers as uncles, her sisters more nearly as aunts: 'What is a sister?' she enquired, examining Matt dressed for a visit to 10 Downing Street (a species of businesswoman approved of at the time: her own management consultancy at twenty-seven).

'Just the two of us?' she enquires (this last child of our marriage, aged nine).

'What shall we do?'

'Dance?'

I put on a record: we dance to a tune much loved by Benjie (before he left for college) – a whining lyric, drowned by its accompaniment: "Would you leave me? Would you love me? Would you leave me here alone?" an incredulity echoed in my mind as I recall this record being played when – like a storm erupting from a cloudless sky – Bea announced, at breakfast, over a cup of tea, 'A most extraordinary thing has happened. I've fallen in love!'

'Love?' ("Would you leave me? Would you love me? Would you leave me here alone?" whined from Benjie's (then occupied) bedroom – the one in which we are now dancing, at the top of the house).

'Isn't it odd?' (The coincidence, I reflect, of the music, or the state of mind itself?). And then, a second cup of tea to follow the first ('Would you like one, darling?'), 'It's never happened before.'

'Never?'

'No.'

'What about us?'

'Never *in* love.'

'I thought it was.' (I thought I was. I thought we were.)

She shakes her head.

'I was intrigued.'

'Intrigued?'

'By your attempt to reconcile God and Mammon.'

'God?'

'Art.' (The working class and everything else.) 'How old was I?' she went on. 'Sixteen? Now, of course, I'm . . .' (she's about to tell me 'fifty-two').

'The same age as your mother when you and I first met.'

'There you are!' She gestures. 'The prime,' she goes on, 'of life.'

Had she, I reflected, ever suspected? She had come across Bella, on one occasion, sneaking a kiss and, unable to explain what was clearly a sensual embrace, I had said, 'Your mother was about to scold me. I was thinking too much of you.'

'Oh, Mum,' she had said, 'can keep you in line,' adding, 'He's like that with all the women, Mum, just as all the men are like that with you.'

'Do you fancy her, sometimes?' she had later enquired.

'As a matter of fact,' I said, but added nothing further for, a moment later, she went on, 'The two of you are often spikey.'

'Spikey?'

'Both Dad and I have noticed. He, after all,' she had gone on, 'was very lucky.'

'Lucky?'

'To have attracted Mum. She could have married any number of men. She still could,' she went on, 'as a matter of fact. She married, as it was, the most handsome one of her time.'

It was in Kells, however – 'Grandpa Kells' – that Bea recognised a challenge (as potent as the challenge – of an altogether different nature – I recognised in her mother). 'To continue,' as she expressed it, 'where Grandpa Kells left off. The war, and the awful Kell Cakes – the uniting of science to a social good – appealed to him in a furtive way as much as it appalled him. I, on the other hand, can see it more clearly: science *and* the social good. The two are indivisible. He, for instance, once the war was over, drifted into supervising the research of others: one of the walking wounded, the ones who were killed but never found out.'

It explained – I always felt – once our children were off our hands, the nights as well as the days spent, in a pool of light,

171

stooped over her microscope – staining her slides, those slivers of cells which came up, under magnification, in a range of colours – lemon, yellow, orange, red – like the pitted surface of a hitherto undiscovered planet. 'I always liked,' she said on one occasion, 'to see you and Mum together. That photograph at the wedding, "like the bride and groom", someone said. Her eyes! I've never seen anything like it! You know her ancestors were pirates and most of the women whores!'

'Supernumerary wives,' I said.

'In a harem.'

'It was described as a private house.'

'In Istanbul?'

'Constantinople.'

'Whores.'

'Concubines.'

'Whores!'

On one occasion, lying in bed, shortly after our honeymoon (spent in a room above a sweet-shop in Camden Town), Bea had said, 'There's something about you which isn't right.'

'What?' I'd asked.

'Something twisted. Even indecent.'

'I wonder what it is,' I said.

'I always felt it,' she said. 'All that innocence,' she went on.

'The first time on the soap-works?' I said.

'The first time you kissed me,' she suddenly confided, 'and, to my surprise, you missed my mouth.'

When I asked her to be more specific, she said, 'Father sensed it. So did mother. They couldn't, at an intuitive level, make you out.'

'Have you never loved me?' I asked her when, in the kitchen, over breakfast (drinking tea), she announced, with characteristic candour, she had 'fallen in love'.

With her mother's gentle smile – that amoral, unassuming smile, the legatee of whores and pirates – she responded, 'I've always loved you, as, indeed,' she'd smilingly continued, 'I love you now, but never,' she had gone on, 'have I been in love. Slightly, perhaps, with that youth from Reading. But not

172

like this. Not really,' she'd concluded, 'like a flame in the bowel.'

'Isn't that uncomfortable?' I'd said, but she'd merely responded, 'Like staining a cell and catching, for the first time, not only the pattern but the purpose of its development.'

'Love and work,' I said, 'in that case, are curiously combined.'

'Yes,' she said, 'I suppose they are,' adding, after pouring another cup, 'It's different for a girl to be in love as opposed to a woman of fifty.'

'Two,' I said, 'to be exact.'

'Over fifty,' she replied.

('Would you leave me? Would you love me? Would you leave me here alone?' whined from the bedroom overhead.)

A tortuous year, that first year of our involvement, her mother and I, one evening, 'caught' by a neighbour in the grounds of the house – a trespasser taking a short-cut from the Ardsley Arms, perhaps, to one of the outlying farms (quicker over the fields) and who, coming across us, late at night, lying on the ground (our 'position' unmistakable) had, Bella suspected, refused to believe his senses: ('I saw his face: I can only conclude he must have seen mine'). A few days later, however, she saw him in the village and he had merely raised his hat in, she confessed, a non-committal manner.

She was seldom, if ever, out of my thoughts: I saw her, or thought I saw her in, if not almost, every middle-aged woman I caught sight of walking in the street, or gazing from a window, or seated in a bus. The risks we took only drove us on (managing, on one occasion, to perform the impossible on the back seat of a bus (how easily one unconsidered act leads to another), she sitting astride my lap, the novelty of the situation – there was one man sitting on his own at the front, the conductor chatting to a chum downstairs, the bus rattling along through the countryside with no one waiting to be picked up – heightened my performance). I had nothing to gauge my actions by: everything was possible (therefore anything was allowed).

'Would you leave me here for ever? Would you leave me here alone?'

I danced with Bella's grandchild. Albert's lover's daughter (the parliamentary private secretary to the Minister of Health: why should he get the benefits of thirty years of marriage?), with H.J. Kells' great-grandchild, the seed of Bea's womb, her magenta hair shining in a swathe the length of her slender back ('I didn't want to come, but Mummy made me!' within minutes of her arrival, jumping on the bed: how like a Kells or a Corcoran to know abandonment when she saw it). 'Is Harriet not coming?' (preferring her brothers to her sisters).

'No.'

'Is Matt?'

'No.'

'Is there anyone to play with?'

'Me.'

'Can we go out?'

'We might.'

'When?'

'You've only just arrived.'

'Daddy Albert takes me out.'

'Where?'

'All over.'

'So do I.'

'You don't.'

'I do.'

'You don't,' (her movements unabating).

While, in a sunlit bedroom, looking out to the English Channel, the possibility, in two or three hours' time, of an airship overhead . . .

A policewoman is standing by my shoulder: she has got on, I am told, at the previous stop (on her way home, I suspect, from duty), her cap at an angle on her coiffured head (the conductor standing behind her): a jowelled jaw, a smear of colouring on each high-boned cheek. 'Your noise is disturbing

174

the passengers,' she says (from 'Happy Land!' to 'Do you love me?').

The engine of the bus, the driver gazing backwards, his head craned down as might a child's in looking through its legs, indicates, with its idling speed, that we are standing at a stop: Thrallstone Park, adjacent to the tinier enclave of Onasett Park, its gates, removed at the beginning of the war, represented by no more than a pair of decapitated pillars (entrance to the architecturally venerated and historically renowned – eighteenth-century 'grand domestic' – Thrallstone House: burnt down and replaced by a comprehensive school – 'impersonal puberty' – erection): beyond, undulating furrowed slopes, scattered here and there with ancient trees, rise to the prominence of Scone Hill, a castle mound, obscured by shrubs which, in their outline against a low, cloud-suspended sky, indicate its man-made profile. 'I've done some of my best pictures,' I indicate the motte, 'from there.'

'As well,' she adds, 'as the dishevelment of your dress.'

'Dress.' I pause. 'I'm wearing trousers.'

'Precisely.'

The woman in the adjoining seat has disappeared.

'A fit,' I announce, 'of absent-mindedness, which,' I go on, 'is the consequence,' (perhaps unwisely revealing this to her), 'of recent medical attention, supervised, I hasten to add, by one of the most resourceful practitioners of mental welfare in the land, not merely the youngest ever to hold the prestigious post of Longcroft Professor at the North London Royal, but a doctor chosen by the wife of H. L. Richards when the poet came over from America to escape the pressures of recognition symptomatic of the insecurities of, and therefore endemic to, that land where – and this, at the time, was widely known – he had been what, in this country, we describe as "sectioned" for behaviour which might, legitimately, be described as manic – and therefore, in my view, he *and* his wife – albeit his fourth – to be respected.'

In parenthesis I add, 'I am,' and proceed to make adjustments. 'The medical treatment, to which I referred a moment

175

ago, has, I'm afraid, left me what, in the old days, was described as absent-minded, to a degree,' I continue, 'not normally associated with a man of my years, in the full flow of his manhood, so to speak, and at the very peak – or would be – of his sexual powers, transposed, in my case – from circumstance, I hasten to add, should you be free, rather than disposition – from the libidinal to the creative. I have come,' I produce my sketchbook, 'to draw.'

'Where are you getting off?' she enquires.

'Spinney Moor.'

'The stop after this,' the conductor declares at her shoulder. The bus is rung off.

Subliminally, I must have been aware of it for some time: we are passing between two hills, the one on the left crowned by the vegetated summit of Scone Hill, the one on the right characterised by the red brick and red-tiled roofs of Onasett itself: between the two, the bus cresting a conjunctive ridge, is revealed a vista of the River Lin; specifically, its upper valley, a tree- and grass-strewn fissure, irregularly obtruded upon by industrial and domestic buildings (the fistulaed intrusion of mill chimneys, the darkened profile of a village) which, against the lowering sky, is sombrely enclosed by wooded hills, their arhythmic undulations fractured further by the profile of a cliff, a ragged edge of blackened rock known as Walton Top.

Houses – the estate is flanked by private dwellings – converge upon the road: hidden, halfway up the slope to my right, is the house in Manor Road where I spent, other than for a few weeks, the first two decades of my life.

'Spinney Moor,' the policewoman says, stepping aside to let me pass.

Nothing is lost: everything is forgiven: 'I have made,' I tell her, 'restitution. I have given up my health, wealth and creativity for those I love.'

'It's not a difficult decision,' Maidstone says, 'disassembling your life. What was characterised by dissonance will be done away with, in all likelihood, for good.' ('And by "good",' he had gone on to announce, 'I infer a moral imperative, not

176

merely an infinitude of time.') 'A wholly felicitous re-arrangement will have been achieved which will astonish as much as it will enhance, facilitate as much as be a cause for wonder.'

The bus comes to a halt and the uniformed figure (a smell of perfume evident at the door) waits, having stepped aside as, encumbered by my slippers as much as by the sketchbook, I descend to the pavement.

'I have stepped down here,' I tell her, 'on many occasions, not least in my childhood, returning from school and, subsequent to that, in my youth, from college. The Linfield School of Art, though "art", in my case, at that time, was something of a misnomer. "Applied technology", in this instance, might have been better: printing, pottery, lithography, etching, as well as a cursory stab at carving. If that's the metaphor. I have, as a consequence of, rather than despite a lifetime of effort, disabused myself of the idea that I could equal the passion, the vigour and the dexterity of – let's choose a minor figure – Cellini – and have reconciled myself to the pleasure of doing what I can, as opposed to what I can't but hope to.'

'Which way,' she says, 'are you going?'

'There is, I take it, no law that prohibits me from walking along this road and talking to you, for instance, about things that count. Experience, after all, without exclusion, is tantamount to the religious, and returns us, if unaware, to the source from which we came.'

The bus has departed: two other figures, having descended, are glancing back as they cross the road to the eponymously named Spinney Moor Avenue to see what conclusions the uniformed figure beside me might have drawn, and what actions will flow as a consequence.

'I was going to see the old homestead,' I suddenly confide, 'and draw, on the way, a couple of sketches,' opening my book at a random page: blank. 'I drew a tree this morning,' I add, finding the image (a trunk, bereft of leaves as well as branches) which, on closer inspection, looks like a mutilated penis. 'Then again, I thought I'd walk to the golf-course which has a hill at the centre from where there is a view of Onasett to the north and the Lin to the south, winding into, or, rather, out of the Pennine hills, from where, via the Aire and Calder valleys, it finds its way to the Humber and, from there, of course, the North Sea.'

She is in two minds: one inclines her (her eyes stark behind a pair of glasses – unnoticed, previously, on the bus) to take me with her, across the road, and wait for a bus in the opposite direction which will take me back to town (there to be lost: out of her jurisdiction); the other inclines her, since she is homeward bound – at the end, presumably, of an exhausting shift – to leave me where I am and hope a passing vehicle – conceivably the returning bus – will knock me down.

'Where is the old homestead?' she enquires.

'Manor Road,' I say. 'Or was.'

'I'm going to Manor Road.' She takes my arm.

'I should say, the golf-course, in that case,' I tell her. 'Nothing personal,' I go on, 'merely a desire to re-acquaint myself with the totality of the landscape before, as it were, I descend to detail, you, no doubt, identifying "home" as a place to return to as opposed to one from which to depart.'

The day is bright (as if in response to my arrival, the clouds have broken): it is not unlike other days in the past when I have alighted at this spot, an invigorating breeze blowing from the north (from, in reality, the direction of the estate itself, rising up the slope before us) and which a smell of coal smoke in no way invalidates – the smoke, I recall, of the fires of home. Leaving the wall of the park, the road winds off along the southern fringe of the estate itself while, directly opposite, stands the hulk, like a chapel, of the Carlton Cinema – now given over, I noticed, to 'Bowls' (the word 'Cancelled' plastered over it, the more challenging, 'Scheduled for Demolition' in its place).

A line of shops (their windows blown out by a land-mine during the war) stand adjacent to the bus-stop on the other side – at which, I notice, a number of people have gathered, curious as to the outcome of this encounter.

'I've often thought, since the advent of women in the Force, in numbers large enough to be noticed, that a trouser-suit would be both more appropriate and more prudent. Police-women's legs, in my view,' her hand still on my arm, 'are no match for the black-stockinged calves – and occasional thighs – of the Salvation Army, whose members are conceivably attracted to the movement by this feature alone.'

I know no other way of explaining it, for it enables them, with the greatest possible decorum, and seemingly the highest motives, to display themselves in a way which, otherwise, would be vulgarly attractive to the opposite sex. Perhaps it is a bonus, if not an appropriate reward for the otherwise thankless task of being a salvationist in an age when their function is largely duplicated by the social services, if not by the wider echelons of the welfare state itself. I could have added – a certain stockiness evident in her build – that criticism of this nature did not apply to someone as attractive as herself, more a rule pertinent to the Force as a whole. If, for instance, there were a suggestion box, it might have been brought to the notice of her superin-tendent. It might influence not only the direction but the vigour of any subsequent recruitment drive and, as a result, have a beneficial effect not only on public support but the alacrity with which she and members of her sex were able to pursue and detain criminals.

'I offer the suggestion, of course,' I add, 'as a tentative outsider, one whose days of impropriety, to say the least, where women are concerned, are long since over. My wife is married to a man who, having served as a parliamentary private sec-retary in the Ministry of Health, is destined, so I am told, to be promoted to the very highest echelons of the Home Office. Thank you,' I conclude, 'for your advice, and thank you, too, for all your help,' setting off, having disengaged my arm, not up Spinney Moor Avenue (to the home I have left), but along the road, bounded by private houses – detached and semi-detached – flanking the estate (red roofs glowing in the light of a setting sun, or magenta in a rising one) – following, in effect, the route of the bus, to my left the houses replaced by a stretch of grass across which stands a Wesleyan chapel – of

179

contemporary construction halfway between domestic-functional institutional-informal, and beside which a pair of gates opens on to a tarmac drive (motor-cars a precedent to worship) which runs in a direct line to a clump of coniferous and deciduous trees: amongst their foliage and beyond their silhouette can be seen the Georgian roofs and chimneys of Onasett Hall – built by and lived in by the (celebrated) first member of parliament for Linfield, 'Jack the Democrat' Thornton, a man whose library was said to be 'the most inclusive in the North of England' (and who drowned in the Lin – which runs a few hundred yards behind the house – endeavouring, during a winter flood, to rescue his son, who drowned with him, a child of seven). 'Jack' had witnessed – and participated in – the storming of the Bastille and had brought back with him a handkerchief soaked in the blood of Marie Antoinette, a dark-stained item of cloth which, on view for many years in his library, was now in the town museum – the old Mechanics' Institute in North Parade – a testament – yet one more (along with myself) – to the longevity of the egalitarian aspirations of this industrial town.

The Hall is currently the headquarters of the Onasett Golf Club (a populist stronghold, vide Jack, as opposed to the more selective Cawthorne Club on the opposite edge of town), whose course extends around but principally to the rear of the house itself, retaining much of its original park – oak and beech and chestnut – and which falls, in an irregularly descending slope, not only to the banks of the Lin but to the parallel canal and railway (traversing the Pennines to Liverpool): a broad perspective of the hills is visible from the Georgian windows, along with the V-shaped gorge through which the Lin descends to its flat, alluvial valley.

I enter between the permanently open gates – for the fences and the walls on either side have been removed, the former for scrap during the Second World War, and never replaced, the latter having succumbed to wind and weather, and the said democratisation of the club which – principle apart – having fallen on hard times in recent years, has reduced its membership requirements, in the shape of its fees, to a level compatible with the economic resources, not of the freeholders whose houses flank the rolling, smooth green acres of its course, but of the not always employed, or employable, denizens of the estate: the house through which Bentham, Gladstone and Disraeli, Wordsworth, Turner, Dickens and Shaftesbury were said, from time to time, to have strolled, echoes now to the weekend carousing of 'the lads from Onasett' – snatches of whose refrains, I am told, can be heard as far away as the fifteenth tee, not to mention the nearest houses.

A path, to my left, leads around the rear of the Wesleyan chapel – a buff-coloured structure with pale 'Onasett' sandstone inset around its tall, leaded windows – and follows the line of the back gardens of the houses flanking the road: hawthorn and elderberry shrubs and a variety of fruit trees divide the gardens from the uniformly-furrowed slope of the course itself whose steeply-ascending central hill – my slippers soaked with dew if not overnight rain – I slowly climb.

A solitary figure, wielding a golf club, traverses the slope: with a distant cry of 'Fore!', a ball, a luminescent yellow, bounces across my path. Behind me, the gardens and the houses bordering the road come fully into view, a bus, like the one from which I have descended, visible above the roofs: ahead, a fringe of trees outlines the summit of the hill – beech, hornbeam, conifer, sycamore and lime – their branches silhouetted against an increasingly lightening sky.

As well as the uppers, the soles of my slippers take in the damp: I am, after all, still in my 'house', the interior that the exterior of my existence has now become, no less a room, the hill, than Etty's kitchen, or the scullery of the house whose roof – I glance behind me once again – must surely be coming into view on the opposing slope: a phalanx of inverted v-shaped wedges.

'Does God exist?' I ask Etty on the morning of the day she arrives to drive me up from London – from our house, mine and Vivienne's in Taravara Road, adding, 'I mean for you and Charlie?' and when, suspecting this merely to be a device to distract her (she is packing my case on the bed), she doesn't respond, I recklessly plunge on, 'Does the question still exist or, in this age of molecular obsession, is it not so much done away with as superseded? Is the real, for your generation, only that which can come apart?'

'I don't know what you mean,' she blithely replies and it is, to say the least, a truism of the time I've lived in that 'God' and 'eternity' have become 'definitions' that 'beg the question', inviting derision to the same degree they parody a good intention.

'There is no such thing, of course, as objectivity,' I tell her. 'It's part of the apparatus with which, through insecurity, we seek to surround ourselves. Is the whole of our existence to be shorn of purpose? How can we arrest it? If two thousand years of appealing to a divine presence has failed, to whom may we appeal? Why,' I tell her, 'ourselves! *We* will be objective, even if that objectivity is threatened by all those things which seek to do it down!'

'Isn't that your illness?' she (calmly) enquires, securing the strap of the suitcase (the sound of our neighbours comes through the party wall of this pokey room at the back of the house). When I don't reply, she quietly continues, 'After all, your illness, as Maidstone and others have often said, has a spiritual, not to say a moral dimension, as well as,' she goes on, 'a medical one. Each of which,' (trying the weight of the case), 'has its relevance yet, at the end of the day,' (testing the weight of the case again), 'I thought you attached more importance to the chemical. I thought,' she concluded, 'you thought it was a biological problem.'

The house is small: the homogeneous appearance of the district – one-storeyed terraced dwellings with rarely more than four or five rooms – each with a correspondingly tiny yard at the back – is reinforced not merely by the common source of the street-names: Corunna, Blenheim, Trafalgar, Taravara (a corruption of Talavera) – but by the convergence of several railway lines which, with their arches and brick embankments, create the impression, as Vivienne remarked, when she first arrived, 'of living inside a castle' (an effect enhanced by the numerous bridges – low, brick-built, round-arched – lacking only, it appears, a portcullis).

'I like living in a castle,' I told her, for the area, unlike most I have lived in in London, did have an air – if a peculiar one – of containment – conveyed not merely by the mellow, ochreish brick and large-windowed façades (relieved here and there by stucco – invariably painted cream or white) and the 'butterfly' roofs, the gutter running centrally down the middle, but by the nature and ancestry of the people who lived there. Though the houses were not infrequently described, in house agents' literature, as 'artisan dwellings' – which may have been true of some – the majority, clearly, were of working-class origin, the domesticated working class of the middle and late nineteenth century: service workers as much as labourers: clerks, drivers, bus and coach attendants, shop assistants and what might have been described as 'the lower commercial orders', the owners of the small businesses located in the yards and alleyways fringing the parapet-like railway embankments across which the steam locomotives hauled their trucks and coaches day and night. Even now, in the early hours, the house shuddered to the diesel locomotives drawing long lines of oil-containers, cement trucks or gantried wagons containing cars, as well as the isolated, single-trucked cargoes of atomic waste. It was the descendants of this nineteenth-century labouring class who still occupied many of the houses – now council-owned – half of them only private dwellings.

'Your attention,' Etty would say, 'moves from one thing to another, seemingly without purpose. I suppose you'd say,' she'd go on, '*you* are the purpose,' and if, in this instance, a description of the district I live in – when, in her own phrase she comes 'to rescue me' – appears to have little connection with the purpose of human existence, it has in my mind, if only in the sudden and vivid evocation of that moment when, packing the case in the bedroom which Vivienne and I had occupied, on and off, for the better part of five years – and in which, unknown to me, she had finally packed her cases before

183

taking them down to the yard below (visible through the uncleaned window) – I recall not only Etty's dismissal of my five years' spiritual progress but the moment when, drawing open the garden shed door – curiously ajar when, unused, it was always shut – I had caught the first glimpse of the cases themselves then, grotesquely, of her cruelly distorted body (the blood and bleached tissue around her mouth).

'You must have misunderstood what I meant by "biological",' I tell her. 'Isn't the physical an embodiment of what I, in my illness, no doubt, would call the divine? Aren't the bricks and mortar of this house, not to mention the cracking plaster, the crumbling ceilings, the tiles and stucco, the splintered front door, as much an expression of the divine as anything more portentous you may care to mention? His church, His people, His ministers, His priests, the infrastructure of religion which is as much to do with belief as your scepticism of my motives is to do with me?'

I follow her down the stairs (the case on the bed) into the tiny hall that runs the length of the house: her own suitcase, packed from her overnight stay, is waiting behind the front door. I follow her into the kitchen which runs out as an annexe at the back – facilitating, through a side window, a view of our neighbour's yard. The female of the couple who live on the ground floor (the house divided into two flats) is hanging out her washing: an elderly woman, of a nervous disposition – a legacy of war-time bombing when a section of the street was reduced to rubble (a council tenement occupies the site) – she glances over the low partition wall aware, if not welcoming, my scrutiny from the other side ('I'm glad you're keeping an eye on us, Mr Fenchurch,' she has said on a previous occasion. 'Our kiddies, now we're getting on, never come and see us.'). She nods: behind my back (washing up tea-cups at the sink) Etty says, 'Let's keep it at a practical level. Everyone, including Maidstone, says you can't or shouldn't live alone,' adding (no ceremony intended), 'No one else will have you. You have to come to Ardsley. You know it. You've lived there. God, and metaphysics, have no part in it at all.'

When, turning from the window, I interrupt, she swiftly continues, 'Your incapacity to relate to anything around you in a way meaningful to anyone else is the only relevant factor. If Matt can't have you – which she clearly can't – and the boys aren't in a position to – then it's up to Charlie and me. The only alternative,' she concludes, 'is Boady Hall.'

'Provided by the estate of F. K. Boady who went mad on these premises,' someone had written on the wall while I was there, to which a subsequent hand had appended, in a larger – and significantly neater script, 'Who wouldn't?' Similarly, a poster starkly declaring, 'Apathy is the greatest sin' across which someone had scrawled, 'Who cares?' Boady, in reality, a clothing manufacturer whose wife had benefited, in his view, if dying, from the medical treatment she had received at the North London Royal of which this was the residential psychiatric wing – and where, a significant number of years later, I had taken up residence myself (on and off, for the better part of five years), an indirect consequence, it could have been said, of Boady over-charging for clothes (sold to people like Mrs Laski next door whose husband, injured in an industrial accident – insufficient provision made for safety – is confined, in his premature retirement, to a wheelchair – the ineffable consequence of the means by which Sir Frederick Boady produced the wealth which in turn takes care of the people driven mad producing it). 'Don't you see the connection which, other than by my asserting there is one, you tell me isn't there?'

'Sentimentality,' she responds, drying the pots and – the last of our washing-up – placing them in the cupboard beside the (still) victorian (black-leaded) cooking range. ('How quaint,' poor Vi had said, 'my parents had one in Scotland': it was in the oven – I discovered too late – she hid not only her drugs but her booze.)

'I live,' I tell her, 'in another world, which is just as real as this one.'

'Which one?' she enquires.

'This!' I tell her. 'This!'

14

I HAVE REACHED the top of the hill: the fringe of trees is interspersed with several rhododendron shrubs, beyond – a vista of the valley: the parkland of the old estate running down towards the river (invisible from this distance other than in the form of the raised, dyked bank of its parallel canal and the embankment of the railway). Only in the upper reaches does a silver-like expanse, shadowed by enclosing trees and buildings, and the shoulder of the valley, indicate where the Lin winds out in a broadening, placid curve from its turbulent course through the Pennine hills – a bulwark of darkness against the lightening clouds.

Directly across the valley is Harlstone, its colliery, too, with its familiar elongated waste-heap, gone, the village no more than a crescent of houses scattered across the brow of a hill: above, looms the shoulder of Walton Top, the soot-blackened outcrop of yellow sandstone, its rain-eroded scars visible at this distance, marked at its base by the sombre fringe of Cornthorpe Wood – a place, in the past, where I have courted Bea and – on one sensational occasion – her mother.

The breeze behind me is brisk and sharp: turning to confront it I am met by a view I have drawn and painted innumerable times: Onasett, a scree of red-tiled roofs rising in a series of interlocking planes like the ill-arranged stones on the wall of a castle, its parapet surmounted by the mill-like church of St Michael's, a pale, low, rectangular structure with a stub of a tower, scarcely more than a chimney, and surmounted, in its turn, by the red brick structure of Onasett School – a one-storeyed building which lies along the crest of what, from this perspective, can be seen to be a protuberant headland, projecting like a cliff from the northern flank of the valley: Ona's Headland; His Place; Ona's Sett (Fenchurch's Folly).

Fenchurch examined the scene before him as he might, on this headland, the embers of a fire, or a scene in a forest: was it here he intended to rest; was it here he had rested before; was it here he had hoped to meet a friend (a companion, a guide) or, as in his youth, had he come to this hilltop to view his home, his native heath, with an impervious if not a God-like eye (his God, his Saviour – the spirit of the place, that numinous presence of which, from his earliest years, he had been aware – essence not only of the place itself but of all who lived and had lived there – the neolithic hunters who had crouched at the foot of the Onasett hill and fished in the waters of the lake left by the retreating ice cap; the Celts, the Britons – the Roman centurion who, two millennia ago, had built his villa and farmed his fields, clearing the woodland long before Ona himself had appeared; the invading armies, the marauding hordes, the civilising Normans (killing everyone north of the river, the land desolate for years – other than for Cawthorne Castle, a visible stump on the southern horizon); himself; his father (first tenant of that house whose roof was indistinguishable amongst so many others) who had tunnelled beneath the hill itself)? The spirit of the place was what? Within himself: God, if he only knew it.

'It's immaterial to me,' he had said to Etty as she placed the last of the pots inside the cupboard. ' "Acknowledge" is an indefinite word, perceivable to some and not to others.'

'I am a humanist,' she had, early on in her college life, declared, and he had said, with something of a laugh, 'someone who sees God within him or herself and, pride inverted, then denies it.'

Now I tell her, 'I see the presence in your hand, the way, for instance, it holds that pot. A pot which, in its turn, has been held by me, *was* held by Vi – and has been, on occasion, by your mother on her infrequent and invariably recriminating visits. It becomes,' I tell her, 'axiomatic and, to the degree of having to point it out, of no interest to me any longer.'

'In that case,' closing the cupboard door, 'why bother?'

'I am,' I tell her, 'sowing seeds and, at this point of my life, interested only in doing that. Through my work I go on living. Through my work, of course, and you. Not the "I" with which I came into this world and which, within myself, will go out of it, but the "I",' I hastily conclude, 'beyond it.'

'What about the child-molester?' she suddenly exclaimed (I could see her protest coming, she much exercised at this time by an incident with Lottie when a man in the village had not only exposed himself but endeavoured to entice her into his car: 'What if she had gone?' she had said, her face buried in her hands).

'This isn't,' I tell her, 'the God of Good. This is the God of Nagasaki, of Buchenwald, of Dachau. This,' I tell her, 'is the God of War. We are no more innocent than He is.'

For over an hour.

'Like God to his daughter,' she finally declared. 'Don't look for your salvation, Father, in me.'

A residue of ashes, I reflect, examining the flame-red roofs before me: evidence of what was there before but which can never be re-ignited.

The breeze blows freshly in my face: with it comes the smell of smoke: Onasett coal, from the Onasett seam, a shaky, friable substance that leaves an orange ash – less 'heat co-efficient' than the denser coals from the deeper seams where time and weight have hardened their texture (burning with a whitish flame).

I begin to draw: two golfers cross the slope: a club is swung: invisible at first, a ball – white, in this instance – bounds across the furrowed grass. I am, as I told myself on those occasions I came here as a youth, in tune with tunefulness itself: praise Him Whose praise we sing below: the graphite smears and smudges.

'Don't tell me,' Etty says, 'you want to drive,' getting in, nevertheless, behind the wheel, while all I can enquire (and complain) about as we drive through the maze of littered streets is, 'Are you sure you locked the door? There are so many papers I've left behind. (So many pictures, too.) I'd hate to find it looted.'

'Matt has said she'll look in. And Mum,' she reminds me, 'has said so, too. They can easily collect anything you want and send it on. Though what you have brought,' signalling behind (a cardboard carton tied with string), 'looks quite enough. After all,' she continues, 'you've written nothing for the past five years. What makes you think you'll be starting now? You're getting away,' she concludes, 'to rest.'

'From what?' I ask.

'From resting,' she says, 'that did you no good.'

'I told Maidstone I wanted to discover how real I am, without the aid,' I go on, 'of medication. "Lithium up your arse," I said, "no longer, love, up mine." I wanted, I told him, to get close to God.'

'Mania,' she told me, in a motorway cafeteria, halfway through our drive to Ardsley, 'strikes you, Father, when I least expect it.' ('Father' denotes irony, 'Dad' affection, silence intimacy – or so I reflect). 'You don't mind me speaking frankly,' she adds (more injunction than enquiry). 'Otherwise,' she goes on, 'with the kids and Charlie, the future will be impossible. I'm taking a risk,' she concludes, 'after all.' One hundred and seventy miles from London, the familiar hills and woodland, the valleys and the rivers coming into view, she suddenly enquires, 'You do love Glenda and Lottie?'

'More,' I tell her, 'than life itself,' and add, 'You don't set a very high premium on it, I know, at present, but, for as much as it's worth, or you're able to judge, as much as I loved yourself.'

'I have never doubted you loved me,' she says, stooping to the wheel, gazing with a peculiar intensity (not far short of serenity) at the road ahead.

'Which isn't quite as strong as saying you were always aware that I did,' I tell her.

189

'No,' she says, 'but then, I was,' adding, 'Do many people travel along this road, I wonder, discussing the nature of God?'

'I don't think,' I tell her, gazing at the vacuous faces in both the oncoming and the overtaking traffic, 'they think of anything I'd care to mention.'

My hand, I notice, has begun to tremble: I have come all this way, I reflect, searching for someone, or something, that doesn't exist: I am, as I told Maidstone, finished.

'You're not much older than I am,' he said. (He was, he'd already told me, fifty-five). 'I expect, when I'm your age, to be in my prime. As you are,' he hastened to add, 'at present. This is merely a reversal before the next prodigal leap.'

'I've made all the leaps I'm going to,' I told him. 'If what I have done is not sufficient I have nothing further to add.'

A pensive man (with a heavy face: a pendulous jaw and soulful eyes) who has said in the past, 'I have no personal experience of what you are going through but, not least from a lifetime's knowledge, I can imagine what it's like,' reflecting, 'There, but for the grace of God,' as he watches each departing lunatic figure (which doesn't obviate his alarm as he watches each subsequent one approach).

The graphite directs my mind to the horizontal line which crosses the paper and which is crossed, in turn, by several shaded patches: I perceive a landscape which, rather than generating awe, precipitates fear – of a magnitude and intensity I can't describe. I shiver: prayers, comprised of the one injunction, 'Help!' alternate with images of Bella – even, absurdly, of Vi: seated at a table in her test for *Hero of Our Time* ('Hoot,' as she described it): the protopsic condition of her eye (swelling at the height of any emotion) for which she saw a specialist in Devonshire Street ('Nothing we can do, I'm afraid,' charging her two hundred guineas).

Figures cross the scene below (I am glancing back towards the river): in pairs, in groups of four: how, I reflect, do they find the time: growers of wheat, hewers of wood, tillers of soil (diggers of coal), builders of houses – those newer structures,

190

I can see now, impinging upon the golf-course, at the furthest end of the slope? 'A collusion of disasters,' as Bea described it, I first seeing Vivienne, on a screen, in a viewing theatre at Boreham Wood, an intensity, not only about her face but, elusively, her figure (the sharpness of her voice – even her smiles: something forbidding and yet, despite the rapacity, forbearing).

'What do you think?' Liam says as, in the darkness, he leans across (her protagonist in the scene Macauley – a fair-haired Scot who became, via the subsequent film, an even bigger star than Vi).

'How I imagined her,' I tell him, adding, 'The character when I wrote it.'

Liam is short and stocky: Irish – O'Donnell: one of the post-war generation of film (and theatre) directors who have had an education: Caius, via Dublin ('Which has done me, I'm afraid, no good at all, merely inbred, in my case, the vice of patience'). He still preserves a light, inconsequential, hopelessly deceptive, native accent: blue-eyed, broad-browed – white skin, wide-boned – round-shouldered, gutted already with too much drink (which, rather than lightening his nature, leaves him curiously phlegmatic): his hands are short-fingered – clumsy (round and smooth) – pale, like fish, his fingers as they dangle, subtended at the end of a dimpled arm, round the back of the seat beside me – he sitting one seat away (much shading in as the clouds descend and, returning to the Onasett side, I fashion in the road).

'Intense,' Warren, our producer, says in the seat behind. 'And possibly short on glamour.'

'Glamour?' The word, in Liam's throat, is swallowed like a pebble.

'Sexuality she has in abundance,' Warren goes on: dour (Scot), red-haired, verging to ginger (pallid face – like Liam), sharp-featured, eyes, pale-blue, like those of someone under water: tall, when he stands, and thin: gawkiness not so much a trait as a weapon.

'She is,' Macauley says, 'like a boxer. Never lets you off the hook, and is light on her fucking toes.'

Warren is young: five years older than myself just as Liam is five years older than Warren: twenty-seven years old, myself, on the occasion Warren rings up and says, 'My name is Warren De'ath ('Day-ath'). I've just been reading your *Hero of Our Time*. I'd like you to meet a man called Liam O'Donnell,' the call not unexpected for De'ath has directed a film himself (from which he has made a fortune, its actors, author and himself in and out of the papers), while, 'Liam is directing a play and could meet us after rehearsals.'

'A catholic, a presbyterian and an anglican,' he once described us: 'a Mick, a Jock and – how would you describe yourself?'

Yet O'Donnell, whose mother's maiden name is Cary, is one of those Anglo-Irish 'presbyterian pederasts who have crawled out of the mother church and fornicated across the border': a religious man whose religiosity is sophomorically expressed by telling God to fuck Himself.

We meet in a pub at the back of the Cambridge Theatre – in a bar which, at that early hour of the evening (half-past six), is full of actors from the play Liam is rehearsing – myself an unknown, post-pubescent author, Warren, red-haired, pale, sharp-nosed, broad-mouthed, his brow and cheekbones lightly freckled ('Liam and I have more than presbyterianism in common, more, even, than the catholic church'), Liam with a leather jacket that, in its tightness, exaggerates the rotundity of his figure, his open-necked shirt with its broad-winged collar framing his head – disproportionately large – as a dish might frame a piece of fruit, a stand a piece of sculpture, a frame envelop a picture ('a highbrow, by any definition,' Warren says): broad-browed, a narrow chin, a thin-lipped and slightly upward-curving mouth – creased by dimples the moment (not often) he smiles ('like,' Warren later says, 'a man might bite on a nerve'). Engaging, cantankerous: 'She has no glamour.'

'Anima,' Warren says.

'Anima.'

'Unlike Miles.'

'Miles.'

'Macauley.'

'Surely,' Liam says, 'that's animus.'

Solace (lead on paper): the interminability of the roofs rising to the scarcely tarnished stone of the church, to the red brick of the school, to the high-walled grounds of the isolation hospital (built on the site of a Roman villa, its fractured mosaic pavement destroyed in the building): the shout of 'Fore!' from the slope, the crinkling of last year's leaves against the rhododendron.

Liam's flaw (his fatal error): 'Wouldn't you like to play the part yourself? No experience as an actor? I think you'd do it well,' his predilection to doomed careers: 'I suppose Viv Wylder was another,' (see his own decline: booze – followed by depression: 'She's good,' he said. 'She's fine: ignore Warren,' on the occasion that we watched her test).

I didn't see Vi again until the novel-as-a-film had started shooting and I heard her say. 'He never thought I loved him, but, Jesus, how I tried,' her back to the camera, while I thought, 'Princess of Lost Causes.'

'Meet Richard,' Liam says, 'who wrote it,' bringing her across the floor, and Vivienne says, 'I was so nervous, hearing you were coming,' her face unreal, or so I thought, with make-up, an apologist for Stratford East, the Royal Court: 'I was a star! In L.A.' (in Capri, Hollywood, New York) 'and now I'm in a house in the back streets of a town I never want to hear about,' saying, years earlier, on the studio floor, 'Don't tell me what you think.'

'Which means she's waiting,' Liam says. 'Which means,' his arm around her waist, 'you'll have to. Say: "Even better than your test",' and laughs.

'There's so much more I can do with it,' she says.

Her eyes expand behind her lashes.

'So much. I've scarcely come to grips with it,' I thinking, 'So we're doomed (such spaces we must plunge to).'

Thirty years elapse before I see poor Vi again (but for one

or two meetings when the film comes out: the start of my career), she coming in, not drunk ('intoxicated, merely') to enquire about a part in *Cage* at the Beaumont Theatre (my last West End production), she the six-years-dispensed-with wife of Zygorski (currently on film posters throughout the town): dark glasses beneath which, absurdly, are a second pair (attached to the upper frame of which are a pair of swivel lenses): honed, her figure, like a fighter's, stripped to a minimum weight, from hours of solitude, booze and weeping.

Her features 'travel' (Liam says – there for this audition), handsome, curiously attractive – full of grace ('no doubt, from all she's been through' (Liam): two publicised abortions, three interim marriages between the two to Zygorski). Her fingers, as she takes the playscript, tremble: 'I don't read well, I'm afraid,' and then, having cleared her throat – returning the playscript to the desk behind and alongside which, respectively, Liam and I are sitting – she declares, 'On principle I never do. My agent, for one thing, doesn't allow it.'

'Too proud,' Liam says, 'to read for friends.'

Turning to me, she says, 'It's no reflection on your play, which, incidentally, I admire immensely. I wouldn't have come if I didn't.'

'How are you, Vivienne?' Liam says.

'I believe,' she says, 'I'm very well. I merely came,' she crosses her legs, 'because I'd been invited.'

'Don't be ridiculous, Vivienne,' Liam says, 'you can read as well as anyone.'

'As long as I can keep in a vertical position, and, when necessary, sustain a horizontal one, I don't see why I should,' she says.

'Why didn't I get the part?' she asked (years later). 'Because you thought I'd never learn the lines? I'd learnt half of them, I might tell you, the night before. Until five a.m., when I snatched an hour of sleep, then had a shower, then walked the streets waiting to come up to that crummy office and be offered the part. Not asked, God damn it, to audition. I made that man's career. And yours. And Miracle Miles Macauley.'

'We made yours, too,' I told her.

'With *Hero*? Before that, all Liam was known for was making documentaries. You thought,' she went on, 'I was on the bottle.'

'More than thought,' I said.

'I hadn't touched a drop for hours. *Hours!*'

'How many pairs of glasses did she have?' the casting director asks after Vivienne has gone (she herself a former actress).

'Two pairs,' Liam says, 'three lenses.'

'She had a glass-case in her hand, with another pair inside,' the woman says.

'Three pairs, four lenses, which shows,' Liam says, 'she came to read.'

'I would never,' the woman says, 'as a *woman*, get into a state like that.'

'Like what?' Liam says.

'I'd have,' she says, 'more pride.'

'Pride, I'm afraid,' Liam says (he to go down that road himself), 'is all that Viv has left.'

'That's not pride,' the woman declares. 'That, I'm afraid, is subjugation.'

'I was never too humble to be proud,' Vivienne said later. 'The last time was in that office at the top of that crummy theatre. The lift didn't work. I walked the stairs, and didn't even get the crummy part. Which is just as well. I'd never have kept it. How long was the run? Two months? Two weeks would have been my limit.'

'Three pairs of glasses, four lenses!' Liam says, laughing (foreshadowing his own disasters: all of my friends and most of my contemporaries dead).

'I fell down the stairs when I left that office and – what you didn't know – I had to be taken home in a cab,' she ringing me a few days later: 'I liked your face. You looked as though you've been through much the same as I have, booze apart, of course, and three or four husbands.'

'Two moths,' Liam said, 'and a single flame: no wonder you both got burned.'

*

195

I brought Bea to this hilltop – twice: once to see the view, the other to make love – and Bella once (the motive much the same). 'It's a sacred place,' I said to Bella when, winded from the climb, she stood panting in the darkness of the trees: the absurdity of requesting her to climb, her vulnerability (humility) in accepting. 'It must have been an island in the neolithic lake. The signs of a settlement have been found at the southern end. Perhaps you'd like to see it?' the lights strewn out beyond the links (the pressure of her hand in mine: 'How much I love you,' I declared. 'I wish that we were married').

'Hence the difference between us,' Vivienne – who was my age – said when I told her about my earlier life. 'You really need a mother. Was she as lovely as you describe? We must have a lot in common.' When I asked her, 'What?' she laughed. 'Women,' she said, 'who were never loved.'

'I loved her more than any other woman I know,' I said.

'Until she grew too old.'

'Not once,' I told her, 'was she ever too old.'

To see her sitting there, or working in the garden, or merely standing at the door when we departed was more than I could bear: I longed to take her in my arms. I would, when we moved to London, lie awake for hours, aching for her touch. She totally possessed me. 'After I was married, after I had children, after I had been with other women, one encounter merely the presage to another. More to me,' I tell Vivienne, 'than life itself,' recalling the occasion when, in the darkness, she had stood here with me, her hand in mine, gazing at the scree of lights before us (Onasett and, behind us, those of Harlstone, across the valley), the swaying presence of the trees (the softness of her touch). 'Making love was a disappointment. It always led to something else. Disquiet. The fact that she was married. The disparity between our ages. The frustration of never knowing in what circumstances we might meet. The longing to be with her was more than I could bear. I would creep into the grounds at Ardsley and wait amongst the trees, hoping I might glimpse her passing by a window. One evening, when I did, she at an upstairs window, gazing out, speculating,

I imagined, what she would do, or merely feel like if, glancing out, she saw me, it was more than I could bear. I stepped out from the shadows. She never saw me. All she could see, she said, was the dark. It was to appease this indiscretion of mine that she took to walking in the grounds in the evening. "To take the air," as she described it, prompting her husband jocularly to remark she must be meeting a lover.'

'I don't know what it was,' I said to Vi. 'The sight of her alone was enough to set me off. I'd be engulfed by feelings which convinced me I was mad. I'd tremble. Her sounds of gratification, the removal of her clothes, the elevation of her hips, the paleness of the garment which, despite my efforts, still concealed her breast, drove me to distraction. "Don't be so wild," she'd tell me (after all, her tone implied, you're getting what you want), and, "Don't be so clumsy," would be her other plea, the final consummation, even now, after all these years, impossible to describe.'

'It's not me you love,' Vivienne, on one sultry evening, casually announced ('I should never have come here to live or had anything to do with you at all,' she added), 'but that woman you see in me. I'm about the age that she was. It's me you're launching into when you come on top. It's her you're making love to,' requesting (something she'd resisted until that moment) I find a photograph amongst the papers I'd brought from Belsize Park to Taravara Road (no search required at all), showing her the most precious – taken in a woodland clearing (with a camera – at my insistence – she'd brought herself), she sitting on the ground, the hem of a summer frock demurely above her knee, her eyes half-closed, her lips parted, the dimples evident in her unlined cheeks. My coat and her own are on the ground, revealing clearly the impress of our bodies (her hair in disarray): sunlight – we are on our memorable visit to Broughton Woods, close to my boyhood camp-site – sprinkles a patina of shadow across her frock, the outline of her thigh, one leg curled beneath her. She smiles as, years later, Bea would smile at the first of our children – bewildered, perplexed (subliminally entranced).

197

'She's very beautiful,' Vi said, searching, indubitably, for a vestige of herself. 'She must have loved you very much. Incontinently,' she added, stammering (a full glass in her hand). 'To have risked not only her husband's but her daughter's love. You said he idolised her, didn't you?' raising her head to examine the kitchen-cum-living-room of that tiny dwelling (no vestige in the photograph, after all, only the residue of where we are now). 'To have risked all that for a boy of – how old were you at the time? Nineteen? It doesn't make sense, and yet, to me, all the sense,' she belched, 'in the world. I idolised my father in a similar way and have been looking for a surrogate ever since. An awful cheat. Zygorski. An awful fucking creep. Twenty-five years younger and the mind of a child of seven.'

She kept the photograph by our bed: 'How beautiful she looks and – worst of all – how innocent. Isn't the key, my darling, she was really much younger than you? What, I wonder, does her daughter think? That inimitable genius who, sooner or later, will come up for the Nobel Prize.'

'She never knew,' I told her.

'Never?'

I shook my head.

'I thought that's why you split.'

I shook my head again.

'Never?'

'Never.'

In two minds, I could see (a handy weapon), to tell her now herself.

'The only person who knows, apart from yourself, is Maidstone,' I said. 'He thought it was something Bea could sense but not define.'

'Which, in any case, came between you,' she said.

'It might.'

She sat in silence for a while: what, she must have reflected, could I do with that? Damage, she must have concluded, commensurate with her own.

Isabella's collar: her arm, her sleeve, the abrasiveness of the material of the coat itself: the extraordinary effect of her perfume in the dark: her smile: 'Is this what you do with Bea?'

'No,' I tell her, and add, 'You'd decided you'd never ask.'

'Nevertheless,' her hair flung back against the grass. 'It must be desperation that makes me.' ('It's more,' she has said on one occasion, 'than flesh and blood can stand.') And adds – or I think she adds – recollection inhibited by aversion, 'This *instrument* that goes in and out of me, goes in and out of my daughter. Does she, I wonder, feel the same? If she found out, is there only disillusionment for both of us?' (Isn't her gratification, she might have gone on, identical to mine – achieved after all, in an identical way?). 'What, I wonder,' she concluded, 'is so different?'

While on the South Coast, in a sunlit room, an airship passing overhead, her daughter is experiencing what she, her mother, experienced then – on the banks of streams, in sunlit woods, on the back seat of a bus (in moonlit copses): 'I seldom feel afterwards I haven't been raped. Odd, when I invite it.'

My dear. My dear! My love!

Or on the bed, when Corcoran is out: in the guest-room where I am staying at present (the view to the trees and the pit-less village); in my lodgings at the Drayburgh when she came to London – which, only moments before, her daughter had left . . .

15

'ARE YOU all right?' the jerseyed (a roll-top collar) zip-jacketed
figure enquires: panting from his climb, a golf-club in his hand,
a companion – female, skirted – some distance down the slope
behind: 'My wife,' he gestures with his club, 'saw you lying
down. She thought,' glancing down the slope, 'you'd fallen.'
He calls, 'I think he looks all right,' vigorous – thick-calved,
broad-chested, face flushed from his exertions: a native,
undoubtedly, of Onasett itself.

'Are you a native of these parts?' I enquiring, aware of sitting
on the ground, my back against a tree, leaning, my elbow
supporting me, over to one side (a dizzy attack or a reflexive
action).

'Linfield.' He names a distant suburb. 'The Cawthorne Club
is difficult to get into. Onasett isn't so choosey.'

'Onasett,' I tell him, 'never was,' conscious of the damp
beneath my thigh: though covered with decaying leaves, the
ground is wet. I can feel further evidence through my jacket
sleeve. 'It took all the people living by the river, in those streets
around the Linfield dock, my parents, as it happened, amongst
them,' half a century or more ago, I might have added but he
is gazing at my sketchbook which, together with my pencil, is
lying on the ground.

'You've got the appearance of it well,' he says.

'I have,' I say, 'and more.'

'Is he all right?' calls a voice from down the slope and, 'He
is an artist,' is offered in reply. 'Would you like me,' turning
back, 'to help you from the ground?'

I take his hand; for the first time – as he takes mine in return – he is aware of my carpet slippers.

'I came out,' I tell him, 'in a hurry.'

'From Onasett?' he enquires.

'Home,' I say, 'is where the heart is.'

'Dougie?' from the slope below: two trolleys parked along the fairway.

'Coming,' he calls, adding, 'Are you sure you'll be all right?'

'Perfectly,' I tell him, he setting off, soliciting a signal, with his golf-club, to which, however, I don't reply.

The etymology of grief is the epistemology of madness, viz:

Grief (*pace* grievance) = injury.

Injury = not right (wrong).

Wrong = unjust (related to wring, awry).

Wring = squeeze, twist (distress, torture).

Awry = crooked (related to wry).

Wry = distort, turned to one side (contort).

(Contort = twist).

Distort (similarly).

Twist = double (twin, twine).

(Double = two).

Two = division:

injury, injustice, torture, distortion: duality – madness, it is conjectured, the logic of grief, its antecedents to be found in injury, injustice, torture, distortion – duality – and self-division.

'Bea,' Maidstone says, 'is no longer a woman,' she is, he is about to tell me, a state of mind, but adds, misjudging my look, 'well known at the Ministry.'

'Ministry?'

'Of Health. Where do you think she gets her money?'

I was about to say, 'Myself,' but go on, 'We separated, would you believe it, after coming to London, and met up again at a college dance: a room full of streamers, played to by a jazz band led by a man with a stammer, his announcements, over a faulty mike, variations on an extempory theme, she a radiant figure – "Beattie" to her pals, principal amongst them her college tutor who, a molecular physicist, was subsequently fired for screwing a student: magenta hair, green-irised eyes, green-coloured dress.'

'Aren't you a student here?' she says.

'The Drayburgh,' I tell her, 'is affiliated to the university.'

'Oh,' she says, and little else, except, as we spin and whirl – she spiralling politely beneath my hand (has she heard, I reflect, about her *mother*?) she adds, 'The Drayburgh, by the way, is known as "The Drain", on account of the people, of course, who go there.'

'Haven't we met before?' I ask.

'Isn't it reprehensible,' she says, 'the way a reputation like that can get around?'

'Take me,' I say. 'I'm known as licentious,' she waiting – our acquaintance once renewed – in her college room dressed in suspenders, stockings, little else (a dressing-gown half-belted), saying, 'Aren't you early? I thought we said half-seven,' the spry, 'My dear!' as I come inside, a Christmas dance, thrown at the Student Union in Malet Street where I'd hoped (intended) to meet her again – and not a week later, of course, her mother ('I thought you and Bea had drifted apart'), she waiting in my room in much the same fashion as Bea in hers, the spry, 'Oh, Richard!' and then, 'My dear!'

'I was studying painting at the time and a student at the Drayburgh was quite a catch. As for her mother: "I really came down, of course to see Bea." '

'Are you a member?' the man enquires.

Unlike the majority of the men who occupy the room he wears a collar and tie: a square moustache, a pale blue eye buttoned either side of a fleshy, mottled nose.

'I'm looking,' I tell him, 'for Mr O'Donnell.'

'O'Donnell?'

'A member here in nineteen forty-five. He lived two doors away in Manor Road, spent more of his time on the tees than he did with his wife.'

'I don't know Mr O'Donnell,' the man replies.

'This would be where Wordsworth, Turner, Castlereagh, on two occasions, Gladstone and Disraeli, at varying times,' I tell

202

him, 'were entertained. You must know Turner's sketch of Onasett Hall, set against the slope, poetically exaggerated, of Onasett itself, the setting sun, the pink eminence of the house in the middle distance.'

'If you're not a member, or invited by a member, you're not allowed in the bar,' he says.

'Any time, he told me, I happened to be around. "You'll be assured," he said, "of a welcome." '

'If you're not a member, nor an invited guest, I have a statutory obligation,' he says, 'to ask you to leave.'

'My father came down here during the Second World War. The Onasett Home Guard occupied premises in what was the gardeners' hut at the back. A unique structure, circular, brick-built, and probably still there, comprised of two rooms, one on top of the other.'

'Nostalgia,' Maidstone says, 'classified as a medical condition, was first noted amongst mercenaries in the European armies in the eighteenth-century wars: stout-hearted men who suddenly acquired the symptoms of depression, not merely a disinclination but an inability to eat, sitting for hours in a stooped or crouched position: men who, when they first left home, had been, where not relieved, jubilant to do so – escaping from marital or parental discord, lack of food or unemployment – only, once away, to curl up and die. Though discarded nowadays as a clinical diagnosis, nosomania is, in my view, under-rated. A longing for one's home is, in many respects, inseparable from a longing for the past: not merely a sentimental aspiration to return to a familiar place and time, but a passionate regard for experiences which may, in reality, never have occurred, a diffusing of experience to which the victim helplessly clings, like a martyr to a cross or a drowning man to a plank of wood, the recollection, in short, of a place or places without which a person, mistakenly, believes he can't exist.'

'As for Maidstone's reference,' I tell the man, 'to my clinging to the past, I only have to refer him to what actually took place, the material set down in black and white.'

'I'll be obliged, if you won't leave, sir, to call on someone to take you out. We have two policemen here as members,' calling, 'Bryan!' to a figure whom, with several others, reflected in a mirror, I see standing at the bar.

'O'Donnell died,' I tell him, 'in 1955, scarcely ten days short of his sixty-fifth birthday. A rent and rates clerk at the County Hall, I saw him, believe it or not, the day preceding the event, walking past our house swaying, as he did so, not merely from side to side but forwards and backwards.'

'He's come here looking for a man who died in 1955.'

'O'Donnell was his name,' I tell the policeman: in civvies, fair-haired, not disinclined, I suspect, to be moved. 'His namesake, not dissimilar in several respects, directed one of my films and a not inconsiderable number of my plays,' I add.

'I'm afraid,' Bryan says, 'this is not a public bar. I shall have to ask you, if you aren't a member, or haven't been invited as a guest, to leave.'

'Jack the Democrat,' I tell him, 'would not be pleased. A populist when populism had more than a pejorative meaning. As for O'Donnell . . .'

The off-duty constable – perhaps sergeant (or, considering the youth of today, conceivably inspector) – takes my arm. 'There's no reason why you shouldn't, on the other hand, invite me as a friend. I am, after all,' I tell him, 'native bred, a son of the Devonian sandstone, the millstone grit – along with the glacial marls and shales, the sands and gravels, the deltaic deposits. Between you and I,' I go on, 'there is no between. That which comprises the between between me and other people has, in the past few years, been set aside. Certainly by me, if no one else. I am almost too free,' I conclude, 'to be alive. Which is why, if the truth were known, I was sectioned by my wife, working in conjunction with a live wire at the North London Royal. Maidstone by name, if rarely by practice . . .'

We are at the door: it looks directly to a smoothly-cut lawn ('Like a bowling-green,' I tell him. 'It is a bowling-green,' he says) bordered in turn by a balustraded wall through a gap in which (decorated on either side by urns in which spring flowers

204

are already blooming: daffodil, crocus, and the like) the first tee of the golf-course can be seen and, in the furthest distance, across a diagonal view of the valley, the pudding-like profile of Cawthorne Castle, the river – hidden by its low embankments and the parallel canal and railway embankments – somewhere in between.

'Which is not unlike being sent outside with the integument of one's skull removed, the abrasiveness of the air so intense a pain as to be,' I tell him, 'impossible to describe.'

'I advise you to leave by the drive,' he says.

The first of my interlocutors – he of the square moustache and collar and tie – points the opposite way to the one I'm going. 'There is no public access across the course,' he adds.

Vivienne, poor Vi, was ensconced at the N.L.R. herself (a different time to me: 'Would you say,' she enquired, 'we're taking it in turns?'), but, unlike me, was never sectioned (no family nor lover to do it for her): subsequently, she joined her chums in L.A.: "mystical analysis", "rational diets", endless hours of driving the freeways, going nowhere, coming back: between her and I there is no between – I bringing her here on one occasion (her incapacity to disengage the seat-belt alone preventing her from falling out).

'I want you,' I tell her, 'to find a root. This is where I started. This,' I tell her, 'is where I belong.'

'Another fucking place to me. Never a one,' she cries, 'to call my own!'

'You left this behind,' the policeman says, handing me the sketchbook.

'That's kind of you,' I tell him. 'I'm on my way home,' the driveway, however, already empty, no one but myself, he a disappearing figure: no curiosity about the present. None, presumably, about the past.

'When you get into these states,' Maidstone says, 'select an image. Preserve it. Concentrate on one thing and nothing else.'

'What I always choose,' I say, 'is Bella.'

'Vi is Isabella,' he says, 'bereft of prohibition.'

"Thanks for everything," Vivienne wrote in her last letter –

leaving it, curiously, with her wedding-ring on the draining-board (where the bleach had stood) beside the sink, I waiting for a call to say she had arrived (conceivably, she'd missed me) – three days, God help me, before I found her (her finger nails filled with garden soil – perhaps, not inconceivably, evidence she'd changed her mind, intending to crawl to the kitchen door, calling me or, God help her, Melvyn.)

A bus goes past: I am once more on the curving, roller-coaster strip of tarmac, rising and falling over ancient, overgrown moraines, which circuits the foot of the estate: an aperture in the façade of red brick and pebble-dash indicates the opening to Manor Road: the familiar verges have been replaced by tarmac, the trees little more than hacked-at stumps: cars, the majority in a dilapidated if not irretrievable condition, are parked amidst pools of coagulating oil: hedges as well as gardens are overgrown and, where the soil has been tarmacked too, vehicles are parked between the houses. The doors and windows have been replaced with inappropriate frames and mountings: out of scale, out of sympathy (out of everything): plebeian exigencies: what was graceful (small and neat) a distortion of the planners' earliest intention: the burgeoning trees, the fresh-cut verges (the smell of grass), the flowered gardens . . .

"Thanks for everything. Love. V."

An overcast sky, the tarmac flanked by the intermittently-tarmacked-over verges (of the trees, where not missing, only one or two are fully grown), the mutilated (or absent) hedges – gaps hacked in to allow access to cars – the decimated gardens, the air of adventitious debilitation: a drive carved out of the soil by tyres; windows punched in inappropriate walls· 'Nosomania,' Maidstone says, 'is cured by a return to the place – or the past – imagined.'

'Only,' I tell him, 'nothing, from being observed, is what it was before.'

Some distance ahead, where the road rises up a gentler slope (never steep enough to sledge down), the front of the house appears: the green paint, inset with yellow, of its window frames and doors is now a uniform brown: the roof is disfigured with wedge-shaped tiles. The front door has changed (a uniform, unmoulded expanse of wood: no relief to its tedious surface), the hedge at the front hacked to waist-height: the gate has gone, replaced by a pair of wooden hurdles which, wedged apart, are already broken. A dilapidated car stands in the gap between the houses (scarcely space to open the door), a make-shift garage blocking the view to the field and – from the enclosing weeds – the overgrown garden behind. The windows are uncurtained, strips of cloth attached on either side.

"Here," Vi had written obscurely in her last letter, "you will find me. We had, did we not, a hell of a time, you fucked up from the inside, I from the outside. 'A woman's work is never done,' ran an advert in my childhood – beside, as it happened, a bottle of bleach. How true! 'Take this cup from me,' Christ prayed in the garden. How, since he prayed alone, did anyone know? When, as a child, I asked my father, all he said was, 'Inspiration!' All I can say to him now, as I say to you. Thanks for everything. Love. V."

In her diary, its writing so small I had to use a magnifying glass to decipher the scrawl: "A sense of obsolescence has preoccupied me all my life: the laughing child, the beautiful daughter, the blushing bride (the fucked-up wife), on each occasion the still, small voice, 'This isn't meant to last.' Nailed to his cross he must have felt the same: 'Don't take it at anything other than face value,' the nails, the hammer, the spear, the sponge – the lament of every woman on earth – and Him: *why hast thou deserted me!*"

My father, pushing his upright-handled bicycle, comes up the path: dark (imprinted, his face, with coal-dust round his eyes and mouth, the cracked lines that retain it beside his lids, the crevices beneath his chin), a short, broad-shouldered, smouldering figure, still at the coal-face at sixty-one – the handlebars grasped in either hand, the querulous, 'It's you?'

'How are you?' I enquire – to which he doesn't reply, laying the bike against the hedge (no longer there) which hides the back garden from the road, stamps his feet on the mat in the porch, ducks his head as he pulls off his cap, stoops, removes his clips, before he thrusts his way inside.

'What did Grandpa do?' the children enquire, years later, as they watch his stumpy, white-haired figure recline in a deck-chair on the lawn of our Belsize Park house – solemn, silent, gazing at the air (rasping in the London pollution), their incredulous looks as they listen to his tales of tunnels, pitprops and collapsing roofs (runaway trucks and crashing engines, floods and falls and fire and dying men).

Taking off his jacket, he washes at the sink, turning, hands wet, to the frayed-edge towel: his boots, coal-dusted, are thrust beneath the mangle: lifting the lid on the plate laid across the top of a pan of simmering water, his head is immersed in a cloud of steam: too tired to eat, he allows my mother, who has come through from the living-room, to take the plate from him. He sits, answering briefly my mother's questions, at the living-room table, the food carried to his mouth unseen: 'The roof half-buried the machine this morning,' eating, two-fisted, like a boxer, the gravy streaked across his lips, eyes like a dog's, hungered from exhaustion, submitting to an appetite his body cannot feel.

'Would you mind telling me what you are doing here?' the woman asks.

'I live here,' I say, and add, 'or used to,' aware I have wandered between our old house and our neighbour's and am standing at the side of a makeshift garage: where once stood a lawn, a rockery and, between the rockery and the field, a vegetable patch, are the accumulated remains of several motor cars: clothes, hung for drying, are suspended above them, while the porch, its coal-house door broken, has its brickwork smeared with the imprint of what appear to be innumerable oil-stained hands.

'You're not, by any chance, called Fenchurch?' she says.

208

'I am,' I say, 'as it happens,' (a commemorative plaque, it's been suggested, should be attached to the front of the house?).

'Someone was looking for you.'

She gestures to the road.

'Who?' I immediately respond.

'A woman.'

Small and stout – a stoutness which, to some degree, belies her age, for she can't, I imagine, be more than in her middle twenties (servile to a savage husband, the mother of more children than she can count: the sound of squawking comes from inside the scullery door: the door through which, for forty-five years, my father daily entered).

'What did she look like?'

'She came in a car. Said, "Has a gentleman been here?" Said you walked with a shuffle, and may even be in your slippers.'

She gazes at my feet.

'Where is she now?'

Gesturing to the road again, she says, 'She drove off when I told her I hadn't.'

'A fan of mine,' I tell her.

'She said she was your daughter.'

'They all say that,' I tell her. I shift my sketchbook to my other hand, recall I may have lost my pencil, and add, 'You have a beautiful dress.'

She looks down at her skirt – stained, ill-fitting, torn at the seam.

'On the line,' I tell her.

'That's a nightdress,' she declares.

'I would love,' I say, 'to see you in it.'

'So would I,' she says. 'I put the wrong heat on and it's gone and shrunk.'

'You're a rough and ready woman, I can see,' I tell her. 'Quite used to your environment, I imagine, and to the rough treatment that you get, no doubt, from your husband.'

'It's a good job he isn't here,' she says. 'Do you want me to ring the police?'

'I merely came,' I tell her, 'to look at the house. I painted my first picture behind that door, composed my first poem, wrote my first novel. For the first twenty years of my life I slept here almost every night, sometimes in the bedroom at the back, more often in the second bedroom at the front. You will hardly credit it,' I go on, 'but I was once put up for the New Year's Honours, until my private life came under closer scrutiny, by which time my reputation, unfortunately, had declined, if not disappeared entirely. Previous to that, several plays of mine had been seen by President Johnson, at the instigation of his wife, Lady Bird – who became, I could almost say, an intimate acquaintance – she arriving at the theatre with her usual guards who not only occupied the best seats in the stalls, the Royal and Dress Circles, but the gallery, each of them armed with an automatic weapon which, on one memorable evening, misinterpreting a line of the play as an attack on her, they drew, pointing them in a variety of directions but principally at the seat in which was sitting the director of the play. I was, for several years, the toast of Broadway and won, for several years running, its principal awards.'

She has turned her attention to a child behind her back, her broad figure stooping to its bare-legged frame which, with a sigh, she hauls to her shoulder.

'Do you mind,' I enquire, 'if I step in the field?' and clambering between the miscellaneous piles of rusted metal, reach the area where normally there might have been a fence and, an instant later, am standing in wasteland (where previously, I remind myself, there had been only grass): here neighbours danced and ate and drank to the music of a wind-up gramophone to celebrate the end of the Second World War and, years later, the coronation of the Queen; here the subsidence that marks the hole where we built our final den, marked itself, like a grave, by weeds; there the cricket-pitch, more pitted than ever; there the slope behind the goal down which the ball invariably rolled after scoring; here – last of all – the level stretch of ground – adjacent to the cricket-pitch – where the tables were set in a single line for the parties to celebrate peace and the coronation – where the women, in their Sunday dresses (overhung with aprons) danced with their waist-coated, shirt-sleeved men, the latter shy to be seen embracing their wives in public, the bolder dancing with their more adventurous neighbours: Mr Clinton (of the large moustache) with Mrs Russell (of the prominent bosom); Mr Walton (with the protuberant waist) with the much animated Mrs Swanson; Mr Wade (bow-legged) with Mrs Braine (from Ireland); my father with my mother, before finding an excuse – the children's demands at the table – to disengage; the golfing Mr O'Donnell with the tennising Mrs Crawshaw, the religious Mr Walls with the irreligious Mrs Shay, the unmarried Peter Waterton (about to be demobbed) with the widowed Mrs Preston, myself an idle youth, leaning on the fence, grimacing at this display of communality...

Burnt, the grass, in one or two places: missing, the fences, behind my back: the desultory windows no longer recall the personalities inside: the Davidsons, the Clarkes, the Petersons, the Smiths.

Dereliction.

Almost idly, Fenchurch takes out a pencil (in his pocket all the while) and, the grass too wet to sit, begins to draw: the line of the field, the inappropriately adapted houses – the battlemented crest formed by the silhouetted roofs – identifying, as he does so, the pattern of the windows – alternating double and single – the alcoves of the porches, the scattered trails of smoke – and decides he is too tired, fatigued (worn-out, defeated): how on earth did Etty know? the woman, he observes, still watching, the child, half-naked, in her arms.

Other figures, too, are watching (other windows, other doors).

'Would you like a cup of tea?' she calls, and disappears inside her porch.

Glancing round, once more, at the familiar façades, I complete the sketch – the lowering excrescences of greyish vapour beyond which, at one time, lurked German bombers (the remainder of my life a remoter threat) – and return, with difficulty – negotiating the rusting metal obstacles – down the

211

remnants of the garden path to the oil-stained entrance to the at-one-time Fenchurch porch.

I tap on the grease-marked door ('Come in,' says a voice immediately inside) and step into a scullery smaller in size than the one retained in memory, the cracked concrete floor covered in linoleum, across which has been laid a tattered mat: a motor-cycle, its engine disassembled, leans against the wall against which, in inclement weather, we propped our bikes. A cooker replaces the gas-fired, green-painted copper, the sink in the corner much the same: beneath the window, looking out to the road, a washing-machine is piled high with washing.

'Come in,' she says again (a kettle plugged to the wall). 'Go through to the living-room, I'll bring the tea through,' she adds, 'in a minute,' the child still in her arms.

Crossing the hall, scarcely broad enough to take two figures standing together, I enter the living-room the other side – a vast interior, in memory, of familial warmth – reduced, in reality, to something not much larger than my Taravara Road kitchen: the closeness of the walls, the lowness of the ceiling, the confinement of the view to the field and road outside – the dereliction of the disassembled cars at the back, the asphalt verge, the overgrown and trampled remnants of the lawn at the front: a decaying, grease-stained settee and two similarly disfigured easy chairs, together with a crockery-encumbered wooden table, take up much of the available space; a television set, turned on, stands adjacent to a fireplace which, tiled, unlike the black-leaded stove of previous years, is occupied by cans of beer, which, on closer inspection, prove to have been opened.

Laying down my sketchbook and pencil I hear a voice behind me call, 'Tea or coffee?'

'Tea.'

The chairs are small.

'Make yourself at home, I shan't be a minute.'

Springs protrude beneath the much-stained fabric. My feet are wet: I clench my toes inside my socks, feel the dampness against the slippers and, having sat, remove them.

Taking off my socks, I put them in my pocket.

Here, on many a solitary evening, I have read *Lord Jim*, *Hamlet*, *A Midsummer Night's Dream*: Dostoyevsky: 'procrastination common to Lord Jim and Hamlet: discuss.'

The paper on the wall, distempered, is marked at a uniform height by children's hands: dark patches enclose the light-switch: a smell of beer is obfuscated, to some degree, by that of rotting meat, the air not only chill but damp: so many evenings have I sat behind a barricade of drying clothes, the dampness permeating the furniture and curtains: the glow of the fire through the different thicknesses of cloth, the chink of flame between adjacent garments, the creak of the leather thongs on the supporting wooden frame echoing that of the table where, on a sheet laid on newspaper, my mother irons.

'Sugar and milk?'

'Milk,' I tell her and, a moment later, the child still in her arms, she brings in a steaming pot.

'Would you like a biscuit?'

'No, thanks,' I tell her.

'A piece of cake?'

I shake my head (uncertain where she keeps it). 'Excuse my feet,' I tell her. 'I wet them in the grass,' and add, 'I came out in my slippers.'

'That's all right,' she says, 'by me.'

She sits, the child, its head averted, twisting in her arms.

'You notice any changes?' she enquires.

A feeling of dispiritation, bordering on despair, and not unmixed with apprehension, absorbs me for a while. 'It seems much smaller,' I finally reply. 'I can't imagine how we all got in.'

'How many were there of you?' she enquires.

'Five. Two parents and three brothers.'

'Where are your brothers now?' she asks.

'Abroad.' I add, 'Since our parents' deaths I rarely see them.' (Nor, I reflect, would they want to see me: disparity of purpose, for one thing; disparity of content, for another).

'I suppose, if you lived here before, you could say,' she says, 'we have something in common,' the child wriggling in her lap. 'Mam! Can I have summat t'eat?' it says (surprisingly: I'd assumed it to be dumb). 'I'd better be getting her clothes on,' she adds. 'She's alus wetting herself at present,' (the vestiges, I assess, of an education – brought to a premature end by marriage: fewer colloquialisms in her speech, for instance, than might reasonably have been expected). 'How many children do you have?' turning to a cupboard by her chair.

'Five,' I tell her, noticing, for the first time, a telephone on a stand behind the door. 'Three grandchildren,' I go on, 'at present.'

A mist comes in, within which the house itself has vanished.

'It's not at all like it was,' I add, enquiring, 'How many other children do you have?'

'Two more at school,' she says, 'though this 'un's nearly ready,' the child's eyes unblinking as, turned in its mother's hands, its final garment is removed and dry ones pulled on.

'It looks much younger,' I suggest, and am about to describe the antics of Lottie and Glenda (of Mathilda, Harriet, Kenneth, Benjamin and Rebecca) but, having got to my feet, intemperately announce, 'I ought to be going. There's so much still I have to do. Your husband'll be at work, I haven't a doubt, and you'll have a great deal to do yourself,' adding, 'I have a house of my own in London. An area to the north of the Euston Road, much frequented by the uprooted and the lost,' making for the door only, with a cry, to return for my slippers.

'Mrs Stott said she'd be here,' she says, 'in a very short while.'

'When did she say that?' I ask.

'When you were in the field I phoned her,' she says. 'She gave me her number and told me to call. She said she'd be here in no time at all.'

'She's a very slow driver, and the road from Ardsley to Linfield,' I tell her, 'is full of bends. She's enough on her hands, as it is, at present, not least of which should have been a definitive study of her father, a singularly neglected figure at the best of times but, in my not unprejudiced view, unlikely to be so in the future. Give her a ring. Tell her,' I pause, a car passing in the road, 'I'll come back on the bus.'

'She says you shouldn't be out,' she says, following me to the door.

'I've been on my own,' I tell her, 'for a very long time. Far longer,' I go on, 'than I recall,' returning to the room to pick up my sketchbook and pencil. 'I have,' I continue, 'never felt better. No day passes,' I tap my head, 'but I wake to a feeling commensurate with being hanged. Hanged, I might add, within the hour. An inordinate sense of guilt masks an indescribable sense of dread. Somewhere along the road, assuming I ever had it, I appear to have lost myself. And yet . . .'

I am looking up the stairs: those tiny stairs, scarcely wider than a ladder.

'I hope you won't mind if I leave behind some money,' emptying my pockets of all the coins I have, laying them on the stairs before me, re-entering the scullery while, behind my back, 'I feel very worried at letting you go,' and, 'Is that man going, Mam?'

'Tell her,' I tell her, 'I went into town. I shall be back home,' I add, 'in no time at all. As quick as a flick,' I call to the child, the walls, I notice, of the scullery, as in my time, damp with condensation. 'I suppose your husband,' I continue, 'is unemployed.'

'No,' she says, 'he drives a taxi.'

'In that case,' I tell her, 'he'll not disapprove of me leaving a tip. I could, if I'd had one on me, have written a cheque. I still can, of course, the moment I get back. I know the address,' I add, 'by heart. The old, old home.' I tap the walls (even damper than I'd thought). 'Things being equal,' I go on, 'I'd have looked upstairs, seen the old bedroom,' turning in the door: in another place, in another time – not bowed down by domesticity, debt and propaganda – she might have been another Vi. But then – this, I reflect, or a garden shed? 'I escaped from this place with an alacrity even now I can't recall. I hated its squalor, its aridity, its lack of scale, its denigration of everything I considered fine.' I shake my head. 'Yet here I am. Looking, would you believe it, for what I lost, hoping for a fire amongst the ashes,' yet all I get, I might have told her, is the smell of beer, the scent of oil, the sight of rusting metal.

'Wouldn't you say,' says Maidstone at one of our meetings in his tiny office (the walnut-fascia desk, the plastic chairs, the postcards from abroad and English sea-side places, pinned to the wall above his head: 'Thank you, Professor Maidstone, for all your help'), 'that life is a deeply depressing experience?' adding, 'Mishima, the Japanese writer, described it as the only definitive view of reality we ever have, and although I have never suffered in the way the majority of my patients have I'm not disinclined to agree with him. As you yourself have remarked, we have been given the means to resolve a mystery which, of its nature, eludes definition. Our tragedy is not only that our minds have outgrown our bodies but that our bodies have outgrown their reason to exist.'

Will this unfortunate woman, I mentally enquire, repeat to Etty what I have told her: tell her, in short, I have returned to town (am returning home: shall be back in Ardsley in no time)? 'His taxi isn't here, by any chance?' I ask, at which, standing in the porch, she shakes her head.

'That's not one of his cars,' I ask her, 'in the back?' and indicate the metal wreckage, at least three models evident amongst the rubbish.

'He hires his car,' she says, 'from a man in town and once he's covered that,' she shifts the child to her other arm, 'everything is profit.'

'Not a great deal of trade, I imagine, with so many out of work, and those in work not earning all they might: industry run down and not,' I tell her, 'being replaced.'

'There's quite a bit,' she says, 'at the station,' and, to clarify this, adds, 'The railway station. There are quite a lot of people go up and down from London.'

Already I am walking down the path, between the houses – the path – obstructed by the dilapidated parked vehicle, and all but obliterated by tyre tracks – down which I have walked too many times to count, the wedged-apart hurdles standing

216

in for gates before me – and fail to recognise the figure getting out of Etty's car drawn up in the road outside.

A man in a corduroy zip-jacket and jeans – an open-necked shirt, the collar of which could do with washing – enquires, 'You're leaving, are you?' and (not unpleasant features: fresh-faced, blue-eyed), glancing to the woman and the child who have now appeared at the top of the path behind me, he adds, 'I can give you a lift, if you like.' (Not Etty's car after all.)

'I haven't any money,' I tell him.

The car, though large – its front wheel drawn up on the tarmacked verge – is old.

'It must cost,' I tell him, 'a lot to run,' and add, 'Did your wife call you, by the way, as well as my daughter?' continuing, as he steps aside to let me pass (determination written in my features, I haven't a doubt, as well as implicit in my figure) 'I have an important appointment. One I've been looking forward to for quite some time,' uncertain still he might not delay me, he clearly in two minds. 'The principal characteristics of someone like myself,' I hastily continue, 'are slyness, self-containment, selfishness, aggression – directed against others as well as oneself: manipulative behaviour, an aversion, overtly as well as covertly expressed, to being influenced by others, an unwillingness, if not an incapacity to give gratification, a basic sense of hostility, the whole suffused by an ineradicable and unappeasable feeling of anxiety, manifesting itself, in my case, throughout my life, in unsolicited and unmotivated attacks of terror. These symptoms are caused, exclusively, by a malfunction of the brain – or by what might even be described as a "colouration" of the brain – like I was born with dark hair, you with light – and can't be altered, except by "dyeing". That is, by chemical infusion, of a kind which, on principle, I eschew. Psychotherapy, I'm afraid, of which I am a connoisseur, is out and, except for the psycho-therapist, a waste of money, the only exception to this rule being that to have someone listen to one's tribulations is not an altogether disagreeable way of spending the time when time, with this particular syndrome, lies heavy on one's hands. Taking

217

all in all,' having proceeded through the gate, 'it may be just as well to let me pass. I take it you haven't read *A New Theory of the Mind* which, in the last two years, has become a best seller, having sold a quarter of a million copies in the United States alone, that land of the ill- or the half-digested, the proceeds of which have been frozen by the bank in lieu of the many creditors who quite outpace my capacity to give it to more worthy causes.'

I am halfway down the road, the taxi-driver and his wife (with child) standing at the gate, the former uncertain – on foot or in his vehicle – whether (promises from Etty) he ought not to follow.

I turn up Hasledean Road.

Hasledean: a former benefactor of the town – one of the four co-founders of the Free Grammar School of Edward VI, a man who, in his time, poked fun at Rayburn, the Free Church preacher who, on a single day, converted five hundred people by offering to walk across the River Lin (above the site of the present weir) and who, being assured by them that he could, desisted on the principle (cf. Christ's mountain-top encounter with the Devil) that a gratuitous indulgence in divine providence was not to their credit. 'Credulity and the English lower orders' Hasledean was alleged to have said, 'are synonymous.' A mill-owner, pre-dating Owens, yet virtually unheard of in his time, he was also alleged to have said, 'If you look after the workers, they'll look after you,' a system he described as 'the reciprocating system of social welfare: what goes up won't go up again unless it first comes down.'

Hasledean: up which I walked each schoolday between the ages of five and ten, occasionally three times, invariably twice on Sundays (morning service, Sunday school, evensong) talking, most of the time, of war: the numbers of Germans and Italians killed, the number taken prisoner, the number of miles advanced (tanks destroyed, planes shot down): the paraphernalia of killing: life extrapolated – (as it turned out) for ever – by what could be done away with (fear, in the form of anxiety, exonerated as social duty: memory, imagination, perception formulated by terror.)

From Hasledean Road into Horsfall Crescent: another co-founder of the Grammar School – plus the Horsfall Hospital (founded 1553 on the road between Linfield and Ardsley – and two fellowships at St Edmund's, still competed for by the pupils of King Edward's, and 'twenty-four quarters of corn yearly for ever to the great town of Linfield' – the houses here, like all those on Onasett, semi-detached, one or two – where the land rises and the air sweeps in unhindered from the Pennine hills – up for sale: if Etty or Matt would release my money, or Bea give me some of hers, I could buy an Onasett home myself, the one, perhaps, in Manor Road. I could even, with hindsight, have brought Vivienne here.

Yet what would a woman who was used to living in Cannes, with an apartment in Manhattan overlooking Central Park, with a home in Beverly Hills (for most of her married lives) have made of living on an industrial housing estate in the industrial north, a place in which she had no roots, neither religious nor artistic nor familial, a sojourner on the jetstreams of this world, from the age of nineteen (her first appearance on the London stage) to her death in a garden shed at the age of fifty-seven? Oh, Vi!

And would Hasledean and Horsfall have recognised their legacy in or on the road and crescent respectively bearing their names: those educators, philanthropists, benefactors whose enterprise saved the sixteenth-century equivalent of the derelict inner cities, those parochial connoisseurs of ignorance, poverty: fear – endowers of Bone (the ecclesiastical scholar), Taplow, the nineteenth-century divine, Foster, the inventor of the 'mechanical jenny' (which revolutionised the manufacture of worsted wool), Freestone and Morton, designers of the 'Free-stone Car', the first 'people's car' in Europe, Simpson, the lexicographer, who institutionalised the teaching of Latin in schools, Stansfield, the scholar, who re-interpreted the Greek Bible, Simmons, 'the poet of the Somme' whose *Letters to Linfield* is still in print, Garside, the cricketer, Monkton, the footballer, Weston, the politician (a pre-war Minister of State), Henderson, the D'Oyly Carte singer, Featherstone, the actor, Hawks, Wentworth and Ripley (producers and directors) and lastly, if not least, Fenchurch, writer, painter, madman (lunatic at large): anxious, humorous, selfish – duplicitous: strong?

I come out of Horsfall Crescent on to Alceston Road (no associations other than a village of that name further up the valley) which, like a backbone, runs along the crest of Ona's headland: geodynamic definition displaces the philanthropic: sandstone, limestone and millstone grit, scoured by river, ice and weather, ameliorated by river, pond and stream (by apathy and despoliation) dissolve into a mist of hill and valley: directly opposite me, behind a six-foot privet hedge (the shrubbery beyond it overgrown) is the brick-built hall of St Michael's church: humouresque in style – lancet (leaded) windows, nail-studded doors, dormer intrusions into its tall, steep-sloping, low-eaved roof – a place of intimacy combined with informal exaltation: scouts, crusaders, Sunday school, youth club: dances, discussions, concerts, shows – its polished parquet floor and blue-curtained stage, its dark-varnished chairs, its domestically-smelling kitchen, its loft where we stored our camp equipment, its posters depicting disabled soldiers, people suffering from loneliness, disease (leprosy and blindness), children, black or yellow, in a variety of clothes. The shrubbery, which shelters the mellow-bricked edifice from the road, is strewn with refuse: paper, plastic cups, cans – a piece of cloth, a tattered shirt: miscellaneous bricks and pieces of stone: the front forks of a bicycle – an itinerary like the contents of a pocket, forgotten, unemptied, ingenuously added to each day. 'Here I have come,' I reflect, 'to do what?' and walk round the hall on a loosely-stoned path to the church.

St Michael's was constructed from a mill: stone by stone and beam by beam, the industrial structure transposed to a terrace dug out of the southern slope of the Onasett headland: a clay-lined, clay-backed, hacked-out trench into which the church was inserted like a ship into a dock: low-roofed, square-structured: its plain glass windows let in an undiluted light.

"His life had been destroyed by a principle (he wrote), though what that principle was he had no idea: from the very beginning to now, as he rounded the corner of the brick-built hall and contemplated the sandstone structure of the church (its mullioned, horizontally-leaded windows more familiar to him than those of any other building on earth) he had been guided by a voice which said, 'For reasons peculiar to your birth you have ascribed to art a significance which is not that which normally exists between an artefact and its creator' (you have taken to yourself, he might have said, a graven image): he had, as the psychologists would now term it, objectified a process, reified his life."

'What's the first thing?' Mackendrick said, 'that you remember?'

I sitting in the celebrated psychologist's consulting room in Belsize Square (the whole house recently purchased from the sales of *The Phenomenology of Experience* (POE, for short), and transformed from separate flats, apartments and bed-sits into a single unit, with Mackendrick's consulting-room and study in the former basement): a view through the recently-installed french windows onto the recently-planted lawn (enclosed on three sides by plants purchased on the final public-viewing day of the previous year's Chelsea Flower Show), overhead the stamping feet of Mackendrick's son (aged three) and his inter-mittent calls (amounting to screams), of 'Selda! Selda!' to the Mackendricks' former East German nanny, the rosy-cheeked, blonde-haired, ample-bottomed Griselda (Mackendrick's wife was also a psychiatrist, but worked away from home).

'My first memory,' Fenchurch said, 'is of being pushed in a pram beneath a bridge.'

My first memory, dear B, is of being pushed in a pram beneath the railway bridge that runs directly out – across Westgate – from Linfield Station:

directly above me are the rusted, corrugated metal sheets which underlie the bridge and across which, at the time, a train is rumbling; water drips from between the metal sheets and falls on the black, gaberdine cover of the pram – one drop, at its source, high overhead, glistening in the light and descending onto the shoulder of my mother's coat.

A second figure walks beside the pram: I merely have the impression of his darkness, of the sobriety of his dress, and of the movement of his arm as he walks adjacent to the handle.

The stain on my mother's coat expands, darkening the reddish fabric as we pass into the light beyond the bridge.

I am bored; I have outgrown the distractions of the field at the back of the house: the world is circumscribed by the garden, the gardens on either side, by the field, by the houses that enclose it. Other roads lead off from our own: they branch out in every direction – to the town, to the park, to the fields (to the golf-course), but, most directly, to the school which, together with a stone-built church and a brick-built hospital, stands at the summit of a hill.

I bore my mother with my summer complaints: 'Go out and play. When you get to school you'll find you haven't the time,' until, when the day arrives, afflicted by apprehension, the portent, merely, of things to come, I become concerned about my bladder. 'Go before you go in. Go,' she says, 'as soon as you come out.'

The torment of not being able to contain himself dominates his other feelings ('You've been asking to go to school for months'), the vacancy of the previous weeks infinitely preferable to the terror which afflicts him now: on the morning that he leaves – clean socks, clean shirt, clean trousers, shoes (clean handkerchief inside his pocket) – five years old and two months exactly – he sets out from the scullery door. At the corner of the road he turns: from the top of the slope he can hear the raucous sound of children's voices.

He goes back to the house, raises the back door sneck and goes inside: his uncle, his father's younger brother, who lives across the field, has come in through the garden. 'Home already?' he says, and laughs.

They have seen him from the scullery window.

'Anything the matter?' his mother enquires.

'Is my cap on straight?' he asks.

'Of course it is,' she says.

She sets it on his head more firmly.

He turns to the door: 'Laugh and be happy!' his uncle says, years later, giving him lifts in his post office van: Bea on his knee in the tiny cab: down to the station or the Ardsley stop.

Re-setting his cap, he sets off once again.

At some point in the day he cries: a Miss Arnold calls him to her desk (his gaze through the window to the stone of the church: its clear-glass windows, its horizontally-leaded lights, its short, square bell-tower like a chimney, the bell visible inside): the confusion of teacherly commands: don't talk, don't stand, don't turn (sit, listen, learn: fold arms). She presses Fenchurch's head against her breast (his first embrace by a woman): there's the smell of chalk-dust and, before he leans against it – before his head is drawn against it – the softness of her breast. 'Against that softness,' he reflects, 'I have been pressing all my life.'

His crying stops and, as far as he recalls, he never cries again.

"The difference between writing a diary," Fenchurch writes in his as he recalls the incidents of his first morning at school, he sitting at his desk in his back-room study in his gigantic house in Belsize Park, "and writing fiction, is that, with the latter (his diary is full of "latters" and "formers", "comparisons between" and "on the other hands") the context within which it exists has to be set down, whereas with the former that element is given (full, too, of incidents witnessed in the street, out-mayhewing Mayhew). The blank page upon which a created world has to be set down is not the blank page upon which the events and the reflections of everyday life can be recorded: the energy as well as the intensity are different; the evocation of a created character within a created context dissipates casualness and even (in me, at least) reflectiveness. I wish it were different (he underlined the last phrase in his mind), that the effortlessness of setting down a thought or feeling, invariably uncorrected, on a page like this could be transposed directly to a novel. It doesn't work (he underlined that, too). It never has, and no amount of effort is going to make it."

"Bea: beatitude," he doodled: "beatific. Beat. Beattie. Beatrice (Beatrix – 'Tricks' – to our children who adopted first the suffix then the nickname at an early age). Mackendrick suggesting today that instead of visiting him in the afternoons at four, when I'm feeling sleepy, I ought to come in at six a.m. When I expressed surprise he informed me it was not unusual for him to see patients at five a.m."

'Who?' I asked.

'A doctor,' he said. 'A civil-servant. A poet who sleeps all day and writes at night. A solicitor. A therapist' (to my surprise).

A portly, genial, black-haired man, dressed in a pin-stripe suit (which I, for one, appreciate immensely), he leans back in his chair (the feet of his demented son across the bare-wood floor overhead: 'Selda! Selda!' the put-upon fascist nanny).

'I thought,' I said, 'you weren't allowed to talk about your clients.'

'What clients?' his hands behind his head: he feels sleepy this time, too, himself.

'Your other clients.'

'I can,' he declares, 'do anything I like.'

"Dear Mrs Fenchurch," I read in a letter Bea received (though no longer living with me at the time), "your husband is seeing another woman. Her name is O'Farrell, though she often goes under her maiden name of O'Connor. Ask him where he was last Wednesday evening. She has been married twice and has four children by three different men."

'Do you think I'm out of my mind?' I ask Maidstone, who has recommended Mackendrick 'as a friend'. 'I often think I'm in it whereas,' I go on, 'to be out of it would be a blessing.'

"Dear Bea, the paint is peeling in the kitchen; mouse-droppings, overnight, appear around the sink. At night there is an owl. I walk in the garden excited by your letter: 'Dear Mrs

Fenchurch (you won't know me but I know you).' Enclosed: someone, it appears, still thinks we're married. (I believe she's referring to Vaughan)."

Bea, Beatrice: Beattie Kells (uses Bella's maiden name in her research).

Must relate to something: Kells, her mother? She is not a PhD for nothing (she is searching at the moment for 'the secret of life'). Her lover, too, is a brilliant man, the parliamentary private secretary to the Minister of Health – divorced and living with a lover who is the picture editor of an international magazine ("such complexity," I wrote, "such singleness of purpose"). Adrian Morley (she calls him by his second name, Albert) is, by any call, a fastidious seducer – in addition to which he has only one arm (a handicap which professionally – certainly politically – has done him a deal of good: he can only write with one hand). His picture-editing lover, too, is something of a charmer: coppery hair, green eyes, a pendulous chin which, not undisagreeably, evokes – misleadingly, I'm told – an air of lasciviousness and languor. B: hair of a lustrous, dark magenta, her colour rich

rich

a northern childhood

her maternal grandfather the one-time syndicalist and latter-day 'democratic communist' H. J. Kells, his *The Locust and the Meaning of Life* being instrumental in the founding not only of his and Bea's careers but of six university embryology departments (three in America, three over here)

overhung, her brows, by that lustrous hair (from beneath which her dark, green-irised eyes gaze out: flecked with brown), the colour, the bloody suffusion of her cheeks

blooming

like the fruit in her father's Ardsley garden (the trees that encroach it on every side).

Her nose is arched: her mother's mother's Sardinian parent, 'the sea,' so she told me, 'in her blood' – evident only, in later

225

years, in the wave-like fervour with which she overlooks her husband's life, smiling

smiling

'no bolts or catches, for instance,' Corcoran tells me, 'on their lavatory door so that, on the occasion of my first visit – when I was courting Bea's mother – *her* mother steps in to clean her teeth, turns on the tap, chatting between scrubs to her daughter's suitor sitting, flushed, on the lavatory seat, caught in the midst of what *my* mother – who was not a primitive woman – was not disinclined to call "my morning ablutions". It's why she and Kells have never got on.'

Mediterranean whore (Bea's mother) mixed with nutty celt (Kells meets Mlle Rievers in Ajaccio, on holiday, in 1912): oriental mixed with occidental: live, dishonest: strong.

"Bea," he wrote about this time, "who has beaten me so badly;

whose pride, after having had five children, has taken a fall;

whose intelligence has been honed by having children;

whose strength has been added to by each mucused streak of bone and gristle deposited on the midwife's table:

Bea: B!"

'Apropos our previous conversation,' Mackendrick says, 'what is revealed in the ideology of confrontation is a shift in the instrumentation of power: behind the nineteenth-century pragmatic idealism is a movement to wrest power from money and invest it in a more expendable commodity: people.'

'People,' I rejoin.

'Note their preoccupation,' he goes on, 'with the "proletariat", a body to be "led", a body "external to the ideology itself" – just as capital is external to the proletariat which, allegedly, it endeavours to exploit.'

'My family name,' he said this morning (not, I might say, at 6 a.m.), his suit uncreased as he lay back in his leather-upholstered chair (how I admire his neatness, a source, to me, of reassurance, providing, as it does, a contrast to my own dishevelment: all the contortions, distortions, dissemblement

226

of the human psyche contained in a pin-striped suit) 'is not Mackendrick.'

'What is it?' (I enquired).

'Butalowski,' (I think he said).

'Butalowski,' (he didn't correct the pronunciation).

'My father came from Russia.'

'When?'

'In 1905.'

'And changed his name.'

'He changed his name,' he confirmed.

'Why did he choose Mackendrick?' I asked.

'He always admired the Scots.'

'In Russia?'

'He was a great admirer of Sir Walter Scott.'

'I thought, in Russia, it was Robbie Burns.'

'This,' he smiled, 'is before the Revolution. He spent his first few years in England in SE 29. After he married he moved to Clapham.'

'What was his christian name?' I enquired.

He smiles again. 'His given name was Yuval.'

'Yuval Mackendrick.'

'He changed that, too, of course to Walter.'

'Apropos Marx,' I said, 'that sounds like the reaction of someone whose family were driven out of their native land and whose father arrived at the London Docks in 1905 and who lived – would it be in West Ham? – before he married.'

'The defensive note in Marx,' he said, 'isn't that of someone defending an ideology against an opponent but that of someone defending a faith against themselves.'

'I, too, have read *Postscript to a Revolution,*' I said.

'In Russian?'

'Paperback.'

Yesterday afternoon he told me that the roots of fascism are to be found in Hegel: the secularisation of the Divine Will: 'It's no coincidence that Stalin and Hitler signed a non-aggression pact in 1939, and the Russians another with the Japanese only a year or two before that.'

Now I ask him, 'What about my wife?'

He is – I am convinced – in love with her himself: after all, we are almost neighbours.

'Bea is making plans to marry Albert if he can get rid of the picture-editing Rose.'

'I thought you weren't divorced,' he says.

'A technicality, in her view, despite our having five children.'

'Your children are all grown up,' he says.

'The youngest,' I tell him, 'is nine.'

'Nine?'

He is about to say, 'Are you sure?' but adds, 'Apart from lovely Rebecca.'

'There is also lovely Benjamin, who is twenty-one, lovely Kenneth, who is twenty-three, lovely Harriet, who is twenty-six, and lovely Mathilda, who is twenty-seven.'

'You can't hang on for ever!' About to laugh, he adds, 'And who is Rose?'

'Rose is Albert's girl-friend, who is six years younger than Albert, and considerably younger than Bea.'

'Rose.' An unself-conscious habit, swivelling in his chair, he slowly picks his teeth: Russian teeth but Clapham-bred.

'Horowitz, neé Schlegel.'

'I don't know the name.' (Cardo, Mackendrick's son, stabs, with his foot, the ceiling overhead).

'Her former husband – Horowitz – is an interior designer.'

'Horowitz.' Listening to Ricardo's voice, he adds,

' "The law protects the ideology of those who have it against the attacks of those who don't and who, possessing no ideology, grow steadily submissive, until, having nothing to define them except their submissiveness, they become," ' his chair comes to a halt, ' "the revolutionary mass themselves." Romanticism, would you say, or faithlessness, or,' avoiding eye contact altogether, 'both?'

The class divides: a few of my (brighter) contemporaries and I, in my second year at Onasett Primary, are joined by others: we enter a room dominated by the tiny Miss Batty: dark hair, dark-eyed, protuberantly featured: on her blackboard are intimidating signs and figures, identified, by her – after a perusal round the class – as mathematical tables: on the top right-hand corner of the blackboard is written the date: a figure in this is changed each morning.

Each morning we inscribe this in our diaries.

Today the sun is out. I ate my dinner,

maturing, years later, into,

'Is Albert very attached?'

'I scarcely know him,' I reply.

'He has been married,' Mackendrick remarks, 'unless I am mistaken, once before.'

'He has,' I reassure him.

'In that case,' Mackendrick observes, 'he's scarcely likely to marry again.'

'Why?' I instantly reply.

'He has two women already (what man,' he is about to add, 'could ask for anything more?' but says), 'The enfranchised proletariat, after all, *are* the bourgeoisie, and where society isn't bourgeois,' he concludes, 'it struggles to become so.'

I am sitting on a slope: a hen has captured my attention: it runs round the back of my mother and, as my father reaches out, the hen runs off. For the first time in my life I stand.

I press my feet against the grass.

I hear my mother's voice call out.

Yet all I am aware of is the thought, 'If I had wished, I could have walked like this before,' and, 'I have walked like this on many previous occasions,' and, like reflections reflected endlessly in opposing mirrors, am conscious of my previous existences stretching out before me.

As, seated in a pew to the rear of the nave, the interior of St Michael's stretches out to the clear-glass, five-lancet window above the altar.

'Surely,' I tell Mackendrick, 'you have removed that from my book,' (*The Logic of Grief*: in reality, a pamphlet – of lectures given at the ICA at the height of my notoriety: "the working classes are the bourgeoisie bereft of their possessions").

It was this pamphlet that brought us together, Mackendrick alluding to it in his introduction to *The Phenomenology of Experience* as well as – and more generously – if equally plagiaristically (Mackendrick is a great synthesiser or, what is referred to benignly as a 'great anthologiser' of other people's work, invariably – after token acknowledgement – subsumed under his own name) – to *A New Theory of the Mind*. In LOG, as it became known, I divide experience into actuality – our awareness of what is happening now – and reality, which includes actuality, but also everything beyond it: actuality is Mackendrick seeing me and me seeing him in his subterranean study in Belsize Park (with intermittent incursions from Cardo and Griselda overhead), and reality, including that, is what is happening in the rest of the house, in all the houses, in all the streets, in the universe as a whole, to the outermost reaches of time, not excluding its potential to go on for ever. Mackendrick's book, not unindebted to my contributions, has become a cult (hence the house) and has been followed by a sequel, *Six Studies in Dementia* which, in the words of one notable reviewer, 'has given psychiatry not so much a new as a novel life', its colloquial style and subsequent accessibility, offensive only to clinicians, contributing in no small degree to the impression created in the mind of the reader that he or she is irretrievably insane.

I dream; I dream quite often in Mackendrick's chair, never sure whether, as was the original case, he was consulting me or I am consulting him: 'Come along and listen to my tapes,' he suggested after the second of our meetings (sure of me at last). 'They're so much like the plays you've written,' tapes which turned out to be of his patients talking of their wives, their husbands, their children, their friends (their mothers, their fathers, themselves). 'What strikes you most?' he genially enquired. And when I said, 'Their exclusivity,' he said, 'Precisely. No one, they are convinced, has suffered like themselves. The subject of comedy, don't you think, as in so much of what you've written.'

"I am lost: I dream of people I have not seen for thirty years:

a teacher at school who taught us tables; a boy I feared; another I admired; a neighbour who died and who had only lived for a year in the house next door. I live," I go on, "in a delirium of terror. I wake: I perspire: my eyes frighten me with what they throw back each day in the mirror. I pray, 'Our Father,' followed by the one injunction, 'Help!' "

Fenchurch, prefixed Richard, regarding, in church, the back of the knees of the boy in front, the profile of his head silhouetted against the southerly-orientated clear-glass (five-lancet) window above the altar: the Crusaders' banners, each with its emblem, at the end of the pews (boys on one side, girls on the other): the Marys and Matthews, the Hildas and Johns: the peculiar scales on St Peter's fish, painted in a luminous silver: 'Give us this day our daily . . .'

"Classes in society are only superficially identified by wealth and possessions: what identifies them more profoundly is expectancy: what each class holds itself in anticipation of – a mental or even spiritual condition which identifies different cadres in society in relationship to what each cadre anticipates drawing to itself. A 'classless' society segregates itself into layers of expectancy each of which, in turn, becomes identified as a class itself." (LOG).

Between my praying hands, Allcock, the vicar, his cassock corded like a monk's, tassels hanging from his waist. Our Father: (the yorkstone paving of the aisle, the columns of sandstone: octagonal shape) walnut pews: hassocks, green on one side, blue on the other: church of St Michael (angel of light).

On the way home (my parents in bed) the buttered-once-a-week-only bread.

'Why Maidstone said he'd found a therapist,' I tell the boy in front, 'who might unearth a hitherto unknown source of anxiety, I've no idea. "I sent a poet to him some years ago," he said, "and though he committed suicide two years later I thought Mackendrick's insights at the time remarkable. He's somewhat softened that existentialist-phenomenologist approach and, in my view, is very much open to new ideas. I've

231

written him a letter. Not mentioning you by name, of course, but enquiring if he'd take on a case not dissimilar to that of the poet. His suicide, by the way, as Mackendrick pointed out, was due to him not keeping to the treatment. He was found hanging from a beam in a lodging house in Kilburn. At the age, I might add, of twenty-one. His poetry had a Dantesque intensity. A remarkable fellow. Mackendrick, I mean. The poet, I guess you could say, was promising." '

'I thought I'd find you here.'

Etty is sitting across the aisle: cheeks glowing, eyes bright, wrapped against the weather (a headscarf disarranged, or perhaps hastily put on): she has taken a look at my sodden clothes, at my sockless feet (my mud-stained slippers) and, with a gesture of indifference, sinks further back in the walnut pew.

'I've been all over,' she adds.

'I don't see why.'

She is gazing at the altar, her profile alone sufficient to convey the gravity (depth, range, complexity) of her feelings.

'When you disappeared from the garden I searched the grounds. I searched the village. Your shoes,' she goes on, 'were in the hall. I didn't think you could have gone far. Then I met someone in one of the shops who recalled seeing you waiting at the Linfield stop. I got in the car and searched the town. Then I thought of Onasett. I called at the house where I thought you'd lived. The woman there must have thought I was mad. Nevertheless, I gave her my number and asked her to call me should you turn up.' Tears glisten in her eye. 'You're worse,' she concludes, 'than one of the children.'

'It wasn't a good idea,' I tell her, 'bringing me up. I'll only be the burden to you that I was to your mother. She, if you recall, absented herself. Her instinct, Etty, is one you ought to follow. Just look at it,' I add, and gesture at the pillars: to each is attached a placard: 'Love,' reads one, 'is what unites.' 'They've even taken down the donated copy of Rubens' "Descent from the Cross" and put it against a window, blocking the light and, because it's silhouetted, obscuring the picture. Can any goodness be left when art is in decline? In the old days, shields, symbolising the saints, of either sex, were hung in profusion at the end of the pews. I was in St Matthew's which had, appropriately, a picture of a book . . .'

She has blown her nose: she wipes her eyes: the coldness of the interior – conceivably, the intensity of her feelings – causes her to tremble.

'Considering my career, something portentous in that, don't you think,' and when she doesn't answer, I add, 'Although, at times, I'm not altogether certain where I am, or what I'm doing – or what, for instance, I set out to do – or whether I'm talking or thinking aloud – I am quite capable, Etty, of looking after myself. At least . . .'

She isn't listening: footsteps echo inside the door from which, in earlier days, the choir and the clergy would emerge: a man in shirt sleeves appears, carrying a bucket.

He turns, aware of our presence and, having lowered the bucket, retrieves it and returns inside the door.

'I came here,' I tell her, 'to confess,' and add, 'I don't suppose it'll do much good.'

'I've got the car outside,' she says. 'Do you want me to wait, or are you coming out? I have to get back as soon as I can.'

'I rather wanted,' I tell her, 'a moment to myself,' at which, blowing her nose again, she rises. 'There's no need,' I go on, 'to take me back. If you give me the bus fare I'll be all right. I gave what I had to that woman at the house. The place, though it's where I used to live, is little more than a rabbit hutch.'

'Perhaps,' she says, 'it was before,' startled by my reaction.

'It saddened me,' I say, 'no end. Or would have done. I've got past being saddened by anything,' and add, 'I gave her the money because I don't believe her husband, once he's paid for the car – he rents it from a man in town – makes enough to live on.'

'I'll wait outside,' she says, and adds, 'I'd like to leave as soon as we can.'

'I wanted to look in the classroom windows. Miss Arnold's and Miss Batty's,' I tell her. 'The one considerate, the other alarming. One three is three. One four is four. Evil is the seat of goodness.'

'Will you be long?'

'Not at all.'

She is, moments later, I am aware, watching me through the glass panes of the door which opens to the porch. She is afraid I might get up and leave by the vestry.

The (blue underpainted) body of Christ, strung, pale, a long, descending diagonal from the arms of the man who has drawn out the nails (standing on a ladder) to those of the women who, weeping, kneel by his feet: I saw such looks in Boady Hall and in my outpatient days at the North London Royal: 'I am sorry and ashamed of my love for Isabella. And yet, dear Lord, I love her now. I disavow . . .' the blue underpainting of the flesh, the rattle of the bucket (the greenness of the paint where the flesh has putrefied): the fleck of red around each hole, ravaged at the edges: the pair of pincers in the workman's hand, the upraised fingers of the praying mother, the half-closed eyes shadowed from a light which, glowing on the face, inspires the question, 'Is he still alive?' ' . . . nothing!'

'Your stratagem,' I tell her, when I get outside, 'was to leave me in there, knowing I had nowhere else to go and would therefore be all the more obliged to come out and join you,' while, inside, before I'd left, I'd perused, from a distance, the T-shaped cross, the centre piece of a triptych, on the wings of which, fore and aft, were depicted four scenes from the lives of the saints (Mark, Luke, Matthew, John) which might well have been appended to those witnessed, daily, in Boady Hall, where 'The Prince of Peace' and 'The King of Love' mingled in the dining-hall, the art therapy room, the corridors, offices and wards (though not the padded cells: much reported on but non-existent) with Napoleon, the Primal Visitor from Space, the Martian Dayman and the Man Who Came From Nowhere.

She is sitting on the wall across the stone-flagged terrace, drawing my attention to the view (south, across the valley, to Ardsley: hedged fields and copses, the silver-lit surface of the winding river: the pitless village of Harlstone, a serrated ridge

234

of silhouetted houses), I gesturing, however, to the low, one-storeyed school visible, across a lane, in the opposite direction (to the north).

'I need to take you back,' she says ('Where are your socks? Look at your slippers!') yet takes my arm (her thoughts, I reflect, on something else) allowing me to escort her up the ramp to the narrow lane which divides the school playground from the church itself.

'That's the first classroom I was in.' I indicate the square-paned window yet, having arrived there, don't glance in. She, for her part, releases my arm, cups her hands and gazes inside.

'I suppose it's not much changed,' she says, and when I reply, 'I can't remember,' adds, 'One classroom, I imagine, is much like another,' a score of tiny heads and one adult one turned in our direction. 'In any case,' she concludes, 'they're coming out.'

'We should have a look at the crypt,' I tell her. 'It's where I attended scouts, Sunday school and the youth club and, in my sixteenth year, painted my "Crucifixion", one which, when exhibited, was described in the *Linfield Express* as "a modernist view of Christ". I painted him surrounded, not by people, but robots,' directing her, her hand, this time, on mine, the way we have come, voices already behind our back.

Something not so much about my voice, nor my manner, but my appearance has alarmed her: 'We'll have to be going. Glenda and Lottie will be home from school. You've led us,' she tells me, 'far enough.'

'The crypt,' I tell her. 'The parquet floor, the row of windows looking out to the valley (the Pennine hills, the sweep of the river, the marching column of smoke that indicates a train hauling its way to or from the Pennine gorge).'

'I shall be *quite* glad to get home,' Vivienne said, pale-faced (stuffed with drugs from a recent stay at a clinic in Blackheath), slouched, her head thrust back, in front of the imitation coal-fire (gas flames flickering around synthetic – unburnable – fuel) in our Taravara Road back kitchen. 'I've been feeling, at last, there's a place to go back to,' her bare feet protruding beneath her winceyette nightie, her hands, short-fingered, clasped around a pot of undrunk tea. 'I don't know what I'm doing here. I don't even know where I am. It can't be in a back street in London. Isn't it true' (a glance to me for the first time since she'd got up that morning) 'I'm dragging you down? Isn't it true we're no good for one another? Your pre-occupation is with your dreadful wife and her dreadful mother and all your children who hate the sight of me, and mine,' she concluded, 'is still with Mel, a bigger shit than all of them.'

Her bloodless lips, her acned skin ('never cleared up from childhood, dear: one reason, of course, I'm not a *star*'), her bitten-down nails, her vacuous look, her tousled hair – thick-textured, curled ('my hair and my legs – though not above the knee – were considered my best features, pal!').

'She is, to my mind, the greatest actress of her generation,' Maidstone said after I had brought her to see him (the window-less room at the North London Royal). What a tragedy, he might have said, to see her in the state she's in at present. 'I'm sure we might do something for her,' he declared but, although he tried, no improvement was discernible to anyone. 'Her problems are intractable,' he announced after – at the end of six months (without any warning) – she took herself off on holiday. 'Has she,' he asked me, 'gone for good?'

'Those awful diets,' I told her (those awful drives she took alone): 'Nowhere is everywhere,' she said, 'when you're looking for somewhere,' and when I told her she had read that in my pamphlet (LOG), she said, 'I knew that a long time, Richard, before you wrote it. Anywhere is better than nowhere. That's why I drive the freeways. Going from nowhere to nowhere has anywhere between.'

'What?' Etty enquires for, assured we are not to be pursued, I have turned once more in the direction of the school, walking parallel to it, along the lane – marking off, as I do so, the classrooms: 'Miss Schofield's, Miss Setchell's – a teacher in that one whose name I don't recall. I learnt my first poem, by Wordsworth, in that room: such simplicity and directness evoking such complexity of feeling. There never was a writer who came so nakedly to the point. And all before his thirtieth

236

year. After his marriage it turned to dross,' recalling how – was it earlier that day? – I had watched my pen making marks on a sheet of paper – scrawls of ink comprised of lines and whirls – an intermittent dash or dot – as might a machine perform a task – the dark excrescence, a residue of vegetable matter, a coagulation – and wonder: where am I – not Fenchurch, prefixed Richard – but the nameless part of me that searches the San Bernardino and/or the Hollywood Freeway (at the same time as it does so calling out a name, 'Vi!'): what is the 'one' that the 'self' is true to? (what is the 'one' that is lost at birth?).

"Dear Mackendrick, the notion that all experience has a particular locale (and its own dynamic) – 'intrinsic referral', you describe it (another lift from me) – begs the question when you go on to assert that, vis à vis the world in general – 'society', loyalties, and the like – 'intolerable consequences' occur if such experience is ignored, a 'malfeasance', you describe it, of the spirit (yet another lift from me: have you ever had such an uncomplaining plagiaree?): the 'degenerative imperative' (ibid) which envelops – in my view (if unacknowledged by you) – the whole of our life and finally destroys it. My immediate wish to go along with this is dissipated by my inevitable enquiry: what about Ricardo? Shouldn't his *mother* be looking after her son?"

'Over here, where the playing-field forms a small enclosure, surrounded by hawthorn hedge, and the ground, here and there, has uneven swellings, stood a searchlight and anti-aircraft gun emplacement during the war: here, adjoining the school gate, stood a guard-house where the soldiers, at playtime, would pass sweets across the fence: there was one called Lofty who was the butt of the other men: they would get him to dance, drill him with his rifle, get him, even though unloaded, to fire it. Once they lit a newspaper he was reading while sitting at the guard-house door and, using the occasion as a pretext, tipped a bucket of water over his head. It gave to the war a feeling of lightness, the guns, when they fired at night, like giant dustbin lids clanging at the top of the estate, and then, the next day, all clean and shiny, the barrels gleaming, the searchlights like dwarfs hunched up on the ground, and we over here, reciting our poems, endeavouring, in my last year, to link, with a horizontal line, the individual letters in each word (the excrescence of ink – a watery blue mixed from a dark blue powder – which years later I came to recognise as less a vegetable or mineral dye than the matter of the mind itself).'

The novel is dead; at least, in its humanist tradition – and I have died with it. I wouldn't wish to argue: my relationships, the few I have managed to sustain, have all but foundered: I maintain, as Vi described it, the residual passions of the morgue. If someone loves me, as I thought she did (though not as obsessively as Mel), I offer them a helping hand: I love – again, as Vi put it – the poor fuckers in return: an engagement which, in my mind at least, evokes the image of a muddy pool: observations on its nature elicit such remarks as, 'It's opaque. It's dark. It appears to contain no life at all.' Yet, as with most dark pools, a great deal goes on beneath the surface: what the surface reflects the depths conceal. Similarly, what the depressive experiences, by second nature – as freshly and as directly as he sleeps and breathes – is the energised negativity which convinces him he doesn't exist in any of the ways accredited to a normal human being: absence, rather than a passive, is an active definition, and 'self' a misnomer for all he experiences as 'self': he is, in short, dehumanised: he doesn't exist: he experiences his non-existence as active.

"Dear Maidstone, is the reality, that the depressive is allegedly out of touch with, reality at all, or merely the bourgeois world of good intentions (providence: doing the best you can)? Hell, presumably, is as real as heaven, if not a great deal more closely related to everyday life. The reality which 'the greatest poet of the twentieth century' has suggested we can only partake of in very small doses is scarcely the reality to which the psychiatrist would wish us to return – whether by pills, psychotherapy, E.C.T., physical exercise or a change of diet. It might, alternatively, be argued that health for the insane, and for the psychiatrist (therapist, analyst) consists merely of the restoration of that thick skin of which the illness has apparently deprived the luckless patient.

In other words, is Eliot's 'reality' a misanthropic fiction?

Or is it the baseline to which no one in their right senses would wish to return? To be capable of relating positively to people (my constant endeavour) might, in this sense, be as shallow an interpretation of reality as Eliot's perception of it was, allegedly, profound."

'Do you,' Etty enquires, 'often talk aloud, irrespective of where you are or who you're with?' and when I reply, 'Each day and each night I go through extremes of emotion which, even after all these years, I find impossible to describe – a sense of loss, for instance, in which the words "sense" and "loss" are inadequate to convey the degree of awareness, in the first instance and the degree of absence, in the second,' she hastily responds, 'It's a good job I brought you up when I did. Leaving you alone in Taravara Road has done you, as Maidstone suggested, no good at all.'

'I was happy in Taravara Road,' I tell her, glancing not at the school, nor any longer at the playing-field – stretching beyond farm fields to the isolation hospital above – but at the church. 'As happy as I was, for instance, sitting in the crypt, in an afternoon daze, the sunlight streaming through the windows, imagining the tribulations and the ecstasies of the saints, men and women caught up in a vision to which,' I concluded, 'I intended to belong,' to which, not listening, she replies, 'You were living in squalor. The place was filthy. You hadn't washed up in months.'

'What's washing-up,' I ask her, 'when you're coming alive? When I was dead,' I went on, 'I was always clean. Despite all I appear to have done in my life, I have, in reality,' I go on, 'done nothing. Nothing at all,' I conclude, 'until now.'

'Have you done any sketches?' she enquires, glancing at the book beneath my arm (glad, at least, I suspect, that I've retained it).

'A tree at Ardsley, a view of Onasett – from the golf-course, one of a hundred, I should think, of that – another of the

239

houses at the back of Manor Road.' I add, 'The characteristics of dementia are not to be taken as peculiar to the sufferer but merely to the illness. Characteristics which the sufferer him or herself would like to do away with.'

'The car,' she says, 'is over here,' for, even while she grasps my arm, I have led her back across the lane and re-entered the yard at the back of the church and although, plainly enough, her car is there – parked, I observe, with the engine running ('I have difficulty starting it,' she tells me later) – I am leading her to the slope at the side of the church and indicating the square, metal-framed windows which offer a view of the parquet floor of the crypt.

'On that floor we played our games, learned our knots, communed with nature, learned first-aid, chanted our oaths, swore our allegiance (dedicated our lives,' I conclude, 'to God),' but, having scarcely glanced in at the room – a fraction of the size of the one I recall – she leads me back up the grassy slope. 'We constructed an overhead railway here, each year, when they held the church bazaar and made more money than the Men's Fellowship, or the Women's Meeting, or,' I tell her, 'both combined.'

'You're getting more childish by the hour,' she says. 'Leaving you in Taravara Road was a foolish step. My mother shouldn't have considered it.'

'Your mother,' I tell her, 'is happy with Albert. And I,' I go on, 'am happy for her. I did her a disservice. One,' I continue, 'I can never repay. (The biggest mistake of my life),' to which she responds, 'In which case, Father, I wouldn't be here. Neither would Matt, nor Ken, nor Benjie, nor Bec.'

'You were all,' I tell her, 'deeply loved,' and, moments later, 'You'll be getting your car stolen, leaving it unattended with the engine running. An open invitation. You can assume, in effect, it's been stolen already. I suppose you've brought no money with you. In which case, we'll be stranded, stuck up here with no means of getting back. I can't walk,' I add, 'much further in my slippers. "The wise man lives in the house of mourning," wrote Solomon. The most important book, I might add, in the Bible (the book to end all books, etc.). Talk about the death of the novel: not another word, I might tell you, was needed after that. Whereas I have followed that advice by instinct, not by choice. "The house of mourning," I told Maidstone, "has been, and still is, my natural abode." '

'Perhaps,' I go on, 'we should have gone down and that man with the bucket might have allowed us to look in the crypt. I know every knot-hole in that wood. The surface of a piece of polished wood is almost as evocative to me as a woman's skin. Did I tell you when *Philistines* was revived in New York one of the actors in the company bought me, as a present, a session with a Hollywood astrologist? I sat for an hour in a borrowed apartment in Greenwich village, just off Washington Square, and, having previously given her the three facts of time, place and date of birth, I listened to an account of my life as accurate as I might have given if I'd had three or four years to set it down.'

I am sitting in the car: how I have got there I have no idea (I don't recall climbing in or closing the door – an elision that characterises much if not most of my present life), the car turning out of the lane that divides the church from the school and into Alceston Road.

'I might come back to that again, the conjunction of Pluto with the sun at the time of my birth: the god of the underworld (the dead and the dying): a peculiar coincidence when you consider that, during her pregnancy, death dominated my mother's life and left its imprint on me for ever (her first child dying, at the age of six, six months before I was born – after a sojourn, I might add, in that isolation hospital at the top of the road). God of the underworld as well as the afterworld, this woman described it: a colourful character with a flowery gown and streaming blonde hair and a lascivious way of saying, "Sweetheart" as she extrapolated from a column of figures – her only points of reference – a psychoramic account of my previous life, down to specific incidents to do with Bea, your Grandma, and even Vi. None of them specifically named, of course. "Being born," she announced, "under the influence

241

of Pluto endows you with the ability to see in the dark. It gives you," she concluded, "the qualities of a shrink." "To probe the unconscious," I told her, "has always been my line. To go where no man (or woman) has been before, or from where, at least, if they have, they have never returned. Only me," I told her, "me alone." (Sole denizen of a world only I can know).'

'Isn't that what astrology is for?' she says, and I recall she has, in fact – before we set out from Taravara Road – listened to the tape (the murmur of traffic from Fifth Avenue, a police siren, the barking of a dog, the slamming of a door announcing the presence of someone else – unintroduced – in the flat).

'I live my life,' I tell her, 'like Penelope with her knitting. It's the way,' I continue, 'I've always worked,' aware, in the warmth of the car, how cold I am – how mania takes a grip without my being aware.

As for the death of the novel – a printer's error: a missing 'r' from the word in question.

A drunken poet in a London street, raising his hand as he sees me pass: 'Hello, there, famous author! Would you lend me a quid?' his less drunken companion (definitely not a poet) calling, 'A fiver would be better!'

Leading to (his last years with Vi) the sequestration of his funds by the more responsible members of his family:

'He gave it to people in the street,' (Etty).

'How much?' the Judge at the enquiry enquired.

'Five hundred pounds in a single day. (Probably more on occasions we never heard about).'

' "The degenerative imperative",' had been the defendant's only reply (by which time, for much of his time, a privileged internee at Boady Hall).

'It's not the disappearing,' she says, 'nor the aggravation you cause to me and Charlie, nor the inconvenience of dropping whatever I have to do to come and find you, as what you might do if one of us who doesn't know you isn't around. That woman at your former home, if I hadn't have been there previously, would have called the police. She must have thought, as it happened, I was mad myself. "If my father shows up," I said, "will you ring me?" as if I were giving instructions about a missing dog.'

' "Madness" has "sane" in it somewhere,' I tell her. 'In my first group therapy at Boady Hall we played, would you believe it, "Twenty Questions", the most extraordinary version of the game you've ever seen. I'd gone, prepared, as per instructions, with an analysis of my state of mind – causes, symptoms, prognosis, et cetera – a mental index with referential points, together with accessible accounts of alternative interpretations – breaking into tears, at one point, as a demonstration of my willingness to involve others. The therapist, however – too young, unfortunately, to know blood from stone – said, the moment we were settled – telling me, incidentally, to blow my nose: "We don't want cry-babies here," she told me – announced, "The first object is mineral with a vegetable attachment," and when someone said, "What is a mineral?" – no great intellectuals on the panel, I have to add – only Isaiah and the Virgin Mary – someone replied, "You buy it in a bottle," and a third young woman announced – who was there after seven attempts at suicide, "I can get three hundred words out of madness, and one of them is sane."

' "That's good," said the therapist, totally confused.'

No one rang me in Taravara Road, other than my children, Liam (once), with whom I immediately quarrelled, and Bea twice ('How are you?' she asked, and added, 'That's good,' without waiting for an answer) in all of six months.

I have never told anyone how I feel without regretting it. ('Why don't you shut your mouth?' I say each day to myself in the mirror.)

'Would you like Bryan to come and look at you?' she says.

'Who?'

'Raynor.'

'I can't see that he'll see much that he hasn't seen already,' I tell her, the Park appearing to our right, Onasett disappearing to our left. 'What did you mean, the other day,' I suddenly enquire, 'when you said, "You are going to die"? It sent a chill right through me.'

'I thought you weren't afraid of death,' she says.

'Curiously,' I say, 'since Vivienne went, I am. Terrified,' and add, 'Was it something that Raynor said?'

'It was,' she says, 'my own conclusion. If you hadn't riled me I would have added, "if you go on as you are." '

Strung up on the x-ray table with a barium enema plugged up my arse while, to help the under-assisted operator, I examine my intestines on the monitor screen and adjust the reflecting plate to his instructions. 'Are you *the* Richard Fenchurch?' one of the group of trainee technicians enquires (boots, jeans and sandals visible beneath their smocks, acned, suppurating fore-heads, cheeks and chins) to which I reply (a definitive), 'No.'

'Has Maidstone said I'm about to expire?' gazing at the profile of the town, directly ahead, from the bottom of Westgate as I enquire.

'I only know what Bryan tells me. I haven't seen your notes,' she says.

'He's afraid I'll go the same way as Vi.'

'That's not what he says at all,' she says.

'I should have been warned. I did my best. All Vivienne wanted was an audience.'

Turning the car towards the centre of the town, she says, 'That's not what you said at the time.'

'I admired her. I admire her still. There were times, sitting there, her feet together, gazing out of the window at the tiny yard, that I thought she'd achieved something little short of sainthood. All she'd been through, her body, as she described it, "gone", her looks ravaged, her hands shaking and, involun-tarily, just watching her, I wept. I've never seen anyone look so . . . blessed. I never guessed. I thought she'd have an easier passage. Easier than the one she chose. And yet, would you believe it? I have to forgive her. It's why,' I suddenly conclude, 'she won't succeed.'

'In what?' We have reached the centre of the town and she turns down, past the cathedral, towards the river.

'In taking me with her.'

As if detached from her as well as I, the car careers along a one-way system: down the Springs, around the market, past a newly covered-in section: the cathedral about to be enclosed by a pedestrian precinct.

'I've brought you back,' she says, 'to get you better. When you are,' she adds, 'you can go back to Taravara Road,' and then, bleakly, 'I hate to see you in that place. Those streets and that house are not for you. All those brutalised faces. Every other one you meet, brutalised or brutalising.'

'Those,' I tell her, 'are the working class.'

'So,' she says, 'are the inhabitants of Ardsley. Yet their faces have dignity, tolerance, strength. Not the mangled features of the London cockney.'

'Why don't we talk,' I suggest, 'of something else. My head,' I tell her, 'has begun to spin.'

'Those characterless eyes, that pasty complexion, those thin-lipped mouths, the scrawny necks, that bow-legged walk that comes, I suppose,' she says, 'from rickets.'

Whereas it is true I have seen more domestic violence in the street than I have throughout the rest of my life, it is still a place where, if only for the briefest time, Vivienne and I were happy.

We cross the river, beyond it, moments later, a hump-backed bridge, the canal visible below us: past the street where one of my father's uncles lived, a colliery sinker with an invalid wife: an only son who was killed on the Somme: 'a street that hides its dead,' my father declared, once, as I sat with him, passing on a bus, adding, as if of something he admired, 'a man who never showed his feeling.'

'So what became of it?' I said.

'Like all feeling, shown or not shown,' he said, a bleakness in his life which, if rarely glimpsed, I always knew was there.

'Why don't you stay up here? You can,' she tells me, 'write and paint,' and when I reply, 'There was a time when I envisaged doing that, painting amongst the fields around Linfield,' she suddenly calls out, 'You're not old enough to give up!' as if, directly ahead, a door has opened. 'Even if you're out of fashion.'

'It's certainly,' I tell her, 'a philistine age, and we can only assume,' I go on, 'it has to get worse,' pausing, startled, at her laughter.

'A joke at last,' she simply says.

16

In his mind's eye his wife and, with his wife, now someone else's, her mother, the coppery gold of their two heads, darkening to magenta, like the heads of two gigantic nails pinioning the palms of the crucified Christ: the green-tinted eye of Isabella: the grey-tinted eye of H. J. Kells, leaping, lithe, from his celtic ocean: 'I wouldn't say I was a marxist,' he says to Fenchurch when, in old age, the locust specialist spends his summer days filling in football pools on the lawn, in the sun, at the front of The People's Palace. 'I'd say, more nearly, I was marx*ian*,' putting down his crosses.

'What would you spend the money on?' I ask. 'Should you win.'

'People,' was all he simply replies, and adds – wisps of unshaven hair around his chin – 'Wouldn't you say,' he watches his daughter pruning roses across the lawn, 'that art, unless it expresses the will of the people, is a waste of time?'

'What is the will of the people?' I enquire.

'Why,' he says, 'you must have noticed, even at a football match, that the crowd is greater than that which congregates for an exhibition of your paintings, or even of the latest prodigal talent on show, shall we say, at the Linfield College of Art.'

'They generate different interests,' I observe, remarking the angle of Isabella's back, her waist, the protrusion of her hips (the position of more intimate features within the suspended folds of her blouse), the placing of one foot before the hem of her skirt which subtly reveals the shape of her calf.

247

'Other than by numbers, which always count,' (chuckles at the joke himself), 'who is to judge whether a popular entertainment is inferior or superior to the interests of an esoteric cult?'

His teeth are brown (if artificial) and his jacket, which he always wears, stained by the food he, at each meal, invariably drops down it: from the third button of his waistcoat to its top left-hand pocket (the folds of the garment, when he sits, enclosing his shrivelled chest) stretch the thin gold links of a watch chain, the watch itself rarely, if ever, lifted out – and wound, curiously, while still inside his pocket, his forefinger and thumb disappearing for minutes at a time.

'Otherwise,' he goes on, 'we are merely left with contempt for the popular judgement. The mass, despite what Shakespeare says, is never, and never has been wrong, particularly,' he concludes, 'when its deepest feelings are aroused.'

'Is this senility,' I ask Isabella, 'or mischief?' when, moments later, disengaging myself from the old man – his long, thin thigh flung, with a booted foot, across the other as he studies the list of football teams again – I cross the lawn, and she – who, her back to us, has listened, I discover, with a smile – smiles again and says, 'The product of experience, Richard. He has lived, after all, a very long time.'

Does he, I reflect, know more about us than, say, Isabella's husband or her daughter: does he suspect, with a father's lifetime's perception of his daughter, that the relationship between us is more than appears at first sight; or, *is* what appears at first sight?

'More means better.'

'Better means most.'

'Where does that leave us?' while she, glancing at her father – a pair of glasses, wire-framed, suspended halfway down his nose – declares, 'I found roses, would you believe it, in the wood?' adding, 'I'm showing Richard the roses, Father,' taking my hand, about the wrist – as she might, in school, encourage a pupil.

'I'm afraid I've told him,' she says, 'about us,' and adds, 'He's quite indifferent,' and when, amongst the trees, I ask

248

her, 'Why?' she laughs and, having released my hand, declares, 'Haven't you been in love and wanted to tell someone all about it?'

'I have,' I say, 'but not him.'

'It's quite all right,' she says (the heavy laugh – guttural – like, or so I'm told, her mother's: the high colour of the cheeks, the incandescence of her eye). 'He was quite pleased,' she goes on, 'to hear it. He was always unprincipled,' she adds, 'with my mother. Or, at least, communality was his principle and my mother, with her background, half-believed it. His interest in people, in any case,' she continues, 'transcends any he has in individuals. He sees life, after all, as a generic whole. Hence the pools: it's the figures, Richard, not the money. The greatest mystery of all,' and, with something of Kells' own expression – but more greatly, I suspect, that of her mother's, whispers, half-smiling, '*chance*!'

Later, returning to the lawn, Kells studies me above his glasses. 'Art,' he says, 'in the way you practise it, is a philosophy of despair, the legacy of an already, in most respects, discarded past. If, in your judgement, you are against the people, you can't be for them. If you can't be for them, you are condemned to a life of isolation. Man is a social animal and if, in society, you are alone, you can't and never will be happy. And,' he laughs, 'are we here to be miserable, do you think?'

'Who is this homo serioso?' he would enquire when, appearing on the lawn, ostensibly to call on Bea, I would cross to where he and, not infrequently, his daughter were sitting. 'Your homo serioso, Bella, is here again! Are you to take him for a walk in the wood?' adding, on one occasion – for when, so prompted, we seldom followed his suggestion, 'Two innocents at large.'

'Wouldn't you say,' he asked me on another occasion, 'that my daughter, your would-be-mother-in-law, is very naive?' adding, 'So was her mother. She gets it from her. So was I, in an underhand way: danced rings round by the anglo-saxonic scientific élite – until, that is, I set my marxian cat amongst the pigeons. A good cat is that, related to the Manx but far more

249

clever – and not only for its transformation, at a stroke, by a single letter.'

'A marxian,' I told him, 'without a cause.'

'Not at all. I did it to confound the English, and much more effectively than those apeists from the public schools who were always confounded by their education.'

'Do you,' he said on a further occasion, leaning forward from his chair (as if to examine something close to his feet) 'make love to both mother *and* daughter?' waiting, head stooped (inspecting the grass) until, assured I would not, perhaps could not offer a reply, he raised his lean-jawed head and laughed – his brown teeth loosened from his gums – gazing at the sky.

Rooks, I recall, rose slowly from the trees: they had – disturbing as it was – heard, I assumed, the sound before.

'He wouldn't tell Freddie, or, indeed, anyone,' Isabella said when, on going into the house, I told her of this conversation. When I enquired, 'Why not?' she said, 'It's not important, though, as a scientist, he sees its relevance to other people. He was always discreet with his indiscretions. This, at least, he feels he owes me.'

'For what?' I asked.

'For all he did to my mother and which she, through her good-nature, forgave. "I made your mother unhappy," he said just after she died. "I shall never – I feel it a bounden duty – do the same to you." Why,' she suddenly went on, 'I can tell my father everything. Everything!' adding, with something of his slyness – the sideways look of the long-lashed eyes, 'But, of course, my dear, I don't have the obligation to tell him anything.'

He feared the old man: he feared what he knew: he feared his life of principle (communality, detachment: amoral): 'You do right,' he told him, 'to fear the Irish,' – the long-angled jaw, the far-from-supplicating eye turned, over the top of the wire-framed glasses ('the glasses that have seen everything!' Bea) in his direction, 'the apostate Irish,' he added as homo serioso approached.

Ah, serious man!

'I wish,' Isabella said, 'you had met my mother,' (one autumn day in the kitchen, waiting for Bea, swotting, in her bedroom overhead). From the mantelshelf above the kitchen range she took down a sepia photograph: a woman sitting sideways, on a bench, her dress short-sleeved, her long, bare arms extended to her knee (her fingers clasped together), a compassionate, warm-hearted, broad-featured face, dark-eyed, broad-lipped. 'Father always called her "Gypsy" ': slim calves, feet, delicately poised in high-heeled shoes, demurely held together. ' "Gave nothing away but love," he said.'

In my head, the Sardinian wife: 'Isabella's mother's background was the bordello,' Kells once said – leaning back, head raised, to laugh (scattering the rooks again in the trees). 'You know what a bordello is, I take it?'

He went into hospital, after I and Bea had moved to London, with a broken hip, caught pneumonia and, with 'Cleo' (a more intimate name for 'Gypsy') on his lips, he died: 'Love personalised, after all,' I said, fearing, for the first time, no rejoinder.

'I never missed anyone,' Isabella said, 'as much as I miss him. Not even you.'

He was tired: he couldn't sleep (the noises of the house, once familiar: no longer so): he had come across the subject in a book of Bea's, propping up the missing castor of their double bed (looking out to their Belsize Park garden) shortly after she had left, with Beckie, and taken the flat in Barnet: Harrison's and Schaadt's experiments, at Berkeley, with pregnant mice, twelve of which had been kept, on fertilisation, in a cage in which the conditions were arranged to cause them maximum discomfort: tilting floors, electric bells, flashing lights, irregular food and – cumulatively – electric shocks: in no time at all, Harrison and Schaadt observed, the mice were subject to 'involuntary trembling', subsequently 'fits and spasms' and, finally, 'catatonic withdrawal' – symptoms which, they further observed, 'disapeared without trace' when, at the birth of their offspring, they were removed to 'a normal environment'.

Except (Fenchurch noted) in their offspring: though only foetal witnesses to the events in the previous cage, they, from birth, exhibited those symptoms which had characterised their mothers' earlier behaviour – involuntary trembling, fits and spasms, catatonic withdrawal – and continued to do so until they died.

'You're not,' Maidstone said, 'making a connection between yourself and a traumatised mouse?' to which, at the time, he replied, 'If smoking can affect a pregnant woman, how about the death of a previous child – precisely at the moment when the central nervous system of the unborn foetus comes on tap, namely, the twelfth or thirteenth week of gestation?'

O homo serioso.

'The more you go into it,' Mackendrick says, 'the crankier it becomes. The prognosis, for instance, in its stress on material functions, is not merely derivative but self-protective: someone whose background impels him to disregard the complexities of any situation other than those he can relate to external events. Idealism extends itself first to define and then to embrace the whole.'

'Hole?'

'The Hegelian whole.' He leans back in his chair: the leather creaks: the patter of his son's feet above our heads and the demented cry of, 'Selda!' – the put-upon East German nanny who came through the Berlin Wall in a van driven by a young admirer: Schnabel, subsequently a journalist on *Die Welt*. ' "If the material causes of greed are removed cupidity will disappear." None of this, of course, is true.'

True.

Like Marx, Mackendrick: a pharisaical tradition ('*my* father did not forsake his religion and turn it into a secular joke'): bohemian (despite his pin-stripe suit: a joke on the world he will never join), theoretical, zealous (a charming plagiarist, to boot): firm, Ukrainian peasant legs inside his trousers: dark-

252

eyed, flat-browed – overtopped, his cunning face, by a frieze of curls – tight-sprung, wiry, greying from each core to an outer fringe of black: an attractive, Panic personality merely bereft of the cloven hoof, the five-barred flute: short, square hands – more used to spade or shovel: 'Who, in a "fulfilled" society would work in the kitchen – wash the floors, superintend the laundry, dig the coal – while we, my friend, are hunting and riding (shooting and fishing), walking in the country, painting and writing, communing, if not with nature, with our fellow men? What, for instance, is the individual going to think who has the floor to wash, the fields to till, the street to sweep, the train to drive, the recalcitrant children to teach when there are others who do not have to do these things because of "different gifts"? Who, in short, Herr Fenchurch, is going to shovel shit?'

Charlie says, 'Why did you run away, then, Father?' sitting on the bed: enquiry rather than reproof, perplexity rather than castigation.

The bed creaks, in the semi-darkness, beneath his weight: the children, I conclude, are both in bed (where I have been since my return), Etty, hopefully, writing up her diary: "This morning/afternoon my father ran away. He had gone back to his childhood home in order, so he said, 'to meet his Maker'."

'The tribulations of the creative life are not to be dealt with lightly,' I tell him, 'nor explained, or dismissed in a conventional way. I am not, after all, a clerk in an office.'

'I never said you were,' his face shadowed by the bedside lamp which, casually, he has turned on while I am speaking. 'It's because you aren't that we're so concerned,' (an unlikely snobbery in Charlie). 'We want, above all, to see you better,' his ample hands spread out across his knees, 'and, if possible, living in London.'

'Doing what?'

'Work.'

'What work?'

'Writing.'

He makes the suggestion with a shake of his head.

'My writing days,' I say, 'are over. Such as they were.'

'Painting.'

'What?'

'The drawings,' he says, 'you did today.'

'Negligible. Bea,' I tell him, 'saw to that.'

The arguments we had, first to persuade her to go back to science then, once she was back, not to overlook almost everything else.

'Careers, I'm afraid, are toys to women. Freedom,' I tell him, 'went to her head. One look down her microscope and she had no time for anything else. The bric-à-brac she left, assembled by her friend Constanza, the absolutely frightful South American (Columbian) interior decorator she got in to desecrate our house.'

'Otherwise,' not listening to this, 'it's back,' he says, 'to the North London Royal.'

'Maidstone has retired. Something to do with his pension. They have a new man in now,' I tell him. 'Waddle. Or Coddle. Or Straddle. In my view, it was exhaustion: Maidstone. That and wanting to write a book about Rossini, Rimbaud, and Piero della Francesca. He had a theory they all suffered from unipolar depression. Unmistakable signs he was cracking up. As for my theory about pregnant mice, not to mention New Mind Theory, further and further evidence he was falling behind the times.'

'Harriet cannot devote the whole of her time to looking after you,' he says.

'I've no wish that she should,' I tell him. Far rather, I am about to add, I'd prefer the reverse, only he swiftly looks up at a sound from outside and, reassured we are not to be disturbed, declares, 'So long as you persist in neglecting yourself,' and is about to continue, 'you leave us no choice,' but, to get the gentle giant off the hook, I announce, 'I might as well specialise in something. Neglect is something I ought to be good at. I've had unlimited training. Indeed, if there is one subject I am familiar with it's the very one, Charlie, you've chosen. I ought to be grateful – indeed, I am – at your offering me not only a

254

lifeline but the prospect of a promising way ahead. Certainly,'
I thank him, 'something to rely on.'

'Wouldn't you say,' Maidstone says, 'that your preoccupation
with your brother is a sign that that preoccupation is doing
you no good at all?'

'No,' I tell him.

'He died six months before you were born.'

'My mother's grief is endemic to my nature. There is no
morning when I wake that I am not aware of his dying. (Despite
every effort to beat it down.) I (even) dream of demands I
become more cheerful – demands which, when I turn round
to see who has made them, I find coming from myself.'

'What Harrison and Schaadt have achieved with mice is not
necessarily applicable,' he says, 'to human beings.'

'Why not?' I ask.

'Why,' he says, and laughs, 'they're mice!'

'We shall have to have a rule. If and when you go out one
of us will have to go with you. Or, at least,' Charlie says, 'be
told precisely where you are.'

How long I've been prattling on I've no idea – evidently
some time, I conclude, for he now announces – i.e., threatens
– more sternly than I have previously heard him, 'It's not, at
least, like Boady Hall, nor the closed ward at the North London
Royal. Other than accounting for where you are going, you
have all the freedom you want.'

'People used to defer to me,' I tell him. 'I had great actors
at my beck and call. I talked, occasionally, to princes. Statesmen
called me on the phone. I could, had I wished, have travelled
round the world simply in answer to invitations, and still have
had enough left over to start again. I was,' I tell him, 'in
demand. Not a night went by but that somewhere in the world
a play of mine was being performed: for every hour of every
day, for every hour of every night, people were watching a play
by Richard Fenchurch, a colliery worker's son brought up on
Onasett estate, near Linfield. Now look where I am,' I
conclude.

'Those days are over, Father,' he says, easing his frame against

255

the bed, his figure more sombre for being beyond the pool of yellowish light. 'I always liked,' I say, 'a greenish shade, yet here I am with a yellow one. (Over,' I tell him, 'and long since gone').

'Will you agree,' he says, 'to what we ask? It'll make Etty's job much easier.'

'When the miners come up the path to the door you have a similar manner,' I tell him. 'Those stalwarts of the Ardsley Constituency Labour Party. Why they agree to being patronised I have no idea. I'm sure they talk behind your back. The good-natured Charlie. We are still a class apart,' I add. 'You and your father, me with mine. Despite the absurdity of what, in a life of absurdity, I've tried to do, the absurdity of what, for a time, I almost achieved – the sums of money, the distinguished friends, the awards, distinctions, honours and prizes, I'm still at heart, unchanged from what I was forty years ago on Onasett estate: gauche, inept, untried, lacking in grace, in faith, in love – bereft, by temperament as well as background, of all that might enhance – all that might, you could say, make life worth while.'

I am even, Charlie, going to fat: when I glimpsed, in a window, a reflection of myself today (in a pane of glass when I descended from the Ardsley bus at Linfield) I didn't recognise – in fact, on first sight, ignored – the figure standing there: grey-haired, obesity at that stage where, on a stocky figure, it might easily be confused with muscle.

Etty – at first I thought Bea, then her mother – has, I've noticed, for several seconds, been standing in the door (the sound which, earlier, had caused Charlie to raise his head): the sleeves of her dress are rolled from having bathed the children or, conceivably, from clearing up her room further along the landing – about to get down (at last) to *The Private Papers of Richard Fenchurch* – or, perhaps, more simply: *A Life.* Charlie, unaware of her, goes on, 'It makes Etty's task more difficult if we can't come to an agreement, Father. All you have to say is, "I'll be in the garden," or, "I'm going out to paint." '

'I haven't the energy,' I tell him, and when he asks, 'To

paint? Or tell us where you're going?' I add, 'I took up art as a means of killing fear. I thought, "When I become an artist it will go away": a sense of loss, a sense of isolation, a sense of being alone so fearful at times I couldn't move. Yet the irony is, of course, it goes the other way.'

Etty, stepping into the room, creaking a floorboard, momentarily distracts Charlie's attention: after all, as a socialist, a humanist, he wants to understand.

'Fear is, in reality, a symptom – of an isolation which was generated before I was born. The use to which I put it, or it put me, exacerbated it in a peculiar way. For nothing quite motivates the artist as the desire for recognition, and yet, the moment that recognition is achieved, his isolation is complete. The longing, would you believe it, Charlie? – the most absurd of all our appetites – a longing to be saved! Vivienne, at the height of her fame, when she discovered *that* – not unlike many in her predicament – despite struggling for years against the inclination – found the realisation too much to bear and, after taking a bottle of sleeping pills, swallowed, for good measure, a bottle of bleach. I will never forgive myself for not going in the yard. I, who suffered in that way, too. Nothing can beat that kind of pain: a sense that all you have struggled for has not only failed, but disappeared. Gone: all your efforts inappropriate.'

I pause, Charlie and Etty now standing together. 'When I came in from the yard I sat on a chair and thought, what effect will this have on Bea, then, more pertinently, on Mathilda, Harriet – on Kenneth, Benjamin, Rebecca? What effect does it have on me? An attempt to obviate the shock – of a sight which, even now, I resist describing: the figure reclining on a pile of compost, the snarl which, with rigor mortis, had stiffened into a ravaged grin: teeth flecked with blood, a fly alighting between her lips, her tongue: the smell. A peculiar codicil, Charlie, to what I've done. A peculiar way to end existence.'

'Let's look to the future,' Charlie says. Subsiding on the bed again, he adds, 'That, and the present, is all we've got. The best thing you can do for Vivienne is to draw and paint, to write.'

'Yet the past,' I tell him, 'is where I am,' (the shadow of Etty, who has come closer, now upon me). 'The past, after all,' I add, 'is here. Bea and her mother sat there, too.' I indicate the bed. 'They, too,' I continue, 'sketched out a future. Into the distance (the long flight I followed, the journey I took). Yet here I am, where I started.'

'You appreciate,' Charlie stands, the bed springing up at the removal of his weight, 'we can't proceed from this point unless we have a plan.' (How the constituency devotees – more the men than the women – admire him.)

'What sort of plan?'

'Of action.'

'I shan't come,' I tell him, 'to any harm. Nor do I intend to harm man, woman, child or animal.'

'It's the damage, Father,' he says, his figure looming above me, 'to yourself. Etty, for instance, has other things to do. She can't confine her life exclusively to looking after you.'

'Nor should I wish her to,' I tell him. 'I have already confided to her a course of action. She could, for instance, write a book. The material, I've pointed out, is close at hand.'

His thick, broad-featured face drives outwards in a smile.

'It might, despite Etty's reservations, solve both our problems,' I go on. 'It would, in a constructive way, employ her skills and gifts – which I, incidentally, hold in very high esteem – and I would be obliged to be here with her, if not in close attendance, while the book is finished. An incidental benefit,' I continue, 'would be, not further notoriety for her, but approbation and the possibility, girded by such praise, that I might return to the work which, as you have pointed out, I have, in middle age, despairingly abandoned.'

'I've asked Bryan to look in,' Etty says, taking, as far as I am aware, not the slightest notice of what I have said. 'He says he'll come tomorrow. You'll stay in, I take it, until he comes?'

'Indubitably,' I tell her. 'No doubt,' I go on, 'there'll be a subsequent consultation behind my back.'

'He'll have his own views on the subject, Father,' Charlie says. 'After all, it's for your good,' he adds, 'that he's coming.'

I'm not sure whether this final remark is directed at me or Etty, or both: he looms for a moment at the foot of the bed, then – a flash of his shirtsleeves – he's gone.

'His torso was dark,' I tell Etty, 'with his wearing a waistcoat, but, for several moments, he reminded me of Corcoran. He, too, would come in here – particularly in the mornings, when I was painting, or writing, there, on a chair, by the window – and make a remark about, for instance, the dignity of manual labour – remarks which, I hadn't a doubt, were intended to point out the strenuous nature of his own employment, and the dependency of so many others on it as well as the irrelevance, if not indulgence of mine.

> So that's today, so desperately begun:
> so much endeavoured, so little done,

I'd quote him – but one of the many poems I wrote at the time,

> so much attempted, so little done:
> so much abandoned, so little won,

another version, he striding off to his yard and his lorries – his men, his coal, his steel, his oil – and I would re-immerse myself in my self-appointed task to show up humanity for what it was.'

As Etty sighs, I add, 'I apologise to Charlie but, most of all, to you, for all the trouble I've caused you. In earlier times, someone like myself would simply walk off, at night, into the trees, or the river. Perhaps, in my own way, that's what I intended to do. Different times, different places. I shall not leave the grounds, or the house, without informing you, or Mrs Otterman, or Charlie, or all three. As for Raynor, he can tell you as much about me as he likes. I doubt, after all this time, there'll be much that is new. Having fouled up my life the last thing I want is to foul up someone else's. After all, if I can do anything at all I can at least set a bad example.'

'After all,' I tell Maidstone, 'the strong may cherish their vulnerability: all those elements which in their lives have previously distracted them, are, by their susceptibilities, brought into focus – and swept aside. Their perceptions are extended: they are obliged to move beyond themselves (they are obliged to move they know not where). In reaching the end of things they arrive at their beginnings.'

Hell has no optimum condition.

The unimaginable is realised and precedes the unimaginable again.

While all Harriet says is, 'We don't want you to feel imprisoned.'

'I don't feel that at all,' I tell her. 'This house is how it was four decades ago, at least. I was just turned eighteen when I first saw it and, while I was a student, I stayed here several times a year – on holidays, at weekends. This room,' I go on, 'is haunted, not least,' I continue, 'by the women that I loved. Principally by two of them, and now, of course, by you. It's no wonder I confuse Corcoran with Charlie: large men, both avuncular, both, in their differing ways, good sports. Your grandfather, of course, was a rabid Tory – the only one in the district at the time – and Charlie is one of your middle-class dreamers, promoting a world which, should it ever come about, would do away with people like himself.'

She has gone.

Fenchurch, I reflect – sketching her introduction – is a complex man: too sensitive to be political, too fair-minded to be partisan, too intelligent to submit the variety of life to a dogma: an amazing conjunction of hypocrisy and ambition, of irresolution and certitude, of absurdity and good sense (of baseness and magnanimity): morbidly introspective, revolutionarily inclined, indisposed to expressions of affection.

Momentously, at the height of his success, he arrived at the conclusion that his life – as he had envisaged it from his youth, if not his childhood – pursuing his goals with an energy bordering on venom – had been based on a misconception. His sense of humiliation in his childhood but, more specifically, in his youth, had indisposed him to society in general, and to certain all-too-clearly identifiable aspects of it in particular: his pessimism – deriving from a source beyond his control – inclined him to an anarchic view of his own existence (one which only belatedly he had come to realise teetered on the threshold of despair). His only antidote, a vitalist belief in self, inclined him to use circumstances and people to increase his power (the product of his insecurity) and to dominate his environment: 'isn't domination,' he conjectured, 'in reality, what life is all about? Didn't Christ dominate the Devil (the priests, the pharisees, his parents, the Romans)? didn't he seek, as a child, to over-rule his mother? (What did his father make of that? What, come to that, did his father make of his Father?)'

Night: his daughter and her husband sleeping: their daughters – with odd cries and shouts which characterise their dreams – asleep as well. 'I might, quite easily,' he reflected, 'be in our home in Belsize Park, the night, for instance, Bea tells me – not the confirmation merely the beginning of his crack-up. And Constanza, the South American brood-mare, as Bea described her, with that psychopathic father who had killed – how many people was it? – three hundred in a day ('almost as many as days in the year'), the Minister of Justice. What about Bea: her drawings, her photographs, the stone (breeding) trough in the boiler-room beneath the front door steps? What about – tears flooding his eyes – the years they'd spent inside that building, in partnership, in comradeship, bringing up their children? 'Our children!' (the only revolution they had witnessed in their lives).

The owls, the mice, the rumble of the trains – the sudden rush, as opposed to the vibration, as they passed a vent, brick-lined and grated, between his and his neighbour's house.

The beginning of what he called his 'grand dispersal'.

He gave away his money: first to charities (who wrote grate-ful, personalised, incredulous replies), then to organisations whose activities he wasn't sure about, then to a variety of individuals, from artists whose work he disapproved of ('I might be wrong') to people whose faces or appearances he didn't like ('they might be beautiful to their husbands/wives' – or, conversely, getting his own back: indebtedness, materialism – all the things he sensed had brought him down). Much, of course, he gave to Bea and, a larger sum, shared amongst the children. It was in response to a letter to Bea from his bank that his affairs, finally, were transferred to her control: he was – in proceedings which he didn't attend – judged to be no longer responsible for his actions. 'I have never been more responsible,' he complained – without acrimony or resentment – the first time she visited him, coming to the end of his first month at the North London Royal. 'I have never, as far as I am aware, been so clear-headed. I have done away with everything,' he told her, gazing from the cupboard – empty, but for his night-clothes and wash things – by his bed to the disillusioned faces which filled the rows of chairs in the television and recreation lounge immediately outside his door. 'People queue up to come in here. My bed is very popular.'

He watched her – as he watched her on most occasions – cry; or, if not cry, endeavour not to. 'I used to know you,' she told him, 'as a child,' and when he answered, 'Surely, Bea, it was after that,' she said, 'I was taken in: all that childishness to do with art.'

('This place,' he told her at the time, 'is a paradox: you can say but not do anything you like.').

He introduced her to Walter: 'Walter,' he first warned her, 'is known as the King of Peace,' his head enclosed in a turban (knotted handkerchiefs) and held permanently to one side. 'It keeps it,' he told Bea with a beatific smile, 'from falling off my shoulders.' Then to Oskar, an Austro-Hungarian avionics, electrical and civil engineer: 'I am civil,' he told her with a bow, 'I have electricity within my system and I have, at night, the capacity to fly,' a sturdy, square-shouldered (bald-headed) man who, Bea declared, looked a smaller version of me. '*Was* he bald-headed?' she said when I pointed this out ('They all look alike to me'). 'This is paradise on earth,' I told her. 'Only a genius could live here, and only a genius, Bea, describe it.'

Then to Daphne (ancient at the age of thirty-five, wizened) who, terrified, dug her nails, behind her, in the wall.

Fenchurch, in his letters – why did he write them? – described what he called 'the improvidence of God': the abandonment with which a caring deity dispenses wretchedness, senility, lunacy, disease and pain – even children, even animals – nothing, not even the smallest microbe, is exempt: 'even babies, minutes old'. In the face of the profligacy of God's disasters, he enquired, why, if he cares so little for us, should we, his creations, care for him: did he, frankly, think twenty-four hours on a cross would be enough? If he, for instance, were subject to the laws of man, he would be in prison – for eternity – for child-neglect: an artist takes more care of his creations, a father of his offspring, than God, in his profligacy, takes care of us.

She listened – Albert waiting in his car outside – with patience to her (then still) husband: 'the ravings of a lunatic,' I heard her once describe them to a colleague when, as a surprise, without warning – my first day 'off' – I visited her in her lab.

"How I love to see you," I wrote to her at this time, "with your lovely hair – as deep and as thick as your mother's – piled on top of your head, stooped, and yet erect, sitting on your stool – square-shouldered – peering (with the intensity, I might tell you, of a child) into the binocular lenses of your microscope, your right hand drawing with a pencil, your left adjusting the focus. How proud your mother would have been! How prouder still your dad! The grandchild, would you believe it, of H. J. Kells!"

'It's not the romance of lunacy,' I told her, 'that makes me warm to a place like this, but a cinquetential structure of the mind I'm sure I have discovered. It will revolutionise psychiatry,' and then, 'There's one thing you can say about madness, it gets you out and about!'

17

'I DON'T THINK I told you,' I said to Etty the following morning,
'the first occasion I saw your mother not as I'd always seen her
but as she is, sitting on a stool in her lab at the MRC, her hair
piled high on the top of her head. She wore a jacket cut square
at the shoulders, with epaulettes and pleated pockets. Her
colour was high: she was on the threshold, if I'd known it, of
making a discovery she sensed was there but hadn't realised.
Her head was bowed, her right hand drawing. Her left hand
held the focus. A beam of light lit up her brow. At first – I'd
been directed to the room by a colleague – I failed to recognise
her. Her eyes, when she looked up, were out of focus.

"Bea?" I enquired.

Perhaps, at that moment, too, she failed to recognise her
husband.

"Yes?" She waited.

"It's your husband," I announced.

The fact of the matter was (I didn't know it) she was waiting
for Albert and the sight of me, I discovered later, filled her
with alarm.'

She wore, in addition to her jacket, a long, blue denim skirt:
not denim. Wool. Beneath its generous folds a pair of boots.
Soft leather. Wrinkled horizontally across her instep. Sitting on
a stool. Flushed. Loved. On the threshold. In reality, expecting
Albert. Good old Al!

'I rang her up the following day and said, "I have never seen
you so absorbed." "Like you," she said, "when you started

264

writing. Or when I came into the studio in the middle of a picture, for all practicalities your attention on the moon." '

It's dark. The curtains closed, Etty – so clear in the dream – not there at all. 'The fact of the matter is, independence, self-reliance, to the point of self-contentment (the one man pitted against the rest) was the one quality I prized above all others. Without it,' I informed Isabella, for want of anyone else to talk to, 'I wouldn't be where I am today,' – here in the bedroom where, for the remainder of his teenage years, she had, on all his visits, brought him a cup of tea each morning – her figure arced, diagonally, as she drew the curtain, the sunlight flooding from the south: the warmth, the glow, the preparations she had made (invariably wearing lipstick), the removal, if the moment were propitious, of all her clothes.

O my dear, my love.

Prized, that is, above all others, a singular, he thought at that time, human virtue: in reality a symptom – his independence – of an illness which, perceivable with hindsight, had, from the beginning, engulfed his life.

Hand in hand, as symptom, went reliance – on one other person who, because of his dependency, he despised.

"Nothing," he wrote to Vivienne in her absence (she lying in the shed outside), "will ever be the same again. All the old virtues – independence, single-mindedness, self-reliance – those, that is, I saw as virtues, are, it turns out in middle age, not virtues after all: self-reliance (self-containment); single-mindedness (isolation); courage (an inability to relate warmly, movingly, entrancingly, effectively to others)."

"It was all," he wrote to all of them, "coming to an end."

All the old virtues, Bella, tested, strong and true!

'What happens after that,' he said to Maidstone, 'I've no idea.'

For the first, and the last time, at the edge of existence.

"When we met in the producer's office at the top of the Beaumont theatre the first thing I noticed were your glasses and, the second thing, your legs. 'She is famous for her legs,' the casting director remarked at the time (something of a feminist: in her office a poster of a men's urinal, men back to camera, the centre of the five figures, urinating, a woman). And, 'I would have more pride,' the moment you departed. 'No man,' she announced (or woman), 'would reduce me to the state she's in.' "

Gibbering Vi: no man would reduce you to the state you're in: no man would know that much of love. Paul's Second Letter to the Philippians recommends not a closer walk with God but the acquisition of neurotic symptoms: fear and trembling of an involitional nature: 'Go mad,' he might have said, 'with Jesus (see if he comes if you don't come back).'

'Pour ne désespérer Billancourt,' wrote Sartre for and to the working class (lying to himself).

Collect his thoughts (like kittens placed in a bag by a neighbour and dropped into a river: 'Is this,' they must have thought, in those dying seconds, 'what life is all about?').

No fire to light in Taravara Road (gas: together with the central heating).

In his youth were many mansions (principally the Corcorans').

He wasn't a poet for nothing.

Domestic bleach is indispensable in every kitchen, said an advertisement at the time. 'Am I a housewife?' Vivienne said.

His father lying on the bed where, hours before, he had almost died, saying, 'Would you do something for me?' in a whisper, Fenchurch stooping closer (to hear his father's dying words): 'Would you cut my toe nails. They've been bothering me for hours.'

Going mad: 'not as easy,' he told Maidstone (in the land of the blind there's no premium on light bulbs): 'a bicycle for two,' he complained, 'with only one set of pedals.'

A tautologous effect: I love you.

Naked ways.

I mean more to me than life itself.

"I no longer have an appetite for writing – of the sort that Etty – and Charlie, would you believe it – recommend."

Plays.

Novels.

Are you there?

Bea?

Bella?

Vi.

Treasures.

"Not treasures, dear, but footprints."

She would sit each morning on or by the bed, hair tied with a ribbon, and say, 'What shall we do today?' he, wondering what Corcoran would think should he come in, replying, 'I hope to go out drawing,' resentful of being asked ('Don't ask an artist what he's doing').

Flogging a dead horse.

Dreamed (borrowing, as it happened, Bea's scissors: would she mind, his father's nails? she insisting, 'for old time's sake' in coming with him).

Linfield Municipal Hospital standing halfway between the King Edward VI Grammar School and the High School, his father's room (provided by Bea, who supervised his money) overlooking an expanse of depleted lawn on which, years before, entranced, he'd first seen a reclining figure: a neo-Aztec configuration set, incongruously, in the heart of a coal-field: Moore.

"Things have not turned out exactly as we planned. It is time," he wrote, "we wrote our memoirs. Etty says I'm going to die. She had, she told me, lost her temper. Who wouldn't with a man of fifty-five? (How about sixty?)"

How about – God help me – sixty-five?

St Paul.

An acute, or sub-acute anxiety neurosis.

"The resemblance," he wrote, "of things to come."

Jupiter.

'The lineaments,' on a phone call to Bea at her Brighton hotel (her weekend away while he looked after Beckie), 'of gratuitous desire.' ('Will you not ring me here,' she said, 'unless it's something important.')

What kind of shit is it who cares if his wife is fucked by someone else?

'The bare-headed Fenchurch,' he read in a review, writing, perplexed to the reviewer who swiftly responded: 'A misprint: for "ar" read "on".'

"O, my dear," he wrote, "two things make a right."

This night: strikes each hour, as then: awake in the old days (imagining Isabella with Corcoran in the other room) to realise two hours had passed without hearing a chime and conclude he had, after all, been sleeping.

The classification of visitors (written at the time): those who were interested in seeing what he looked like; those who came because they thought they had to; those who thought they'd better stay clear and this was the necessary inducement to do so; those who felt flattered they had been and survived; those who were curious about what a lunatic asylum looked like; those who thought they might write about him in their diaries (memoirs, columns in the press); those – the one person – who thought they loved him; and his wife and children whose motives came under the generic heading which, after a great deal of reflection, and much rubbing-out, he identified as 'love'. All of them, he concluded, acquired a relish for their own existence together with a disinclination to endorse the one they were leaving behind.

"My mind," he wrote at this time, "is in the region of – by my calculation (rough at the best of times) – two hundred and fifty thousand years old: more images flow through it in one night's sleep (and one day's reflections) than pass through a normal brain in three or four years. Since my discovery that the mind, in sleep, disintegrates into a psychotic state – the five cellular structures which comprise the composite self distinguishable, uniquely, one from the other – the significance of my dreaming has vividly increased. I can elucidate dreams like no one's business: indeed, no one's business is what dreaming is all about."

He understood it clearly: in sleep, as in breakdown, the

psyche devolved into its constituent parts. Dreams were the dramatisation of the process.

"Dear Maidstone, odd how we never got to first names – despite the informalities, despite the intimacy, the delicacy – indeed, the outrageousness of much of what was revealed. There we are: doctor and patient; emeritus professor and psychotic – acute or sub-acute anxiety neurosee. Maybe, in retirement, you have discovered that what goes on in the psyche goes on in the universe as a whole (we are plugged in to eternity): systems are elaborated, patterns evolve, processes reveal themselves – everything is in motion. If the black holes of astronomical speculation are one of the wonders of the universe, entities a billion times more powerful than the sun, switching themselves on and off in a time interval equivalent to two earthly days, then so, in my view, is the black hole of depression into which all matter seemingly descends and where the organism ceaselessly absorbs itself."

The waste, he was about to write, that characterises space – all those galaxies going on for ever, matter evolving and dissolving without purpose – was echoed by the wastefulness of the human brain (see Fenchurch: its unused resources, its neural profligacy unmatched by a proportionate function).

"Dear Mackendrick, I wasn't at all convinced by your performance on television the other night: 'Politics and Madness: are the two irretrievably combined?' No one, for instance, attending courses for training in the practice of counselling or psychotherapy can have failed to have noticed, let alone to have been affected by, the party games or group disciplines involved, where insights are encouraged to appear and manifest themselves, and are accredited, by the deployment of mechanistic verbal and/or non-verbal techniques: neutralised personalities are both attracted by and vulnerable to these neural engagements, and non-neutralised personalities to controlling them.

Yet the rationalisations engendered in and by this form of play, harmful or harmless as it may seem, can just as efficaciously be assigned to the same category of empirical observation as the Virgin Birth, the bodily ascension of Christ, or the service of ritualised cannibalism which lies at the heart of Christian worship. Or – and I come to the point I am making (and you undoubtedly will steal) – the tracts of any political theory."

No light shows beneath the curtains.

Four must have passed without his hearing.

Conversely, regarding his temperature, he might have been asleep.

There is hope for everything, he concluded.

There were those who came to clarify what they thought about themselves; there were those who thought they felt the same and wondered if it mattered: there were those, of course, who didn't come at all.

Those, the latter, he saw little of.

In my mind, I reflect, I see them all the time.

She sat on a log, her legs astride: 'When I am eighty, you, my dear, will be forty-five.' ('Forty-six,' he told her).

Coming to the point when, once again, he would take up drawing.

I have lost, in order of importance: Bella, Bea, our children, Vi, recognition, my vocation: an avalanche before that: Liam, Mackendrick . . .

Here, in the room, I recall, where the mischief started.

The equilibrium he found in dementia towards the end of a faithful life.

"Fenchurch's discovery of the process of dreaming is the logical result of his discovery of the structure of the mind, essentially an n-dimensional concept allied to his observations on the radial nature of perception and its lateral suffusion, or association, throughout the system: the mind perceives radially (he asserts), translating its perceptions through lateral connections which have acquired as well as intrinsic characteristics transfigurations which determine not only what is perceived but how it will be perceived in the future."

Consider the nasturtiums in the garden, they strangulate the lesser plants, yet they weep not, neither do they labour.

'What, in my youth,' he told Mackendrick, 'was of interest no longer is: personality, idiosyncracies, *character*. Do you occupy the same hinterland of terror?'

The tertiary way of doing things (testing, he thought, the lateral extensions).

'What is mind?' Mackendrick said: 'the dirty sheet on which society writes its incorrigible message.'

'What is my mind the window on if not its own reflection?' Fenchurch said.

Vivienne said, 'You have given me such a happy time. Do you remember the day we spent by the river – was it Maidenhead or Marlow? – even if you can't otherwise bear the sight of me.'

'I never said,' he said, 'I would.'

The physiognomy of love: 'Just look at my nose!' (as she examined it in the mirror).

The night: how long the night is when you're on your own: how swiftly it goes in the company of another.

Who was the one that the other lay close to?

He heard the children scamper down the stairs: scrape chairs and clatter cups and open doors: 'I am closer to Isabella's great-grandchildren than I am to my own: there I can see the separation, whereas the my that the self is close to is invisible to me.'

Homo serioso.

'I engineer,' he told Maidstone, 'the engine of the mind,' (selling off the spare components).

'I can't cope with children,' the child psychotherapist said as the secretary led in the next child patient (unaware that the therapist's sole aim is to subsume his or her irrationalities in those of other people), her husband, a celebrated paediatrician – 'killing two birds with one stone', he described it – explaining how the extraordinary size of his fees facilitated his purchasing of our house in Belsize Park, intended to be turned by the pair of them into 'a mecca for child care: cure the parents with very large bills: it is, after all, an open market.'

Rising from the floor, he saw – in the morning light – the ghost of Isabella.

Kells and Corcoran: Irish priests (two men to be relied on).

'Nothing,' Kells says, 'is what it seems,' following, in the sunny garden, the movements of his daughter (stooping, in her middle years, to the flowered beds).

Then Etty got up.

Two selves: what price, he thought, in staying one?

What a lot to be taken for granted, not least the room provided by his daughter, the company that she provided.

'My daughter,' Kells said, 'is a happy woman. She would be happy if she wasn't married. She would be happy if she didn't know you. She is, by nature, a happy woman, in the same way as, by nature, her mother was: a child of God,' a daughter, Fenchurch took it to be, of H. J. Kells.

'My close relatives,' he told Mackendrick, 'are powerful people (how powerful, he went on, you'd be surprised).'

In the night: 'instead of writing a radial novel (which all novels, until now, have been) I shall write a diametric one, which traverses rather than travels in and out.'

('That,' Bea said, 'is good enough for me.').

He dreamed.

Overhead, scratching on the tiles, a rook, he conjectured, or a pigeon.

He no longer cared whether he wrote at all: what came to hand was dispirited, de-energised – unrepresentative of what he was himself.

'Between Linfield and Ardsley: somewhere on that road,' he said, measuring the distance, 'is a quotient of myself.'

He would rise, go down to the shop, owned and staffed by Pakistanis, in Sebastopol Street – hardly more than a converted front room in one of those narrow, one-hundred-and-fifty-year-old houses – and buy a paper and two cartons of milk. Vivienne, meanwhile, would be in bed: the endless charade with her glasses, her compulsive buying of several more, together with a variety of clip-on lenses – until he persuaded her to give them up ('they will not change the nature of what you see,' he said): 'our naked selves,' as she described it – regarding herself, eyes almost closed, as she did each morning in the mirror.

272

It's cold: despite the introduction of central heating since the days, in Isabella's time, when the inside of the panes, in winter, invariably were frozen up, the room does not retain its heat for long: at night, when the boiler switches off, the warmth disappears in seconds. Charlie is always threatening to improve it: 'These old houses,' he complains, as if his being here is Etty's fault entirely, 'are not designed for easy living: their level of comfort, at the time of their construction, was determined by that prevailing in a cave.' Yet, despite his threats, the windows, for instance, have not been double-glazed: there is no insulation in the roof and draughts whistle in not only from beneath the doors (and from around the windows) but from underneath the floor itself – one vacated knot-hole being a favourite where a stream of air, as if from a bellows, is, on windy days, as undiminished in its velocity as it was when Isabella used to stand there, dressed in a housecoat, and complain, as I do now, about the fact that, despite her protestations, Corcoran, in those days, Charlie now, did, or has done, nothing about it. 'I am,' she would tell Corcoran, 'a Mediterranean woman with a passion for the sun.'

I would see her, on occasion, walking amongst the stalls in Linfield market – held beneath the northern walls of the, at that time, coal-black cathedral – her unmistakable head of hair (around which a green silk scarf would occasionally – strikingly – be fastened) conspicuous amongst the drab-coloured awnings and the colourless figures of the colliers' wives. I would delay, for instance, going up to her, merely for the pleasure of observing her from a distance – as might a devotee of wildlife observe a creature he had long admired but, in its native habitat, never glimpsed. I would follow her amongst the stalls, deriving pleasure of an ecstatic nature from contemplating the inclination, at one stall, of her head, from the extension of her arm at another, from the sway of her body at a third. All the while I would be aware of the glances of the other shoppers, not least the fixated gaze of the men – contrasting sharply with the sideways but nevertheless all-consuming gazes of the women – and the often bizarre effect her face and figure and her manner (her clothes, that is, and her manner of address) had on the stall-holders themselves – invariably resulting in her being offered a bargain rather than, as might have been expected, her being exploited because of the exoticism of her dress). 'Look at this,' she would say, like a child, smiling, when I finally came up – and, with the greatest propriety, she had offered her cheek. '*Half* the price I would have to pay in Ardsley, and for something twice as fresh,' showing me a savoy (a savoy: her 'favourite' vegetable, she more than once announced), a piece of fruit, or – one of Corcoran's favourites – a veal and ham meat pie.

Laden with her shopping we would make our way to the semi-derelict room I occupied over the barber's shop in Southgate, on the opposite side of the cathedral's coal-black hulk, and there, having made a cup of tea, we would, as she, on occasion, described it, 'endeavour to amuse ourselves'. 'Isn't this innocent?' she asked, with surprise, when I remarked, if we were conscious of (the implication of) what we were about, it couldn't be innocent any longer, adding, 'After all, my dear, I see you as a child.'

She was more duplicitous than I imagined, or, rather, wished to acknowledge: was she as unaware, for instance, of being observed as I, in my innocence, or seeming innocence, imagined? Was she oblivious of the effect our relationship would have on Bea had she, either before our marriage or after, been aware of what was going on? Was she as unaware of her attractiveness to me – the, at times, mesmeric effect she had – as she, from time to time, bemusedly made out? 'I don't see what you see in me,' she would protest. 'I am a woman, as far as I can see, without an attraction in the world,' affecting reluctance, when she posed, not only to remove her clothes (which she did willingly enough on other occasions) but to pose at all. 'You'll see how much is wrong,' she'd happily complain, coaxed into submission with gestures which, with hindsight, I see she was soliciting all the time.

Perhaps she was mad. Perhaps she didn't believe in Bea. Perhaps she didn't believe in anything: unquestioning,

274

unasking, untormented – except on those occasions when she identified – or thought she did – something morosely none of these things in me. Perhaps she was an exotic, brought back, unwittingly, by Kells from the Middle East (caught up in his baggage) – something founded in thousands of years of desert life, as unreal, as unlived, as inauthentic in this northern clime as the exotic plants she cherished.

'Not one of Kells' locusts?' Maidstone wryly enquired, while I protested, 'I re-live my life at that time over and over again, as if, after all this time, it will never come into focus. I not only seem to see but need to see something in it which eludes me all the while. An embodiment of a faith in something which I know to be there but which, other than in her, I shall never recognise,' he crossing his legs, inscribing his notes, propped on his knee, murmuring through pursed lips, 'I wonder what that is?'

'Eyes that can see that,' I tell him, 'have not yet been invented.'

'Nothing,' I told her at this time, 'is clear. (Everything, of its nature, is bound to be confused.)' Except, of course, his pictures – and his drawings (principally of her): sitting, for instance, in the third-class compartment in Linfield Station the day he left for the Drayburgh – Bea, whose term started later, coming on behind (with, he understood, a new friend: a pupil from King Edward's who, the same subject, had enrolled at the same college) – his paints, in a tin, above his head, on the rack, buried inside a suitcase: 'My passport,' he'd told his parents – and there, framed in the window, suddenly, her face which, after this date – despite their holiday with Clare and 'Venny' – and Bea (perhaps because of it) – he'd assumed he'd rarely if ever see again.

'How are you?' she enquired, and when he asked, startled, 'But Bella, my love, are you coming to London?' (abandon everything: come with me), she had merely responded, 'I am seeing you off.'

'I live, and let live,' he told Maidstone, 'and fail to come alive,' and he, fatigued (having, that day, announced his

275

coming retirement), had responded, 'You don't let live long enough. You don't, when it comes down to it, give anyone a chance.'

When he replied, 'But I give everyone a chance,' Maidstone wearily rejoined, 'Only a chance with chance. Not, I'm afraid, a chance with you.'

It was the turning-point, he'd thought, in his recovery. 'He thinks,' he'd reflected, 'I'm holding something back. After all this time. I wonder what it is? Something solid, something elusive: something, in the light of his condemnation, I can grasp at last.'

'We have the chance, now that Bea may well be embarked,' I tell her, 'with someone else. Come with me.'

'Permanently?' she says, half-smiling. 'Or for a while?'

'Forever,' I tell her. 'I would like to have you with me.'

'This argument,' she says, 'goes on for ever,' (I have, by this time, stepped out from the train).

'Why not run away for good?' (my arm around her waist).

'I only came,' she says, 'to see you off. This,' she goes on, 'is as good a time as any,' and when, my lips against her cheek, she adds, 'to break away for good,' I whisper in her ear, 'My love! My love! Just step into the train. We'll send a letter. I'll telephone. Your father, I know, will understand. Corcoran, too, no doubt, in time. I can't exist,' I go on, 'without you!'

'This break,' she says, 'will do you good. You,' she continues, 'must go ahead, and I,' she concludes, 'must stay behind.'

She allows me for a while to kiss her lips (months before I had the chance to kiss her again – at King's Cross Station, meeting her with Bea after she and I are re-united: 'on a maturer basis, after each of us has had a "fling",' as Bea described it, Isabella there to visit her daughter). "In her lips," I wrote that night in my room in a hotel in Cartwright Gardens, "I felt the distance that has come between us: the force – for the first time – of those thirty-two years: 'half a lifetime', she described it. Goodbye, my dear, my dear, my love," without, to my surprise, the slightest regret.

That night, sitting in a window of a café in the Euston Road, a stone's throw from my lodgings, I watched the crowds flood by and realised that, for the first time since we had met, my thoughts had moved on to something else: the noise, the surge, the grip of something which, I knew, could only be ambition. 'It is,' I concluded, 'to justify her (all my achievements to justify Bella).'

I watched the dull red glow of the lamps which, spread at intervals along the street, slowly increased in incandescence, changing imperceptibly to a transfiguring orange then finally to a translucent gold. "I wouldn't change my being here for anything," I further wrote that evening.

"Dear God, tolerate my worst excesses for my best are meant for you alone," I might have written at the time, for my decline began the moment that my fortunes rose, the path downwards never, from that instant, more clearly defined.

All I recall is the steam of the engine, the metalwork structure above the platform, the look of relief as we said goodbye.

I hadn't left, after all, but arrived.

18

First, there is the room, twenty feet in height, glazed panels on the upper walls, supplemented, in darker weather, by neon lights. A model, reclining on a cushion, is positioned on a platform: around her, sitting on donkeys, or standing at easels, are a variety of students, tall, short, fat, thin, old, young: male – the women's life-room occupies a similar interior on the opposite side of this ancient, neo-classical, Greek portico-fronted building. The light, on an early winter's afternoon, is fading: the neon strips, an hour earlier, have been switched on: the clock on the wall is approaching five. The model, who has been posing, with rests and an interval for lunch, for the previous eight hours, eases her weight against her arm: her shoulder stirs; a hand is raised, the fingers shaken. Someone, at one of the easels, and two others, seated on donkeys, begin, after glancing, head-sideways, at their drawings or paintings, to pack their things.

Feet stir: there's a distant hum of traffic: the college, its main entrance off, nevertheless backs onto the Euston Road, its presence obscured by a façade of shops, a restaurant, and an amusement parlour.

Someone looks up: the minute hand on a clock set high on the wall approaches twelve, quivers, reaches its zenith and, after coming to a halt, quivers once again.

'Rest.'

'Thanks,' come up on every side.

Groaning, despite her recumbent posture, the model stretches.

One of the students – a stocky, well-built figure (dark-haired and of a saturnine expression) – cleans his brushes and packs his equipment and, taking down his painting from an easel, leaves the room with a briskness which marks him out from the others. Depositing his work in a rack outside, he passes along a corridor which runs underneath the centre of the building (with its antique-room and studios overhead), past the student common-room where a sideways look of regret animates his features as he glances at the students congregating in groups and making plans for excursions to the West End that evening, and reaches a back door of the building from where, down a narrow alley, he emerges into the lamp-lit glow of the Euston Road. He walks, increasing his pace, eastwards until, opposite St Pancras Station, he enters a narrow street and, from there, the door of a terraced building, set at the corner of a crescent and, in several rapid bounds, climbs a winding flight of stairs.

He enters an attic room: the walls are lined with pictures (others, of varying sizes, propped against the walls themselves) and on the floor of which are stacked piles of (mostly) second-hand books. An easel, holding a painting, stands beside the window, the uncurtained panes of which look down to a tennis court set in the centre of the crescent's gardens.

Drawing to him a sheaf of papers, he takes out a pen and, sitting at a table immediately beneath the window, a light beside him, begins to write.

A political view of his life was coming to the surface: 'It isn't me,' he reflected, 'but the life I lead which creates the impression of a divided world, dissonance and vulgarity on one side, refinement and perspicuity on the other,' his life, indeed, fragmented, at that time, in more ways than he imagined, Bea (and her mother) on the one hand, the girls he was attracted to, on the other: the working and the (largely) middle classes which, separately, absorbed his artistic and his social lives, providing, the one, the dynamic which, he suspected, energised his work, the other the impetus necessary to his ambition.

Each morning he got up, wrote, walked briskly to the college, entered his name in the Drayburgh register (lying on a shelf of one of the rotunda windows which illuminated the spiral-staircased entrance), descended to the locker-room to retrieve his materials, then made his way to the life-room to which he had been assigned or, if he were working on a composition, to the antique-room where, amidst the casts, the plants and the multitude of easels, he set up his hardboard (cheaper than canvas) and, for the remainder of the day worked as steadily as distractions (too numerous to mention) in such a large interior might allow – not excluding an occasional break for coffee and one for lunch and for earnest chats about 'art' with the men and about 'life and love' with the women.

At some point he went home and wrote, steadily, for several hours: in the evenings, if he didn't draw (or write) or paint, he visited Bea in her room or she came to visit him, or, if he were deceiving her, he visited or entertained someone else.

He was a 'card'; on the other hand, a bundle of conflicting yet nevertheless dogmatic views (he had opinions about everything, a compendium of the most divergent and contentious elements in the world he lived in, a synthesis – and the principal protagonist of – the same within himself: 'A liver and lover,' he said to Bea, 'if only because the extremes I live at are common to no one else.')

Even after the pipes start ticking beneath the floor – the expansion from the heat as, at intervals, audibly, in the basement of the house, the boiler fires – it is cold: 'These old houses,' I reflect, 'and this one in particular, the one in which I have loved and which has brought me to this pass (unloved by anyone at present), are not for me.'

The girls are romping in their room, sent up, I assume, after breakfast, to prepare themselves for school: Charlie, having come out from the bathroom into his bedroom, is whistling (as, no doubt, he fastens on his tie beneath his triplicated chin), examining, with equanimity, warmth and candour those

280

eyes which, reflected in the mirror, convey nothing but the same in return).

'Breakfast, Charlie!' (from Etty, below).

I've been awake for hours, absorbed in the persona of a twenty-year-old youth (a child, his body and his mind divided, his heart, like his soul, in two).

I used to wake like this at camp: the other sleeping figures, the muggy air, the pigeons in the wood and, at Broughton Springs, the distant sound of the sawmill: the dew, as I crawled out beneath the brailing, first on hands and then on feet (the cool, sharp shock abrasive), the clarity of the air, the shadowed humps across the valley of the medieval mine works, the cows standing in or browsing by the stream, or drifting in a line to or from the dairy on the opposite valley slope: the visit to the toilet, already thick with flies, the smell of the damp, the dust and stone in the decaying game keeper's cottage: the stillness of the wood which, hours before, in the darkness, lit by the flickering camp-fire flames, had sent me to bed with a pang of fear – to be infinitely extended in future years – a deeper darkness, untouched by the flames, lying dauntingly beyond them.

'I thought, this morning, I might go to Broughton Springs,' I say to Etty as she comes in carrying not, as I'd thought, a pot of tea (or my breakfast) but several buff-coloured letters. 'What are those?' I ask to which, seeing me awake, she says, 'Charlie's,' drawing back the curtains.

'Does it require you,' I ask, 'to bring him up his letters? Won't he get them the moment he goes down to the hall (to find,' I am about to add, 'unlike myself, his breakfast waiting)?'

'I thought you'd be asleep,' she says, turning with a smile, and adds, 'If I don't put them in his hand he forgets them. I've brought them to put in his briefcase,'

'Nothing, I suppose for me?' I enquire.

'No one knows,' she says, 'you're here. As for Taravara Road, Matt has said she'll keep an eye on things and post anything that comes.'

'I used to get ten, sometimes twenty, occasionally thirty or forty letters a day,' I tell her, 'at the height of my notoriety,' and add, 'I've been lucky, in the recent past, to get as many as that in a year. Sometimes, in Taravara Road, nothing comes for over a month. That,' I go on, 'despite forty-five years as a writer. And a few other activities as well.'

'They must think you dead.' She smiles.

'Irrelevant,' I tell her.

'Are you getting up, or shall I bring you something?' still smiling in the door.

'What's got into you?' I ask her.

'I have decided,' she declares, 'to make a fresh start.'

'Does that include the first draft of *The Private Papers of Richard Fenchurch*?' I enquire.

'It doesn't.' She smiles again.

'I hesitate to call it a revolution, but what,' I enquire, 'has caused this change?'

'Nothing I can think of,' she says, 'except when I was driving you home, after picking you up at the church, I realised there was nothing more I could do. It took a great weight,' she adds, 'off my mind. No longer do I need to care, slippers or no slippers, sketching or not. You are not my responsibility any longer.'

'I never said I was,' I tell her.

'No,' she says, 'but the whole of yesterday, after you'd disappeared, I'd begun to think you were.'

'You sound,' I tell her, 'like your mother.'

'Exactly.'

Having closed the door behind her, she opens it again.

'As for Broughton Springs, that's up to you,' she says. 'I wouldn't recommend it. And I shan't,' she adds, 'if you fail to come back here, come all that way to fetch you.'

'Then, again, there's Ardsley Edge.'

'There is.'

'And Cawthorne Castle.'

'That, too.'

'Places which, in the past, have inspired, some would say, my better work.'

282

'You are as free,' she tells me, 'as a bird.'

But I can see, apart from discussing me with Charlie – during the dark hours of the night, or perhaps the previous evening – she is saying this not merely to keep her spirits up but to put me on my guard – not against her, but against my own misgivings. She is doing it to alarm me: I have no one, she is saying, but Charlie and herself: biology alone, she might have said (taking a leaf from my book) is the cause of your distress, and not the conditions you were born in.

The embolismic structure of – let us choose a mind at random – that of a once well-known author, playwright, painter and draughtsman, is exacerbated by circumstance, or what the theorists describe as nature, and that, too – though discounted by his second daughter – may be taken into account when assessing how responsible or otherwise he or other people are for his unprecedented actions.

Verbosity was his greatest sin, she might have said, not least at the moment that he suspected that, against the odds (and the prognosis of his doctors) he might recover his peace of mind (never there to be recovered, he'd omitted to tell them, in the first place).

'I've been tormented,' I tell her, 'the whole night long by the thought of mediocrity: all those practitioners of the same who comprise virtually the whole of those engaged on those activities I have been so busily engaged upon myself and who, by self-definition, come under the sobriquet of "failure".'

Her feet come from the stairs: 'I've got your correspondence, dear. I've put it in your briefcase,' and, 'Glenda! Lottie! Time for school! We're leaving in a minute!'

Charlie, I assume, is late, or is delaying his departure in order, as is his not unusual custom, to give me the benefit of his advice sans wife and children in the background: 'You are an old phoney,' he told me, on one occasion, in Taravara Road, on a London visit, before he realised – or had it from Maidstone – I was already mad.

'What is madness,' I can see his much-chinned face enquire, 'if not a cop-out we could all subscribe to?' revising his view, alarmingly (and, incidentally, to my disappointment), on his first visit to Boady Hall: I'd been counting on cop-out, at the time, myself: that innocent, socialist vision that included all things but the view that life intrinsically is bad.

'The final page,' I tell Etty when I go down, 'should have a single drawing – of the one woman who – I might as well admit it – dominated and still dominates my life, namely,' I am about to tell her, 'Isabella,' only, with a suffusion of alarm (a shock of recognition) she declares, 'You've come down without your clothes,' for, in the mirror of the kitchen I can see, my upper (and I presume my lower) body is as naked as the day when, traumatised by an earlier death, it came soundlessly from between my mother's thighs.

"This is the man I gave birth to: heredity in action, a close-up of death, a foetal spasm at the graveside of his eldest brother:" there, with the grace of God, go I.

As the children arrive she offers me a towel and I say, 'I'm on the way to the bathroom,' with something of a laugh, at which, the moment I have gone, they begin to giggle.

'Has Grandpa come down,' I hear them say, '*like that?*' and later, to Charlie, before she takes them off to school, Etty says, 'He came down like that to shock us.'

'We shall have to send you back,' says Charlie when he comes up to my room (Mrs Otterman already flushing a vacuum outside the door) and when I say, 'To where?' he says, 'To a place that Raynor recommends.'

'Private,' I ask him, 'or National Health?'

'The latter,' he says, and adds, 'knowing your appetite for social justice.'

'I never sent my children to a private doctor – except, of course, in emergency (which happened twice) – nor to a private school,' I tell him (as, no doubt I have, many times before), and when he replies, 'Hypocrisy was always a dominant feature of your life,' (does he talk like that to the local constituency Labour Party?), I respond, 'Even when my wealth was sufficient to buy up a private school (one such became available, while

284

we were living there, at the back of our home in Belsize Park – an area given over, almost exclusively, to private and therefore privileged education) I never had a second thought about sending any of our children to a state school, all of which, with one exception, gave them an education which you would have to travel for ever to find an equivalent in paucity of imagination, enterprise, credibility, professionalism and moral strength. I fought for years to raise their standards, entirely on my own, and for most of that time without success, only in the final years, having taken several years off my own life in the process, and when most other middle-class parents had removed their children to the private sector, did I finally come up trumps.'

He has left the room – yet only to fetch his briefcase, for, returning to the door, he stands there, at my declaration, 'come up trumps', fastening the catch (the old-fashioned type, characterised by a flap, and not the miniature suitcase variety popular today), and adds, as if a postcript to his final remark, 'The choice is yours.'

'The choice was mine,' I tell him, 'a long time ago (and see where I am now,' I add).

'You can button up,' he says, fastening, head stooped, the middle button on his pin-striped jacket – a rotundity below the waist the only blemish on a not unyouthful figure, 'or,' raising his head, 'be buttoned down. The choice is yours,' he says again.

'You are kicking,' I tell him, 'against the pricks, a euphemism, in biblical times, for a genetic disability manifesting itself in the form of a disingenuous indisposition to fulfil the expectations of others,' he already turning from the door, something in his pocket absorbing his attention, his briefcase now beneath his arm. 'This came, by the way,' he says, handing me an envelope. 'The writing looks familiar,' he continues as he lays it on the bed.

'In that case,' I tell him, 'it must be from Bea. Bea,' I continue, 'and the private parliamentary secretary to the Minister of Health, the ubiquitous one-armed bandit who is never off the news-screens at present, much, I might add, to Etty's pleasure. *All* our children appear to delight in their mother's choice of husband – her first not being a choice, she says, and therefore doesn't count,' and when, picking up the envelope (without a second glance), I conclude, 'Their father, I'm afraid, they've no time for at all,' he declares, 'At least he makes a go of things,' turning once more so that his final phrase he gives to the stairs – and Mrs Otterman, not oblivious, despite her vacuum, on the landing, 'from a background, I might add, as unpromising as yours.'

'One arm versus half a mind,' I tell him, at which he is about to add, 'She must have a penchant for cripples,' at least, I do my best to imagine so, only, glancing at his watch, I hear a strangulated, 'I'm late, Mrs Otterman. Mrs Stott isn't back yet. Could you keep an eye on Father?' – the sixty-nine-year-old proletarian fake with his faded if once-pristine reputation for being the only outstanding depicter of working-class life since that androgynous aesthete Lawrence, the one compounded of the elements of earth and water (phlegm), the other of air and fire (bathos).

I hear his car a moment later and the (pregnant) silence from the landing as Mrs Otterman, switching off her vacuum, contemplates, in the absence of her mistress (let alone her master), the possibility of being – it must have crossed her mind – assaulted by the mindless mogul in the bedroom who was once described in a national journal as 'the only writer who, in his depiction of the *material* of English working-class life, illuminates *ideas.*'

'Are you all right, Mr Fenchurch?' comes from the heart of Yorkshire: guttural in its strength: no thoughts of anything other than combativeness promised there.

'I'm well,' I tell her, and when she calls, 'Anything I can get you?' immediately respond, 'No, thank you, Mrs Otterman. I shall, in a moment, be getting dressed,' (an invitation to the picnic, the dissolute old devil whom even a potential Nobel-Prize-winning wife could not constrain) at which, after a pause, the vacuuming begins again.

How much I should have liked the previous mistress of the house, as she did on so many occasions, to have come in the door and enquire, 'Where are you going to draw today? If you'll tell me where you'll be (when I've done the shopping, chores, housework, lunch) I'll come out and join you. I fancy a walk in Ardsley Wood,' I choosing a suitable rendezvous in which to sketch, and pleasurably anticipate her arrival: the reeded stream, the leaf-strewn grass, her summer dress, the sheen of her stockings.

There were times, on these occasions, when I suspected that Corcoran might be, contrary to appearances, a patron of the arts; that, having come to a judgement about my potential, he had decided to contribute his wife, a testimony to and an encouragement of my talent. 'You walk in the woods, if you like!' I heard him – in moments of reverie – exclaim. 'Never mind the neighbours. For the sake of his art, which I know is buried in him somewhere, allow him to take with you, as well as your reputation (for housewifeliness, domesticity, fidelity, etc.) whatever liberties he likes. Go with him! Give the genius what he wants!' I endeavouring, on our next encounter to identify in his smiles and frowns, his gestures and appearance, if not an endorsement a hint of a contributory fervour which might, in the name of inspiration, betray a complicity in his handing over his wife.

How I loved her! When, on one occasion, lying beside me in Ardsley Wood, the sunlight in the ferns above her head, she enquired, tracing my lips beneath her finger, 'Would you give up writing and painting if it threatened to come between us?' I responded, without a second's thought, 'Of course!' at which she laughed and, not for the first or last time, exclaimed, 'You're such a rotten liar! Let's hope you never have to make the choice,' nestling her deliciously smelling hair against my cheek as, side by side, we gazed up at the ferns together.

Sometimes in the wood we lit a fire, a bundle of twigs, a rotted log, and, with a pleasure derived from domesticity as much as anything else, watched the flames flicker beneath the trees, the smoke drifting up against the darkness. 'How nice it would be,' I'd say, 'if we could be married. I'd never have to paint, or write again: just to wake to you each morning,' to which, invariably, she'd reply, 'When I am eighty, my dear, you will be forty-five.' ('Forty-six,' I would correct her.) 'Beauty of your sort,' I'd tell her, 'doesn't fade. (It deepens and increases.)' 'So speaks,' she'd say, 'a young and, if I may say so, not only inexperienced but dishonest man.'

The writing is my own: "Dear Richard Fenchurch, this is written in case (when your daughter arrives to take you 'home' – to that damned house which (nowadays) brings you no pleasure – because in the past it brought you so much) you find, once there you are out of your mind. Recall how much peace, despite loathing it, your Taravara home brought Vi: 'I want to be a star!' and, 'I am the legend that dreams are made of: when I am dead there will be films about my life played by actresses who couldn't hold a candle to me. I call that irony: you, I believe, a suitable reward.'

No doubt this finds you as it's leaving me: confused (terrified), waiting for relief from the tribulations that have plagued my life in general but specifically the last five years when not one morning has there been when I have not woken to a degree of fear and dispiritation that would drive any normal person mad (and this abnormal one also).

"No other writer in his time" is crossed out and replaced by, "No other woman (I am speaking of Bella) ever did me so much good. 'Isn't it strange,' she told me one day in the wood, 'you're the only man I know on whom to gaze has been enough.' What Christ was to the author of the Philippian letters she has been to me: an illumination that transfigures (the radiance of her looks – and, let's face it, the dexterity of her touch).

Now you're in that room you've thought so much about; now you're in that bed; now you're gazing, each morning, at the village – bereft of its pit, headgears and slag heap, now the whole place has returned to something not indistinguishable from its medieval past – its one or two burghers, the 'big man' in the manor, endowed with the debilitating accoutrements of a post-socialist existence – you'll know what it's like to be out of touch – in a way you never were, and never will be, in Taravara Road with its brutalised and brutalising neighbours, its graffiti, its dereliction, its public squalor and its private – how would you describe it? – indolence."

'All right?' A pink-cheeked face around the door: breathlessness within the aproned bosom (head of vacuum in her hand). 'Had a letter?'

Speaking to an idiot: but then, of course, I reflect, I am.

'From myself.'

'Yourself?'

'Addressed to me at this address. Written before I came here.'

More redolent of masculine assertiveness than receptivity, her bosom.

'Keep you up to date?'

'It does. If not,' I tell her, 'a little in advance.'

'On your way to the bathroom?' Indicates the towel. 'Why don't you get dressed?'

'I thought,' I tell her, 'I'd have a rest,' and then, 'I'm about to do some writing.'

'In the buff?'

'I often write like this.' I let the towel drop, and recall that she has seen more naked men in the bath-tub by the fire than I have had hot dinners, as companionable, and as discounted, Mrs Otterman, as any domestic pet.

'Best not let Mrs Stott know about it!' with something of a laugh.

'Or,' I tell her, 'Doctor Raynor.'

'Nor Doctor Raynor!' Another laugh. 'He'll have you locked up in no time,' a threat which, casually delivered, has an immediate effect.

'Think I'll get dressed,' I tell her, at which she leaves the room.

"This is from a chum of yours whom you may have forgotten, the one who lived, disguised as you, in Taravara Road the week before Etty was due to arrive: the one who butters your bread and toasts your toast and goes to bed as you at night in that Vi-less room at the back of the house where the sounds from the neighbours are least intrusive – and the sounds of Vivienne, when she lived there, less extreme: 'I'll never be a star!' "

'No point,' she tells me, 'reading that letter if you've written it yourself,' leaning in the door.

I woke this morning to the rhyme in my head, 'Reason and its guide: reason and its pride,' and thought, 'That presages a return to painting,' and later came the thought which never troubled me years ago but which now troubles me almost daily: 'How could a woman fall in love with her daughter's lover without the slightest guilt, remorse or, as far as I could discern it, (not simply unease but) anguish? At the time I took her to be naive, then I took her to be cunning, then, after talking to her father, that it was due to 'genes' – the sea, the sand, the sub-tropical beaches, the whore-house ridden coast of that almost-inland sea: yet all these, I considered later, were excuses to pacify a sense of fear which, on all those occasions I waited at a bus-stop, approached the house, sauntered up and down a road, sat on a log, preceded our encounters – until I saw the turn of her head, the swing of her skirt: her high-heeled shoes, her low-heeled sandals, her blouse (her jumper, her scarf, her coat).

'Naivety,' I thought, 'must be the answer,' as if, in reality, Bea were not her daughter ('Don't you need a coat? Have you put away your books/clothes/things upstairs?' as she might enquire, not of her own but anyone's child). 'She is of a race with which the Anglo-Saxons have never come to terms,' I thought – the one from the shores of a turquoise sea, the other from pitch blackness: the mine, the cauldron, the pit.

'Naivety,' I said, 'of course,' and add, 'Of which I took advantage. Bea idolised her mother,' and when Mrs Otterman says, 'Who?' the vacuum cleaner in her hand, its orifice directed at me, I continue, 'My wife. She thought her mother a remarkable woman. "A child of nature," she being a scientist and not a poet. "It's why my father married her. *Her* mother, too, was

290

much the same, with the reputation, rumoured in the family, of being a Turkish prostitute." '

In Taravara Road, from my workroom window, I see, each morning in an adjoining garden, the wife of a neighbour: in a benign and wholly passive way, even when Vivienne was alive, I fell in love with her stocky figure, stooping to the plants (another horticulturist), only to discover that she is Greek by birth – and then, not even Greek, but Turkish (a cross-border liaison in a war-torn land) and, God help me, the same age as Isabella when we first met – that fateful glance, open and accepting, through the living-room window to the evening-lit figure in the garden outside. 'How I loved her,' I announce, but the termagant Yorkshire miner's wife, the vacuum turned on behind her, is already thrusting at the floor and, above the wailing, calls, 'I want to do in here.'

'Alki', I discover, is her name, the neighbour's wife, and though her beauty is of the sort that can, with discretion, only be admired from a distance, her smile and her composure (a garden-to-window wave) are enough to reassure me.

Etty is back: 'Sorry I'm late, Mrs Otterman,' the lowered tone, 'Is he all right?' and the breathless, flushed-cheeked face, 'Mrs Otterman says you're dressing.'

'So I am,' I tell her.

'Magnificent,' I announce and when she asks, 'What is?' reply, 'All that life entails.'

She is sitting at her desk, the window of her study looking out to the trees at the back of the house – a room which, in my youth, was Bea's bedroom and from the window of which she waved on the memorable day Bella and I climbed Sugden's Bank, lying immediately before us, to look at the Swansons' house.

'What,' I ask her, 'are you writing?'

'I am tinkering,' she says, 'with a life of Cotman. It comes,' she goes on, 'as some relief.'

'A self-effacing fellow, whose personality,' I tell her, 'had little appeal but whose work can only be matched with that of Girtin and, with reservations, Peter de Wint. A genius,' I continue, 'before his time, the progenitor of much in twentieth-century art, not excluding Cézanne and Picasso, and prone to depression at the end of his life, caused, to some degree, I haven't a doubt, by neglect and the consequent cultural isolation,' adding, 'Why don't you choose a living model? No one else will have the chance. If it turns out you've picked a dud – another Haydon, say, rather than a Christopher Wood – you can, when I'm gone, turn back, if not to Cotman – a worthy subject – someone else. Constable, of course, I've never liked. I can't stand the coarseness of his textures, the paint put on as if with a trowel, and Turner is far too literary for my taste. Except, of course, for the first decade of his century, when he painted like a dream. But whores: his life has whores, and misogyny,' I go on, 'in plenty. If you follow my advice on this occasion you'd make a killing. As for myself, I'm astonished that someone hasn't tried already. A film,' I conclude, 'would be the least of your worries.'

Removing her glasses she massages the bridge of her nose. She frowns.

'Cotman wasn't *prone*,' she says, with surprising intensity, 'he was *ill*.'

'He suffered,' I tell her, 'from timidity and a lack of resolution. Timidity of execution and irresolute ambition. A parochial English figure. Or do you, unlike with Caravaggio, see much of him in me?'

The frown intensifies between her puckered eyes: the spontaneity – the turning over of a new leaf – of earlier that day has gone.

'I can't stand these English mediocrities,' I add. 'They dominate the scene but when I'm gone we'll see who's been the master.'

Her gaze, like mine, is on the trees: the bare oak and beech and poplar: I am, rather than defining a position, digging my own grave.

'What's so wrong,' I ask, 'in writing not about something

292

you've studied but something you've observed? You can incorporate that part of my life before you even knew me. You have, before you,' I conclude, 'a seminal source.'

'Perhaps,' she says, 'his reticence is inseparable from the quality of his work.'

('A quality,' she might have concluded, 'I very much admire.')

'When he should have ventured all he plumped for patronage,' I tell her, 'of a particularly unenlightened sort. What originality he did possess, to, as I've said, no small degree, he meticulously squandered. If only Girtin had had his life span. Dead at twenty-seven.'

It rains: or is the wind flailing dust, from the gutter and the roofs, against the panes?

In the rain, one evening, Isabella and I lay beneath the ferns in Ardsley Wood: 'Pretend this is a house,' she said, while the drops – she laughing – fell across her face.

'I am,' she says, 'too close to the subject,' and returns her gaze to the paper strewn across her desk. 'If,' she adds, her head still bowed, her glasses replaced, 'you're such an interesting subject, why not try yourself?'

I am in this house with Isabella: we embrace: the windows are blacked out with tar – sprayed on by a figure in overalls outside. I crawl out from a crashed and burning car and find my glasses frosted: 'I shall never,' I tell Bella, 'see you again. (I shall never write and paint)': a dream the night before I heard she'd died (Bea, but not Corcoran, with her).

'If you're going out let's keep to the arrangement we've worked out already,' she says, 'and let me or Mrs Otterman know.'

Meanwhile, at the back of Fenchurch's mind, spring, like feathers, *wings*.

"The writer, painter, raconteur, plagiarist, poseur and charlatan (he raised charlatanism to the heights of a respectable profession) was born in the city of Linfield in 1934 (or was it five – or '33?), date, as yet, to be decided: he had no education other than the one normally available to the majority of children at that time: drilled in spelling, writing and arithmetic (a spouter of mathematical tables backward by the time he was seven), he advanced from one educational peak to another with a dexterity which was the envy of his peers and aroused much pride in his family (if enmity amongst his brothers)."

'I thought I might go to Cawthorne Castle.'

'Isn't it far?' without looking up.

'No further than yesterday,' I tell her. (And yesterday no further than the day before). 'I would like,' I go on, 'to sum up my life (draw a line beneath the account; find out, for instance, how much I owe, how much I am in debt, how much, if anything, is left over.')

'What has that to do with Cawthorne Castle?'

Not that there's much castle, to speak of, there at all.

'I drew up sums in the past while standing there.' Many a sunset watched with Bea: many a sunset watched on my own: the path across the fields, for instance, which led, via a footbridge across the Lin, across the golf-course to a back-garden ginnel leading, through someone's garden (a fretted look from the scullery window), to Manor Road itself. 'It is time,' I say, 'to make amends, to come to a judgement, to recognise all I've been through in the hope I shall not have to go through it all again.'

He heard Alki, from time to time, busy with her pots (preparing her husband's lunch) in Taravara Road, welcoming the sound (all domestic sounds audible in that tiny London back-street house) as evidence of a life other than his own.

'I sacrificed everything,' I tell her, 'for art,' while she, above Cotman's 'Greta Bridge', adjusts her glasses on her nose.

If I released the nude I painted of her, in the room above the barber's, in Southgate, all those years ago, no one would recognise, I'm sure, anything other than another female.

'Many people make the mistake of equating madness with irresponsibility. It's nothing of the kind,' I tell her. Bea, for instance, and that woman in the neighbour's garden who came out each day to tend her plants, and whose appearance, from a distance of twenty-five feet, I mistook for that of Isabella, she

294

and Isabella two figures in one, a definitive form of femininity, the possibilities of which I saw no end. 'The first thing a madman discovers is his obligation to duties which he not only had never responded to before but had never even recognised. First and foremost,' I add, 'his duty to God. Not to his wife, not to his children, not to his vocation, but, above all else ("above all else" a phrase not chosen lightly) to . . .'

She has, that morning, plaited her hair (it must have taken quite a while: up early after a night spent talking to Charlie) and has coiled a plait above each ear – in a manner that reminds me, with a shock – a sensational spasm of recognition – of her grandmother sitting in the same room on her daughter's bed, where I have found her as if by chance – allowing me to stroke her neck, which led moments later to her lying back, the vibrations of the floor beneath us echoed on the kitchen ceiling, Mrs Hopkins (Rose) enquiring, 'What on earth was going on up there?' when we went down, Bella, calm as a dove on a summer evening, responding, 'Richard was helping me to move Bea's bed: there's so much dust collects beneath.'

' . . . higher things. Madness, after all, devolves from grief, and grief, in turn, devolves from loss,' and when she says, 'There's so much, this morning, I'd like to do,' stooping closer to her desk, 'A View of Richmond, Yorkshire' absorbing her attention, I respond, 'If you don't take note of what I tell you there's no way for either of us to look ahead. Charlie's aspirations to a general good are no more realisable than they were two thousand years ago when the first theologian of the Christian religion enjoined us to seek our salvation in fear and trembling, that is, within the parameters, clinically defined, of a sub-acute anxiety neurosis.'

'If you're going to Cawthorne Castle,' raising her head, 'put on your shoes and winter coat. We bought them, if you recall, expressly for this weather. And take enough money to get you there and back and, if you are going to be late, have the courtesy to ring us. I'll give you the number.'

'I know this number,' I tell her, 'by heart.'

'It's changed.'

'Changed?' I am, without intending to, pausing in the door.

She is writing – has been writing on a piece of paper which, getting up, she places in my trouser pocket.

'Remember where I've put it.'

'You look so much like,' I tell her, 'Isabella. Is it one of her photographs you've been looking at?' to which, ignoring the enquiry, she adds, 'Bryan Raynor will be here in half an hour. Don't even go into the grounds until then.'

'This higher responsibility,' I tell her, 'is all that it's cracked up to be. The physiological implications of which I don't even have to go on about.'

So that one morning, in the garden, looking down – the heat of the summer (a July afternoon) – the humid heat that strikes these airless back-street yards – I see her in a low-cut blouse, stooping to her roses (in no way as effulgent as those of Bella) and, from this angle, glimpse her breasts, shadowed, within the collar of her blouse, and recall a not dissimilar occasion when, stooping, Bella too, inadvertently, had disclosed her breasts, stooping to me in her evening gown (twin fruits of femininity transcending transcendentity itself).

'In half an hour?'

'I'll come down,' she says, 'and see him with you.'

'No doubt he will see you without me as well.'

When, after returning to her desk, she doesn't look up, I announce, 'If you look like that in seven years' time, when Lottie brings her first boyfriend home – conceivably from King Edward's – you will find yourself in an impossible situation. You will fall in love with an eighteen-year-old youth and neither the grounds nor Ardsley Wood, nor the entire fields and surrounding copses will be sufficient to contain what it is you are endeavouring to hide; not even the railway line, or the motorway from here to London. Wherefore, I ask you, where will you hide that which years later, you will find, there is no confessing?'

For the first time since I have come into the room she glances up directly: she examines my gaze for several seconds – and I see that Etty is, by no stretch of the imagination –

despite the plaits – an Isabella: she is not her grandmother's grandchild so much as the daughter of the opportunist, subvertionist, duplicitous Richard Fenchurch – as inclined to betray his class as he is his family: 'all for art!' he might have said as vehemently as now he cries, 'all that I can gather unto myself!'

Raynor is a small man: at our previous meeting – a week, ten days, a month before? – he has told me in his youth he wished to be a jockey: 'Until I saw the horses: I've never looked at another since.' Slight, with sharply fashioned features: 'Like a bird of prey,' I told Etty on that occasion the moment he had left, with no interest in the past ('The past, Mr Fenchurch, is only a fiction'), he comes into the sitting-room, distinct from the living-room (the children largely excluded) and says, 'So you've been running off again. We'll have a rope around your ankles, like Corcoran's horses had, they tell me, when he hobbled them in the yard.'

'I take it I'm to be seen as something other than a dumb animal?' I enquire.

'Far from it!' cheerily, as he looks round for a chair, selecting a straight-backed one as if to signal he has more important things to see to (and far more important on his mind).

'I have dispensed with pills,' I tell him. 'And I have not caught a fever. No chills or sneezes or pains in the chest. I am, in short, in tip-top condition.'

His pale blue eyes, veiled by light, thin lashes even lighter than his thin, fine hair: auburn ('He is,' Etty explains, previous to our first encounter, 'a shy and self-effacing man.'

'We have, in that case,' I rejoined, 'much in common.').

Bares my arm, takes my blood pressure: makes no comment. 'The worst moment of all,' I tell him, 'in the maze is to discover that the minotaur is preferable to any other choice. That one is the minotaur and there is no better offer.'

'Mrs Stott has asked me to recommend a doctor,' he says.

'I thought you were a doctor,' I tell him.

A window looks out to the front of the house: the descending slope, the remnants of the beech hedge, the crescent beds of roses (pruned) inset at each corner of the lawn – and a window at the side of the room, framed, to its right, by the massive fireplace, looks out to the iron-gated arch which, in the old days, led to Corcoran's yard: nothing but neatly-tiled roofs is visible above the old stone wall.

'A psychiatrist,' he says.

He sits, as might a petitioner, on his hard-backed chair, I, for my part, reclining on a couch (as close to the confessional as, I imagine, will set him at his ease).

'I've seen all the psychiatrists I intend to,' I tell him. 'Many, in fact, have followed my example, having moved on to, or homed in on my discovery of the super-authorial self, a multi-dimensional phenomenon and the closest thing we know to God. Indeed, it's more than my contention that it is the God in all of us, unique, articulate, all-comprehending, our miraculous window on paradise.'

'Doctor Robeson is an admirer of your work,' he says.

'If we know enough,' I say, 'already, why on earth should we need to know more?'

'Another view,' he says, 'is helpful,' in no way swayed, I observe, by my beneficent smile.

'Are you a native of these parts?' I ask.

'As a matter of fact,' easing his trousers around his knees, 'my father was a local doctor.'

'In Ardsley?'

He shakes his head. 'Several miles away.' He adds, 'I was always interested in the mines.'

'After horses.'

'Oh, horses came much earlier,' he says. 'I had ambitions, at one time, to be a vet, but the examination requirements were more demanding than those for medical school, so I followed the family practice. My uncles and brother are doctors, too.'

'In these parts?'

'In London. One of them,' he adds, 'was a former colleague of Professor Maidstone.'

'Oh, Maidstone,' I reflect, inwardly comparing his avuncular frame with the ascetic one before me.

'He, too, has a high opinion of your work.'

'But, then,' I tell him, 'he's retired. The fate, I'm afraid, of all those who have had a high opinion of me. Or my work. It appears to be a pre-condition, a high opinion of Richard Fenchurch and retirement going,' I continue, 'hand in hand.'

'He refers, in his notes, to your habit of giving subjective reactions an air of objectivity,' he says, adding, 'Maidstone,' as I frown.

'He never mentioned that,' I tell him.

'I'm sure he did.' He bows his head (leaning forward, his hands clasped loosely between his thighs).

'I'd have remembered if he had.'

'You may, on the other hand,' he says, 'have chosen to forget.'

'And forgotten,' I tell him. 'I've forgotten.'

'Precisely.'

'I'm far too clever,' I tell him, 'for that.'

'None of us are, I'm afraid,' he says. 'Which brings me back to why I would like you to see my colleague.'

'Not Donny Robeson?' I ask.

'His name is Donald Robeson,' he says.

'I knew him at school, if it's the same Donald Robeson,' I tell him.

'He never mentioned that,' he says.

'I'll run rings round him,' I tell him. 'What new observations will he have to make that I and others haven't made already?'

'It's not so much a question of something new as merely to have an outside view. And one up to date, of course,' he adds.

'To date?'

'Something,' he says, 'to bounce things off.'

'I've bounced a few things off Robeson in the past, a few more,' I tell him, 'shouldn't do him any harm.'

'Having known you in the past might,' he tells me, 'be of assistance now. Particularly,' he goes on, 'at a time of your life when none of your other advisers knew you.'

'Is he tall and thin?' I ask.

He nods.

'Red hair?'

'Balding.'

'Oxford.'

'He was.'

'One of the school's great scholars,' I tell him.

'Was he?' Getting up he re-opens his bag. 'I thought,' he says, 'I might look at your chest.'

'Heart?'

'If you wouldn't mind,' he says.

When, a little later, he re-packs his bag, he says, 'I'd like to prescribe some pills. See what effect they have over the next few months.'

'You might prescribe,' I tell him, 'but I'm afraid, even with Donny on your back, I shall not be inclined to take them.'

'They're a precaution, rather than a cure,' he says. 'Rather like lithium in the past, they'll help you to live a fuller life.'

'I live a full enough life,' I tell him, 'already. When the time comes to go you'll find me,' I add, 'at the head of the queue.'

'What if you only half go?' he says. 'The life of an invalid, after a cardiac attack, isn't something, I'm sure, that you'd welcome.'

'I've had these pills,' I tell him, 'before. They didn't do me any good then. They won't do me any good now,' and, at a knock on the door, Etty pausing on the threshold a moment before entering, I add, 'See what your chum is up to. Prescribing pills he knows I won't take. From now on, Etty, it's mind over matter.'

'Mind devolves from matter,' Raynor says (portentously, in my view: not the sort of statement either welcome or expected from a village doctor), 'not the other way around.'

'I shall get well,' I tell him, 'in my own good time, and by good,' I go on, 'I mean good of my own prescription.'

"Nothing," Fenchurch wrote, "was resolved by this meeting with the doctor, in his liveried pin-stripe suit (light grey in (vivid) contrast to Maidstone's charcoal), but," he paused, "the prospect of running rings round Donny Robeson after all these years (he beat me in the mile and got a scholarship – after special coaching – to St Edmund's College) brings me – more than the threat of partial paralysis – back to life."

'He says your pulse is high ("fevered", he describes it), your blood pressure is no better, if not slightly worse, than it was before, and he says your mood is too volatile to be allowed to go out on your own. He's concerned,' she adds, 'you're taking no medication.'

'I am not,' I tell her, 'a chemical bin,' (though I have been, even more than Vivienne, in the past), she having spoken to Raynor in the hall for several minutes – then several minutes (considerably) longer in the yard outside – even stooping to his car door after he's got inside: 'He's doing us a favour coming to the house: most patients, other than the terminally ill, have to go to him.'

'He doesn't consider that a favour, he feels flattered,' I tell her. 'Called out, in this provincial backwater, Etty, to see the scribe, plagiarist, grovelist and playwrong, friend of the grate and the gourd, novelless, playless, plagueless, friendless: good God, he'll make a fortune with his memoirs.'

'Will you see Robeson?' she says.

'Once I've run Donny,' I tell her, 'round this provincial patch I shall be fit and ready, my dear, for anything!'

19

CAWTHORNE CASTLE overlooks the upper reaches of the Lin: a bend of the river skirts it to the north, flowing along a broad, alluvial bed, while to the south, the east and the west, lies the wooded hill-land of the lower Pennine slopes. On an opposing hill, beyond the river, stands the Onasett headland.

I am too tired, I am tempted to tell Etty, to go out, having discovered, after sixty years (doesn't do to be precise), that my body isn't my own, merely the property of an artificer who has little, if anything, to do with what's inside (the facility, Etty, of everything I've done), leaving the house, however, in Charlie's boots (stronger than my own) and my winter coat, with (as if I needed them) precise instructions ('they have moved the stop') where to catch the bus, for, if I go the 'back' way to Linfield, through the lesser mining villages to the west (a favourite route in the past, but now awash with drugs), instead of the more familiar route to the north-north-west, I can get off close to the castle where, at the zenith of my powers, I wrote, 'Meditations Standing on a Hilltop at Cawthorne' – yet minutes later see Raynor leave his car, parked at the kerb, and enter a shop and come out carrying a bag (the shop's a chemist's). Having glanced in my direction he shakes his head (face flushed above his light grey suit: no overcoat for him), gets in his car, adjusts his mirror (a reflection of myself) and, re-adjusting it, drives off.

A stiff breeze is blowing on Cawthorne hill: the town lies in a haze across the valley: to the west, obscured by cloud, is the fissure in the Pennine wall through which the upper river flows (cascading through a limestone gorge: sandstone at a lower level, its ochre boulders strewn in its bed).

I enjoy the bus ride more than (an unfinished sentence is, if frequently repeated, an invariable sign, Maidstone says, of a schizoid condition).

The disassociated frame of mind.

The disassembly of his head.

I am still at the stop (the other side of the road to the direct-to-Linfield stop) waiting for the 'back way' bus.

After a moment of reflection, Fenchurch bows his head, contemplates the footpath by his feet (the eroded flags) and returns, past the church and the rectory, to the door in the old stone wall and makes his way, up the steepening slope, beneath the trees, to a recently-installed wicket-gate in the beech hedge (Charlie's idea, matching the one that leads to the orchard), entering the front garden of his daughter's house, his wife's childhood home and, glancing in the window of the living-room with the hope of glimpsing the love and longing of his life, the woman without whom his existence has no meaning, re-enters the front door which, by his estimation, he has left only moments before.

'The inclination never to complete a sentence is invariably a sign of,' Maidstone pauses to illustrate, unwittingly, the state of mind in question.

'Back?' the vacuuming, at least in the hallway, finished, Mrs Otterman popping out from the kitchen.

'Back?' Etty coming out, spectacles raised above her head, from her study (once Bea's bedroom).

'I have,' I tell her, 'changed my mind. My mind,' and such a mind, tuned, I reflect, to molecular phases, 'is susceptible to change,' I add.

I mount the stairs, still in Charlie's boots and my winter coat. 'I had envisaged taking the back way bus, through those villages which, now the pits have gone, are seldom seen – domestic scree, the grey and crumbled houses amidst the fields and copses, the little streams and dells, the unexpected ponds and lakes, the whole awash, I am told, with drugs, theft, burglary, violence to obtain the same – a sea which will finally engulf this village, this house – everything we have known and loved – you see them now, waiting at the stop, behind the houses, in windows and doors, unemployed miners, their wives, their children, waiting, watching every move – "What," they are asking, "did we dig all that fucking coal for, to be cast on the waste-tip with everything else?" but found that a discontinued course of action is as relevant, in this instance, as a discontinued sentence. Stop.'

'Maidstone said,' however, I go on, 'that a cyclonic depression of the sort I've got is invariably the preamble to something worse. I had such visions, Etty, of the castle, the town spread out below, Onasett across the valley, its ridge poking up beyond the trees.'

He couldn't write,
nor could he right
the wrong
that writing of his wrongs
had done.

The thought occurred, 'I don't feel well,' (decide to tell her), lying there, moments later, boots still on, 'I'll go to bed.'

'Are you all right?'

She coming in.

'That doctor.' Said, 'I think I'll rest. (Think I'll go to sleep). Even though I've just got up.' Shouldn't have dressed. Threats from Charlie. Best behaviour. Found a place not far from here. 'Greater responsibility to greater things unseen when not insane,' et cetera. One thought is always back of brain. Has no one found a master?

Two:

'Caught a chill,' flu (from walking in his slippers).

All day he lay there.

Bells.

Church.

Midday: rhetoric was his strongest suit.

If writing didn't work he could always paint; if painting didn't work – he didn't recall the score exactly: hydrochloric acid mixed with amphetamines.

Well, then, Fenchurch, what sort of person am I? Strong, as a youth; stronger as a man: dependent, despite that, on women as vulnerable as himself: picture entitled by others, not himself – Maidstone, Mackendrick, Raynor, et al, *always looking for the bottom line*: inverted paranoia.

Last night he had had a peculiar dream: he had brought an old steam engine up from London and parked it – to people's amusement – in the field at the back of the house at Manor Road: crowds had collected – figures from his past, contemporaries who, as the saying goes, he had left behind: doltards, thickheads, provincial oafs. He joined in, along with his engine, a 'festival of art': films and pictures (poems and books: songs and dancing) ending, anachronistically, in a football match of the kind he had played at school but involving, rather than a team, these figures (and many more) from his past. At the end of the dream the field, flattened by the festivity, was deserted: the engine stood alone, gigantic and absurd in its garish colours, with its giant metal wheels and its smoking funnel. He set off, directing it from behind, on the long road back to London: no one, other than a policeman, came to shake his hand: no one, he observed, was there to see him off. He had one last ambition – to park the engine in front of his house and allow his parents to see it: that ambition, too, he set aside – for he was, he reminded himself, already on the road and, once started, he knew from experience there was no turning back.

He woke with a clear view of his past: he woke, he recalled later, not to a familiar sense of terror – fearfulness, apprehension – but to a peculiar sense of calm: he and Bea, he reflected, had never lived: they had been joined, throughout their adult lives, in a common venture: the steam engine, with its gargantuan wheels, its hissing valves, its gigantic funnel, its superfluous power, was a symbol of his writing and painting: he had worked to achieve, not so much fame as recognition and she to raise a family of – as it turned out – five vividly

305

contrasted children. He had failed, she succeeded: 'Bea,' he said, on waking, aloud, and then, curiously, in the same loud voice, he had added, without the thought having, until that moment, been in his head, 'That's why she took everything I had: the house, my writing, my money – even our children: she knew about her mother, and this, she felt, is what she deserved – what she was owed by the man who had betrayed her in a way that could, even if explained, or understood, never be forgiven.'

She has come to success by climbing on my back, the Nobel Prize acquired, he reflected, at my expense. And I thought last night I had never slept!

I am ill, unwell, as a consequence of Raynor's visit, that putative jockey (doctorial vet: diminutive build and threat of confinement) and the most absurd suggestion of all I should see a contemporary of mine with whom I was in competition throughout my school career.

And then, she knows: 'Are you going mad?' she would, ingenuously, at the time, enquire as she might, 'Is this the right way to stain a cell?' This – he clutched his heart – is a consequence of that. 'That's why, of course, she instantly agreed,' aloud, 'to my coming here: "*You* go *there*": to rub it in ("Meet my Nemesis" the title of the picture).'

Bereft of wife (possessions) God: she wishes me to be confronted by what I am (defined by my omissions). 'If this is her way of telling me she knows then I have nothing left to fear,' he told her: he was, he reflected – with a peculiar calmness, considering his position – about to fall.

She knows.

I know she knows.

I know she knows I know she knows.

"Dear Bea, not only have I discovered that your theory that the stream that runs (a polluted beck) through the middle of Ardsley, and which, you suspected, was flanked by reeds in medieval times, and thereby gave its name to the house built on this site previous to The People's Palace, is wrong, but that this original house derived its name from the colour of the sandstone of which it was built: red (hence, Rede House). Which brings me to a lesser point, namely," I made a pact with fate (read 'fete', the subject of my dream last night), the lore of self-expression. I lost my art to Beatrice Kells (her professional name) but really to her mother, "the doctor came today and wants to place me in the hands of a quack – a putative quack when I knew him at school. Didn't you go out with Robeson (D.), he wanting to put one over on me, you wanting to get back at me also? Tall, thin, sporty, but not as good as he thought, and with parents who had a chauffeured limousine?

Etty is convinced I'm out of remission.

P.S. Mrs Otterman says the principal industry in the village is the procurement and the sale of drugs which makes it surprising that the Hall, unlike most houses in the village, hasn't been broken into more often (twice: nothing of interest taken), but it does suggest – despite Charlie's New Labour Line – conceivably because of it – they won't (we won't) be here for long: a more modest dwelling closer to Linfield – or even in London (though never mentioned) – is on the cards, Charlie champing to get his hands on *global* abuses of humanity again, the local ones too horrible to mention: debilitation of a class, almost of a race, certainly a species, that proud, autocratic (conservative), *humanist* fervour associated with what, at one time, was a necessary profession ('a rat in a hole,' my father described it).

P.P.S. I am better than I've ever been."

'Do you want,' she says, 'to take your pills?' (She has been to the chemist to get them: holds them out).

'I caught a chill,' I tell her. 'I shall stay in bed. Nothing to write home about – apart,' I go on, 'from a note to your mother.'

'Are you taking to heart what Raynor said?' glasses pushed to the top of her head – a mannerism I never liked (two supernumerary eyes, etc.).

'I've decided,' I tell her, 'to stay in bed.'

'I ought to call Raynor back,' she says.

'Carry on with Cotman,' I tell her. 'I,' I assure her, 'will be all right.'

The etymology of grief, the epistemology of madness.

The plight of the middling asses.

'I shall,' I further reassure her, 'draw the line (beneath all these armless jesters). Is your father farther from the truth than your father's father ever was? What's it like,' I further enquire, 'to be embraced by a single arm? Does he use it to support himself or embrace where others have embraced before?' adding, 'I saw Raynor shopping in the village and felt so ill I came back home to bed. All those hours of introspection on which,' I conclude, 'there's been no return,' (a terror of being re-interned).

Neurones and syntases.

'One other thing,' I interrupt, 'I weigh too much. I shall have to slim.'

He went, in the end, in Charlie's car, though it was Etty who came with him. 'Charlie, I suppose, has gone to work?' I enquire as we drive into the grounds of the North London Royal and when I observe we are parking in the forecourt of Eastley Hall, the former Linfield Municipal Lunatic Asylum – passed by, on numerous occasions, on the way to school (its grey brick, mullion-windowed, gothic façade) – having driven all the way in silence – she says, 'He has,' manoeuvring the car into a vacant parking bay.

'It's not,' I tell her, 'so different from Boady Hall.'

'Pleasanter,' she says.

'Worse.'

'Some things get better, Father,' she says, and might have added, 'and some get worse,' but continues, 'It has greatly improved in recent years.'

'Little that I can see,' I tell her.

'But then, you've seen it so little,' she says. 'At least coming out has done some good. I hope you're not going to show Robeson how well and how frequently we quarrel.'

308

'I didn't ask you to bring me here,' I tell her, stiffly climbing out.

Rain flecks the windscreen of the car: it falls on my grey and grizzled head: my arm in hers, the car door locked, we proceed up a flight of worn stone steps to a glass-panelled porch.

Lunatics are visible inside: a mosaic floor inset with a design which appears to incorporate, to my discerning eye, a flower. 'Didn't Van Gogh shoot his brains out,' I ask her, 'after visiting a place like this?'

She appears to know her way, gripping my arm beneath hers then, having negotiated a flight of stairs, we turn along a corridor which echoes (more mosaics) to a woman's high-pitched voice calling, 'I shan't! I shan't!' and then, as if re-programmed by someone as positive in their thinking as Etty, 'I shall!'

We enter a room: we have, a nurse informs us, been expected. We sit, with several others, on wooden benches: figures pass to and fro obfuscated by a layer of liquid which hangs, in permanent suspension, in front of my eyes.

I see a facsimile of a figure I knew before, erect, slim, balding: the epitome, I reflect, of a self-made man, except, I recall, so much more has gone into his creation: a suit as dark and as elegantly striped as Maidstone's, and singularly less creased.

'Forty-three years,' I tell him, 'is a very long time,' to which, unsmiling, he remarks, 'I make it nearer forty-five,' grasping, however, my outstretched hand – smiling at Etty (shaking hers), I convinced he has met her already.

'So much,' I tell him, 'is still the same. As if,' I add, 'we were back at King Edward's,' the smoothness of his chin (so many lunatics have passed his way before), the coolness of expression (eyes, light blue, cast, distractedly, to a far horizon). 'You announcing your intention of thrashing me in the mile.'

'I don't think I ran the mile,' he says. 'Cross-country,' he adds, 'I did for a while,' continuing, 'I've had a long talk with Doctor Raynor, and a longer one still with your daughter,' smiling at Etty again, and when I enquire, 'Did you come

309

to any conclusions?' he replies, 'We're not here to come to conclusions. We're only here to help.'

Put him in perspective.

'On the other hand . . .'

He indicates the way to a door marked 'Annexe': we pass along a corridor with a wooden floor: a line of elderly figures, holding hands backwards and forwards, approaches us from a lighted space: a key is taken from Robeson's pocket and a door inscribed with his name is opened.

He indicates, with an outstretched hand, a chair that Etty might sit in, directly to one side of a wooden desk – indicating a second as Etty signals I sit in the first. He takes his place not behind but, not unlike Maidstone, beside the desk so that, confronting Etty, he is diagonally across the desk from me.

'How are you?' he enquires, glancing from me to Etty, and when she replies, 'Not well,' he adds, 'Doctor Raynor, in his letter, sounded intimidated by your father.'

'He's more at home,' I say, 'with miners, at least, with those that used to be miners. Particularly,' I go on, 'their wives and children.'

Robeson's legs are crossed: long and lean, with prominent, sharply-pointed knees and one bared ankle above a sock which reminds me of the short-trousered, red-haired, lanky youth squeezing spots in a glass-fronted cupboard. Now consultant at Eastley Hall, re-named, he must, on not a few occasions, encounter not a few of his former chums (rivals, fellow entrants for the Horsfall fellowship to St Edmund's).

'Good old Edward's!'

'I beg your pardon?'

'One Old Edwardian to another,' (creatures from a bygone age). 'The parameters are perimeters only,' I tell him. 'Beyond them,' I continue, 'everything is allowed.'

'Let me,' he tells me, 'make a note.'

A pad, taken from the desk, replaces the file on his knee. A pen, taken from an inside pocket, is – Old Robeson! – carefully unscrewed: nothing changed in three thousand years. 'Perhaps you remember Beatrice?' I enquire. 'A putative beauty with magenta hair likened by some to a ptolemaic cat. A leading light,' I go on, 'at the High School.'

Previous medical history, he enquires, glancing at Etty, to which I reply, 'I was consulted by the infamous existentialist Robert (known as "Bobby") Mackendrick whose father was a Ukrainian cobbler who plied his trade in places as far apart as East Ham and Clapham, in years as divergent as 1906 and 1937, he killed by a bomb at the grand old age of seventy-two in an air-raid shelter with a suspect roof which received a direct hit in 1941. "Bobby" asked me if I would listen to his tapes, a preamble to his writing his celebrated *The Phenomenology of Experience,* an amalgam, not entirely inaccurate, of much of what I told him. It is, in short, a study of me, unannounced and something of a parody of my less successful but more influential *A New Theory of the Mind* and my equally influential *The Logic of Grief,* without a doubt,' I wait for acknowledgement, 'you must have read them all.'

'We read nothing, I'm afraid,' he says, 'up here.' He glances not at me, but Etty.

'In which case,' I tell him, 'let's stick to the facts,' giving him my date of birth and marital status, number of children and financial position. 'The future has been mortgaged to the past by mortgagees who made commitments which had nothing to do with me,' I tell him. 'Insanity is a motor impairment which, like everything else, has a spiritual dimension, one, however, which conditions, rather than is conditioned by.'

'What feelings, for instance,' he asks me, 'are you having now?'

'I might as well confess it, dissimulation is my ruling passion. I am that not uncommon phenomenon, a vocational liar. All my life,' I add, 'is a fiction. Not a day has gone by in which I have not added another word, another deed, another event, another action.'

'Is he,' he enquires of Etty, 'as defensive with you?' and when she answers in the affirmative, I add, 'Opposition, in the past, has been all I've had. (Me against the school, remember?) Not invited back in my final year at the Drayburgh, for – I was told,

311

by Sir Felix Pemberton, the Principal at the time – you've seen, I take it, his pictures at the Tate? – failing to attend statutory classes in Perspective, Anatomy and the History of Art and, a peculiarly venturesome subject for that time, the Moral, or was it the Immoral Principles of Design. I was, in reality, writing novels, not painting the pictures and drawing the drawings I should have done. Furthermore, for the next few years, I taught in schools in the East End of London which were – at least three of them – counted amongst the worst in Great Britain, the venomous Tudor Street School between the Whitechapel Road and Cable Street in Stepney, and the odious Windsor School in Hackney, to name but two, after which I applied for jobs as diverse as a refuse superintendent (the only white man in the queue of West Indians and Asians, losing out to one of the latter) at a departmental store in Oxford Street, as a stock-clerk in a steam-casings manufacturer's office in Clerkenwell, an exhibition-stand erector for a firm in Southwark, at the southern end of Blackfriars Bridge, as a copy-writer at the corner of Wardour Street and Shaftesbury Avenue, as a journalist on the in-house magazine of a well-known manufac-turer of household soap: a cleaner, a bouncer, a washer-up. I ended up starving in a room above a sweet-shop in a street not far from where I am living at present, collecting discarded vegetables and half-rotten fruit from the gutters as the day-long street markets closed. Meanwhile of course,' I glance at Etty, 'our first two children were born and I was writing and painting every minute of every hour when exhaustion didn't engulf me.'

> I laid it on the line:
> I gave it to him proper:
> no good not lying when you're down:
> o give the sod a copper.

'And all the while,' I add, 'you were studying at the Radcliffe.'
He is writing with a thick-nibbed pen – a present from Mrs, or perhaps Ms Robeson at Christmas, or bought at the Swan

Press, the only bookshop in Linfield: no books by the author whose tortured revelations are a postscript to his life in Linfield.

'Then, of course, with *A Hero of Our Time*, I became,' I add, 'a household word.'

And so forth, as Isabella, in her retirement at Torquay would say ('nothing like the Riviera') when the delirium of recollection got beyond her: 'Those picnics that we had (when Bea was a child) in Ardsley Woods, *and so forth*,' waving her delicately wrinkled hand.

'How I loved her. Above all else,' I am about to add, but remark, 'And never looked back until, approaching my fiftieth year, but, more closely, my fifty-fifth, I was overwhelmed by forces which youth, energy, certainly passion had, until that moment, kept at bay, a species of terror, the intensity and extensiveness of which, even now, after all these years, I hesitate, indeed, am unable to describe.'

'Experiences,' Robeson says, referring to Raynor's letter, 'you've had since childhood.'

'I believe you were in Junior King Edward's?' I enquire.

'King Edward's Juniors,' he replies.

'Fee-paying at the time.'

'I was a fee-payer all the way through school,' he says, and adds, 'At least, my parents were.'

'I was at Onasett Juniors.'

'A good school, too, I hear,' he says.

'Only a few passed to the Grammar.'

'That's right.'

'Equality restored by administering to the sick in your home town,' I tell him.

'It wasn't my home town,' he says. 'My parents lived abroad and, when not, in a variety of places. However,' he pauses, 'I have made it my home town,' and adds, 'Would you say you were feeling depressed?'

'Dispiritation,' I tell him, 'has been my way of life. I wake each morning as do the bereaved. *Someone has gone.* In my case, my mother's eldest son who died six months before I was born.'

'Your mind harks back to it continually,' he suggests.

313

'Not,' I tell him, 'any longer.' (I have, I might have told him, outgrown it.)

'We all have our portion of bad luck,' he says. 'Some infinitely more than others. The question we have to ask isn't,' he continues, 'why or how, or even when and who, but what are we going to do about it?'

The words taken, or might have been, out of Maidstone's mouth (a pragmatist!).

'A life,' he continues, 'of initial hardship, followed by one of considerable success.'

'A classic pattern,' I tell him, 'of decline.'

Etty is subdued. 'Perhaps you'd feel easier,' I suggest, 'if my daughter wasn't here.'

'On the contrary,' he says, 'I'm interested in what she has to say.'

'Over the last few days,' she says, 'he has rambled in his speech, has been unable to focus his thoughts, is totally self-absorbed, and appears oblivious of any help anyone may give him.'

God help Cotman! is what I am about to say, but, if shocked, swiftly reply, 'That's not entirely true. I am more aware than ever of my faults and do my best, despite dispiration and attacks of terror, to set them right.'

Robeson writes – left-handed, I note, recalling this mannerism in the Sixth Form Library, his pen held in such a way that, as he wrote, the nib was pointing at his chest: something narcissistic, careerist, even, in this gesture – less so, I reflect now, as if, self-possessed, he is privately lost.

'In addition to which there are,' I tell him, 'moments of self-preoccupation that induce a feeling of my being lifted from the ground. I float. A curious sensation I can't,' I conclude, 'otherwise describe.'

'Would you describe it as ecstatic?'

'On the contrary,' I tell him, 'I invariably feel reflective, as if this form of elevation is, or should be, my normal state of mind.'

A sense of normality, he might have written, he ascribes to an abnormal state of mind.

'Who, in this situation, is to define normality?' I enquire. 'Or do we take a hippocratic view that that which is not experienced by the observing mind is not to be considered normal – is, if not corroborated, to be considered pathogenic, etymologically deriving from, in short, a grief-stricken source?'

Such abstruseness (a view of Linfield's inner suburb – rows of semi-detached houses – visible through the window and, closer to the building, a mildewed, stone-flagged yard) is not to Robeson's liking: his pen, its cap towards me, is arrested in its track: the self-directed scribbler, the other-directed scribe, the silver clip enquires, have you come here to decide?

'Were you,' I enquire, 'at the Allgrave party that summer when "the best generation KEGS has ever had", as the Head described it, met for, as it turned out, the very last time?'

'I was one of the few,' Robeson said, 'who didn't go.'

'Why not?'

'Because,' he says, 'I wasn't invited.'

'I wonder why that was?' I ask.

'Because,' he says, 'I was in the bug-house,' smiling at Etty to add, 'The boarding-house where us poor boarders slept, socially unacceptable,' he goes on, 'to the town boys,' and, still smiling, 'You're the third person from that party I've seen in the past few months,' continuing, 'not socially,' the pen still in his hand, 'but in this room.'

'Depression of the kind I have described is the equivalent,' I tell him, 'of having your skin peeled back, or your skull removed. All those things that normally protect you have been displaced. The whole metabolism quivers and shakes, is ceaselessly tormented.'

I tell him this to have the satisfaction, the cap of the pen once more towards me, of watching him make a note on his pad.

'You're the seventh psychiatrist I've spoken to, at length, over the past ten years – one, roughly, every eighteen months – and though our encounters have never led to much – as much a fulfilment of their expectations, I might add, as mine – it has nourished in me a scepticism of my own reactions. Am I, for instance, I ask myself each morning when I wake – gripped by alarm, anxiety, dread – *as mad as I make out?* Is this a reasonable expectation? i.e., a sensitive and intelligent man, imbued with understanding, sensibility, taste, even with the gift of self-expression. Will it, unless I am brutalised like everyone else, ever be any different? Am I condemned to be an aberration, a sensitised monstrosity, thrown up by nature which only evolutionary indiscretion will bring to an end? It's not, for instance, by chance, that when I look up the antecedents of a case like mine – unique, I would have thought, in many respects – I am not directed to psychology, or even analysis, let alone philosophy or God, but to teratology, the science of vegetable and animal monstrosities, and the famous Harrison and Schaadt experiments, at Berkeley, on pregnant mice.'

I am scarcely, at this stage, in a state to go on (his pen feverishly active on the paper before him – how like those lectures in Natural Science, he, as always, sitting at the front).

'I haven't heard of teratology,' he says, smiling at Etty, 'applied to this particular subject. Nor,' he goes on, 'of Harrison's – and did you say Shat's experiments on pregnant mice?'

'I want! I want!' comes a voice outside the door, followed by a banging at the one adjacent.

Robeson's pen is still. The adjoining door is opened: 'What is it, Hilary?' a male voice enquires.

'*Can* I smoke?' a woman's voice replies.

'Only if you have to.'

'You said only one a day.'

'Only one.'

'I've had one, Doctor Freeman, already.'

The door of the room is closed.

'What relevance,' Robeson says, 'do these experiments have for you?'

'My mother suffered,' I tell him, 'in a similar way when,' I add, 'she was pregnant with me.'

316

'You're not equating yourself,' he smiles once more at Etty, 'with a mouse?'

'With several.'

'Or even,' a further smile at Etty, 'with several.' Leaning to the file, he adds, 'Your psychiatrist at the North London Royal was inclined,' he consults an appropriate sheet of paper, 'in fact, was anxious to discount it.'

'We are talking about a physiological entity,' I tell him. 'Like having, for instance, red hair, or being born with only one foot.'

'At least, not three,' Old Robey laughs.

I laugh as well: so does Etty, who, until now, has watched Robeson's expression with a frown.

'If,' he goes on, 'it happens to be – shall we say, not "true", but relevant – it doesn't change in any way what you intend to do about it now. A mouse, I suspect, has no powers of reflection. Consciousness it might have, in a passive but not an active sense, of things mulled over and acted on. And we,' he smiles again at Etty, 'are mullers, and you, if I'm not mistaken – according to the *The Edwardian*, which I still receive, at the end of every term,' he gestures in the direction (I take it) of the school, 'are a muller-in-extremis, your books, whereas unread by me, have been commented upon almost, it seems, on an annual basis – until, that is, the last few years. I take that to be congruent with your illness.'

'It was more my illness was congruent with something else,' I tell him. 'My wife leaving me, for instance, first for the sake of science, then for the sake of the parliamentary private secretary to the Minister of Health and subsequently, in a re-shuffle, to a junior minister in the same department.'

'Your wife's departure was congruent with your illness?' he enquires.

'Coincidental,' the patient declares. 'I was already in extremis,' (the foetal prodigy of those early months, locked in with its placenta, had, after sixty-odd years, finally shown its hand).

'What brought you to me?' he suddenly enquires and, as I

317

turn my head from the window, perceive that this enquiry is directed not at me but to the, until now, relatively silent figure beside me who, pre-empting my desire to say, 'Brought is the operative word: I didn't choose to come,' says, 'He appears, despite you being with him, to be speaking to someone else. That, and his irresponsible and at times nonsensical actions, his inclination to sit, his arms folded across his stomach, and rock himself in a chair, his tendency – which, at this stage, I wouldn't wish to put any higher than that – to weep, involuntarily, without provocation, sometimes, with only one or two intermissions, for several hours on end.'

'What do you weep about?' he asks, and adds, 'It's unusual for a man to weep so long,' as if, in reporting this behaviour, Etty is being, if not deceptive, misleading.

'I don't know why I weep,' I tell him. 'It happens, as it were, without my knowing. First of all,' I go on, 'there's fear, a feeling of desolation, of loss, so complete that, even after all these years, I couldn't begin to describe it.'

'Why not,' he tells me, 'make a start?'

'First of all,' I tell him, 'there's the fear that is on me the moment I wake. There is no morning, for instance, when it isn't there, and no day when it doesn't persist until the evening. At times it is so intense, so comprehensive, so all-embracing that, involuntarily, I weep.'

'What sort of fear?' the pen pointing once more towards his chest.

'A passive fear, synonymous with waking to the realisation that during the night a death sentence has been passed, and an active fear synonymous with the realisation I will never see another dawn, another night, my children, my wife, or anyone I love, again. Underlying this sensation is a feeling of guilt which not merely absorbs but consumes the mind entirely, so monstrous and complete, so all-pervading and all-enclosing, that there is no hope – no conception, even – of forgiveness or atonement: gripped by this dementia, the mind can think of nothing else. Yesterday, for instance, I persuaded myself I was on the threshold of going mad. This was prompted by the severity of a bolt depression which struck me, unaccountably, when I glimpsed my daughter's doctor, Raynor, in the village, doing nothing more significant than carrying a bag of shopping to his car. Immediately I thought, "My last hope has gone!" though what that hope was, and why it should be abandoned at such an irrelevant moment, I have no idea. This attack, appeared to be related to the shallowness of everything around me: the people in the street, the face of Raynor with his bag of shopping – the fact that he had something meaningful to do in life and I, transparently, had not – and with the face of Etty and the cleaning-woman as I came back inside the house. I immediately thought of Bea and the shallowness of our marriage, of a relationship diverted from its course by something as inconsequential as a laboratory experiment and a relationship with a one-armed opportunist whose name at school, I understand, was "Bandit". The fatuity, as I say, not only of all these people but of such reflections reducing me to a state not indistinguishable from that of a condemned man who steps out to the yard and, after one or two faltering steps, onto the scaffold. A certain complicity in what is about to take place absorbs him, alongside the feelings of terror and despair, a dispiritation so profound he can't even speak, as if, in desperation, he is about to slip the noose from around his neck. Yet the noose, in this allegory, is reality itself, and the irreality he would have to endure in taking it off is worse than the reality he faces at present, a realisation which pitches him into a despair greater than anything he has previously imagined.'

The room is quiet: a door opens in the corridor outside. 'One more,' says a woman's voice, followed, from inside the adjacent room, by, 'Perhaps you'll miss one tomorrow.'

A door is closed: feet fade towards the sound of distant voices.

All this, I reflect, is induced by what? Not hunger, not electric shock, not a lack of shelter, nor a lack of love but, despite the absence of such things, an organic, physiological condition endemic to my system.

'I think,' Robeson says, writing again, 'you give me a very clear picture.'

When I enquire, 'Of what?' he replies, 'A tired mind.'

'My God!' I cry. 'I only need a rest!'

'A rest,' he says, 'wouldn't do any harm.'

'What do you think, Etty?' I ask. 'Does that complete the clinical picture?'

'I think it's gone further,' she says, 'than that. We need,' she continues, 'a practical solution.'

Robeson raises his head: he is not sure what a remark like that is intending to suggest.

'You think your father,' he pauses, 'ought to come in.'

'I'm not sure I can handle him,' she says, 'in the mood he's in at present. He can't, quite clearly, be left in London or up here to live alone.'

'Do you want to come in?' Robeson says, addressing me.

'I'm quite all right on my own,' I tell him.

'You're currently living with your daughter,' he says as if, having identified a coffin, he is tapping in a nail.

'It was her, and her mother's suggestion I should come up here,' I tell him. 'My wife, as you know, has now re-married. "A run-away romance", it was described in the papers. Though where they ran to I've no idea. They were both back at work inside two weeks.'

'That is an indication of the difficulties my husband and I are under,' Etty says, obscurely, interrupting this remark.

'The only point,' I tell Robeson, 'I wish to make is that I was living contentedly in London, and though one or two neighbours had made complaints, they were nothing that, on reflection, I couldn't contend with.'

'What complaints?' Robeson says, closing the file on the desk and re-adjusting the pad on his knee.

'I solicited, in a wholly innocuous way, the wife of my next-door-neighbour and the wives of two other neighbours across the street. With women particularly I have difficulty in distinguishing between what I wish them to be – loving, warm, all-embracing, providing the affection I never had – and what they

320

are: attached to, and strongly imbued with the values of their husbands. Now I've recognised this as a characteristic of my illness – which, like most disabilities, requires a little while to get used to – I can and, indeed, shall refrain from doing the same again.'

'What would be the same?' he says, this a turn-up, his look suggests, for a former hero of King Edward's whose name, for several decades, has figured prominently in the termly published *Edwardian*.

'I commented on their make-up as well as their appearance, in terms which were approving but which were regarded by them as, if true, intrusive. Yet how can truth be intrusive? I'd enquire, their husbands, of course, taking a more forceful line, disinclined to have their wives approved of in any way at all.'

'How approve?' He re-crosses his legs, preventing the pad, as he does so, from falling on the floor.

'I embraced each one of them and, in one specific instance – that of my immediate neighbour – solicited a kiss.'

'Were you aware of this?' He directs his enquiry to Etty.

'It was my mother who visited him,' she says, 'and found him unable to work or even properly feed himself. Both his general practitioner and the psychiatrist, Maidstone, suggested it would be a good idea to bring him away, as an alternative,' she adds, 'to returning either to the North London Royal or Boady Hall.'

'I went prepared,' I tell him, 'to a group therapy session, with an account of my past history at my fingertips, to find only four other people there, in addition to the psychotherapist, as a consequence of which, on the therapist's instructions, we spent the entire hour playing Twenty Questions. How, with an intellect like mine, with a wealth of social, cultural, moral and spiritual, not to mention domestic experience behind it, am I supposed to recover? I'm afraid confinement, apart from keeping me off the streets, never did me the slightest good.'

'I had no alternative,' Etty says, 'but to bring him home. But I'm not sure his eccentricities fit into a home with two young children, and I'm loath to have him returned – since he so dislikes it – to Boady Hall.'

'Eastley Hall,' I enquire, 'is a suitable alternative?'

'Doctor Raynor,' she goes on, 'suggested we got in touch with you, not merely,' she adds to me, 'as a matter of form but because he believes we need advice.'

'There are halfway houses,' Robeson says – with, I notice, a return of his smile. 'But none that I know of would be suitable for a man of Richard's background.'

'Why not call me Fenny?' I ask.

'Fenny?'

'The name I had at school.'

'I don't remember that,' he says (his own, too, I presume, forgotten).

'I don't see why my wife should interfere,' I tell him. 'It's only guilt. She came, I might add, without any warning. Two days, as it happened, after she'd got back – though I wasn't to know it at the time – from an overseas trip with Albert. Tanned. I hadn't, she discovered, read about her in the paper – the sensational run-away bride and groom, and the difficulties both the Ministry of Health and the Medical Research Council might be in having the soliciting of funds, by the latter of the former, compromised by what was described as "practically an inter-departmental marriage". Politics,' I add in parenthesis, 'is a tricky business. As it is,' I continue, 'she caught me by surprise, opening the door, as I did so, to find her on the step, no food in the kitchen, a pile of unwashed pots, unshaven – "unapproachable," she announced, "merely the shadow of my former self, the man she had married some thirty-odd years before." Albert, I scarcely need to add, I never brought up. Sexual jealousy is the most painful of all the emotions, outside of anxiety and terror, and their cohort, despair, I being a specialist in all three. Nevertheless, if I had had the opportunity, I wouldn't have had the slightest compunction – would, indeed, have derived a great deal of pleasure from it – in killing Albert, and a great deal more, not from killing – I wouldn't like to do her down (after all, I love her) – but from conveying to my former wife the scale and intensity of what I felt at being abandoned in favour of a one-armed mandarin whose own species of suffering is infinitesimal beside my own.'

'I believe you were deeply affected,' Robeson says, 'by the death of Vivienne Wylder.'

'I was,' I say, 'and am,' and then enquire, 'Who is Vivienne Wylder?'

'Vivienne,' Etty says.

'I know no one of that name,' I tell her.

'You lived with her,' Etty says, 'for over five years.'

'It couldn't have been over,' I tell her, 'I would have noticed.'

'Under five years,' she says. 'The dates aren't that important.'

'She had a great deal of money of her own,' I tell her, 'but never any cash. The greatest disturbances to our relationship were less to do with drink and drugs and professional failure – the latter, otherwise, apart from Melvyn, her constant pre-occupation, but money. I'd given all I had to Bea who, unlike Etty, took it without the slightest hesitation. I've earned – or, perhaps, I deserve, she might have said, every single penny. For putting up with me,' I add to Robeson.

'She enjoyed being a mother,' Etty says.

'She enjoyed,' I tell her, 'being my wife, until she was per-suaded not to.'

'Who by?' Etty asks.

'I never found out,' I tell her. 'The place, the times. All the women at that time were giving up on marriage, only – within days, in some instances – weeks, months – taking up with someone else, invariably,' I go on, 'a facsimile of the one they'd left behind.'

'Like you, in Mum's case,' Etty says.

'I doubt it,' I tell her, and add, 'I wonder.'

'It had, nevertheless,' Robeson says, 'a profound effect.'

'My assets,' I enquire, 'or my wife's re-marriage?'

'The death of Vivienne Wylder.'

'That was several years ago,' I tell him, and add, 'Two and a half, to be precise,' or was it eighteen months (two weeks, three days, and thirty-seven minutes? according to the coroner's report). 'She'd been lying there for nearly two days, or was it four, her suitcases packed and hidden in the garden shed, I assuming she was visiting friends, the few she had left, in L.A., one in particular, a diabolic presence, addicted to a diet which when she was over there, reduced Vi to little more than a match-stick, something she redressed with booze the moment she got back. Initially,' I go on, 'she came whenever she'd started drinking, having been turned out or down by most if not all of her other friends. In her final years she'd turn up directly from the airport, having flown in from L.A. or New York, or even Chicago where she used to go and dry out. A taxi-load of cases, like moving half a house, none of which she opened. Sometimes she'd stay a month, sometimes a day, sometimes – on two or three occasions – for only three or four hours. Sometimes six months. Sometimes a year. "Partners in distress," she'd say, and bed down, or otherwise, without another word. She'd been threatening to kill herself for seventeen years, and had even tried it two or three times, on one occasion driving a car into a motorway bridge, having previously, however, fastened her seat-belt. She came out with a dislocated shoulder and a broken wrist which, for two or three days, sobered her up. As for psychoanalysts: she joined me at the North London Royal. Maidstone, the Sub-Dean of the Medical School and the Longcroft Professor of Psychiatry, fell on his knees before her. "The most remarkable woman," he told me, "I have ever met," taken in by her assertions she intended to reclaim herself. "My Academy performance," she described it. He let her out after seven weeks on that occasion and two weeks later she was dead.'

I weep. 'In,' I tell Robeson, 'a disenchanted way (no notice to be taken of it: in another man such an affectation might just as casually be conveyed by the scratching of his head: an itch occurs which induces tears, a melancholia so profound it can neither be described nor analysed).'

The writer takes a rest, absorbing himself in thoughts of the countryside, or the wife of his next-door neighbour, the impracticalities of a relationship with whom must be as clear to her as they are to him: thoughts of immortality cross his mind, together with intimations of senility (currently undiagnosed).

'My principal concern,' I add, 'is to find a companion of the opposite sex with whom I can have a relationship at least as rewarding as that which, for the better part of thirty-odd years, I had with my wife. A woman, in short, who is companionable and strong, intellectually assertive, physically engaging, and who has lived a life, ideally, as unpredictable and as charged with adversity as my own.'

Robeson is writing once more on his pad.

'Do you require,' he suddenly enquires, 'a sedative?'

'I've dispensed with drugs,' I tell him, 'some time ago.'

'I'd recommend you re-start your course,' he says, 'of anti-depressants. We might,' he goes on, 'try a different kind. Once this phase is over I'd recommend a return to lithium. It doesn't necessarily require,' he adds, 'a lifetime commitment.'

'I'm afraid,' I tell him, 'I've been this way before,' glancing at Etty and adding, 'Have you brought me here to be sectioned? Is that what Raynor's up to?'

'No,' she says, and shakes her head.

'As a child,' I tell Robeson, 'she loved me very much. So did all the children. When I was a husband and a father, for days, quite often, at a time, I felt, in light of my temperament, unreasonably happy.'

'It's your welfare,' Robeson says, 'we're concerned about. But that doesn't preclude,' he goes on, 'the effect that that welfare, and the provisions we may make for it, may have on others.'

Maidstone said, 'I have never been depressed myself, as opposed to being dispirited, nor have I ever been anxious to a degree which makes it impossible to function, as a consequence of which I can only imagine what it's like, in your analogy the equivalent of endeavouring to imagine a new colour or the limits of a limitless universe. I have only your symptoms to go on, indications which, as you can see, distress me as much as anyone. If I respect your suffering there is an obligation on you, not to defer to, but to recognise mine. The

325

treatment I am recommending I am obliged, in all cases but your own, to prescribe with the knowledge that if I failed to do so I would be open to accusations of professional neglect. I have no alternative therefore but to insist you take the medication and, failing that, to make it mandatory that it is administered to you, if not by me, then someone else.'

Robeson says, 'If you don't take the prescription, in the doses I recommend, to the satisfaction of your daughter and/or Doctor Raynor, I shall have no alternative but to have you brought inside.'

I weep.

'The dispensary,' he adds to Etty, 'you'll find downstairs. If any further difficulties arise you will, of course, let me or Doctor Raynor know.'

On a separate sheet of paper he writes a number.

'Telephone that number at any time and bring your father in directly if you're in any doubt at all.'

To me, he continues, 'I'm giving you the benefit of the doubt. Freedom outside as opposed to confinement here.' He raises his arm, as he might on winning the mile that he says he never ran. 'The choice,' he concludes, 'is yours.'

'Not that it's any concern of mine,' I tell him, 'but at the time of the events I have previously described I was plagued by reporters, as indeed were my neighbours, who wished to take photographs of the shed in question. Though failure is a cloak that few people can afford and none, as far as I am aware, wholeheartedly welcome, despite its being so freely dispensed, it is not one which even now obscures me entirely. I am still susceptible to being recognised and responded to in a wholly unacceptable way.'

'I am sure your name,' Robeson says (his smile returning), 'will be of no interest, if it's known at all outside the pages of *The Edwardian*, to anyone at Eastley Hall.'

Eastley was a man of action and lived in a house the foundations of which are still, allegedly, in place beneath the present building: he built a five-arched bridge across the River Lin ('one for each of the senses'), hunted in South America, was famous for riding a crocodile with a bridle and bit, and built the first hospital in the district, in the grounds of his house, for the treatment of the mentally ill: a taxidermist, naturalist, water-colourist, philanthropist, engineer (his son assisted George Stephenson in the construction of the station in Linfield) he bequeathed his house and grounds to the hospital which bears his name.

'I gave,' I tell Robeson (Eastley, too, of course, was considered mad), 'all my money away, although a sum has been retained by my former wife, and is administrated by her and my children in conjunction with the bank and the Board of Inland Revenue. I have a residual income which would inconvenience the proverbial mouse, though not at all one of Harrison's and Schaadt's notorious menagerie who subsequently lived, despite their hereditary problems, in, I understand, luxurious retirement, in the form of royalties on plays and novels and from the sale of occasional paintings and drawings, most, too, of which, I gave away. I don't belong to the government scheme for paying authors on the basis of copies borrowed from public libraries, on account of the principle, adhered to, as much as possible, throughout my life, that an artist should be independent of statutory procedures, such independence being the only valuable thing he or she may have. I'd rather starve to death, and, on occasion, have almost done so, rather than accede to state support, not least – the most invidious of all motives – because it's well intentioned.'

I am about to continue but observe that Robeson has already risen (the slurring of his chair). 'The pills are to be taken initially,' he says, 'in very small doses. There'll be no effect for five or six weeks, during which time,' he confides to Etty, 'I want you to call me should you ever feel the need. I'll see your father this time next week. Will you be free,' he enquires, 'to bring him?'

'I,' she says, 'or someone else.'

'The other point I wish to make,' I tell him, unable to recall precisely what it is, 'is that there are certain qualities common to us all, the "all" I refer to,' I continue, remaining in my chair, 'being those afflicted by an unreasonable dependency on others.'

'I'll see you and your father out,' Robeson says (after all, at one point, he was courting Etty's mother and, should Albert fall at the final jump – a one-handed leap at the prime-ministership – might still see himself in there with a chance: from provincial anonymity to metropolitan (Kellsian) notoriety: fame, for fuck's sake! I can see it in his glance).

'This, in turn, is occasioned by what I would describe as an absence of self, a phenomenon I can only describe as being akin to a fall from grace, an absence of, or a removal from God. No language adequately describes it, and though it may have prompted Major Eastley to donate his home, in the late eighteenth century in an unprecedented fit of generosity, to the community in which he lived, for the healing, by seclusion, of those who were mentally ill, the only comment it would draw from me is that it is indistinguishable from a feeling of perdition, the absence of something within one's body without which communication with anything outside, temporal or divine, is not only indescribably painful but impossible. In short, I am not the person you thought I thought you thought I thought you thought I was.'

We are sitting in the dispensary amidst a multitude of over-coated figures who are waiting, via an illuminated sign, for their number to come up: Etty has gone off to get a coffee, returning with a plastic cup which, despite being encased in another, is still too hot to hold.

'Am I to be like this for ever?' I ask her. 'For ever like this to the end of my life?'

'You're lucky he didn't take you in,' she says.

'It's at moments such as this that reality becomes a mockery of my strongest feelings,' I tell her. 'A further reality takes over, comprised of violence, malevolence and destruction, the whole of it suffused by a feeling that life is comprised of nothing else – love, friendship, goodwill – not to mention hope – species of appearance, until appearance becomes our springboard for living and, the ultimate deception – the final irony, Etty – the core of life itself.'

She isn't listening (sipping her coffee) crossing her legs within the confines of the chair and glancing up at the illuminated sign above the dispensary porthole. We have, evidently (glancing at the ticket in her hand) several numbers to go.

'All this,' I tell her, 'is a waste of time. When you were young and happy, and we were living in Belsize Park, one big, happy family, or, if not happy, boisterous, things like this would have seemed unreal. Untenable. Inconceivable. Out of this world. As if I have been cast into inner darkness. Where,' I enquire again, 'did it go wrong?'

'I shall arrange for Charlie to come with you when you next see Robeson,' she says. 'He may be more constructive than I appear to have been.'

'You've been,' I tell her, 'constructive enough. What more could anyone want? My principal impulse,' I go on, 'is to protect you. You have done more than enough,' I add, 'already. No man, considering his history, could have been more sympathetically looked after than I have been. Manipulative, self-centred, cantankerous, uncaring – cowardly, to boot – what more could I have asked for?'

We are being observed by several attentive faces. ('Take no notice of these,' I tell her. 'Most of them are mad.')

'This is a general dispensary. Eastley Hall is part of a general complex,' she says.

'As for being sectioned, I don't believe my behaviour warrants it,' I tell her. 'As for these pills. I wondered if Bea and Albert wouldn't have me. Being a junior minister in the Ministry of Health, having a madman in his home might do him, professionally, a great deal of good. While life might seem to be vicious and bad he would have the invaluable satisfaction of proving it is not so.'

'I don't think, Father,' she says, formally and calmly, 'you have anywhere left to run.'

This phrase I not infrequently used with Bea: having written myself, as it were, to notoriety, and complemented this achievement by painting pictures – several of which, though rarely hung, were purchased by the Tate – and discovering that my propensity to subside at intervals into the profoundest gloom was, despite all my efforts to resist it, unassuaged, I frequently remarked, 'I have nowhere left to run,' to which Bea would respond, with her unfathomable stare, 'Except here.'

'The other thing I wanted to tell him,' I tell her, 'was that long into my adult life I was firmly convinced that everyone endured the things that I did. Everyone, I foolishly assumed, woke each morning to a feeling of terror and, throughout the day, their principal energies were engaged in attempting to overcome not only that but its indefatigable ally, dispiritation. Fear, combined with despair, produced an awesome dread, the most fearful of all the human emotions. Everyone, I was convinced, experienced the same. I took it for granted – in the same way I could assume that, despite wearing shoes, everyone had five toes on each foot. I even assumed Bea, even you, suffered in a not dissimilar way, that all the principal questions of human existence came terrifyingly to the surface at the moment of waking, but that she, and you, and everyone else, had not only a greater degree of resourcefulness in combating the condition but, the most debilitating emotion of all, infinitely more courage in covering it up. Only in the last few years have I come to recognise that the degree of fear and dispiritation that has greeted me each morning on waking, and which, in struggling not to show, I merely showed to everyone, is the prerogative, if not of me alone, of a small percentage of the human race who suffer in a not dissimilar fashion. Imagine my surprise when I discovered that what came to my mind as effortlessly as the joy of living was confined, in my personal experience, to me alone. Surprise, that is, and dispiritation, a fear and a despair at my isolation greater, terrifyingly, than the original symptoms. I was, as the saying goes, engulfed.'

'That's our number.'

My daughter stands: I repair to the porthole and, through the sliding panel, take the pills myself. When the pharmacist –

a girl, in appearance at least, of seven – enquires, 'Mr Fenchurch?' I am more than convinced that in her unseemly madeup face there is a flicker of recognition.

'It was merely,' Etty says, when I point this out, 'the loudness of your voice. In respect of remaining anonymous, you having only yourself to blame.'

'As always,' I rejoin as we descend the steps to the car. 'Guilt at feeling guilt,' I add, 'and so on.'

Peas, broccoli, baked potato and ham are, peculiarly, all we have that day for lunch.

We eat in silence (a brief call from Etty to Charlie to tell him the outcome).

'I don't think,' I tell her when she returns from the phone, 'I'm ill. Some experts call it "a problem with living", varying degrees of experience of which are common to most if not all people's lives.'

To which, with typical Kellsian asperity, she replies, 'If you're not ill then I am.'

'Perhaps you are,' I tell her, to which, with not unKellsian vigour, she responds, 'That's how you used to undermine Mother. You won't do the same with me.'

'I was most gentle with your mother,' I tell her. ('There was no one I loved more,' etc. 'She couldn't have had a finer husband.') 'She was much envied by the women in the street (whichever street that was). There was no woman in the neighbourhood more idolised by her husband.'

'Why not make it London?' she says.

'Why aren't the children home to lunch?' I ask.

'I made arrangements,' she says, 'for them to have their lunch elsewhere. I didn't know,' she adds, 'how long we'd be.'

'Good job you did,' I tell her, yet wonder at the emptiness of the house. It was never, I reflect, as empty as this: there was always someone or something in it.

'We'll be leaving, in any case,' she says. 'There's a partner of Charlie's who's willing to buy it.'

'I never knew that,' I tell her, looking out, for the first time, at the garden and trying to imagine, after all these years, those flowerbeds – and those trees, the beech hedge – in the hands of someone else. The last vestige of Isabella, with that garden, I reflect, will be gone, but say aloud, 'It sounds to me a good idea.'

'We've found a pleasanter house,' she says, 'closer to Linfield.'

'Not London?' I enquire.

'I've had enough of London,' she says. 'It's paradise on earth up here,' (a recent, and derisory conclusion, I reflect).

'You're beginning to talk like me,' I tell her, to which, without interest, she replies, 'I am.'

Nevertheless, consulting Robeson (not least, a figure of authority) has given her some relief: I hear her singing in the kitchen, later in the day, and moments later, humming on the stairs: shortly after that comes the sound of recorded music from her room (as she works, no doubt, on 'Greta Bridge' – all those tones and planes and textures, the miraculous abstraction and miracle invention). Mrs Otterman, who normally leaves each day after preparing lunch, returning later, if requested, to prepare dinner or supervise the children, comes in, around tea-time, and calls – from the back door of the house, 'I've brought you up some flowers, Mrs Stott,' naming the gardener as her source and, in response to a call from Etty, adding, 'I thought the house needed cheering up.'

'Oh, we're cheerful enough already,' Etty calls – on with 'Ships off Gravesend' now, no doubt. 'Which isn't to say they won't be welcome.'

I have, at her suggestion, remained throughout the afternoon in bed and when I go down to the kitchen, Mrs Otterman, who has evidently come in to prepare the dinner (several guests are due at seven), the miner's wife, daughter, grand-daughter and great-grandchild remarks, 'You're looking well. How did the hospital go this morning?'

'You'd better ask Mrs Stott,' I tell her. 'She did all the talking.'

'That's unlike Mrs Stott,' she says, and adds, 'Nevertheless, I

332

can see it's done some good. You're far less dark beneath the eyes.'

'That,' I say, 'is because I've washed. You should know, being the daughter of a miner.'

Her sharp-featured, dark-eyed face lightens with a smile.

'You're pulling my leg, Mr Fenchurch!' turning to the sink.

'I'm too old to pull anybody's leg,' I tell her, at which, turning once more, she cries, 'I'm sure you're much younger than I am!'

'I'm sixty-five,' I tell her, 'or nearly, and look half as much again.'

'I'm not quite as o'd as that,' she says. 'But feel it, at times, I can tell you.'

'I hope this house,' I tell her, 'will never change. That you, or I, or someone known to me, will forever be at work in the kitchen, in one or other of the rooms upstairs, in the garden or the yard outside. That the trees will bud, the flowers bloom, the fruit ripen, with a Kells or a Corcoran or a Fenchurch somewhere about, painting or writing or hammering or drawing, the window open, on a sunny day, to the sound of Celtic or Saxon voices. Too much has happened here, too much has been felt, endured, survived. Our blood is in these stones.'

'I thought you were from Onasett,' she says.

'What have you been saying to Mrs Otterman?' Etty says when, later, she comes up to my room. 'She was ever so bright when she first came in.'

'I won't, if you don't mind, come down to dinner,' I tell her, for the children, already, are playing in their room (the sound of Mrs Otterman's voice as, earlier, she bathed them) and Charlie has returned and is already dressed, his voice coming from the hall and then the sitting-room as he first greets then solicits with drink the first of his evening's guests.

'Everyone will expect you,' she says, (the occasion, she is about to tell me, will do me good).

'Tell them,' I tell her, 'I'm unwell. It's happened often

before,' and when she says, 'They won't believe it. You're supposed to be up here and getting better,' I respond, 'I am much better,' (in my shirt-sleeves, she in a gown that scarcely covers her shoulders). 'I intend in the morning,' I continue, 'to go back to London. There's nothing left for me up here.'

A look of extraordinary gravity lightens the skin around her eyes.

'When did you decide that?' coming one step further into the room.

I am sitting at the table, beside the window, where, from my youth onwards, I have sat many times before.

'I am writing up,' I tell her, 'my memoirs. The embryo, as it were, of *The Private Papers of Richard Fenchurch*, revealed to the world by his second eldest daughter or, failing that, the author himself, the ultimate, if unreliable, authority on the subject. Previous studies have merely moved my work on the one step from penultimate neglect to conclusive obscurity.'

'It's not a good time to discuss it,' she says, a flush rising from her throat, more nakedly exposed than ever. 'Which,' she adds, 'is probably why you chose it.'

'It's too late to ring up Robeson. He'll be out at dinner, or, if I'm any judge of character, in front of the television,' and when she turns to the door, I add, 'I welcomed seeing him this morning. I welcomed you taking me as well. Don't you see I've come full circle? Robeson and Linfield is where it began: the old school tie, the élitist education, that ardour that goes with the provincial grammar-school boy: that plum-cheeked look, like the crest of the school, which accompanies him throughout the rest of his life. There's one such youth, with that same parochial, charming, bright-eyed look, who presents a television programme on the arts in an identical manner, adenoidal, sincere, that earnest, community-serving expression (the persona of the actor not far behind). It's a world I eschew. I loathed it then. I loathe it now, buried, as it was, in the London mists, the London fog, the effete artistic drizzle that, throughout these years, has numbed me to the bone. I've buried my pills, by the way, in the garden, a foot apart. The worms, I can assure you, over the next few years, will turn into happy toads.'

And when, moments later, Charlie comes up, dressed for the evening, after Etty's gone down, I say something of the same again: 'Robeson has done me the world of good!'

'I hear,' he says, 'you're leaving, Father.'

'I feel much better,' I tell him, 'for seeing Robeson. It's brought my old motivation back, contempt for parochialism and an avid desire – which has nothing to do with you – to escape.'

'Where would you escape to, supposing we were inclined to let you?' Charlie says, sitting on the bed (very much, I reflect, in a pre-match fashion: elbows on thighs, a thick-necked stoop, leaning forward as he gathers his strength: an Old Edwardian, of course, himself, as was his distinguished father).

'Taravara Road,' I tell him. 'Apart from one or two tourists, curious to see where Vivienne swallowed her bleach, I should settle in quite quickly. I even thought,' I go on, 'I could rent or buy a miner's cottage – there are a lot standing empty in the back-way villages where the pits have gone – and paint and write to my heart's content. I've been admiring the sunsets since I came up here, specifically the one,' I continue, 'we had last night, with a lurid band of green above a screen of red, a crimson orifice darkening to blue, an orange sheen around the sun, a turquoise and magenta cloud one side, and fangs of vapour, like wings, gold and silver along each edge.'

He fists one hand in the palm of the other.

'The fields and hedgerows,' I conclude, 'where my youth and dreams began.'

He fists his hand once more (before he runs out with the First XV: 'Play up, KEGS! Play up, play up, for fuck's sake, play the game!').

'And you've buried all your pills.'

'I'm grateful to Raynor,' I tell him. 'And more grateful still to Robeson. And most grateful of all to you and Etty. Without the former, of course, and the latter, the second wouldn't be there. I've come full circle. I feel a new man. I can't tell you,

Charlie, how glad I am that you and Etty had the idea of bringing me here. It's done me, I assure you, the world of good. On top of which, the news of you selling up the house – too big, too impractical, too vulnerable – it scarcely needs explaining – has clearly done the trick. I gave away, over the past fifteen years, something in excess of half a million pounds, none of it recoverable. I have a house, of modest proportions, and a residual income which will enable me not to have to scour the gutters after the local street market has been cleared up. As I say, when I've settled in, with a little subsidy, perhaps, from you, or Bea, or both – or, even, the sale of a picture, an unexpected run on a book, a revival of a play – I can come up here, rent or purchase a cottage – one up, one down – and paint and write, and think. Respice finem, Charlie.'

'Are you coming down?' he says.

'I'm staying up here,' I tell him, 'to write.'

'We'll discuss it in the morning,' he says. 'I'll delay going in to Linfield. These phases,' he goes on, 'require that someone should be with you all the time.'

All is not well in the Land of Uz, said Hiro of the Chaldeans.

Cannibalism in Ardsley as the miners eat their wives.

'You can't be left alone,' says Charlie.

(I've been there all my life).

I remember very well how, in her last days, Vivienne was convinced she was being followed in the street – 'by an actress' who, 'portraying' Vi, was being filmed in a film commissioned by her former husband, 'in order,' she complained, 'to justify his life.' On occasion, out together, we would come across this woman disguised, variously, as a bus conductress, a police officer, and an usherette in a cinema – and once as a stranger who approached us in the foyer of a theatre and asked Vivienne the way to the ladies' toilet. 'That's *her*!' she said as the woman walked away. Much subsequent fleeing from scenes (she said were) being filmed while all I saw was a passing car, a woman glancing in her handbag, a tourist with a camera. 'They're everywhere,' she said, running videos of her films twice hourly

336

through the night, 'looking,' as she said, 'for clues. I'm con-vinced they hired her to watch me as I failed.'

Poor Vi.

Poor Hiro.

Poor wives.

Our telephone was tapped: a 'detective' followed her from bar to bar (from car to car, shop to shop): everywhere was somewhere.

'Why should they make a film?' I asked. 'They haven't got the rights.'

'Rights?'

'The rights,' I tell her, 'to your life.' (The rights to the story which, she says, time alone can tell.)

Her midnight calls to Hollywood: to a director she had worked with, to a dietician, to a Scotsman she had met on a studio lot who professed to have known her father: 'A saint! A saint!' The writing on large (discarded) sheets of paper, in coloured crayon, 'the story of how,' she'd cry, 'I was crucified by men!' ('That's why,' she'd say, 'I live with you: look at the way you treated your wife.').

'Look at the way,' I'd tell her, 'she's treated me.'

'With contempt! (Don't you think you didn't deserve it!),' lying on the couch in the tiny Taravara Road back kitchen. 'My admiration for your wife goes up in leaps and bounds. It wasn't large-heartedness that prompted you to give away your money.'

'I haven't gone back on anything,' I tell Etty when, her guests departed, she knocks on the door, seeing the light beneath. 'I promised nothing at Eastley Hall, nothing to Raynor, nothing to Robeson, nothing to you and Charlie, nothing even to Maid-stone, who was far more pressing than all of you. I intend,' I go on, 'to make a new start.'

'I'm not sure Robeson, or Raynor, would agree to your going, nor your doctor in London,' she says, implying it only takes two of them to put me away for good.

'I'm so much better,' I tell her. 'I was telling Charlie, that meeting with Robeson has done the trick. I can't tell you how grateful I am to you and Raynor. Without you bringing me up here nothing like this would ever have worked out.'

'It's too late to discuss it,' she says, and when I enquire, 'Too late in the day, or too late in the cycle of events?' she merely shakes her head. 'We'll discuss it in the morning.'

'In the morning,' I tell her, 'I'll be gone. My whole life has been based on spontaneous reaction. In such a way I got all my jobs, got to the Drayburgh, wrote my books, painted my pictures, became, in short, what I am today,' and when she replies, 'A fool,' I laugh. 'To be insane, with me, is to be dead with any other person.'

'That's not much of an endorsement of Charlie,' she says. 'And even less of me,' to which I respond, 'Charlie is as mad as I am. At least I represent a range of disaffection which would put me on a level with those iconoclastic heroes he and his chums affect to admire. How, for instance, would you have spoken to Van Gogh? Aren't I a Gogh of the northern counties, a parochial buccaneer?' she waiting in the door, arm raised towards the lintel (a childhood gesture) as if searching for support. 'I'll pack my bags,' I add, 'tonight. Without your help, as I told Charlie, I couldn't have achieved this peace of mind.'

'Is it peace of mind?' she says.

'I feel a new man,' I tell her, 'already.'

'This morning,' she says, 'you didn't feel well.' ('Creased over in that chair when I came in,' she adds, indicating the one in which I'm sitting – terrified (let's face it) of what might happen at Eastley Hall.)

'I shall miss this place,' I tell her, 'and yet it's necessary,' I add, 'to let it go,' while, from behind her back, across the landing, Charlie enquires, 'Why don't you leave it, Etty, tonight? There'll be plenty of time in the morning,' his voice no different from when, earlier, I had heard him calling, in the yard behind the house, 'Goodnight! Goodnight!' to his cheerily departing guests. ('He'll not do a midnight scarper.')

20

IN THE MORNING I am ill: 'A rheumatoid condition,' Raynor says when, alarmed, Etty calls him in. 'His blood-pressure,' he tells her, 'is far too high and there's congestion in his lungs. His glands, too,' he adds, 'are up. In other circumstances,' he addresses me directly, 'I'd have you taken in.'

I dream: there is an argument (in an ancient building, not unlike a temple, across a landing) about the medication I might be given. 'He planted the pills,' I hear, 'in the garden, and all sorts of peculiar things came up,' (flowers bloomed, plants burgeoned, the house, after a while, began to fall down).

'It's been coming on,' she says, 'for days. (Ever since I brought him up.) His feet were steaming in the car.'

'It's a wonder,' I tell her, 'I didn't die (He takes no regard of other people.) In sleep, the mind is disassembled, like petals close at sun-set, opening (I go on) at sun-rise. Figments,' I add, 'are the fruit of the tree that you have at the back of the house, adjacent to the Dell, into whose pool it drops its leaves (in autumn when they die).'

When she says, 'You needn't act, you *are* delirious,' I reply, 'Put me on the train to Taravara Road (or the bus to Camden Town),' the place, had I known it, I set out for sixty-five years ago (pushed beneath the bridge of Linfield Station while overhead a single drop of water falls, darkening the fabric of my mother's coat).

'I dreamt last night,' I tell Etty when she next comes in, 'that I fell ill,' and when she says, 'Like the time I called on you in London and found Vivienne, drunk, beneath the sink,' I respond, 'She was. She was mending the plumbing,' recalling the incident far too well. 'She hit her head on a pipe.'

'What was all the vomit?' she says.

'Vomit?'

'She was,' she tells me, 'very sick.'

'Dizziness from the blow,' I tell her, perceiving the room through a veil of tears.

I make my way up the slope then across the fields and down the, at one time, winding lane (that led, by a circuitous route, to Ardsley Wood) – now a broadened, straightened highway – to the station.

'Where's the station?' I enquire of a man in a passing car and when the car has stopped and the man got out, enquiring, 'Are you all right?' I remark, 'It used to be here, by this bridge,' lines running off in both directions.

'The station hasn't been here for years,' he says – a youngish fellow, a woman still in the car, its engine running.

'I spent hours,' I tell him, 'by the siding. It was my principal occupation when I'd nothing to do. I drew the buildings, and an ancient metalwork bridge that crossed the lines and through the planks of which you could see directly down the engines' funnels (the demise of the steam engine the end of the world of course, for me).'

'The nearest station,' he says, 'is Linfield.'

'Isn't there one,' I enquire, 'much further away?'

'Further?' He glances towards the car. 'There's Darton,' he says, mentioning a village in the opposite direction.

'I might try that,' I tell him, looking along the road (any moment Etty and Charlie setting out to search).

'I can drop you there, if you like,' he says.

A sporty model, the car, like the man himself. 'I'd be much obliged,' I tell him.

The boot is opened, my suitcase placed in.

'We're giving this gentleman a lift,' the man remarks to the figure inside and, with signs of displeasure, the woman gets out: sliding the front seat forward, she indicates I get in behind.

'You get in, Shirl,' the man suggests, but churlish Shirl remains by the door and, hearing a car engine approaching from the village, I swiftly squeeze in.

A car – neither Etty's nor Charlie's – passes, throwing up a cloud of spray.

'We're going to Darton,' the man informs the woman and she – no comment – gets in in front. 'We almost knocked you down,' he adds to me, over his shoulder, as he closes his door.

The car moves off: the road, unfamiliar in its straightness, is neatly attenuated between their heads. They are young: a disembodied gesture of goodwill. 'It must be some time,' he goes on, 'since you came down here,' the last houses of the village, set amongst fields and against the profile – still there, thank God – of Ardsley Wood, passing by on either side.

'I was only,' I tell him, 'passing through,' noticing, for instance, the neatness of his hair (how ill-judged, I reflect, of Etty to suggest my interest in people has been impaired), the neatness, too, of hers, and the fragrance that comes through to the back of the car. 'Though I knew it well when I was younger. So much of my life,' I go on, 'was spent amongst these fields and woods, by Ardsley Dam, in Ardsley Wood,' gesturing as the trees of that – I now observe denuded – plantation disappear: a large, prefabricated structure – not unlike an aircraft hangar, and presumably a warehouse – has been set incongruously in the long-loved fields the other side.

Beginning his last adventure at the age of sixty-five.

'I'll be forty-six next birthday.' An incongruous message which has little effect on the heads in front.

I resist observing the landscape on either side or directly ahead and merely concentrate on the surface of the road itself: the alternate flicking of a broken line and the variegated texture of the tarmac.

'Nothing is what it seems,' I am about to add, but say instead, 'I hope it doesn't take you out of your way.'

'Hardly,' the youthful, clean-shaven, fair-hair-styled man declares. 'A couple of miles at most.'

341

He has, possibly speeding, almost knocked me down and is anxious, I reflect, to make amends.

'I thought I might make for Glasgow,' I tell him, reflecting ('Lunatic Picked Up by Disingenuous Couple'), should he be questioned, this should be enough to put pursuers off. Such a primitive device, however, depresses my spirits and, recalling there is no chemical agent in my digestive system that can arrest or subdue my current excesses, I add, 'Or Sheffield. Being,' I go on, 'of independent means, the world, as, indeed, it always was, is still my oyster,' on the absurdity of this confession wondering if I haven't gone too far. 'Or Blackpool,' I suggest.

All is not well in the Land of Ur.

'The advantages of the independent life – the independent mind apart – is that freedom and liberty are often confused, the one not being a concomitant of the other, defined, as they are, by separate rules which, on the surface, appear to confound the element they're defining. The man, for instance, in the middle of the desert might assume he is free, but, on further reflection, conclude he is not. At liberty would be a better description, for he is not free from hunger or thirst, or, let's face it, the longing for someone to love. Freedom, in short, has to be defined, and mine is defined by its limitations. I am free, for instance, from the burden of earning a living, for it's difficult to starve in a country with such a profusion of goods and so richly endowed with charities. Is one's freedom defined solely by the limitations one places on oneself, inculcated, the majority at least, in childhood, which in turn is the period when the adult mind brings to bear upon it the discipline required of the adult mind in order to function in an environment governed exclusively by technological prescription which is itself the product of an adult mind? Indeed,' I add as a car sweeps past to the young man's consternation, 'a vicious circle.'

Two vehicles are overtaken by the young man in turn: the car ahead – unfamiliar, not one I recognise – disappears over the brow of a wooded hill: we are moving through a landscape I recognise with a pang of pain: here I walked with Isabella, here I strolled, on summer afternoons, with Bea: here, on one occasion, I wheeled Etty in her pram, sitting down on a fallen tree and, admiring her sleeping head against the pillow, reflected, 'What on earth will become of her?'

'It's odd, Ardsley station being removed. It had such character,' I tell them. 'On the one hand, the expresses thundering through, approaching ninety miles an hour, on the other, the stopping trains, together with the long coal trains from Ardsley pit, and the long, returning trains of empty wagons,' while, further afield, at Onasett, as a child, I and my companions would follow a path across the fields, beside the golf-course, to the parapet of a bridge which allowed us access to a similar, cross-Pennine line where we laid coins on the rail to be flattened by engines.

'So you come from here?' the man enquires.

'A child of Ardsley, an old son of the village,' I tell him, 'who has seen,' I continue, 'better days. I came in by bus and couldn't believe my eyes, my favourite station, the one from which I left on many adventures, to school, to college, on holidays, on travel to foreign lands, had disappeared.'

'We haven't lived long in the village ourselves,' he says. 'Since the pit went we thought it looked quite pretty. We're in one of those new estates at the top of Ardsley hill, next to the old house and Rectory, close to the church.'

'A sort of mews,' the woman declares.

'The Hall,' I tell her.

'That's the one. Lived in by a solicitor,' she adds.

'A barrister,' the young man says.

'A lively place in the old days,' I tell her.

'You knew it, then?' She turns her head.

'I knew the family living there,' I suddenly explain.

'The ones there at present are relatives,' she says. 'A grandchild, or, at least, that's what they say.'

'You go to work in Darton?' I enquire.

'Near there,' the young man says, naming a town some miles away. 'We have a shop. We set up in business this time last year and so far,' he glances at the woman, 'so good.'

343

'Fashion and sportswear,' the woman says.

'It'll be quite late before you get back home,' I tell them. 'And hear the news in the village.'

'We don't hear much,' the woman says. 'Unlike the old days, I imagine.'

'The only village activity nowadays,' the young man says, 'is to do with the consumption and sale of drugs.'

'By which time I'll be in Glasgow,' I tell him.

'Or Blackpool,' the woman says.

'I think I'll press north,' I tell her. 'I've a particular reason for doing so,' I add.

'Relatives?' comes the man's enquiry.

'Someone, at one time,' I tell him, 'I thought I might marry.'

'Where do you live yourself?' the woman enquires.

'I'm on the move, at present,' I tell her and, the conversation having achieved a degree of tedium I can, in the comfort of the car, no longer sustain, the old rail junction of Dalton (lines from the east and west meeting those from the north and the south) comes into sight, its colliery, I notice, too, having disappeared.

Rows of terraced houses enclose the road: shops (the majority of them, eerily, boarded up) and, some distance through the village, beyond where the colliery at one time stood, the station is visible above an embankment of slag.

'It was very kind of you,' I tell the couple as I disembark and my suitcase is set down in the station yard.

'Any time,' the man says as he gets back in, waving, moments later, as the car drives off.

'They nearly knocked me down,' I inform the man I assume to be the station official but he merely remarks, 'Cold day for sandals. Off on your holidays?' indicating the overcast sky – resonant, still, of course, with winter, even though the flowers of spring, in one or two places (plastic tubs, for instance, on either side of the tarmacked entrance) are pushing through.

I plan a route that will take me not to King's Cross but Euston and, using the money I have taken from Etty's purse, a little more from a drawer in her desk, the children's piggy-bank and the pockets of Charlie's overcoat (and Mrs Otterman's in the kitchen), I purchase the relevant ticket.

Trains of a local nature pass in and out, none, however, on the route I want: a phalanx of passengers finally alights. The name of my first destination is called.

My suitcase, I observe as the train pulls out, I leave behind, glimpsing it as I might a child deserted on a railway platform. It is midday by the time I arrive at Euston.

I catch a bus in Drummond Street: familiar shops and offices pass: the dull façades of Victorian houses, the Georgian lineaments of Mornington Crescent obscured beyond adjoining roofs, the detritus of Camden High Street and, after a change of bus, the oppressive, winding route, along a narrowing road, between decaying offices, shops, yards and blocks of flats: the darkening, suddenly, beneath a bridge, the emergence into the fracas of traffic and people the other side: within minutes of getting off the bus I am in Taravara Road, an interstice between the diminutive, butterfly-roofed houses with their ochre brick façades and white and cream-painted fascias.

I unlock the front door: an aroma of cold air, a hint of gas, perhaps of vegetation (the drains nothing to write home about), stale food: the welcoming hall (illuminated from the fanlight above the door): the room, to the left, knocked through from back to front and cluttered with canvases and sheets of paper – hardboard, easel, paints – the light suffused through dusty glass. Immediately ahead, beside the stairs, the passage leading, down two steps, to the room at the back: I open a door and reveal an interior divided between a sitting-room and kitchen: a gas-mantled fire (the cooking range the opposite end), a door and two windows looking out to the yard (a vista of encroaching houses).

I sit in a chair and allow the house to re-absorb me.

The telephone rings. Not many hours after that there's a knock at the door. 'What is madness?' Maidstone enquired. 'I'm not even here,' he went on, 'to discuss it.'

Food. Am I capable of living on my own? The cuckolded

345

husband, the writer and artist (incompetent father, improvident son). Where do I go, I reflected, from here?

I went out shopping; returning, I sat for hours: noises from the house next door: the clatter of pots in the adjoining kitchen. Voices.

All is not well in the Land of Ur.

From a curtained window I glimpse my eldest daughter Matt first getting out of then into her car parked down the street: the intervening ringing of the bell, the rush of blood to the heart: paroxysmal tachycardia (that rushes round the head): a tall, lean girl with her mother's freckled skin: long-skirted, booted, with a tight-waisted, round-cut jacket (secured by a single button): visible, behind the windscreen, Dan, her Scandinavian husband, taller, slimmer: blond: they gaze up at the house for several seconds: they must be discussing the possibility of summoning the police.

Christ crucified ('I know what I am doing'): he had it all worked out.

Looking for a cottage – vandalised, of course, while he was out: out-of-work miners trample on his goods, write 'Here we go' across his pictures: "the miracles of art outweigh," he wrote to Bea, "the miracles of science". "How are you?" she enquires in a letter I pick up, amongst circulars and bills behind the front door (recognise the writing). "I've suggested to Etty she takes you north," ("home" crossed out: 'at least,' he thought, 'we have that in common, our children and our past'), "there's plenty of room at Ardsley," enough, I reflect, to do her research, me in one wing, she in another, divorced from Albert, staining cells: all my pictures, from now on, will be in yellow.

The bell rings at the door: it's followed by a knock ('I know you're in there, Father!').

'Perhaps the door is jammed,' (Dan's voice the other side: the Scandinavian reporter).

'It's bolted,' (as the door is tried again).

Rain fell, the day we married, but the sun came out in the afternoon: Isabella's friend (from the WI) had a cinematic camera and took pictures of us walking, through the grounds and past the Rectory, to Church and – a single cut (no cameras allowed in the church itself) – walking back again.

Bea's daughter beats on the door the other side and, after a pause, calls, 'Dad?' and then, more formally, 'Father!'

Etty must have called her.

And pictures, too, of the reception on the lawn, the looming presence of the Hall, Fenchurch in his morning-suit (despite it being the afternoon), with his grey top hat, Bea in her tight-waisted, flare-skirted wedding dress (which lay like a lost cause for years in a cupboard above the sweet-shop in Camden Town), the relatives and friends – and Isabella, radiant, incandescent, like a bride herself – all fifty-seven years of her, Fenchurch subdued (fired from the Drayburgh the previous summer, his art in tatters, Bea still one year to do at college) the final shot on the station platform, the train to London drawing in: Bea, Isabella, Corcoran . . .

'Dad?'

Tenacity a Kellsian trait.

'I've gone to Scotland,' I tell her through the door.

'Open up,' she says. 'We want to come in.'

'Don't ring me,' I tell her, 'I'll call you:' cheeks suffused by the exertion of pushing, knocking, stooping, pressing – calling out to a recalcitrant father as I open up the door.

Who breathes, perspires, creates, aspires: 'You've got here, then,' she says.

'I'm just about to leave,' I tell her while Dan, smiling, brushes back his fringe of hair. 'Where are you going, Richard?' he says, as if other plans in mind.

'I thought I'd try the north,' I tell him. 'Or, then again, the south.'

'You're in the south,' he says, 'already.'

'Further south,' I tell him. 'Where the bluebird flies and the sea is green and people can lie all day in the sun,' only Mathilda says, 'You've done enough lying already. How much money did you pinch?' as if this invoking of the preceptorial self will bring the composite back in line.

'The awful irrelevance,' I tell her, 'of all we do – in art, that

347

is, as well as silence,' and when she says, 'Do you mean
"science"?' her pale green eyes – almost grey in colour –
looking into my darker ones, I add, 'Names of painters, poets
and whores – dramatists, Mattie, and musicians – people whose
work is of no consequence at all, while mine goes unattended.
There was not one letter here when I arrived that has anything
to do with me, Bea writing to a man at this address whom she
assumes to be her former husband,' turning down the passage
while the tall, slim figure of Bea's child casts a tall, slim shadow
before me.

'My mind is in pieces,' I remind her. 'I have no intention it
should be other than it is,' drugs which I took under Bea's
influence, 'which wasn't true,' I add, 'at all,' uncertain which
words of these I've spoken. 'Only the other day, for instance,
I stood on the hill at Onasett golf-course and did a drawing of
Onasett against its headland, Harlstone pit no longer there. It
has a pre-industrial freshness, like an athlete in peak condition
arriving at a race already run.'

Leather boots, creased horizontally around her instep: a full-
length, full-skirted dress, the upper half of which, with its high-
necked collar (secured by a glittering brooch), is concealed
beneath her round-cut jacket (no corner on it anywhere): 'the
turbulence of genius,' I might have said (the buzzing of a fly
in a long-still room where, once, Vivienne, with the incongruity
of the Hollywood whore she was, stretched out on a couch –
where Danny sits, his wife still standing by the door).

Contemplates her father: all my previous triumphs – posters,
of his plays – stored with the miscellaneous bric-à-brac of Vivienne's upstairs.

'I had her for weeks,' I tell her, 'on the mantelpiece in a
plastic jar provided by the Golders Green crematorium, several
of her drinking pals imbibing from the bottle while the priest
intoned the non-sectarian rites and we chanted, absurdly, in
the local church (no organist provided) the fifteenth psalm
which identifies those who, in the last analysis, will not be
allowed into the kingdom of heaven – excluding not only
Vivienne herself, and all her pals, but yours truly, Richard

Fenchurch,' my long-loved daughter at the peak of her career, her bronze hair, plaited, coiled in a crown at the top of her head, her pale, hollow-cheeked face turned not in my but her husband's direction ('Say something, Dan,' her look suggests).

'We've come,' Dan says, 'to take you back.'

'How can you spare,' I enquire, 'the time from work?'

'This doctor, Robeson, Etty has found, is prepared,' Matt says, 'to sign you into Eastley Hall.'

'It's all a question of rhythm,' I tell her, 'how and where you put the words, less the ones you've chosen,' and add, 'I shall be happy living here, much as I was before Etty fetched me.'

The telephone rings: Matt, half-startled, glances round.

'You're looking very well,' I tell her.

'That'll be Etty,' she says and when Danny picks it up, his tall figure uncoiling from the couch, stooping, dark-suited, to where the instrument lies by his feet, he listens for a while then says, 'Matt is here, if you'd like to speak to her,' and adds to her, 'It's your mother.'

'Immensely well. I've never seen you looking better. Your work, I conclude, is going well.'

She takes the phone and bows her head, raising a strand of hair from her brow and securing it behind her ear.

'No,' she says, and after a murmured enquiry from the other end glances up and answers, 'Do you want to talk to him?'

When I take the phone the receiver has been replaced the other end.

'I am,' I tell her, 'interned by love. I don't wish to go,' I add, 'to Eastley Hall, nor to the North London Royal. I am quite prepared,' I go on, 'to live on my own. A visit each day, or alternate days, or even alternate weekends, should be enough to reassure you. I intend, for instance, to go out shopping,' and when she says, 'It appears you've been already,' I conclude, 'That's what I mean: I'm perfectly capable of looking after myself.'

She sits, bemused, across the tiny room: a couch and two chairs confronting each other, the latter at right angles to the gas-mantled fire. Bea at one time accused me of loving Matt and Etty and Beckie too much: 'You are too fond of your daughters: your sons could do with care as well,' but when I pointed out I spent more time with Kenneth and Benjie, she blithely announced, 'Time alone will tell.'

'Aren't they daughters a father could be proud of?' I'd tell her. 'Aren't they daughters who, despite an inner-city education, have done immensely well, one a financial adviser and management consultant, another a scholar – and who knows what Beckie will become?' (she about to start at college). All, in any case, I concluded, gifts inherited from her.

Now when I declare, 'Your mother accused me of caring about our children far too much, supervising your education in those crummy schools without, so she said, a care in the world. Private education – which, she said, would have suited you better – was, I told her, an abuse, not least of a democracy's primary tenet that education was a right, not a privilege to be purchased by the few.'

'Isn't guilt part of your illness?' Matt enquires – or is it merely, I conjecture, her observation?

'I've forgotten all the parts,' I tell her. 'And all the questions and answers, too. Why don't you pop in in two or three days' time? Apart from the odd people who want to see where Vivienne died, and come, invariably at weekends, to take pictures, no one calls. I'll have no one to relate to and if you wish, on the front door, I can hang a notice which says, "Before you go out adjust your dress," and look in one of the drawings to see if I'm properly attired. No one, otherwise,' I conclude, 'would know I was here.'

When she continues sitting there, one booted foot swaying above the other, and Danny, close-cropped, continues sitting on the couch, I reclining in the other chair, I announce, 'To behave, in the past, in the way I've done, isn't a critique of anyone. Material possessions, to me, have always obscured what it was I wished to do. I've never felt so well, for instance, since the day I gave to Bea, and you, everything I had. My only qualm was the damage it might do. But Bea is used to wealth, or was, until her father died.'

I gave away everything I had in the hope that by getting rid of it I would re-vivify my talent: such a simple precept. Initially, of course, I was thought quite mad: I didn't realise what I was up to: the absurdity of giving up a house worth half a million pounds. 'You don't seem happy,' someone said. 'The world is bedevilled by material things,' I told them. 'I am better off without,' scrawled, or so she said, in a casual letter to Bea.

"Dear Bella, if only you could see me now."

How might the fallen rise, etc.

The airship drifted overhead while to the south (seventy-two miles, to be precise) her mother lay in the arm of her lover.

'Bea and I are now divorced. She has no rights of any sort. My sectioning,' I add, 'has been rescinded. I don't wish Etty to apply for it again, even though she has this psychiatrist and her own G.P., a man called Raynor, at her beck and call. Both are bedazzled by her books, though she only has one to her credit.'

I met a woman novelist once.

'Each day,' she said, 'I write a little.' 'Why, in that case,' I asked, 'don't you write a lot?' 'A lot would be a little too much,' she said. I asked her for a date. 'The plums,' she said, 'are not in season,' (the sea at the seaside, the cork in the bottle).

Jocular: the hieroglyphics.

'You want to be left alone?' Matt says.

'I do.'

'I'm not qualified to decide,' she says.

'Ring up Maidstone.'

'I already have.'

'Don't try Mackendrick,' I go on. 'He'd put me inside to prevent me writing the sequel to *A New Theory of the Mind*, the epilogue of which he wishes to write himself, having pinched, on his own admission, most of it already. "I am an anthologist," he said when, putting my mental life in his hands, I went to the trouble of pointing it out. What did Maidstone say?' I ask.

'He said he was retired and we should consult with his successor, which, as yet,' she says, 'we haven't done.'

'What have you decided?' I hastily enquire (like asking Joan of Arc to set herself on fire). 'Etty,' I tell her, 'even as a child, was always an alarmist.'

'You'll be all right on your own?' she asks.

'My sentiments exactly,' as I slowly rise. 'We had an argument before I left. Charlie, Etty and I. Etty was haughty, I was naughty and Charlie was very sad. I'd lost interest, he said, in the things that count. I had no interest, *she* said, in people. "I've got past what you mean by people," I said. (I am deep inside their minds.)'

After my daughter and my son-in-law depart (offering, the former, to go out shopping 'to buy anything you want') I walk, for a while (amounting, I suspect, to several hours), around the house. Danny is saying to Matt as they walk to their car, 'He has to make his own decision,' while Matt, waiting for him to release the door, says, 'What about the doctors?' ('Robeson' and 'Raynor' framed on her lips through the reflected light of the windscreen) while, with a cheerful wave, I watch them depart, their vehicle turning from our narrow street, enclosed by irregularly terraced houses, into the broader one beyond.

All is not lost in the Land of Ur, wrote Hiro (people's motives for doing what they do are never what they seem).

In the back-street kitchen, with its back-street yard and its back-street windows overlooking

a man as cantankerous as I.

'The peculiar thing is,' he told Etty when she rang, 'I left my suitcase on Darton station. My sketchbook and a life of della Francesca, Botticelli and Mantegna are also inside. (What have these three,' I ask her, 'in common?)'

The night, alone, with Sebastopol and Corunna Streets adjoining: the sound of music from The Spion Kop thundering through the weekend air: flats on one side, a house on the other.

"He was starting," Fenchurch wrote, "where he left off (to have no idea where he was going)," lying in bed, the glow from

352

his neighbours' windows shining in his own. He had done too much: 'If I love you will you love me?'

'If you love me will I love you?'

"Such thoughts are reassuring."

His sleep: on a log, in Ardsley Wood, 'Would you give up writing and painting if it threatened to come between us (would you give up everything)?'

His heart, for instance, wasn't strong: the pills he took for tachycardia he had long ago dispensed with, along with those for (non-specific) anxiety and depression.

"I take nothing now but cups of tea (and have done away with alcohol and women)."

The house was falling into ruin: twice the size of Fenchurch's, it was nevertheless tall and narrow: the ceilings had broken away from the rafters, the stairs come away from the walls; rain, when it fell, poured through the roof: pots and pans, aimed at collecting it, were scattered across the upper floor. It was like, he often reflected, boarding a sinking ship, the swaying of the stairs (the creaking of the timbers), the tarpaulin sheets suspended like sails directing the rain ineffectually to the appropriate containers (the odour of decay and, unless he was mistaken, rats).

Yet Siobhan, alias Mrs O'Farrell ('Vaughan' to him and his fellow students at the Drayburgh forty years before) appeared to be above all this: ebullient – a Scottish mother, and Irish father – broad-bosomed, with a lyrical inclination to transmogrify in paint her domestic life, she had remained throughout three marriages, four children and as many live-in lovers ('my body is worn out, where not with love, of course, with kids'). Blonde, stout, the rotundity of her figure enhanced by shawls and gowns: 'Where have you been the last few weeks?' she enquiring, the door having fallen open at his knock.

'Ardsley,' Fenchurch said. 'They've been trying,' he told her 'to lock me away.'

He went inside to look at her pictures: scenes from her childhood, portraits of her children, one of a husband, two of a lover. 'My capacity for love is limitless,' she had often said, 'yet I never took money from any man.'

A turbulent, troublesome woman, her hair tumbling to her shoulders: pale eyes gazed out from a broadly-featured face, with a full-lipped mouth and red-flushed cheeks which, in the summer, shone like the sides of an apple. Furrows lined her brow over which a fringe fell in a frieze of curls: broad-beamed, broad-hipped, 'as long going across as coming up,' she had told him, taking him through to the kitchen: cats sprang off a chair (cat-food – brown and blood-coloured rusks – scattered across the floor). From the cluttered sink she removed a pot (pans and bowls from a week of cooking, more than the whole he had in his house). 'Coffee?' her fingers vivid with colour. 'So they want you back inside?'

'I intend,' I tell her, 'to put up a struggle.'

'You can come and stay here, if you like,' (the smell from the sink, the decaying food, the fissures in the walls, and holes directly through the ceiling, exposing the beams of the floor above).

'I'm all right where I am,' he told her.

'Nevertheless,' she said, 'it's always here if you want.'

Was this the 'success' (of failure) he had, in the past, gone on about: was this the antithesis to Vi, the bleach and mogadon-soaked killer? Was this what life was all about: the where not grease- graffiti-streaked walls, the (startling) pictures, pinned carelessly above the stove along with telephone messages yellow with age – a life he could not in any way encompass, or become a part of? This is Vaughan, he reflected, and I really have no place with her: out of chaos, order (her colours, shapes, her belligerent, sketched-in pictures: 'tactile', 'plastic', 'relevant', fine.)

The sister, he had told her, he had never had, not someone he could turn to (her method of support as helpful as a hammer to the head): someone with whom he could celebrate success, the opening out of his life at the publication of a novel, the production of a play, the completion of a picture, events which, with a peculiar wryness, she never, as far as he could ascertain, very much enjoyed.

The greatest moment of his life: when Isabella acceded to those intimacies which, in their final stages, involved the removal of her clothes (and which she, with an intoxicating delicacy, effortlessly assisted). She wasn't vulgar, by any means, he reflected, 'her sensitivity and openness of an order I have never encountered in anyone before.'

'I've missed you, the past few days,' she said. 'I miss our talks about art. No one talks to me about painting, it's all about men or this bloody house,' a dribble of dust from the laths overhead.

The vomit from a cat lay in a pool on the table before him.

Having put on the kettle, and set down his pot, she wiped it away with a sheet of newsprint on which she'd idly drawn a head.

'Do they intend,' she says, 'to take you back?'

'I've been put,' he says, 'on my best behaviour. No more late-night phone calls to Bea, no more protests in the street, no more soliciting of neighbours' wives, nor, indeed, of anyone,' he adds. 'Or lapses of taste when talking to women. A by-product of my current disability, which might be likened to despair, is,' he goes on, 'I can't get women, either individually or corporately, into focus. I am, when addressing or merely observing them, whether old or young, thin or fat, degenerate or angelic, driven by a desire to be embraced,' whereupon, stooping, she places – as he has hoped – her arms around him, a difficult manoeuvre which he only finally eases by standing and allowing her to draw him to her.

His hands encompass her solid hips: his fingers delve at the flesh of her back.

'This is more like it,' he sighs as, behind him, the kettle gives out the shrillest shriek.

'I'd better get the coffee,' she says and he, releasing her, goes over to the kettle, turning it off and announcing, 'I've changed my mind to tea.'

Picking up his pot, he looks round for another (they are all

355

in the sink) and when she says, 'I've had one, thanks,' he puts in a tea-bag and pours in the water.

Steam rises in the chilly air: the house, other than by an electric fire, is unheated.

'Let's go to the studio,' she says, he reflecting with any other man she would have said the bedroom.

As he follows her up the swaying stairs – fresh areas of brickwork revealed behind the disintegrating plaster, fresh laths exposed by descending plaster, fresh areas of wall and ceiling stained by damp – these thoughts preoccupy Fenchurch unduly: 'Isn't Vaughan, in a unique way, an amalgam of all the women I have known as well as of certain aspects of myself I have protected or concealed in a way which she, within herself, has never felt obliged to? Isn't she the woman I thought I was working from but, in reality, towards, over all these years?' recalling the fresh face of the twenty-one-year-old he had glimpsed standing at her easel in the mixed life-room at the Drayburgh forty-five years before: the sturdiness of her figure, the candour of her look (which, despite her three husbands and four children, had never left her): the blueness of her eye, the curve of her smiling, if not laughing mouth, the cascade of curls from her tossed-back head (the fullness of her throat, the amplitude of her breast), the characteristic sway outwards and downwards as she walked or stood, legs parted, at her easel (no decorous jabs or titillations but broad, expansive sweeps of the brush: never anything less than primary colours).

'What do you think of this?' as they come into the principal first-floor room which, through a tall, uncurtained window, looks onto the car-parked street below (several streets' walk away from his own).

The scroll of colour, the streak of paint, the fractured, jagged, vibrant line.

'Based,' she adds, 'on my notion of a woman. One not altogether unlike,' (she gives a laugh, throat bared, curls cascading to her shoulders), 'myself.'

'One of your best,' he says, his mind not on the picture but Vaughan herself, the angle of her body, the way it superimposes

356

itself against the discarded drawings that litter the floor, a table, two chairs, the paint and crayon-scoured walls themselves, embodiments of plants and figures on the plaster. She was, he reflected, not merely a handsome but a beautiful woman – in a way that all women were to him now, but more so: she exuded grace, she exuded strength, she exuded beauty – to a degree he had, except in Isabella, never experienced in another woman. 'And this is someone,' he further reflected, 'who is perceptibly stiff-limbed, marked – vividly – by her experience as a wife and mother – as three wives, and four mothers: how could I have not noticed her over all these years?'

'Or this one?' turning to a section of the wall to which numerous sheets had been attached, aimlessly, or so it seemed, one on top of the other.

'Like all your pictures,' he said, realising, for the first time, she dyed her hair and that, unusual for her, she was wearing make-up. 'When I was first successful,' he added, 'I thought I would be besieged by women. When I wasn't, I felt let down – unaccountably so, in many respects – and, as a consequence, redoubled my efforts. When, with my second success, I met with the same result, I can't describe the degree – and intensity – of my frustration. Yet, once on with a fresh piece of work, it was quickly forgotten. Now,' he went on, 'the work has gone, and my reputation with it. Perhaps the work, which absorbed me so completely, was merely a distraction. I've certainly, in the past, made mistakes which can only be described as cataclysmic, and, to that extent, we have a great deal in common,' and when she said, 'I don't see my life in terms of mistakes, nor,' she continued, 'failure, either,' he responded, 'It's one of the things I have to give up, or, if not give up, at least control, a disinclination not to talk when neither thought nor feeling warrant it. You see why I frighten people off, not least of all my family.'

When, for a while, she gazed past him to the picture, he suddenly added, 'It's what has led to accusations that I have no interest in people: everything is reduced to verbiage. Nothing,' he concluded, 'matters any more.'

357

'I wouldn't say that,' she says. 'It matters to me,' continuing, 'You don't seem interested, at the moment, in pictures. I can't blame you,' and with an aimlessness he had always associated with her, 'Let's go back down and get more tea.'

So this is what it's like, he thought. All these years I never knew: all these years and I forgot. I don't wish to be shackled to anyone – not wives, not children – not art: the first time in my life I'm free, not merely, he reflected, at liberty.

Vaughan, he suspected, was relieved that he should leave (perhaps had been, in any case, expecting someone else). 'All is not lost,' was his immediate response (walking back through the streets). 'Going to Ardsley and coming away from it,' he further reflected, 'was the best thing I ever did. And although this feeling won't be with me all the time, on those occasions that it is I can recoup sufficient of its strength to carry me through the intervals between. I shall outlive the pain that engulfed me, outlive my art, outlive the means by which I put it into practice. Reality, after all, goes on for ever and, to the degree that I am part of it, so will I.' In the decadence of Vaughan's existence he had found a source of strength: in the arbitrary way she supervised – or refused to supervise – her life (disinclined to arbitrate in the existences of others) he had found an antidote to the way he had lived himself (the prescription he had written from an early age and which – in fulfilment through women, an unrepayable obligation – had driven him mad). He had – he had not been aware of the process, merely of the pain – been re-united, in a tangible way, with that source of reality which was within him, not outside. 'Such a casual visit,' he thought, 'and yet, as if, in a curious way, I've been planning it all my life: right up to that moment when (her bell not working) I knocked on her door, found her doodling on the newsprint in the kitchen, made the tea, went up to her room, looked at her pictures then, with a peculiar contentment, came away,' (she undismayed at his leaving): all those forces that had, waveringly, characterised his existence in the past had been brought into focus. 'Of course, at the instant she showed me the painting – the woman rising, as if

358

from a bed – I took it as an invocation, the one thought came to me, through the mists and clouds, of Isabella,' as if, with dread as well as understanding, with a sense of enchantment as well as fear, in fear and trembling, he were moving closer to the one he loved.